IPSec:
SECURING VPNs

IPSec: Securing VPNs

Carlton R. Davis

Osborne/**McGraw-Hill**
New York   Chicago   San Francisco
Lisbon   London   Madrid   Mexico City
Milan   New Delhi   San Juan   Seoul
Singapore   Sydney   Toronto

McGraw-Hill

A Division of The McGraw-Hill Companies

Osborne/**McGraw-Hill**
2600 Tenth Street
Berkeley, California 94710
U.S.A.

To arrange bulk purchase discounts for sales promotions, premiums, or fundraisers, please contact Osborne/**McGraw-Hill** at the above address. For information on translations or book distributors outside the U.S.A., please see the International Contact Information page immediately following the index of this book.

IPSec: Securing VPNs

  2 3 4 5 6 7 8 9 0 FGR/FGR 0 1 9 8 7 6 5 4 3 2 1

ISBN 0-07-212757-0

This book was set in New Century Schoolbook by V&M Graphics, Inc.

Printed and bound by Quebecor.

Throughout this book, trademarked names are used. Rather than put a trademark symbol after every occurrence of a trademarked name, we use names in an editorial fashion only, and to the benefit of the trademark owner, with no intention of infringement of the trademark. Where such designations appear in this book, they have been printed with initial caps.

Publisher: Brandon A. Nordin
Vice President & Associate Publisher: Scott Rogers
Executive Editor: Steven M. Elliot
Acquisitions Coordinator: Alex Corona
RSA Press Project Manager: Mark Luna
Project Manager: Dave Nash
Technical Editor: Bronislav Kavsan-RSA
Cover Design: William Chan

 This book is printed on recycled, acid-free paper containing a minimum of 50% recycled, de-inked fiber.

To my mom Curline,
for the support she gave as a mom
that went beyond the call of duty.

CONTENTS

PREFACE

The Internet as well as most packet-switching networks are based on the Internet Protocol (IP). IP, however, is inherently insecure: it is relatively easy to capture IP packets that are in transit, modify and replay them without the destination host being able to detect the modifications. IP uses a 16-bit header checksum to validate the integrity of IP datagrams.

This is a rather rudimentary security mechanism, since the checksum can be recomputed after the modification of a datagram, and the new value re-inserted into the checksum header field. One therefore has no guarantee that an IP datagram originated from the source it claims to originate from; nor is there any guarantee that it has not been modified while it is in transit from the source to the destination.

The IP Security (IPSec) protocol provides a viable solution for securing IP traffic. IPSec uses strong cryptographic authentication and encryption algorithms to protect the integrity and confidentiality of IP traffic. The protocol however, is quite extensive and complex; as a result, it is sometimes regarded as a puzzle.

It is our aim for this book to present the components of this important protocol, in a form that is easily understood; and show how they can be utilized in the form of virtual private network (VPN) to secure IP traffic. The scope of the material presented is of such that it is insightful and a good source of reference for seasoned IT professionals (network/security engineers, administrators, developers or programmers); yet individuals that have little network security related knowledge can equally benefited from this book.

Audience

This book was written for three principal audiences: IT professionals, students and anyone desiring to get a better understanding of IPSec, relevant encryption and authentication cryptographic algorithms and VPN. The book is written in a modular form. For each new topic, the subject matter is explained in such a way that prior knowledge is not required to grasp what is present. However, as a topic is developed more and more details are presented.

The scope of the material is quite broad. For example, there are full details on symmetric-key and public-key cryptographic algorithms, digital signature schemes, Diffie-Hellman key exchange and hash functions, such that this book can be of much value to university students taking cryptographic courses, or professionals developing security software applications; yet, it can be equally valuable to individuals who desire to get a simple understanding of cryptography.

The topics we presented are quite extensive; of such, this book can be an invaluable reference for IT professionals or students who periodically need to reference relevant information about IPSec, TCP/IP, cryptography, PKI, LDAP or VPN.

Organization

This book provides information and insight in five principal subject areas. We listed them below in the order they are presented.

TCP/IP

In Chapter 1, we gave a detailed overview of the TCP/IP protocol suite. Our presentation involves discussions on (IPv4, IPv6, TCP, UDP, ICMP and IGMP).

Cryptography

Chapters 2 to 4 contains in depth description and analysis of cryptographic schemes (encryption algorithms, digital signature schemes, Diffie-Hellman key exchange, hash functions and message authentication codes) that are relevant to IPSec.

PKI

In Chapter 5, we presented an overview of X.509, PGP digital certificates and their components, and showed how they are used to provide Public Key Infrastructure (PKI) solutions.

LDAP

Chapter 6 provides a primer for the ubiquitous Lightweight Directory Access Protocol (LDAP).

IPSec

The remainder of the book: Chapter 7 to 13, contain detail description of the IPSec protocols and technological components, and insights on how these protocols can be used to secure IP traffic via VPNs.

ACKNOWLEDGEMENTS

First, I would like to express my sincere gratitude to the Lord Jesus for being my saviour and for helping me to complete this project. Next, I acknowledge my family and friends for their encouragement and support. I also would like to say thanks to Luc Boulianne, formerly of McGill University, for arousing my interest in network security and IPSec.

There are a number of individuals that helped to make this book a reality. It is important for me to take the time out to mention a few names and say a big thank you to these individuals for contributing to the fruition of this project. First, I must say thanks to Steven M. Elliot and Alexander Corona (Executive Editor and Acquisitions Editor at McGraw-Hill) and Mark Luna (from RSA Press) for their patience and encouragement. Thanks to Joanna V. Pomeranz, Joseph Cavanagh, Peter Karsten and other members of the team at V&M Graphics for the excellent copy-editing job they did. Thanks to Bronislav Kavsan (from RSA) for providing the technical review. Thanks also to William Chan for designing the book cover; to Maria Tahim for compiling information for the cover; and to David Nash, the project editor at McGraw-Hill.

ABOUT THE AUTHOR

Carlton R. Davis has undergraduate and graduate degrees in Computer Science from McGill University, Montreal, Canada. Over the years he has held a number of IT Security related positions which provided hands-on experience with VPN applications and other network security tools. These positions include Senior SE for PGP Security—a Network Associates business unit (Santa Clara, CA), Unix System Manager for Bell Canada (Montreal, Canada) and System Administrator at the School of Computer Science, McGill University (Montreal, Canada).

About the Reviewer

As the leading publisher of technical books for more than 100 years, McGraw-Hill prides itself on bringing you the most authoritative and up-to-date information available. To ensure that our books meet the highest standards of accuracy, we have asked a number of top professionals and technical experts to review the accuracy of the material you are about to read.

We take great pleasure in thanking Bronislav Kavsan for his insights. Mr. Kavsan is a Vice President at RSA Security, where he is leading an engineering organization developing an Advanced PKI family of products.

Mr. Kavsan joined RSA Security in 1999. His areas of interest include Data Communication Protocols, Network Security and Public Key Infrastructure. He has more than 25 years of information systems data communication experience, including architecture and implementation of VPN/IPSec systems (SafeNet, Inc) and research/development in the area of Data Communication Protocols (Bell Laboratories, AT&T/Lucent Technologies).

TCP/IP Overview

Overview of Chapter 1

In this chapter, we discuss the following topics:

- History of TCP/IP
- TCP/IP Protocol Architecture
  - Data-Link Layer
  - Network Layer
    * Internet Protocol
    * Internet Control Message Protocol
    * Internet Group Management Protocol
  - Transport Layer
    * Transmission Control Protocol
    * User Datagram Protocol
  - Application Layer

The Transmission Control Protocol/Internet Protocol (TCP/IP) is the most widely used network protocol. TCP/IP can be considered the engine that powers the flow of data, the vessel that transports the data, and the controller that navigates the flow of data on the Internet. The Internet is being utilized for just about every transaction imaginable. You can buy groceries online and have them delivered to your door within an hour. Online trading will become ever more commonplace in our lives as time progresses; it therefore certainly helps to have some knowledge of the operation of this ubiquitous infrastructure—the Internet—that has become such an integral part of our lives.

Since it plays such an important role, we should all be concerned about the security of the Internet. Unfortunately, there are still a number of companies out there whose security infrastructures leave much to be desired, and yet they are wooing us to conduct online transactions with them. It is definitely advantageous to be aware of, if not abreast with, network security concepts and terminologies. This is not just for the "techies." This applies to all of us. Before we click the button and send our credit card or banking account information over the Internet, we should all be able to click the "security" link on the Web page of the company that we are considering doing business with, and make an informed opinion as to whether or not the security mechanisms are adequate for online trading. If we are capable of making this important judgment, we might just save ourselves from the predicament of our credit card number or bank account and PIN number getting into the wrong hands.

For a good understanding of IPSec or any other security protocol, a sound knowledge of TCP/IP can be considered a prerequisite. In this chapter, we are going to give—in some instances—a detailed review of the components of the TCP/IP protocol suite that are relevant to IPSec. If you are not interested in the detail, please feel free to skim through and just direct your attention to the portions that you consider relevant. We will start by giving a brief history of the Internet and TCP/IP.

1.1 Some History

In the mid-1960s at the height of the cold war, the Department of Defense (DoD) wanted a command and control network that could survive a nuclear war. The DoD consequently commissioned its research arm—ARPA (Advance Research Projects Agency)—to invent the technology that could get data to their destination reliably even if an arbitrary part of the network disappeared without warning as a result of a nuclear attack.

The technology, called *circuit switching*, that existed back then and is still used today to transmit wired-telephone data, had serious drawbacks. In circuit switching, a route for data to get from one point to the next needs to be set up using relays that make physical connections among pieces of cable. Consequently, if part of the circuit fails, a new circuit must be set up, which could be quite difficult and time consuming depending on the severity of the damage.

To overcome these problems, ARPA used the technology called *packet switching*. The idea of packet switching networks was proposed by Paul Baran in the early 1960s [Bar64]. With packet switching, data to be sent over a network are divided up into discrete parts called packets. Each packet is routed independently from one computer to the next over the network until it reaches its final destination.

The first experimental network—called the ARPANET—went into operation in December 1969. It consisted of subnets and host computers. The subnets consisted of minicomputers called IMPs (interface message processors) connected by transmission lines. This network contained four nodes, one each at UCLA (University of California at Los Angeles), UCSB (University of California at Santa Barbara), SRI (Stanford Research Institute), and University of Utah. Each node of the network was made up of an IMP and a host in the same room, connected by wire. For the purposes of our discussion, a host is synonymous with a computer. These four sites were chosen because all had large ARPA contracts; additionally, all four sites had different and completely incompatible computers. This experimental network grew rapidly: in July 1970 it grew to 8 nodes, by March 1971 it had expanded to 16 nodes, in April 1972 it grew to 23 nodes, and by September 1972 it consisted of 34 nodes.

This network worked well in its early stage when there were few nodes. However, as the number of nodes increased, the network experienced a number of system crashes. Additionally, when satellite and radio networks were added to the ARPANET in the early 1970s, Network Control Protocol (NCP) [NKPC70], the existing protocol of the ARPANET, had trouble working with these networks. As a result, research started in the early 1970s for a new protocol that was robust and able to work well with different kinds of networks. The research effort culminated with the development of the TCP/IP protocol suite in 1974.

The TCP/IP protocol suite proved to be quite robust and was very adaptable to different networks. Because of this and because it was an open protocol, was freely available, was developed independently of any specific computer hardware or operating system, and was simple and easy to implement; TCP/IP became very popular. By 1983 TCP/IP was integrated into release 4.2 of Berkeley Software Distribution (BSD) UNIX—which was the operating system of choice back then. In the same year, the DoD adopted this protocol suite as Military Standard (MIL STD) and it became the standard of the ARPANET, the precursor of the Internet.

Today, TCP/IP continues to be the standard for the Internet. The fact that this protocol was designed to be independent of any specific physical network hardware has allowed it to be integrated into many different kinds of networks. TCP/IP is currently integrated into Ethernets, token ring, dial-up networks, and just about every other type of physical transmission medium, and virtually all modern operating systems.

1.2   TCP/IP Protocol Architecture

Networking protocols are normally developed in layers, with each layer responsible for a different facet of the communication. Layers are more desirable because changes can be made to a given layer without affecting the functionality of the other layers. The TCP/IP protocol suite consists of four layers. Each layer has distinct functions and consists of a combination of different protocols as illustrated in Figure 1-1. The functionalities of the layers are discussed below.

1.2.1   Data-link Layer

The *data-link* layer is also called the *link* or *network access layer*. It is the lowest layer of the TCP/IP protocol stack. Example of data-link layers are *Ethernet* (IEEE 802.3), *token ring* (IEEE 802.5), and *ATM* (asynchronous transfer mode). Of the three, Ethernet is the most widely used for local area networks (LANs). At the time of writing, Ethernet cards support transmission speeds of 10 or 100 megabits per second (Mbps) and 1 gigabit per second (Gbps), i.e. 1000 Mbps. Ethernet is essentially a *broadcast network* that is based on bus hardware architecture.

What is a broadcast network? In a broadcast network, small messages called *packets* are sent on the network. Along with the data they are transporting, packets contain information such as the source and destination

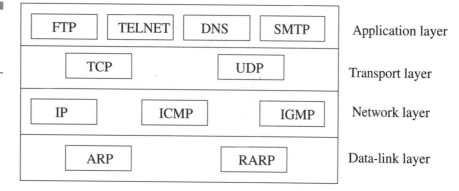

Figure 1-1
Protocols at the Four
Layers of the TCP/IP
Protocol Suite

addresses, and protocols. Each machine on the network examines the packets to ascertain whether or not its *medium access control* (**MAC**) address—also called *hardware address*—matches the address in any of the packets' destination address fields. If a match occurs, the responsible host removes the packet from the network and processes it; if no match occurs, the packets are left alone.

Ethernet uses an access method called *carrier sense multiple access with collision detection* (CSMA/CD). Typically, when a host on the network wishes to send data to another host, it accesses the transporting medium and checks if there are any data signals; if no signal is detected, the host sends the data. However, if it detects data on the channel, it backs off, waits for a few microseconds, and checks again to ascertain if the channel is free. It continues doing this until the channel is free, at which time, it sends the data. If more than one host on the network transmits data at the same time, a data collision likely will occur. However, the CSMA/CD technology allows the hosts to detect when a collision occurs, and the hosts consequently will retransmit the data that were involved in the collision. For details on how a host detects collisions, a good source of reference is [Tan96].

We mentioned previously that the host on a network examines the packets transmitted on the subnet that it is on, to ascertain whether any of the packets' destination addresses match their MAC address. The next topic that we will address is the MAC address. A MAC address is a 48-bit unique address that is assigned to each Ethernet card. It usually is represented in hexadecimal numbers. On most Unix systems, MAC addresses are represented by six pairs of hexadecimal digits separated by a colon; for example, 08:00:20:3E:0C:11. On Windows systems, the six pairs of hexadecimal digits are separated by an en dash, for example, 00–AA–00–15–20–0F. On Windows NT systems, the command `ipconfig /all` displays the MAC address; on most Unix systems the equivalent command is `ifconfig -a`.

The first 24 bits of a MAC address are the *organizational unique identifier* (OUI): this a unique number that the Institute of Electrical and Electronics engineers (IEEE) assigns to each manufacturer of Ethernet cards. For example, the MAC address for all Ethernet cards manufactured by Intel starts with `00AA00`, whereas, those of SUN start with `080020`. RFC 1700 [RP94] lists the number assigned to each Ethernet card manufacturer. The remaining 24 bits of a MAC address are assigned by the manufacturer of the cards. It is the responsibility of each manufacturer to ensure that each card that it assembles has a unique MAC address.

When the data-link layer receives a packet from the network layer—the layer above it—it encapsulates the packet with the appropriate header, for example, the Ethernet header for the Ethernet data-link layer, before sending it to its intended destination. The Ethernet header contains information such as the source and destination hardware addresses. For details on the different fields in an Ethernet header see RFC 1042 [RP88], which contains the original specification. The layers above the data-link layer have no knowledge of hardware addresses: they use IP addresses to identify networking elements. However, the data-link layer operates with hardware addresses, and it consequently needs to fill in the destination hardware address field of the Ethernet header.

How do IP addresses get translated into Ethernet or other hardware addresses? The data-link layer *Address Resolution Protocol* (ARP) takes care of this. The process that ARP uses to map IP addresses to MAC addresses can be described as follows: when a datagram—for now, think of a datagram as a synonym for a packet—arrives from layer 2 to the data-link layer, the ARP module extracts the destination IP address from the datagram, and then checks its ARP table—a dynamically updated table that stores IP-to-hardware-address mappings—to determine if there is an entry with this IP address. If there is an entry, it uses this information to fill in the destination hardware address field in the Ethernet header and sends the packet. However, if there is no matching IP address in its ARP table, the ARP module on the host sends an *ARP request* broadcast to the hosts and routers on its subnet. The ARP request message announces that the host with the specified hardware and IP address needs to know the hardware address of the network element whose IP address is indicated in the ARP request message. If the IP address matches any of the hosts' IP addresses, the ARP module on the corresponding host sends an *ARP reply* message indicating its hardware and IP address. If none of the IP addresses of the network element on the subnet match the IP address whose hardware address is being sought, the packet is routed on to other subnets. The process continues until the ARP request message reaches the host with the hardware address being sought, or the time-to-live value (this will be explained later) of the message expires. When the host that sent the ARP request message receives this ARP reply message, it uses the information in this message to fill in the destination address field in the Ethernet header, adds the Ethernet header to the datagram it had received from layer 2, and sends it to its destination; then it updates its ARP table with the IP-to-hardware-address mapping information it received in the ARP reply message. If the host has not received an ARP reply message within a certain predefined time, the ARP module sends a message to the layer 2 protocol, indicating that the host for whom the message was intended is not reachable. For further detail on ARP, see RFC 826 [Plu82], which contains the original specification.

The Reverse Address Resolution Protocol (RARP) does the opposite of what ARP does: it maps hardware addresses to IP addresses. RARP is mainly used by diskless machines to discover their IP addresses at boot time. RFC 903 [FTMT84] contains the original specification of RARP.

It was explained above, in the discussion on ARP, that when the data-link layer receives a datagram from the network layer (the layer above), it encapsulates the datagram with a data-link header before sending the datagram via the physical network to its destination. The reverse occurs when a packet arrives from the physical network to the data-link layer: the layer removes the data-link header and then sends the packet up to the network layer for processing. This is illustrated in Figure 1-2.

1.2.2   Network Layer

The *network layer* is also called the *Internet layer*. This layer is responsible for the routing of packets from the source to the destination. The protocols at this layer that are of interest to our discussion are the Internet Protocol (IP), the Internet Control Message Protocol (ICMP), and Internet Group Management Protocol (IGMP). A discussion of these protocols follows.

1.2.2.1   Internet Protocol

IP is the protocol that holds the whole TCP/IP protocol suite architecture together. The data of the protocols in all the layers of the TCP/IP protocol

Figure 1-2

Encapsulation and decapsulation of data as they go down and up the protocol stack, respectively.

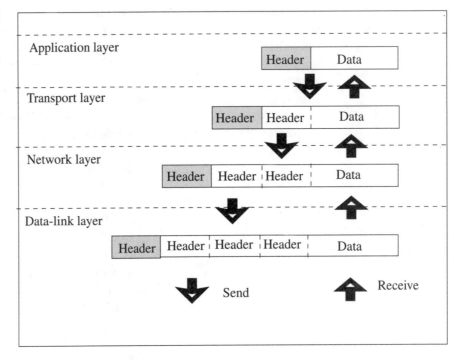

stack, except the data-link layer, are transmitted as IP datagrams. IP allows hosts to inject packets into the data-link layer—which eventually puts them on the physical network—and have them travel on potentially different networks to their final destination. IP offers a *connectionless* service. In connectionless services, each message or datagram carries the full destination address and is routed independently of the other datagrams. With connectionless services, it is possible for the datagrams to arrive at their destination in different order than they were sent. This is not possible with *connection-oriented* services since these are like a telephone system that establishes a connection or a path from the host to the destination, uses the path to send data, and then releases the connection after the data transmission is completed.

There are two versions of IP that are available for use with the TCP/IP protocol suite: IPv4 and IPv6.[1] The format of the datagrams and the addressing mode of these two protocols will be presented in the discussion that follows.

---

[1] IPv5 is a real-time stream protocol.

IPV4 DATAGRAM FORMAT

An IP datagram consists of a header portion and a data portion. The header portion consists of a 20-byte fixed part and a variable-length optional part. The data portion is of variable length. Figure 1-3 shows the format of an IPv4 datagram. An IP datagram is transmitted in *big endian* byte order: from left to right; that is, lower-order bytes are transmitted first. This is the byte ordering required for all binary integers in the TCP/IP headers as they traverse a network and is called *network byte order*. Machines such as Pentiums that use a *little endian* byte ordering format must convert header values to network byte order before transmitting the data. Let us now examine the IP header fields.

The *version* field indicates the version of the IP protocol to which the data belong. This field is usually used for backward compatibility.

The *Internet header length* (IHL) field is the length of the header in 32-bit words. The minimum value is 5 words (20 bytes), which is the case when no options are present; the maximum value is 15 words (60 bytes), which applies when the options field is 40 bytes.

The *type of service* (TOS) field indicates the traffic requirement of the datagram in terms of the combination of delay, throughput, and reliability.

Figure 1-3
IPv4 Datagram

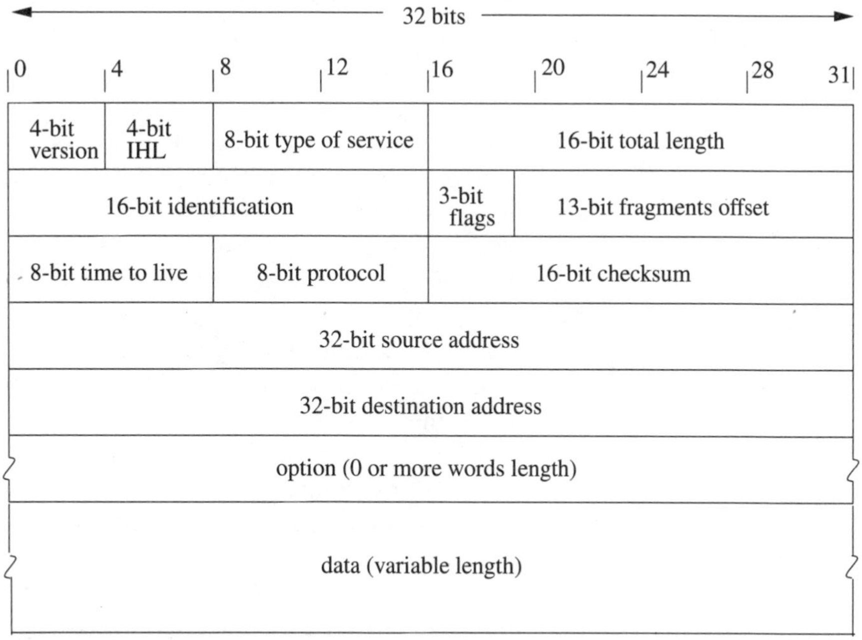

The *total length* field is the total length of the IP datagram—header and data—in bytes. The maximum length is 65,535 bytes. This field is used in combination with the IHL field to indicate where the data portion of the IP datagram begins.

The *identification* field allows a host to determine to which datagram a newly arrived fragment belongs. Each datagram has a unique identification number, and each fragment of a datagram has the same identification number.

Only 2 bits of the 3-bit *flags* are used. The first of the 2 bits is called the *don't fragment* (DF) bit; it indicates whether or not the IP datagram should be fragmented. If this bit is set, it indicates that the datagram should not be fragmented. When a router receives a datagram with the DF bit set, it usually sends back an ICMP message to the host from which the datagram originated indicating its *maximum transfer unit* (MTU). This bit is therefore used to determine the path MTU: the maximum size of an IP datagram that will be allowed to pass through a given network path to the destination without being subjected to fragmentation. The next bit is called the *more fragment* (MF) bit. This bit indicates when the last fragment of a datagram arrives. This bit is set for all fragments of a datagram except the last fragment.

The *fragment offset* tells where in the current datagram this fragment belongs. The first fragment has offset zero. All fragments except the last one in a datagram must be multiples of 8 bytes.

The *time-to-live* (TTL) field is used to limit the lifetime of a datagram, thus preventing the datagram from looping infinitely within a network segment. The TTL field is set to a default value by the host. Each router that the datagram passes through decrements the TTL value by 1. If a router receives a datagram with a TTL value of 1, it discards the datagram and sends an ICMP message to the source indicating that the TTL value of the datagram has expired.

The *protocol* field tells which transport protocol is used for the data encapsulated within the IP datagram. It allows destination hosts to demultiplex IP datagrams among the different transport protocols.

The *header checksum* is computed on the IP header and is used to determine the integrity of the IP header. It should be noted that the checksum is not encrypted and can be forged easily.

The *source address* and *destination address* fields indicate the 4-byte IP address of the host that generated the datagram and the destination host, respectively.

The variable-length *options* field carries optional information about a datagram such as the security and handling restriction. This field is rarely used and is usually ignored by most routers.

The *data* portion of the IP datagram is of variable length and contains the IP payload.

For further details on the header format of this protocol see to RFC 791 [Pos81], which contains the specifications of IPv4.

IPV4 ADDRESSING

Each host or router that is connected to a network must have an IP address. The IP protocol uses IP addresses to identify network elements. Machines that are connected to more than one network must have an IP address for each network that they are connected to. An IPv4 address is a 32-bit number. It is usually represented by a 4-byte decimal number from 0 to 255, where each byte is separated by a period.

IPV4 ADDRESS CLASSES

There are five classes of IPv4 addresses. Table 1-1 summarizes the attributes of the five classes. An explanation of the columns in Table 1-1 follows.

- Higher-order bits: This column represents the higher-order bits that the first byte of all the IPv4 addresses of the respective classes must begin with. For example, for all class B addresses, the eighth bit (counting from the left) of the first byte must be set; therefore, the first byte of the smallest class B address is 2^7, which is equal to 128. Similarly, for all class C addresses the eighth and the seventh bits of the first byte must be set; therefore, the first byte of the smallest class C address is $2^7 + 2^6 = 192$.

- Net ID: This is the number of bits in the network portion of the IPv4 address.

- Host ID: This is the number of bits in the host portion of the IPv4 address.

- IP range: This is the range of IPv4 addresses for the respective classes.

TABLE 1-1

Summary of Attributes of IPv4 Address Classes

Class	Higher-Order Bits	Net ID	Host ID	IP Range
A	0	7 bits	24 bits	0.0.0.0 to 127.255.255.255
B	10	14 bits	16 bits	128.0.0.0 to 191.255.255.255
C	110	21 bits	8 bits	192.0.0.0 to 223.255.255.255
D	1110	28 bits	None	224.0.0.0 to 239.255.255.255
E	11110	27 bits	None	240.0.0.0 to 247.255.255.255

Class D addresses are special addresses called *multicast addresses* that are used to address hosts that belong to special groups called *multicast groups*, which is the reason why there is no host ID portion of these addresses. Similarly, class E addresses have no host ID portion because these addresses are reserved for future use.

TYPES OF IPV4 ADDRESSES

There are three types of IPv4 addresses: unicast, broadcast, and multicast:

- Unicast addresses: A unicast address is an address that is assigned to a single host.

- Broadcast addresses: These are used to address all the hosts on a given network. All the bits of the host ID portion of a broadcast address must be set to 1. Therefore, class A broadcast addresses are of the form X.255.255.255 where X is a decimal number between 0 and 127 inclusively. Class B and C broadcast addresses are of the form Y.Z.255.255 and W.U.V.255 respectively, where Y is a decimal number between 128 and 191 inclusively; Z, U, and V are decimal numbers between 0 and 255 inclusively, and W is a decimal number between 192 and 223 inclusively. A special broadcast address that is used to address the local host is 255.255.255.255; that is, if a host sends a packet with the destination address field being 255.255.255.255, the host is essentially sending the packet to itself.

- Multicast addresses: These are used to address a group of hosts that are part of multicast groups. As noted above, the class D addresses are multicast addresses.

In addition to these types of addresses, some addresses are designated as *loopback addresses* and *private addresses*. Loopback addresses are the network interface of the local host. These addresses are used for testing purposes to ascertain whether the network interfaces of the local host are functioning. The address block 127.0.0.0 to 127.255.255.255 is reserved for loopback addresses. Private addresses will be discussed shortly.

CLASSLESS INTERDOMAIN ROUTING

Due to the shortage of class B addresses, the Network Information Center (NIC), the agency that is responsible for assigning IP addresses, has been allocating blocks of class C addresses instead of single class B addresses. A class C address allows $2^{21} - 1 = 2,097,151$ (the maximum decimal number that can be represented with 21 bits) networks with up to $2^8 - 1 - 2$ = 253 hosts each. Two hosts are subtracted from the number of hosts because the addresses with the host ID portion consisting of all 1's or all 0's are special addresses that refer to the network that a host is on, and the broadcast address for all hosts on a network, respectively. A class B address allows $2^{14} - 1 = 16,383$ networks with approximately 65,000 hosts each. The allocation of class C addresses helps to slow the depletion of available IPv4 addresses. However, it also introduces another problem. In order to route packets to any host on the Internet, routers need to know about every network that is a part of the Internet. Routers gather the information about the different networks dynamically, using different routing algorithms, and store the information in their *routing tables*. With this scheme, if 1 million class C addresses are allocated, the routing table of each router connected to the Internet would have a million entries. If this were to happen, there would be a significant increase in the amount of time that routers take to ascertain the paths to hosts to which packets are addressed; consequently, there would be a noticeable increase in the time it takes to transmit data from one host to another. *Classless interdomain routing* (CIDR) is a proposal that has been implemented to address this problem. The idea behind CIDR is presented in RFC 1519. CIDR is also referred to as *supernetting*.

CIDR stipulates that when a set of class C address is to be assigned to an organization, contiguous blocks of these addresses should be allocated in variable sizes, depending on the number of IP addresses requested. For example, if an organization needs 1200 IPv4 addresses, it would be given a block of 1280 addresses (5 contiguous class C networks); similarly, if an organization needs 10,000 addresses, it would be given 10,240 addresses (40 contiguous class C networks) instead of a class B address.

In additional to the above, CIDR also suggests that the remaining class C addresses be partitioned into eight equal address blocks, each block to be allocated as follows:

- 192.0.0.0 to 193.255.255.255 for multiple regions
- 194.0.0.0 to 195.255.255.255 for Europe
- 196.0.0.0 to 197.255.255.255 for future use
- 198.0.0.0 to 199.255.255.255 for North America
- 200.0.0.0 to 201.255.255.255 for Central/South America
- 202.0.0.0 to 203.255.255.255 for Asia and the Pacific regions
- 204.0.0.0 to 205.255.255.255 for future use
- 206.0.0.0 to 207.255.255.255 for future use

Each block consists of $2(2^{24}) = 33,554,432$ addresses. Therefore, each region has approximately 33 million addresses to allocate.

In addition to the above, CIDR requires that addresses be represented by two entities: an address plus a netmask. A *netmask* is a 32-bit mask such that when it is Boolean ANDed to the address, the result is a 32-bit address that is identical to the original address, except that the host ID portion of the address is zero. In other words, when the netmask is Boolean ANDed to the address, the result is the network address portion of the address. For example, consider the class C address 192.1.1.1. In CIDR representation this address would be represented as 192.1.1.1 with a netmask of 255.255.255.0. The binary representations of this address and the netmask are 11000000 00000001 00000001 00000001 and 11111111 11111111 11111111 00000000, respectively. When these two bit strings are ANDed, the result is 11000000 00000001 00000001 00000000, which is the binary representation of 192.1.1.0; that is, the network of which the address 192.1.1.1 is a part. The short form of representing the above address and netmask combination is 192.1.1.1/24; this indicates that the network and host portions of the address are 24 and $32 - 24 = 8$, respectively. Netmasks are also referred to as *masks* or *subnetmasks*.

We will now address the topic of how the CIDR representation of addresses helps to reduce the number of entries in the routing tables of routers. As we mentioned previously, CIDR stipulates that addresses be allocated in contiguous blocks. Suppose, for example, an organization is given 12 blocks of class C addresses ($256 \cdot 12 = 3,072$ addresses), which contain IP addresses 195.30.1.0 to 195.30.15.255. Without the CIDR method of routing, these 12 class C networks require 12 entries in the routing tables of the routers on the Internet; however, with CIDR, these blocks of addresses can be represented as a single network with address 195.30.0.0 and netmask 255.255.240.0, or simply as 195.30.0.0/20. Consequently, only one entry would be required for these blocks of addresses in the routing tables of the routers on the Internet. The routers that are on the internal network with these address blocks, however, would have additional information in their routing tables with regard to the 12 different networks that make up the block of addresses.

With CIDR address representation, the host ID portion of an address no longer needs to be confined to the 8-bit boundary of the old class A, B, and C representation. The host ID portion of a network can be from 2 to 24 bits inclusively. Thus, a class C network, which in essence is a single network with 254 IP addresses, can be subnetted to various numbers of subnets with a reduced number of IP addresses. For example, it can be subnetted to two subnets of 62 hosts each, etc. It should be noted, however, that although subnetting provides additional networks, it also reduces the number of address spaces, since the first and the last addresses of a subnet, that is, X.Y.Z.0 and X.Y.Z.255, cannot be used because they are reserved as network and broadcast addresses, respectively.

PRIVATE IP ADDRESSES

The three blocks of IP addresses listed below are designated to be used on private networks only; consequently, they are not assigned by NIC:

- 10.0.0.0 to 10.255.255.255
- 172.16.0.0 to 172.31.255.255
- 192.168.0.0 to 192.168.255.255

These addresses are referred to as *private, illegal,* or *ambiguous* IP addresses. Unlike *public* addresses—also referred to as *unambiguous* or *legal* addresses—private addresses are often not unique since they can be found on several private networks.

What is the motivation for the use of these IP addresses? First, they are free: one does not have to pay to use them. Second, organizations sometimes do not have enough public IP addresses to meet their needs adequately. The drawback in using these addresses is that networking elements with these addresses cannot communicate directly with other networking elements on the Internet. For a host on a private network to communicate with a peer on the Internet, the private IP address must first be translated to a valid public IP address before the peers can establish a communication path. The Network Address Translation (NAT) Protocol, RFC 1631 [EF94], is responsible for translating private addresses to public addresses and vice versa. For the translation to occur, an implementation of the NAT module needs to be installed on the private network gateways[2] and be allocated a pool of valid public addresses that will be assigned individually, either statically or dynamically, to network elements on the private network that need to communicate with other network elements, whether on or via the Internet.

This concludes our discussion of IPv4; we will now turn our attention to the new version of IP: IPv6.

---

[2]Gateways are entry points to or from a network segment.

IPv6 DATAGRAM FORMAT

IPv4 suffers from a major limitation: it limits IP addresses to 32 bits. With the current rate of growth of the Internet, there is a real possibility that if the size of IP addresses does not increase, then there might not be enough IP addresses to meet the demand. IPv6, the designated successor of IPv4, overcomes this limitation, as well as simplifying the IP header and adding more flexibility to the IP datagram. Some of the changes from IPv4 to IPv6 are as follows:

- IPv6 increases the IP address size from 32 bits to 128 bits, thus increasing the addressable nodes by $(2^{128} - 1)/(2^{32} - 1) \cong 10^{28}$-fold.
- The number of header fields is reduced from 13 in IPv4 to 7 in IPv6. The smaller number of headers allows routers to process packets faster and therefore increases throughput.
- IPv6 provides better support for options. The options are treated as separate headers instead of being a part of the IP header. This change allows routers to skip over headers that are not intended for them. This feature speeds up packet processing time; it also allows for less stringent limits on the length of options and provides greater flexibility for the introduction of new options in the future.
- IPv6 provides new capabilities to label packets belonging to a particular traffic stream for which the sender requests special handling, such as non-default quality of service.
- IPv6 does not support any fragmentation for packets in transit. The host that generates the packet must perform path MTU to ascertain the maximum size of the IP datagram that will be allowed to pass through the network segment on route to the destination host.
- IPv6 specifies extensions to support authentication, data integrity, and (optional) data confidentiality.

Figure 1-4 shows the required IPv6 fixed headers. A description of the fields of these headers follows.

The *version* field indicates the version of the IP protocol the data belong. This field is usually use for backward compatibility.

The *priority* field is used to indicate the quality of service that a packet requires.

The *flow label* field is still experimental, and currently not being used.

The *payload length* is a 16-bit unsigned integer that indicates the length of the IP payload, that is, the rest of the packet following the IPv6 headers.

Figure 1-4
IPv6 Header Format

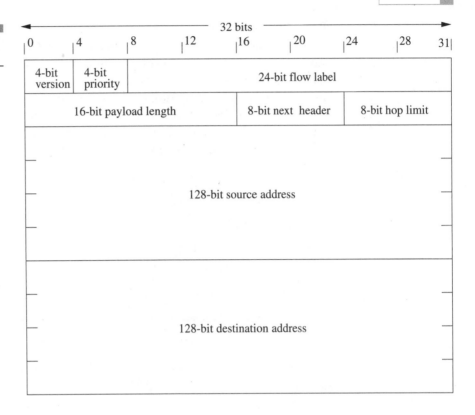

The *next header* field identifies the type of header immediately following the the IPv6 header. This field facilitates a reduction in the number of fields in the IPv6 header compared to that of IPv4. It tells which extension header, if any, follows this one; if this header is the last IP header, it tells which transport protocol the packet should be passed to. RFC 1700 [RP94] contains the list of the numbers assigned to each protocol.

The *hop limit* field is the same as the TTL field in the IPv4 header and is used to limit the lifetime of a datagram, thus preventing a datagram from looping infinitely within a network segment. The hop limit field is set to a default value by the host. Each router that the datagram passes through decrements the hop limit value by 1. If a router receives a datagram with a hop limit value of 1, it discards the datagram and sends an ICMP message to the source indicating that the hop limit value of the datagram has expired.

The *source address* and *destination address* fields represent the 128-bit IPv6 addresses of the source and intended recipient of the packet, respectively.

EXTENSION HEADERS

IPv6 introduced the concept of optional *extension headers*. These headers can be supplied to provide additional information. There are currently six extension headers defined by IPv6, and each has a unique identification number; the identification numbers are described in RFC 1700. The extension headers, if present, are inserted between the IPv6 header and the transport header. If more than one extension header is present, the order of the headers is important and should be as follows:

- Hop-by-hop options header

- Destination options header

- Routing header

- Fragmentation header

- Authentication header

- Encapsulating security payload header

- Destination options header

- Upper-layer header (for example, transport layer protocol header)

Note that if the destination options header is to be processed by the first destination that appears in the IPv6 destination address field, plus subsequent destinations listed in the routing header, it should be processed immediately after the processing of the hop-by-hop options header; whereas, if this header is to be processed only by the final destination of the packet, it should be processed just before the upper-layer header. Let us now take a brief look at these extension headers.

- Hop-by-hop options header: This extension header is used to carry optional routing information that must be examined by every node on the path from the packet's source to its destination. The hop-by-hop options header is identified by a value of 0 in the IPv6 *next-header* field.

- Destination options header: This header carries optional information that needs to be examined only by the packet's destination node(s). This extension header is identified by a value of 60 in the next-header field of the immediately preceding header.

- Routing header: This extension header is use by the IPv6 source to list one or more intermediate gateway(s) through which a packet should pass on its way from the source to the destination. The routing extension header is identified by a value of 43 in the next-header field of the immediately preceding header.

- Fragmentation Header: An IPv6 source uses the fragmentation extension header to send packets that are larger than the maximum transfer unit (MTU) for the path from the source to the destination. Fragmentation in IPv6, unlike that for IPv4, is performed only by source nodes, and not by routers along a packet's delivery path. The fragment extension header is identified by a value of 44 in the "next header" field of the immediately preceding header.

- Authentication header (AH): The AH carries information about AH options when IPSec is enabled. The AH extension header is identified by a value of 51 in the next-header field of the immediately preceding header.

- Encapsulating security payload header (ESP): This extension header carries information about ESP options when IPSec is enabled. It is identified by a value of 50 in the "next header" field of the immediately preceding header. We will discuss the AH and ESP in greater detail in later chapters.

For additional information on the format of any of these extension headers, see RFC 1883 [DH95], which contains the specification of IPv6.

IPv6 ADDRESSING IPv6 addresses can be represented in three forms:

1. RFC 1884 [HD95b], which specifies IPv6 address architecture, indicates that the preferred form is eight 16-bit hexadecimal numbers separated by a colon. The leading zeros in these 16-bit hexadecimal numbers can be omitted; however, at least one digit needs to be in each field. An example of this representation of an IPv6 address is 1C02:5:0:0:0:F2:D250:75E.

2. Multiple groups of 16-bit zeros in the representation described in form 1 above can be suppressed with a double colon. For example, the address, given in form 1 can be represented as: 1C02:5::F2:D250:75E; similarly, the IPv6 loopback address 0:0:0:0:0:0:0:1 can be represented as ::1.

3. When dealing with a mixed environment of IPv6 and IPv4 addresses, IPv6 addresses can be represented as X:X:X:X:X:X: d.d.d.d, where the X's are the six higher-order 16-bit hexadecimal pieces of the address, and the d's are the decimal values of the four lower-order 8-bit pieces of the address. For example, the address in form 1 can be represented as 1C02:5:0:0:0:F2:210. 80.7.94, or as 1C02:5::F2:210.80.7.94 in compressed form.

There are three types of IPv6 addresses: unicast, anycast, and multicast. A description of each type follows:

- Unicast address: This is an address that is assigned to a single host. The higher-order byte of a unicast address can have any value except FF (that is, 11111111), which identifies a multicast address.

- Anycast address: This type of address is an identifier for a set of interfaces, not necessarily on the same host. A packet that is sent to an anycast address is delivered to the interface that is the shortest path from the source node. Anycast addresses are taken from the unicast address space, and they are not syntactically distinguishable from unicast addresses.

- Multicast address: This addresses a group of hosts. Packets sent to a multicast address are delivered to all interfaces that are a part of this address. The higher-order byte of all IPv6 multicast addresses has the value: FF.

There are no broadcast addresses in IPv6. IPv6 multicast addresses take the place of broadcast addresses.

This concludes our discussion of the IPv6 addressing scheme; for further details, see RFC 1884, which outlines the addressing architecture of IPv6.

1.2.2.2 Internet Control Message Protocol

ICMP is the protocol that is used to communicate error conditions that occurred during the transmission of IP packets. ICMP specification RFC 792 [Pos81] defines eight types of ICMP message formats. These message format are presented in the following sections.

ICMP MESSAGE FORMATS

All ICMP messages are encapsulated in an IP datagram. The first byte of the data portion of the datagram is the ICMP type field; the format of the remaining data of the datagram depends on the value of this field.

DESTINATION UNREACHABLE MESSAGE

This message is usually sent by a router when it receives a datagram whose destination field specifies an IP address in which the network portion corresponds to the subnet that the router is on, but for whatever reason, the network element with the specified IP address is not reachable. The format of this message is as illustrated in Figure 1-5. A description of the fields of the destination unreachable message format follows:

- Type: The value of this 8-bit field for the destination unreachable message format is 3.

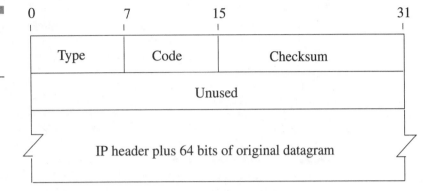

Figure 1-5
Destination
Unreachable
Message Format

- Code: The possible value for this 8-bit field are shown below.

  0–The network that the destination host is on is unreachable.

  1–The host is unreachable.

  2–The protocol specified in the protocol field of the IP header is unreachable.

  3–The destination port specified in the transport layer protocol header[3] is unreachable.

  4–The size of the packet is too large; it needs to be fragmented, but the DF bit of the IP header is set.

  5–The source route fails, that is, there is no route back to the source host.

- Checksum: This is the 16-bit one's complement sum of the ICMP message starting from the type field. The checksum field is first set to zero before the one's complement sum is calculated.

- Unused: The 32-bit unused field is reserved for future use.

- The last field is of variable length and it contains the IP header plus the first 64 bits of the original datagram's data. The first 64 bits of the upper-layer protocols, such as TCP or UDP, contains information such as port number that the process[4] for which the data was intended, listens. This data are used by the host to match the message to the appropriate process.

---

[3]We will discuss the transport layer protocols shortly.

[4]In simple terms, a process is a computer program that is being executed.

TIME EXCEEDED MESSAGE

This message is sent when a router receives a packet with the time-to-live field being zero. The format of this message is identical to the destination unreachable message format, except that the value of the type field is 11, and the code field has the following values:

0–Time to live exceeded in transit.

1–Fragment reassembly time exceeded.

PARAMETER PROBLEM MESSAGE

This message is sent when a host or a gateway has a problem processing the header parameter of a datagram because of error condition(s) such as an incorrect argument in the header field. The format of this message is similar to Figure 1-5, except that there is an additional 8-bit field after the checksum field, and the unused field is 3 bytes long. Figure 1-6 illustrates the format for this message. The values of the fields that are different from those previously discussed are as follows:

- The type field has the value 12.
- The code field has the value 0.
- The pointer field identifies the byte where the error was detected.

SOURCE QUENCH MESSAGE

This message is sent when a host or gateway temporarily runs out of buffer space because it is receiving data faster than it can actually process the data. The format of this message is identical to the destination un-reachable message format, except that the type field has the value 4 and the code field has the value 0.

Figure 1-6

Parameter Problem
Message Format

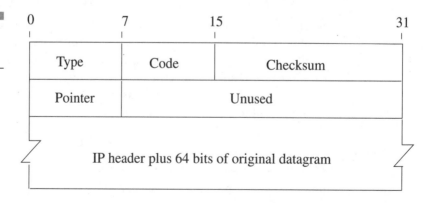

REDIRECT MESSAGE

A gateway or a host sends a redirect message when it receives a datagram that traverses an unnecessarily long path on route to this gateway or host. The redirect message contains the IP address of the gateway that the source of the datagram should use, in order for the datagram to take the shortest path to the destination host. The format of this message is similar to that of the destination unreachable message, except for the following differences:

- Instead of the unused field, there is a gateway address field, which contains the IP address of the gateway that is on route to the destination host, but is on a shorter path from the source of the datagram than the host or gateway that generated the redirect message.
- The value of the type field is 5.
- The values of the code fields are:

    0–Redirect datagram for the network.

    1–Redirect datagram for the host.

    2–Redirect datagram for the type of service and network.

    3–Redirect datagram for the type of service and host.

ECHO AND ECHO REPLY MESSAGE

Echo and echo reply messages are used mainly for debugging network connectivity problems. The popular debugging tools Traceroute and Ping utilize the echo and echo reply message format. If a gateway is configured to answer to echo messages, then it is required to return in a echo reply message, the data it receives in the echo message. Figure 1-7 represents the format of this message. The values of the type field are:

Figure 1-7
Echo and Echo Reply
Message Format

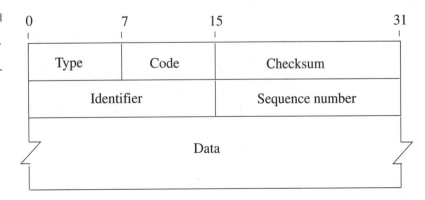

8–for echo message

0–for reply message

The values of the code, identifier, and sequence number fields for this message format are all 0.

TIMESTAMP AND TIMESTAMP REPLY MESSAGE

The ICMP timestamp message allows a system to query another for the current time. If the system being queried is configured to respond to these queries, it will respond by sending a timestamp reply message. Figure 1-8 illustrates the format of these messages. The values for the type field are:

13–for timestamp message

14–for timestamp reply message

The code, identifier, and sequence number fields are all 0. The three timestamp fields are all 32 bits long and their contents are as follows:

- Original timestamp: This is the number of milliseconds since midnight UT (Universal Time) and the time that the sender last touched the message before sending it.

- Receive timestamp: This is the number of milliseconds since midnight UT and the time that the system replying to the query first touched the message on receipt.

- Transmit timestamp: This is the number of milliseconds since midnight UT and the time that the system replying to the query last touched the message before sending it.

Figure 1-8
Timestamp and
Timestamp Reply
Message Format

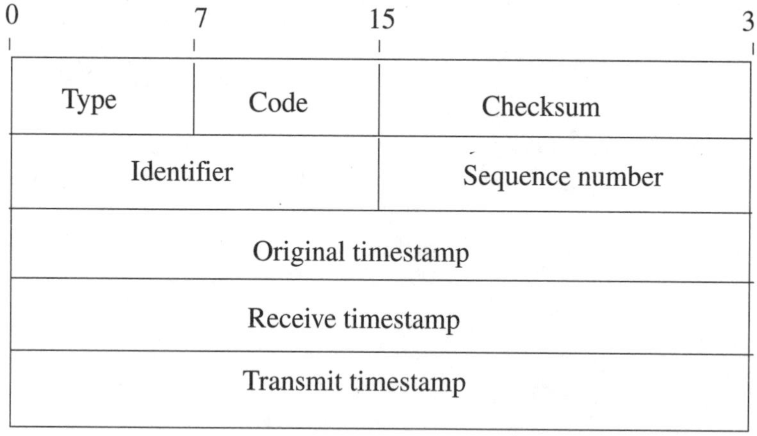

Type	Code	Checksum
Identifier		Sequence number
Original timestamp		
Receive timestamp		
Transmit timestamp		

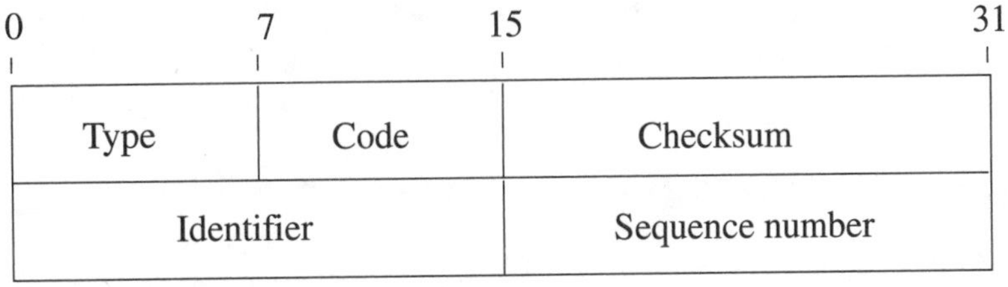

Figure 1-9
Information Request
and Reply Messsage
Format

0	7	15	31
Type	Code	Checksum	
Identifier		Sequence number	

Figure 1-9
Information Request and Reply Messsage Format

INFORMATION REQUEST AND INFORMATION REPLY MESSAGE

This ICMP message allows diskless network elements to ascertain their network address at boot time. When a diskless system is in the process of booting, it broadcasts an information request message to the hosts on its network. A host replies to this message using an information reply message. As is the case with all ICMP messages, this message is encapsulated by an IP datagram. The source address field in the information reply message will contain the IP address of the system that is replying to the information request message. The diskless system, on receiving the information reply message, will be able to ascertain its network address from the IP address in the source address field of the IP header, since both peers are on the same network. The format of this message is illustrated in Figure 1-9. The values for the fields of this message format are identical to the values of the respective fields of the echo/echo reply message, except that the values for the type fields are:

15–for information request message

16–for information reply message

This concludes our discussion of ICMP. For further details on this protocol, see RFC 792, which contains the specification.

1.2.2.3   Internet Group Management Protocol

Of the three network layer protocols, IGMP is the least used. It is used by hosts and routers to ascertain information about the hosts in multicast groups: groups of hosts to which IP datagrams are to be sent simultaneously. RFC 1112 [Dee89] contains the specification of this protocol. We will now turn our attention to the next layer in the TCP/IP protocol stack.

1.2.3   Transport Layer

The layer above the network layer in the TCP/IP protocol stack is the *transport layer*. This layer provides a flow of data between two hosts for the application layer above. Two protocols are implemented at the transport layer: TCP and User Datagram Protocol (UDP). Let us take a look at these two protocols. We will start with the more complex of the two, TCP.

1.2.3.1 Transmission Control Protocol

TCP is a reliable connection-oriented protocol that allows byte streams from a host to be delivered without error to any other hosts on networks that are reachable. We will begin our discussion of TCP by first examining its header format.

TCP HEADER FORMAT

TCP packets are encapsulated in IP datagrams. When the protocol field in the IP header contains the value 6: the number that the Internet Assigned Number Authority (IANA) assigned to TCP, the TCP header immediately follows the IP header. Figure 1-10 illustrates the format of the TCP header. A description of the fields in the TCP header follows:

- Source and destination ports: These are 16-bit fields that contain the source and destination ports, respectively, that are used for the TCP connection.

- Sequence number: This field contains a 32-bit number that uniquely identifies each byte of data that a host sent during a TCP session. If the SYN bit is set, the value in this field is the initial sequence number (ISN) (we will elaborate more on the ISN later). After the

Figure 1-10
TCP Header Format

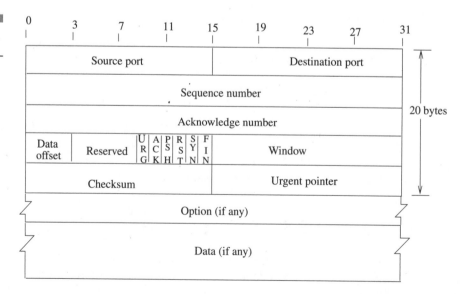

datagram with the SYN flag is transmitted, the sequence number is consequently incremented by 1, each time that a byte of data, or a datagram with the FIN flag set, is sent.

- Acknowledge number: This 32-bit field contains the value of the sequence number of the next byte of data that the sender is expecting, provided that the ACK bit is set. If the ACK bit is not set, the value in this field has no significance.

- Data offset: This 4-bit field contains the length of the TCP header in 32-bit words. This field indicates where the data in the TCP payload begin.

- Reserved: Reserved for future use.

- URG: When this bit is set, it indicates that the urgent pointer field is significant.

- ACK: When this bit is set, it indicates that the acknowledge number field is significant.

- RST: Setting this bit results in the resetting of the TCP connection.

- PSH: When this bit is set, it indicates that the receiver should pass the data to the application as soon as possible.

- SYN: When this bit is set, the sequence number field contains the sender ISN.

- FIN: This bit indicates that the sender has no more data to send.

- Window: This 16-bit field contains the number of bytes of data, starting with the one in the acknowledge number field, that the sender is willing to accept.

- Checksum: This 16-bit field contains the one's complement sum of all 16-bit words in the header and data portions. If a segment contains an odd number of bytes, the segment is padded to the right with zeros to form a 16-bit word for the checksum calculation. The padding, if added, is not transmitted with the data. The checksum field must be set to zero before the checksum is calculated.

- Urgent pointer: This 16-bit field is valid only if the URG flag is set. It contains a positive offset that should be added to the sequence number of the segment to give the sequence of the last byte of urgent data. The TCP urgent mode provides a way for a host to send data urgently to a communicating peer.

- Option: This field is of variable length. If options are present, they must be padded to ensure that they end on 32-bit word boundaries.

■ Data: The variable-length data field contains the TCP payload. The data portion of the TCP header should also be padded, if necessary, to ensure that it is a multiple of 32.

What are the services that TCP provides, and how does it provide these services? TCP provides the following services:

1. Reliability: TCP provides the mechanism to recover data that is lost, duplicated, or delivered out of order. It does this by assigning a sequence number to each byte transmitted, and requiring acknowledgement (ACK) from the receiving TCP peer. If an ACK is not received within a specified time period, the data are retransmitted. At the receiver end, the sequence number is used to correctly order the packet fragments and to eliminate duplicates. The receiving peer also uses the checksum to identify damaged segments. If segments are damaged, the receiver will request that the sender retransmit them.

2. Flow control: TCP allows a receiver to regulate the amount of data a sender sends. The is accomplished by the receiver sending the range of sequence numbers, in the window field, that it is willing to accept.

3. Multiplexing: TCP provides the mechanism for a number of processes on a single host to use the TCP communication mechanism simultaneously. It does so by providing communication ports that are used in conjunction with the interface address to provide connections. A connection is identified by a pair of sockets, which consist of the source IP address and port number and the destination IP address and port number.

4. Connections: TCP maintains certain status information about about each data stream it transmits or receives. This information is what constitutes a connection and it includes information about the sockets, sequence numbers, and window sizes. A connection is established when TCP initializes the status information on each side. Similarly, the connection is released when TCP frees up the resources and makes them available for use by other processes.

INITIALIZING TCP CONNECTIONS

As mentioned previously, TCP uses a 32-bit sequence number to uniquely identify each datagram segment that a host transmits. The first sequence number, the initial sequence number (ISN), that a host employs during a TCP session must be randomly generated. The sequence number of the remaining data fragment will be the ISN plus the segment sequence. For example, the first data segment will have sequence number ISN + 1 and the second, ISN + 2, etc. Note that the fragment with the ISN as the sequence number contains no actual TCP data because the connection has not yet been established. As mentioned in the previous section, during a TCP session a host uses the sequence numbers associated with the datagram segments it receives from its communicating peer for a number of important functions, such as to reassemble the data fragments and to perform flow control. Therefore, the peers need to inform the other peer about the ISN it generated for the session, before the TCP connection can be established. The steps involved in exchanging the ISNs are illustrated below. In the illustration A is the initiator of the TCP session and B is the other peer.

```
1) A--> B: SYN bit set; sequence no. field contains A's ISN.
2) A <--B: SYN and ACK bits set; sequence no. field contains
           B's ISN. Acknowledge no. field contains A's ISN.
3) A--> B: ACK bit set; Acknowledge no. field contains B's ISN.
```

The above exchange is commonly referred to as the TCP *three-way handshake*. Let us now look at the different states of a TCP connection.

TCP CONNECTION STATES

A TCP connection progresses through a series of states during its lifetime. We will now take a brief look at these connection states:

- LISTEN: The state in which a process is waiting for a connection request from any remote TCP port.

- SYN-SENT: The state in which a process is waiting for an ACK after sending a connection request.

- SYN-RECEIVED: The state in which a process is waiting for a confirming connection request acknowledgement, after both receiving and sending a connection request.

- ESTABLISHED: The state immediately after the three-way shake is completed. It represents an open connection where data can be delivered to the user process.

- FIN-WAIT-1: The state in which a process sends an FIN (a datagram segment with the FIN flag set) to its remote peer and it is waiting for an acknowledgement.

- FIN-WAIT-2: The state in which an FIN has been sent and an ACK received.

- CLOSE-WAIT: The state in which TCP is waiting for a connection termination request from a local user process.

- CLOSING: The state in which TCP is waiting for a connection termination request acknowledgement from a remote host.

- LAST-ACK: The state in which TCP has received an acknowledgement for a termination request it previously sent, and has sent an acknowledgement for the acknowledgement it received.

- TIME-WAIT: The state in which TCP is waiting for enough time to pass to be sure that a remote TCP process receives the acknowledgement to its connection termination request.

- CLOSED: The state in which there is actually no connection state.

On most systems the command `netstat -a` displays the states of all the current connections to or from the system. For further details about these connection states, or any other information about TCP, a good source of reference is RFC 793 [Pos81c], which contains the specifications for TCP.

1.2.3.2   User Datagram Protocol

Unlike TCP, the User Datagram Protocol (UDP) offers an unreliable connectionless[5] service. It does not perform any error checking or flow control; it just sends a datagram from one host to another and does not provide any guarantee that the datagram will get to its destination. There is much less overhead involved in processing UDP datagrams than in processing TCP packets. Consequently, the throughput for UDP datagrams is usually greater than that of TCP. UDP usually is used by applications for which prompt delivery is more important than accurate delivery, such as in the transmission of speech or video. RFC 768 [Pos80] contains the specifications for UDP.

UDP HEADER FORMAT

UDP is assigned the protocol number 17 by IANA. Therefore, when the IP header protocol field contains the value 17, the UDP header follows the IP header. The UDP header has fewer fields than any of the protocols we have discussed so far. It has only four fixed-length fields of 16 bits each and a variable-length data field. Figure 1-11 illustrates the format of this protocol header. A description of the fields follows:

---

[5]See Section 1.2.2.1.

Figure 1-11
UDP Header Format

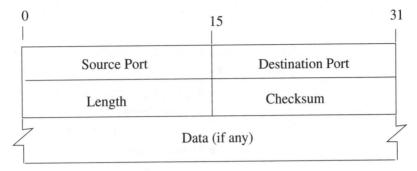

- Source and destination ports: These 16-bit fields contain the source and destination ports that are used to send and receive UDP datagrams.

- Length: This is the length, in bytes, of the UDP datagram (the header plus the data).

- Checksum: This 16-bit field contains the one's complement of the one's complement sum of the 16-bit words in the UDP header. If the datagram has a data portion, if necessary, it is first padded with zeros on the right to make its total length a multiple of 16, before the checksum is calculated. The padding, if added, is not transmitted with the data. The checksum field must be set to zero before the checksum is calculated.

This concludes our discussion on the transport layer. We will wrap up our discussion of the TCP/IP protocol suite by taking a brief look at the application layer, the final layer in this suite.

1.2.4 Application Layer

The top of the TCP/IP protocol stack is the *application layer*. This layer includes all processes that use the transport layer protocols to deliver data. Application layer protocols usually provide services to the users of the system. There are many application layer protocols. The ones that just about all TCP/IP implementation provides include the following:

- Telnet: Network Terminal Protocol, which provides remote login.
- FTP: File Transfer Protocol, which is used for file transfer to or from remote hosts.

- SMTP: Simple Mail Transfer Protocol, which delivers electronic mail.

- SNMP: Simple Network Management Protocol, which is used for monitoring network segments.

- DNS: Domain Name Service, which is used for mapping host names onto their IP addresses.

- HTTP: Hypertext Transfer Protocol, which is used for fetching Web pages on the World Wide Web.

CHAPTER **2**

Symmetric-Key Cryptography

Overview of Chapter 2

In this chapter, we discuss the following topics:

- Historical Perspective of Cryptography
- The Data Encryption Standard
- Design of Symmetric-Key Cryptosystems
  - Security Issues
  - Implementation and Performance Issues
  - Modes of Operation
- The Advanced Encryption Standard
  - MARS Cryptosystem
  - RC6 Cryptosystem
  - Rijndael Cryptosystem (AES)
  - Serpent Cryptosystem
  - Twofish Cryptosystem
  - Performance Comparison of the AES Finalists
- Other Symmetric-Key Cryptosystems

Cryptography involves the study of the enciphering, deciphering and authentication of data. There are essentially two methods of enciphering data: one approach uses symmetric cryptographic keys and the other uses asymmetric keys. The former methodology is referred to as *symmetric-key cryptography* and the latter as *public-key cryptography*. Symmetric, or private-key, cryptosystems use the same cryptographic key to encrypt and decrypt data, whereas public-key, or asymmetric systems utilize one key for encryption and another for decryption. In this chapter we examine symmetric-key cryptography; in Chapter 3 we discuss public-key cryptography, and in Chapter 4 we focus on hash functions and message authentication code. We begin our discussion by first taking a look at the evolution of symmetric-key cryptography.

2.1   Historical Perspective

The history of cryptography extends back more than 2000 years. It is believed that Julius Caesar, the Roman emperor, utilized a cryptosystem that is now commonly referred to as the *Caesar cipher*. This enciphering system is an example of a *shift cipher*. A shift cipher involves assigning a number to each letter of the alphabet as shown in the two tables below.

A	B	C	D	E	F	G	H	I	J	K	L	M
0	1	2	3	4	5	6	7	8	9	10	11	12

N	O	P	Q	R	S	T	U	V	W	X	Y	Z
13	14	15	16	17	18	19	20	21	22	23	24	25

Then the position of each letter of the alphabet is shifted by a number k. For example, if $k = 7$, then A becomes H, H becomes O, and Z becomes G. The Caesar cipher is the special case of a shift cipher where $k = 3$. Let us look at an example of the enciphering of a text with this cipher. Suppose Caesar wished to send the following message to one of his generals:

Youmustattackatmidnight.

The first step in enciphering this message—usually referred to in cryptographic parlance as the *plaintext*—involves converting each letter of the plaintext to an integer, using the two tables above. The result is:

24 14 20 12 20 18 19 0 19 19 0 2 10 0 19 12 8 3 13 8 6 7 19.

Next, shift each letter in the plaintext by three spaces; that is, add 3 modulo 26 to each of the numbers above.

Before we proceed, let us review some mathematical concepts. To compute $a + b \bmod n$, we take the sum of a and b; let us assume that $a + b = x$. If x is smaller than n, then the result of $a + b \bmod n = x$. However, if x is larger than n, then $a + b \bmod n = r$, where r is a positive integer such that $0 \leq r < n$ and $x = i * n + r$, where i is a positive integer.

The result of adding 3 modulo 26 to each of the numbers above is:

2 17 23 15 23 21 22 3 22 22 3 5 13 3 22 15 11 6 18 11 9 10 22.

In the final step, the integers that resulted from the addition operation are converted to the letters they represent, using the tables, to give the *ciphertext*. Therefore, the ciphertext for the message is:

CRXPXVWCWWCFNWPNCWPLGSLJKW.

The deciphering process is the reverse of the enciphering procedure: first, the letters in the ciphertext are converted to their corresponding integers, and then each integer is reduced by 3 modulo 26. Finally, the resulted integers are converted to their corresponding letters to give the decrypted message.

Evidently, this is not a secure cryptosystem: it can be broken quite easily. Breaking it essentially involves identifying the key k. Since k is an integer between 1 and 25 inclusively, it can be identified via an exhaustive key search in at most 25 attempts. Note that, as stated earlier, the Caesar cipher is just a special case of a shift cipher where $k = 3$, but for a shift cipher, in general, k can be any integer between 1 and 25 inclusively. To do an exhaustive key search on this or on any other cipher, one simply would use all possible values of k to in turn decrypt the ciphertext until a message that is in some intelligible form is obtained.

The next generation of ciphers were called *substitution ciphers*. In actuality, shift ciphers are a subset of substitution ciphers. There were a number of commonly used substitution ciphers. For a description of these ciphers see [Sti95]. Substitution ciphers differ from shift ciphers in that, instead of just shifting the letters k spaces, each letter is substituted for by another. Consequently, the key, instead of being an integer, it is a permutation. An exhaustive key search on a substitution cipher is much more difficult since the key space consists of all possible permutations of 26 symbols. There are 26 factorial (26!) possible permutations of 26 symbols—an exhaustive key could take as many as 26! attempts. Recall that for an integer a, for example, such that $a \geq 5$, $a! = a * (a-1) * (a-2) * \cdots 2 * 1$; so $26! = 26 * 25 * 24 * \cdots * 2 * 1 \approx 4.0 * 10^{26}$. An exhaustive key search of substitution ciphers requires considerable effort; however, they can be broken quite easily using *statistical cryptanalysis* techniques.

Cryptanalysis is the study of the techniques of breaking cryptosystems. Statistical cryptanalysis uses statistical information to break a cipher. Let us take a look at how this technique can be used to break a substitution cipher.

Each letter of the English language has a certain probability of occurring in a text. The probabilities are summarized below:

1. E has the highest probability of occurring in any written material—its probability of occuring is approximately 0.12.

2. D and L have a probability of approximately 0.04.

3. A, H, I, N, O, R, S, and T have probabilities between 0.06 and 0.09.

4. B, C, F, G, M, P, U, W, and Y have probabilities between 0.015 and 0.028.

5. J, K, Q, V, and Z have a probability of less than 0.01.

The frequencies of digrams and trigrams—two- or three-letter consecutive sequences—have also been documented; see [Sti95]. Therefore, one can perform analysis on the ciphertext outputted from a substitution cipher using the probability of occurrence of each letter, along with the frequency of digrams and trigrams, to easily identify the encryption key and consequently break the cipher. Thus, a simple substitution cipher does not offer much security.

Another cipher that was in use hundreds of years ago is the *permutation cipher*; it is also called *transposition cipher*. The permutation cipher is different from the ciphers we have discussed so far, in that permutation ciphers leave the letters unchanged, but change the relative positions of the letters, whereas shift or substution ciphers replace letters in the plaintext by other letters. This technique is still used quite extensively in modern cryptosystems. Examples of the application of this ciphering technique in cryptosystems are discussed later in this chapter.

2.1.1 Modern Cryptographic Techniques

Claude Shannon is considered by many to be the father of modern cryptography. He introduced the idea of making *diffusion* and *confusion* be essential elements of the building blocks of cryptosystems. As we have seen during our discussion of substitution ciphers, it is relatively easy to use statistical analysis to break a substitution cipher. Shannon proposed that the way to thwart these attacks is to use some form of diffusion technique that will cause the statistical composition of the ciphertext to have no relation to that of the plaintext, and to combine this with confusion techniques that make the relationship of the statistical composition of the ciphertext and the value of the encryption key as complex as possible. This result is achieved by using complex substitution algorithms that ensure that each character in the ciphertext is determined by as many characters as possible in the plaintext. The *Feistel cipher*, published by Horst Feistel in 1973 [Fie73], was the first cryptosystem to incorporate the ideas of Shannon. The network schemes that Feistel used in designing his cipher are still widely used today in a large number of cryptosystems. The unique design features of the Feistel cipher can summarized as follows:

- It employed product ciphers that perform two or more basic substitutions and/or permutations in sequence.
- It performed several rounds of substitutions using a substitution function.
- It utilized a key schedule algorithm to transform the key bits into subkeys that the cipher used for the different rounds.

These design features are used currently in just about all symmetric-key cryptosystems.

In 1973 the National Bureau of Standards (NBS), currently known as the National Institute of Standards and Technology (NIST), issued a request for proposals for a national cryptosystem standard. A number of cipher systems were proposed. After a review of the proposals, in July 1977 NBS adopted the cryptosystem developed at IBM in the 1960s, by a group of researchers led by Horst Feistel, as the Data Encryption Standard (DES). This cipher system is based on a cryptosystem called LUCIFER [Fie73] that is essentially an extension of the Feistel cipher. DES became the most widely used cipher system in the world. It was reaffirmed as the national standard in 1983, 1988, and 1993.

In 1997, RSA Laboratories issued a challenge with a reward of $10,000 to find the DES key of a ciphertext that was preceded by a known block of text, which contained the the phrase "the unknown message is:" A project headed by Roche Verse—an independent consultant—which involved over 70,000 computer systems linked over the Internet, used a brute-force[1] program to find the correct DES key in approximately 96 days [RSA97]. In July 1998, a machine built by the Electronic Frontier Foundation (EFF),

---

[1]A brute-force attack involves trying all possible keys until the correct one is found.

which cost \$250,000 in 1998, cracked DES in less than 3 days; for further detail, see the document on the EFF home page at *http://www.eff.org/des cracker.html*. These successful attacks on DES accelerated the search for a more secure replacement.

In recognizing that DES was near the end of its useful life, NIST announced a plan in January 1997 to select a candidate for the Advanced Encryption Standard (AES): the new standard that would replace DES. In the interim, on October 25, 1999, NIST adopted triple DES—a more secure variant of DES—as the national standard.

In response to the NIST solicitation for candidates for the new encryption standard, 15 cryptographic algorithms were submitted by mid-1998. On August 9, 1999, NIST announced that it had chosen five finalists for the second round. Finally, on October 2, 2000, NIST disclosed that it selected Rijndael, one of the five finalists, as the candidate for the AES. It is expected that the AES candidate algorithm will be be unbreakable for at least the next century.

2.2 The Data Encryption Standard

DES has been in used for almost a quarter of a century. It has been studied extensively, and its structure is well understood. DES has proven to be quite resistant to cryptanalysis. The problem with DES is not with its design, but rather its key length. It uses a 56-bit key to encrypt blocks of 64-bit plaintext. Given a 64-bit plaintext x and the corresponding 64-bit ciphertext c that resulted from enciphering x with DES, the 56-bit DES key K can be found within 2^{55} operations. As the speed of computing systems increases, it becomes much more feasible to perform large number of operations within limited time periods. In the light of the increasing capabilities of computer hardware, a cryptosystem that uses a 56-bit key is by no means secure. For a reasonable degree of security, an algorithm that utilizes a key that is at least 128 bits long, is required.

We will now take a detailed look at DES, and use it as our reference when we discuss the design of symmetric ciphers later in this chapter.

The DES algorithm proceeds in three stages:

1. The 64-bit block plaintext x is first run through an initial permutation function IP, which gives a 64-bit output x_0. We can represent this as $x_0 = \text{IP}(x) = L_0 R_0$, where L_0 represents the the first 32 bits of x_0, and R_0 represents the last 32 bits. The permutation

function IP is shown on the left side of Table 2-1. It is interpreted as follows: the first 3 bits of the output from this function are the 58th, 50th, and 42nd bits of the input to the function; similarly, the 62nd, 63rd, and 64th bits of the output are the 23rd, 15th, and 7th bits, respectively, of the input bit string.

2. x_0 is then subjected to 16 iterations of key-dependent computations involving a cipher function f and a key scheduling function KS. If we represents the output from each iteration as $x_i = L_i R_i$, where $1 \le i \le 16$, then

$$L_i = R_i{-}1$$
$$R_i = L_i \oplus f(R_{i-1}, K_i)$$

where $\oplus$ denotes the exclusive-OR of two bit strings. The K_i's are 48-bit blocks that are derived from the original 56-bit key using the key scheduling function KS. The key scheduling function, the derivation of the K_i's, and the cipher function f are discussed later.

3. The inverse permutation function IP^{-1} is then applied to $R_{16}L_{16}$ to give a 64-bit block ciphertext c; that is, $c = IP^{-1}(R_{16}L_{16})$. Note the change in this order of R_{16} and L_{16}. The inverse permutation function is shown on the right side of Table 2-1. It is the inverse of IP: if it is applied to the output of IP, the result is identical to the bit string inputted to IP; that is, $IP^{-1}(IP(x)) = 1$. Figure 2-1 illustrates the DES algorithm.

The cipher function f involves the following steps:

- The R_i's are subjected to an expansion permutation E that takes as its input the 32-bit block R_i and yields a 48-bit block output.

TABLE 2-1

Initial Permutation (IP) and Inverse Permutation IP^{-1} Functions

IP								IP^{-1}							
58	50	42	34	26	18	10	2	40	8	18	16	56	24	64	32
60	52	44	36	28	20	12	4	39	7	47	15	55	23	63	31
62	54	46	38	30	22	14	6	38	6	46	14	54	22	62	30
64	56	48	40	32	24	16	8	37	15	45	13	53	21	61	29
57	49	41	33	25	17	9	1	36	4	44	12	52	20	60	28
59	51	43	35	27	19	11	3	35	3	43	11	51	19	59	27
61	53	45	37	29	21	13	5	34	2	42	10	50	18	58	26
63	55	47	39	31	23	15	7	33	1	41	9	49	17	57	25

Figure 2-1
DES Encryption
Algorithm

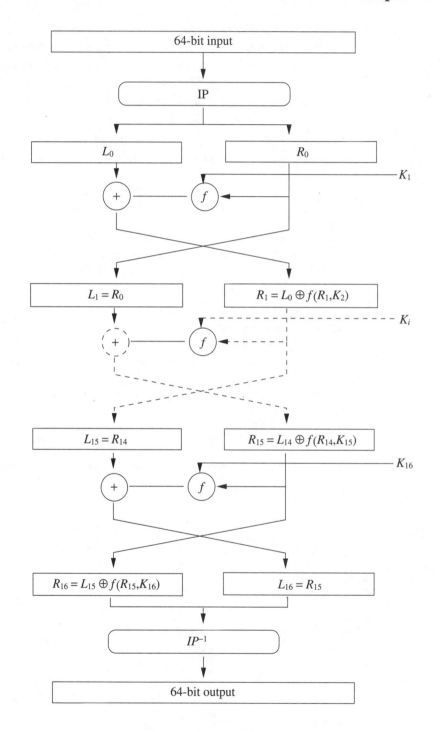

The expansion permutation is shown on the left side of Table 2-2. It is interpreted as follows: the first three bits of the 48-bit output $E(R_i)$ are the bits in positions 32, 1, and 2 of R_i; whereas the last 3 bits of the output are the bits in positions 31, 32, and 1 of R_i.

■ The 48-bit output $E(R_i)$ of the expansion permutation is exclusive-OR with the 48-bit K_i.

■ The 48-bit output that resulted from the $E(R_i) \oplus K_i$ operation is broken up into eight 6-bit blocks and each block is passed through an S-box that gives an output of length of 4 bits. The eight S-boxes are shown in Table 2-3. The permutation of the S-boxes can be described as follows: the first and the last bits of a 6-bit input to a given S-box S_i form a 2-bit binary number to select one of the four rows in S_i; whereas, the inner four bits form a binary number in the range 0 to 15 to select one of the 16 columns in S_i. For example, if an input to S_1 is 101011, the 2-bit binary number obtained from the first and the last bits is 11, the decimal equivalent is 3; therefore, row 3 is selected. The inner four bits are 0101, the decimal equivalent is 5; therefore, column 5 is selected. The number in the 3rd row and 5th column of S_1 is 6; therefore, the output from S_1 for this example is 0110, which is the 4-bit binary representation of 6.

■ The 4-bit output of each of the eight S-boxes is concatenated as shown in Figure 2-2 to yield a 32-bit output, which is then fed into a permutation function P. Finally, P yields an output of 32 bits, which is the result of $f(R_i, K_i)$. The permutation function P is shown on the right side of Table 2-2, and Figure 2-2 illustrates the computation of $f(R,K)$.

TABLE 2-2

Expansion Function and Permutation Function P

E Bit-Selection Table						P			
32	1	2	3	4	5	16	7	20	21
4	5	6	7	8	9	29	12	28	17
8	9	10	11	12	13	1	15	23	26
12	13	14	15	16	17	5	18	31	10
16	17	18	19	20	21	2	8	24	14
20	21	22	23	24	25	32	27	3	9
24	25	26	27	28	29	19	13	30	6
28	29	30	31	32	1	22	11	4	25

TABLE 2-3

DES Eight S-boxes

								S_1							
14	4	13	1	2	15	11	8	3	10	6	12	5	9	0	7
0	15	7	4	14	2	13	1	10	6	12	11	9	5	3	8
4	1	14	8	13	6	2	11	15	12	9	7	3	10	5	0
15	12	8	2	4	9	1	7	5	11	3	14	10	0	6	13

								S_2							
15	1	8	14	6	11	3	4	9	7	2	13	12	0	5	10
3	13	4	7	15	2	8	14	12	0	1	10	6	9	11	5
0	14	7	11	10	4	13	1	5	8	12	6	9	3	2	15
13	8	10	1	3	15	4	2	11	6	7	12	0	5	14	9

								S_3							
10	0	9	14	6	3	15	5	1	13	12	7	11	4	2	8
13	7	0	9	3	4	6	10	2	8	5	14	12	11	15	1
13	6	4	9	8	15	3	0	11	1	2	12	5	10	14	7
1	10	13	0	6	9	8	7	4	15	14	3	11	5	2	12

								S_4							
7	13	14	3	0	6	9	10	1	2	8	5	11	12	14	15
13	8	11	5	6	15	0	3	4	7	2	12	1	10	14	9
10	6	9	0	12	11	7	13	15	1	3	14	5	2	8	4
3	15	0	6	10	1	13	8	9	4	5	11	12	7	2	14

								S_5							
2	12	4	1	7	10	11	6	8	5	3	15	13	0	14	9
14	11	2	12	4	7	13	1	5	0	15	10	3	9	8	6
4	2	1	11	10	13	7	8	15	9	12	5	6	3	0	14
11	8	12	7	1	14	2	13	6	15	0	9	10	4	5	3

								S_6							
12	1	10	15	9	2	6	8	0	13	3	4	14	7	5	11
10	15	4	2	7	12	9	5	6	1	13	14	0	11	3	8
9	14	15	5	2	8	12	3	7	0	4	10	1	13	11	6
4	3	2	12	9	5	15	10	11	14	1	7	6	0	8	13

								S_7							
4	11	2	14	15	0	8	13	3	12	9	7	5	10	6	1
13	0	11	7	4	9	1	10	14	3	5	12	2	15	8	6
1	4	11	13	12	3	7	14	10	15	6	8	0	5	9	2
6	11	13	8	1	4	10	7	9	5	0	15	14	2	3	12

								S_8							
13	2	8	4	6	15	11	1	10	9	3	14	5	0	12	7
1	15	13	8	10	3	7	4	12	5	6	11	0	14	9	2
7	11	4	1	9	12	14	2	0	6	10	13	15	3	5	8
2	1	14	7	4	10	8	13	15	12	9	0	3	5	6	11

Figure 2-2

f(R,K) Calculation

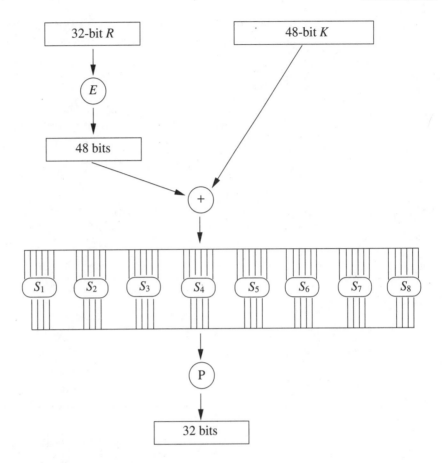

The *key scheduling function KS* is used to generate the 48-bit K_i's from the 56-bit original key. Actually, DES keys are 64 bits in length. However, 8 of the bits are used for error detection: the bits in positions 8, 16, 24,..., 64 are used for assuring that each byte has an odd parity, that is, that each byte has an odd number of 1's.

KS involves two permutation functions: permutation choice 1 (PC-1) and permutation choice 2 (PC-2). The functions are shown in Table 2-4. The algorithm for determing the K_i's, where $1 \leq i \leq 16$, can be described as follows:

1. Given a 64-bit key K, discard the 8 parity bits and apply the fixed permutation PC-1 to the remaining 56 bits of K. We can represents this as PC-1 $(K) = C_0 D_0$, where C_0 and D_0 represent the first and last 28 bits of K, respectively. In Table 2-4, PC-1 is

divided into two halves. The first half determines the bits in C_0 and the second half determines the bits in D_0.

2. Compute C_i and D_i, such that

$$C_i = LS_i(C_{i-1})$$
$$D_i = LS_i(D_{i-1})$$

where LS_i is either 1 or 2 and it represents the number of cyclic left shifts by which the bits in C_i or D_i are to be shifted. Table 2-4 shows the LS_i's for the 16 iterations.

TABLE 2-4

Tables Used for DES Key Schedule Calculation

PC-1						
57	49	41	33	25	17	9
1	58	50	42	34	26	18
10	2	59	51	43	35	27
19	11	3	60	52	44	36
63	55	47	39	31	23	15
7	63	54	46	38	30	22
14	6	61	53	45	37	29
21	13	5	28	20	12	4

Schedule of Left Shifts															
Iteration number 1	2	3	4	5	6	7	8	9	10	11	12	13	14	15	16
Left shifts 1	1	2	2	2	2	2	2	1	2	2	2	2	2	2	1

PC-2					
14	17	11	24	1	5
3	28	15	6	21	10
23	19	12	4	26	8
16	7	27	20	13	2
4	52	31	37	47	55
30	40	51	45	33	48
44	49	39	56	34	53
46	42	50	36	29	32

3. Concatenate the bits of C_i and D_i and apply the fixed permutation PC-2 to the result. The output from PC-2 is the key K_i, that is, K_i = PC-2 (C_iD_i). The key schedule computations are illustrated in Figure 2-3.

This concludes our presentation of the DES enciphering algorithm. The *deciphering* process utilizes the same key and algorithm as are used for enciphering, except that the algorithm is applied in the reverse order.

A complete description of both the encryping and decrypting process is presented in the Federal Information Processing Standards Publication 46-3 (FIPS PUB 46-3) [NIST99]. This paper is a very good source of reference if further detail is required.

Figure 2-3
DES Key Schedule
Calculation

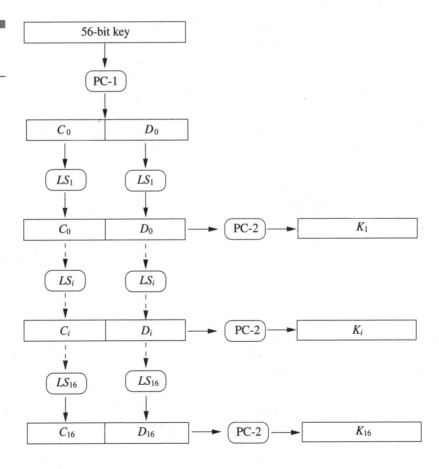

2.2.1 Triple DES

As indicated earlier, NIST assigned triple DES the interim encryption standard in 1999. Triple DES is a more secure variant of DES; however, it encrypts data much more slowly compared to DES.

The triple DES algorithm can be described as follows: let $e_k(x)$ and $d_k(x)$ represent the encryption and decryption of the 64-bit bitstring x using the DES algorithm with key K; then the 64-bit ciphertext c is obtained by performing the following operation:

$$c = e_{K_3}(d_{K_2}(e_{K_1}(x)))$$

where K_1, K_2 and K_3 are 56-bit DES keys.

The deciphering of triple DES to derive the plaintext x from the ciphertext c is the reverse of the enciphering process, and it can be described as follows:

$$x = d_{K_1}(e_{K_2}(d_{K_3}(c)))$$

For greater security, the three keys should all be different; this in essence corresponds to enciphering with a key of length 168 bits—which should be relatively secure against brute-force attack for many years. For data requiring a lesser degree of security, K_1 can be equal to K_3. In this case, the key is effectively 112 bits in length.

Triple DES is considered to be the most secure of all the commonly used 64-bit block ciphers; but, in software, it is also the slowest of these commonly used block ciphers. However, there are hardware accelerators for triple DES that speed up the runtime considerably. With these accelerators, triple DES can outperform any of the other block ciphers in software.

2.3   Design of Symmetric-Key Cryptosystems

All of the cryptosystems that we discussed so far are refered to as *block ciphers*. Block ciphers are cryptosystems that encrypt the plaintext in blocks of x bits and output blocks of x-bit ciphertext. Some ciphers use variable block sizes, whereas others uses fixed size. Most of the ciphers in the DES era use a block size of 64 bits; however, the more recent ciphers utilize block sizes of at least 128 bits.

Block ciphers differ from *stream ciphers* in that stream ciphers encrypt one character of the plaintext at a time. The uses of stream ciphers are rather limited. For this reason, most of our presentation is concerned with block ciphers.

It is now time to address the important parameters that must be considered in designing any cryptosystem. The element that is of paramount importance is the security of the cipher. If the cryptosystem is not secure, it will not be of much value. Let us now look at issues that affect the security of cryptosystems.

2.3.1 Security Issues

There are a number of elements that have a direct bearing on the security of a cryptosystem. We discuss these elements in this section. Let us start with the size of the encryption key.

2.3.1.1 Key Size

The key size is the length of the encryption key in bits. Bits, in this sense, are synonymous with binary form: they are just 1's and 0'. For example, the bit representation of 99 is 1100011. Therefore, 99 in binary form is 7 bits long. As we have seen in our discussion of DES, it took a machine that was specially built in 1998 for cracking DES, less than 3 days to break DES, via an exhaustive key search. This machine executes about $2 * 10^{11}$ instuctions per seconds. The speed of computer hardware is increasing at a phenomenal rate. The Internet also makes it possible to have thousands or even millions of computers working in parallel to crack a cipher. This needs to be taken into consideration when designing cryptosystems. The key length for a secure cryptographic algorithm should be long enough that it will be infeasible to use hundreds of thousands of computers—that are a million times faster than the fastest known machine—working in parallel—to break it.

NIST stipulated that the candidates for the new encryption standard should use a minimum key size of 128 bits. Let us do some analysis here: assume that it was possible to build a computer that was a million times faster than the one used to break DES in 1998. This computer would be capable of executing approximately $2 * 10^{17}$ operations per second. How long would it take a million of these computers to complete an exhaustive key search of a cryptosystem that uses a 128-bit key? If the cryptosystem is symmetric, it requires approximately $2^{128}/2 = 2^{127} \approx 1.7 * 10^{38}$ operations. One million of these "super computers" working in parallel would be able to execute about $10^6 * 2 * 10^{17} = 2 * 10^{23}$ operations per second. Therefore, it would take approximately $\$1.7 * 10^{38}$ divide by $2 * 10^{23}$, which is about 10^{15} seconds. 10^{15} seconds is approximately 31,623,153 years! This is an estimate of the time that it would take 1 million computers that are 1 million times faster than the one used to crack DES in 1998 to complete a brute-force attack on a cryptosystem that uses a 128-bit key. Obviously, this is impractical, but no one knows what new hardware inventions are going to surface in the next decade; consequently, it is imperative that provision is made for the highly improbable when designing a cryptosystem that is expected to be secure for the foreseeable future. For a high degree of security, the length of the key for a symmetric-key cryptosystem should be at least 128 bits.

2.3.1.2   Block Size

As explained previously, block ciphers encrypt blocks of x-bit plaintext at a time and output blocks of equal-size ciphertext. The block size is another important element that affects the security of a block cipher. In general, the security of a cipher typically increases with increasing block size because it is more difficult to perform cryptanalysis on large blocks of ciphertext since larger blocks of ciphertext have more possible plaintext candidates.

However, there is a disadvantage to using too large a block size: the encryption overhead generally increases with an increase in block size; that is, the larger the block size, usually the greater the encryption time. Therefore, it is important that the right balance be found between the added security of larger blocks and the faster encryption speed of smaller blocks. A block size of 128 bits is typically ideal for most applications.

2.3.1.3   Key Scheduling Function

A key scheduling function is a design feature of most block ciphers. These functions are used to distribute the key bits to the different parts of the cipher that need them. In most ciphers, key scheduling functions expand the keying material and create subkeys that are utilized in the different rounds of the cryptosystem. The design of the key scheduling function is very important. It should be designed so that the key bits that are used in each round are unique to the round. If the key scheduling function is poorly designed, it could result in properities—such as different keys producing equivalent ciphertext—that can help cryptanalysts to break the cipher. Therefore, it is imperative that much consideration be given to the design of the key scheduling function because this element of a cryptosystem often determines the strength of the cipher.

2.3.1.4   Number of Rounds

The number of rounds in the encryption process is another important element that affects the security of a cipher. The ciphertext obtained from a single round of a cipher can often be decrypted to the equivalent plaintext, by way of some cryptanalysis techniques, with considerable less effort than if several rounds of ciphering were utilized in the encryption process. Typically, each additional round that a cipher utilizes should provide added security for the cipher. However, the throughput of the cipher decreases with the number of rounds. Thus, as in the case of the size of the encryption block, the right balance between the added security of an increased number of rounds and the better performance of a smaller number of rounds needs to be found. The degrees of security associated with the number of rounds of different ciphers are in general not equivalent: the security associated with one round of one cipher may be equivalent to that of two rounds of another cipher, and visa versa. The level of security of a round depends on the overall design of the cipher and often to a large extent on the design of the key scheduling function. To determine the number of rounds that is appropriate for a cipher, the cipher's designers need to perform the necessary analysis to ascertain the number of rounds that will render adequate resistance against cryptanalysis.

2.3.1.5   Resistance to Cryptanalysis

Another important parameter that affects the security of a cipher is its resistance to cryptanalysis. Cryptanalysis is the study of the techniques of breaking cryptosystems. In our discussion of classical ciphers that were used in previous centuries, we mentioned the relative ease with which these ciphers can be broken using statistical cryptanalysis. As a refresher, statistical cryptanalysis is the technique of breaking a cipher using statistical analysis of the characters in the ciphertext. This approach attempts to relate the frequency of characters or group of characters in the ciphertext to the probabilities of them occurring in written text. Statistical cryptanalysis can be quite effective in breaking simple ciphers; however, it is ineffective against ciphers in the DES or post-DES era. The DES and post-DES era ciphers employ the Shannon ideas of diffusion and confusion (discussed earlier) to ensure that the statistical component of the ciphertext has no relation to that of the plaintext.

There are two relatively new cryptanalysis techniques, however, that can be used with some measure of success against modern cryptosystems. These techniques are quite complex: they incorporate the use of complex mathematical procedures. A high-level description of these cryptanalysis techniques follows.

1. *Differential cryptanalysis*: Differential cryptanalysis is the technique that involves analyzing the effect of particular differences in plaintext pairs on the corresponding ciphertext pair; the differ-

ences are then used to assign probabilities to the possible keys in an attempt to identify the most probable key, and hence breaking the cipher. Differential cryptanalysis was first reported in open literature in 1990 by Murphy [Mur90], where he outlined the methodology he used to cryptanalyze a cipher known as FEAL. Following Murphy's paper, there were a number of papers by Biham and Shamir on similar techniques for cryptanalyzing DES-like cryptosystems. In 1993, Biham and Shamir published a differential cryptanalysis method that can be used to successfully cryptanalyze DES in an order of complexity of 2^{47}, requiring 2^{47} chosen plaintext [BS93]. Essentially, this method involves starting with two plaintexts m and m' with known exclusive-OR difference $\Delta m = m \oplus m'$, and then considering the difference between intermediate message pairs [that is, $\Delta m_i = m_i \oplus m'_i$, such that $m_{i+1} = m_{i-1} \oplus f(m_i, K_i)$ for the rounds i, $0 < i < 16$, where f is the key scheduling function for DES], utilizing the subkey K_i. Similarly,

$$\Delta m_{i+1} = m_{i+1} \oplus m'_{i+1}$$

$$= \left[m_{i-1} \oplus f(m_i, K_i) \right] \oplus \left[m'_{i-1} \oplus f(m'_i, K_i) \right]$$

$$= \Delta m_{i-1} \oplus \left[f(m_i K_i) \oplus f(m'_i, K_i) \right]$$

If many pairs of inputs to the function f with the same exclusive-OR difference, using the same subkey, yield the same output difference in the ciphertext; after a large number of tests, it is likely that one can predict with some degree of certainty the changes in the plaintext that will cause particular changes in the ciphertext. This information can lead to the identification of a subkey for a given round. If a number of subkeys are identified, this can lead ultimately to the identification of the encryption key.

2. *Linear cryptanalysis:* Linear cryptanalysis is the technique that attempts to find linear approximations based on the transformation that a cryptosystem performed on a plaintext. Matsui outlined in an article published in 1993 [Mat93] how this technique can be used to successfully cryptanalyze DES using 2^{47} known plaintexts. This technique, like differential cryptanalysis, is very complex; and its description is beyond the scope of this book. If more information is required, Matsui's article [Mat93] is a good source of reference.

Both differential and linear cryptanalysis belong to the class of cryptanalysis techniques known as *known plaintext exploits* because they utilize known plaintext to perform the attacks. These attacks, although they are more of theoretical interest because of the large number of plaintexts they require, are nonetheless significant, particularly when either method requires less effort to break a cipher than a brute-force attack requires. For a secure cipher, the general principle is that the order of magnitude of the effort required to successfully cryptanalyze the cipher should be greater than that which is required to break it via a brute-force attack.

2.3.2   Implementation and Performance Issues

It is not just important for a cryptosystem to be secure; it also needs to be relatively easily implemented in both software and hardware. Moreover, it needs to have good encryption throughput in both these mediums. If a cipher does not satisfy these requirements, its use will be rather limited. Let us look at some of the elements that affect the implementation and performance of a cipher.

2.3.2.1   Primitive Operations

The primitive operation that most symmetric-key ciphers employ can usually be performed very efficiently in both software and hardware. This contrasts with public-key cryptosystems,[2] which involve computationally intensive operations, such as the modular exponentiation of very large numbers. For this reason, applications such as IPSec that require large encryption/decryption throughput almost exclusively utilize symmetric-key cryptosystems as opposed to public-key cryptosystems.

The operations that can be implemented most efficiently are those that are native to the hardware instruction set. These operations include: addition, subtraction, exclusive-OR, and bitwise-AND. Multiplication and bit rotation operations are rather special in that their efficiency depends on the type of hardware that they are implemented in, or the hardware that the software runs on. This is because the multiplication operation is not native to the instruction set of most hardware. For example, in the original SPARC architecture, a multiplication operation takes about 50 cycles, compared with about 10 cycles in the Intel Pentium and approximately

---

[2] Public-key cryptosystems are discussed in the next chapter.

2 cycles in Intel Pentium Pro/II/III, Ultra-SPARC, or Alpha architectures. Cryptosystems that utilize multiplication and/or bit rotation operations extensively will therefore experience performance degradation on certain hardware architectures.

2.3.2.2 Memory Utilization

The amount of memory that a cipher utilizes is an important parameter that affects its performance. If a cipher uses too much memory, then it will be unsuitable for utilities such as Smart Cards. The use of Smart Cards is becoming more and more widespread. Consequently, the cryptosystems that will experience the most extensive use are those that require a limited amount of RAM—less that 100 bytes—since 8-bit Smart Cards usually have between 128 to 256 bytes of on-board RAM. Some of the parameters that affect memory utilization of a cipher are as follows:

1. *S-boxes:* S-boxes are nonlinear substitution operations that are used in most ciphers. They typically increase what is called the *avalanche effect* of a cipher. The avalanche effect is the property whereby a change in 1 bit in the plaintext results in several bit changes in the ciphertext. This property is desirable in that it can help to thwart certain cryptanalysis attacks.

   S-boxes can be either large tables—as in the case of DES—or they can be derived algebraically. The implementation of algebraic S-boxes usually requires less RAM, since they do not involves large lookup tables; however, they can result in S-boxes that are vulnerable to differential cryptanalysis [Mur90]. Tabular S-boxes take x-bit input and output y bits; hence, they are described as x-by-y-bit S-boxes. For example, DES has eight 6-by-4-bit S-boxes. The amount of RAM that S-boxes use depends on their actual sizes, and more particularly, on their input size: the larger the input size, the greater the RAM size required.

2. *Subkey computation:* The other factor that can have a significant bearing on the RAM requirement is the way that subkeys are derived. If subkeys can be effectively computed on the fly, then the memory requirement will not be significant. However, if the subkeys have to be precomputed and stored in memory—as in the case of RC6[3]—the RAM requirement can be quite high.

---

[3] We discuss the RC6 algorithm later in this chapter.

2.3.3 Mode of Operation

Block ciphers can operate in four possible modes. A brief description of each of the four modes follows:

1. *Electronic codebook (ECB) mode:* This is the direct application of the cipher's algorithm: given a bit-string of plaintext $x = x_1 x_2 \ldots$, break up the bit-string in blocks of b-bit x_i's, where b is the block size of the cipher, and apply the algorithm to each x_i to produce a block of ciphertext, c_i. We write $c_i = e_k(x_i)$, where e_k is the enciphering algorithm. The complete ciphertext c is the concatenation of the c_i's in numerical order; that is, $c = c_1 c_2 \ldots$.

2. *Cipher block chaining (CBC) mode:* Given a bit-string of plaintext $x = x_1 x_2 \ldots$, where the x_i's are b-bit blocks, the first block x_1 is first exclusive-ORed with a b-bit initial vector IV. Then the encryption algorithm is applied to the result to give the first block of ciphertext, c_1. The consequent blocks of plaintext, x_i's are then exclusive-ORed with the previous block of ciphertext, c_{i-1} and the encryption algorithm applied. This can be represented as: $c_1 = e_k(x_1 \oplus IV)$, $c_2 = e_k(x_2 \oplus c_1)$, and $c_i = e_k(x_i \oplus c_{i-1})$. Initial vectors are used in this mode of operation to ensure that the ciphertexts that result from plaintexts that are similar in the first few bytes—for example, the header of IP datagrams—are different.

3. *Cipher feedback (CFB) mode:* This mode uses previously generated ciphertext as input to the cipher's algorithm to generate pseudo-random outputs which are exclusive-ORed with the plaintext to produce the ciphertext. The steps can be described as follows: apply the algorithm to an initial vector IV to produce a cipher output z_1, and then exclusive-OR x_1 with z_1 to produce the first block of ciphertext, c_1. The subsequent blocks of ciphertext, c_i's, are produced by applying the algorithm to the previous block of ciphertext, then exclusive-ORing the output with the corresponding block of plaintext, x_i, that is, $z_1 = e_k(IV)$, $c_1 = x_1 \oplus z_1$, $z_2 = e_k(c_1)$, $c_2 = x_2 \oplus z_2$, $z_i = e_k(c_{i-1})$ and $c_i = x_i \oplus z_i$.

4. *Output feedback (OFB) mode:* This mode is similar to the CFB mode, except that OFB does not chain the ciphertext; instead, the initial vector IV is encrypted in turn to produce the z_i's. Thus, $z_1 = e_k(IV)$, $c_1 = x_1 \oplus z_1$, $z_i = e_k(z_{i-1})$ and $c_i = x_i \oplus z_i$.

2.4 The Advanced Encryption Standard

In 1997, NIST solicited submissions from the cryptographic community for candidates for the new Advanced Encryption Standard (AES). NIST stipulated that the candidates should satisfy the following requirements:

- The ciphers must be unclassified: they must not be protected as trade secrets.
- The full description of the algorithms must be publicly disclosed.
- The ciphers must be available for use royalty-free worldwide.
- The cryptosystems should support a block size of at least 128 bits.
- The ciphers should support key sizes of at least 128, 192, and 256 bits.

By August 1998, 15 candidates were submitted for the AES. NIST announced on August 9, 1999, that it had selected five candidates as the finalists for the second round. NIST disclosed on October 2, 2000, that it had chosen Rijndael as the candidate for the AES. The finalists and finally, the AES candidate, were chosen based on the following distinguishing characteristics:

- Security
- Ease of implementation, performance in hardware and software; and memory requirement.
- The flexibility and simplicity of the cipher.

The officials at NIST who conducted the review process were convinced that Rijndael provided the best combination of security, performance in hardware and software, low memory requirement, and flexibility of the 15 candidates that they reviewed.

In the following sections we give a detailed description of all five AES finalists. We also present the C and Java source codes for AES, in Appendices A and B, respectively.

2.4.1 MARS

MARS was developed by a group from IBM. The developers of MARS filed a patent application; however, they stated that if MARS was chosen as the candidate for the AES, then MARS will be available for royalty-free use worldwide. MARS homepage is *http://www.research.ibm.com/security/ mars.html*. MARS uses a block size of 128 bits and variable key sizes ranging from 128 to 448 bits. The primitive operations that MARS utilizes are additions, subtractions, exclusive-OR, table lookups, and both fixed and data-dependent bit rotation; in addition, it utilizes 16 multiplication operations. We give a high-level description of this cipher, and then present a detailed description, using mainly pseudocodes.

2.4.1.1 High-Level Description of MARS

MARS takes as its input four 32-bit data words containing plaintext and produces the same number of data words in the resulting ciphertext. The algorithm proceeds in three phases:

1. *Phase 1:* In this phase, the n 32-byte key words—n is an integer between 4 and 14 inclusively—are expanded to forty 32-byte key words, using a key expansion function. The data words are then added to the key words, followed by eight rounds of S-box based unkeyed mixing in "forward mode."

2. *Phase 2:* The second phase is the "cryptographic core" of the cipher. It employs 16 rounds of keyed transformation, 8 in the forward and 8 in the backward mode. Each round uses an expansion function E, which takes as input one data word and two key words, and outputs three words.

3. *Phase 3:* The last phase is essentially the reverse of the first phase. It uses eight rounds of the same unkeyed mixing, except that it is in "backward mode." This is then followed by subtraction of key words from the data words.

2.4.1.2 Notations

We use the following notation in describing the algorithm and its components:

- $x + y$ is addition modulo 2^{32}.
- $x - y$ is subtraction modulo 2^{32}.
- $x * y$ is multiplication modulo 2^{32}.
- $x \wedge y$ is the bit-wise AND of x and y.
- $x \vee y$ is the bit-wise OR of x and y.
- $x \oplus y$ is the bit-wise exclusive-OR of x and y.
- $x \lll s$ represents the cyclic rotation of the 32-bit word x by s positions to the left.

- $x \ggg s$ represents the cyclic rotation of the 32-bit word x by s positions to the right.

- $Y[i]$ represents the ith element of an array $Y[\,]$.

- $S[0,\ldots,511]$ is an S-box consisting of 512 32-bit words. The first 256 entries of S are denoted as $S0$ and the last 256 entries as $S1$.

- $(x_n,\ldots,x_2,x_1) \longleftarrow (x_1,\ldots,x_3,x_2,)$ represents the n-wise swap operation of 32-bit words; for example, $(D[3],D[2],D[1],D[0]) \longleftarrow (D[0],D[3],D[2],D[1])$ represents the rotation of the 4-word array $D\,[\,]$ by one word to the right.

- In the presentation of the pseudocode for the algorithms, information on a given line that follows // is not a part of the code; it is meant just for comment.

- The pair /* and */ is used to enclose comments that extend over multiple lines.

Before we present a detailed description of the enciphering process, we first examine the components of the cipher. Let us start with the key expansion function.

2.4.1.3 Key Expansion Function

The key expansion function takes a key array $k[0,\ldots,n-1]$ consisting of n 32-bit words—n is an integer between 4 and 14, inclusively—and produces an array $K\,[\,]$ of 40 words. The key expansion function can be described as follows:

```
Key-Expansion (k[0,...,n-1],n)
// This function takes as input an array k[] and an integer n,
// such that 4 ≤ n ≤ 14.
// K[] is an expanded key array consisting of 40 words.
// T[] is a temporary array consisting of 15 words.
// B[] is a fixed table consisting of 4 words.

// Initialize B[]
B[0,...,3] = {0xa4a8d57b, 0x5b5d193b, 0xc8a8309b, 0x73f9a978

// Initialize T[] with key data
T[0...n-1] = k[0...n-1], T[n] = n, T[n+1...14] = 0

// Four iterations, each computing 10 words of K[]
for j = 0 to 3 do
    for i = 0 to 14 do        // Linear transformation
        T[i] = T[i] ⊕ ((T[i-7 mod 15] ⊕ T[i-2 mod 15])
            <<< 3) ⊕ (4i + j)
```

```
    repeat four times      // Four stirring rounds
      for i = 0 to 14 do
      T[i] = (T[i] + S[low 9 bits of T[i-1 mod 15]])
             <<< 9
             end repeat


  for i = 0 to 9 do      // Store next 10 words into K[]
    K[10j + i] = T[4i mod 15]
end for


// Modify multiplication keys
for i = 5, 7, 9, 11, ..., 35 do
    j = the least two significant bits of K[i]
    w = K[i] with the two least significant bits of K[i]
        set to 1


    // Generate a bit mask M
    M  = 1 iff w  belongs to a sequence of 10 consecutive 0's
      1        1
         or 1's in w and 2 ≤ 1 ≤ 30 and w -1 = w  = w
                                        1      1    1+1


    //Select a pattern from the fixed table and rotate it
    r = least five significant bits of K[i - 1]
    p = B[j] <<< r


    // Modify K[i] with p under the control of the mask M
    K[i] = w ⊕ (p ∧ M)
end for
```

2.4.1.4 S-box Design

The 512 32-bit word entries of the S-box are generated pseudorandomly and tested—and replaced if necessary—to ensure that they conform with certain properties; the properties are outlined in [IBM99]. We use the following notations to describe the generation of the elements in the S-box:

- $S0[]$ and $S1[]$ are the arrays that contain the first and last 256 32-bit words entries of the S-box.

- $x_1|x_2|\dots|x_n$ represents the concatenation of the bit representation of $x_1 \dots x_n$.

- SHA-1 $(x)_j$ represents the jth word in the output of the message digest of x using the hash function SHA-1.[4]

---

[4] Hash functions are discussed in Chapter 4.

The generation of the elements of the S-box can be described as follows:

```
// Initializes constants
c₁ = 0xb7e15162
c₂ = 0x243f6a88
c₃ = y such that 0 ≤ y and the generated S-box entry satisfy
     properties outlined in [IBM99]

for i = 0 to 102 do
    for j = 0 to 4 do
        S[5i + j] + SHA-1(5i|c₁|c₂|c₃)ⱼ

// Fix entries in the two halves of the S-box
for i = 0 to 225 do
    if S0[i] ⊕ S1[i] has two or more zero bytes, then
        S0[i] = 3 * S0[i]
```

2.4.1.5 Expansion Function

The expansion function E-function takes as input a data word *in* and two key words *key*1 and *key*2 and outputs three words L, M, R. and the E-function can be described as follows:

```
E-function(in, key1, key2)
M = in + key1            // Add first key word
R = (in <<< 13) * key2   // Multiply by second key word,
                         // which must be odd
i = lowest 9 bits of M
L = S[i]            // S-box lookup.
R = R <<< 5
r = lowest 5 bits of R   // These bits specify the rotation
                         // amount
M = M <<< r         // First data-dependent rotation
L = L ⊕ R
R = R <<< 5
L = L ⊕ R
r = lowest five bits of R
L = L <<< r   // Second data-dependent rotation
output(L, M, R)
```

2.4.1.6 Enciphering Algorithm

The MARS enciphering algorithm takes as input the array $D[]$ consisting of four 32-bit data words containing a 128-bit block of plaintext, the expanded key array $K[]$ consisting of forty 32-bit words; and output the array $D[]$ containing the resulting 128-bit block of ciphertext. The algorithm can be described as follows:

MARS encryption ($D[0,\ldots,3]$, $K[0,\ldots,39]$)

Phase I: Forward Mixing

```
// First add subkeys to data
for i = 0 to 3 do
    D[i] = D[i] + K[i]
// Then do eight rounds of forward mixing
for i = 0 to 7 do          // Use D[0] to modify D[1], D[2],D[3]
    // four S-box lookups
    D[1] = D[1] ⊕ S0[low byte of D[0]]
    D[1] = D[1] + S1[second byte of D[0]]
    D[2] = D[2] + S0[third byte of D[0]]
    D[3] = D[3] ⊕ S1[high byte of D[0]]
    // Next, rotate the source word to the right
    D[0] = D[0] >>> 24
    // Followed by additional mixing operations
    if i = 0 or 4 then
        D[0] = D[0] + D[1]
    // Rotate D[] by one word to the right for next round
    (D[3], D[2], D[1], D[0]) <-- (D[0], D[3], D[2], D[1])
    // End of forward mixing
```

Phase II: Keyed Transformation

```
// Do 16 rounds of keyed transformation
for i = 0 to 15 do
    (out1, out2, out3) = E-function(D[0],K[2i+4], K[2i+5])
    D[0] = D[0] <<< 13
    D[2] = D[2] + out2
    if i < 8 then          // First eight rounds in forward mode
        D[1] = D[1] + out1
        D[3] = D[3] ⊕ out3
    else          // Last eight rounds in backward mode
        D[3] = D[3] + out1
        D[1] = D[1] ⊕ out3
    end if
    // Rotate D[] by one word to the right for next round
    (D[3], D[2], D[1], D[0]) <-- (D[0], D[3], D[2], D[1])
end for
// End of key transformation
```

Phase III: Backward Mixing

```
// Do eight rounds of backward mixing
for i = 0 to 7 do
    // Additional mixing operations
    if i = 2 or 6 then
        D[0] = D[0] - D[3]
    if i = 3 or 7 then
        D[0] = D[0] - D[1]
```

```
    // Four S-box lookups
    D[1] = D[1] ⊕ S1[low byte of D[0]]
    D[2] = D[2] - S0[high byte of D[0]]
    D[3] = D[3] - S1[third byte of D[0]]
    D[3] = D[3] ⊕ S0[second byte of D[0]]
    // Next, rotate the source word to the left
    D[0] = D[0] <<< 24
    // Rotate D[] by one word to the right for the next
    // round
    (D[3], D[2], D[1], D[0]) <-- (D[0], D[3], D[2], D[1])
end for
// Then subtract subkey form data
for i = 0 to 3 do
    D[i] = D[i] - K[36 + i]
// End of algorithm
```

The decryption process is the inverse of the encryption process.

This concludes our presentation of MARS. The description was adopted from [IBM99], which contains the original specification, along with detail about the design philosophies and an analysis of MARS. [IBM99] is available at *http://www.nist/aes*. This is no longer the case.

2.4.2 RC6

RC6 was developed by Ronold Rivest and a group from RSA Laboratories. The name RC6 is protected by a copyright. The RC6 algorithm is protected by U.S. patents. The homepage for RC6 is *http://www.rsasecurity.com/rsalabs/aes/*. RC6 uses variable word sizes, a variable number of rounds, and key sizes up to 2040 bits. However, for the AES submission, RC6 employs a word size of 32 bits, 16 rounds, and key sizes of 128, 192, and 256 bits. RC6 uses the following primitive operations: addition, subtraction, exclusive-OR, and bit rotation, in addition to 32 multiplication operations. RC6 does not utilize lookup tables; however, the key schedule requires 176 bytes. We will present a detailed description of both the encryption and decryption algorithms using pseudocodes; however before we proceed let us look at the notation that we will be using to describe this algorithm.

2.4.2.1 Notation

We will use the following notation in describing the algorithm (the algorithm uses variable word sizes of w bits):

- lg w represents $\log_2 w$.
- x + y is addition modulo 2^w.
- $x - y$ is subtraction modulo 2^w.
- $x * y$ is multiplication modulo 2^w.

- $x \oplus y$ is the bit-wise exclusive-OR of x and y.
- $x \lll s$ represents the cyclic rotation of the w-bit word x by the least significant $\lg w$ bits of s.
- $x \ggg s$ represents the cyclic rotation of the w-bit word x by the least significant $\lg w$ bits of s.
- $Y[i]$ represents the ith element of an array $Y[\ ]$.
- $(A, B, C, D) = (B, C, D, A)$ is the parallel assignment of values on the right to the registers on the left.

2.4.2.2 Key Scheduling Function

The RC6 key scheduling function takes as input variables a b-byte key and r number of rounds and computes and stores $2r + 4$ w-bit round keys in an array $S[0,\ldots,2r+3]$. The b-byte key is appended with sufficient zeros so the resulting key length is an integral number of words. The padded key is loaded into c w-bit word array $L[0,\ldots,c-1]$ in little endian format; that is, the least significant byte of the padded key is in the lower byte of $L[0]$. The function utilize two constants P and Q that are derived from the binary expansion of $e - 2$, where e is the base of natural logarithm function; and $\phi - 1$, where ϕ is the Golden ratio $\left\lceil \left(\sqrt{5} + 1\right)/2 \right\rceil$, respectively. The key schedule function can be described as follows:

```
RC6-key-schedule (L[0,...,c-1],r)
/* Two inputs: the user supplied b-byte key, padded with the
necessary number of zeros and preloaded into a c-word array
L[0,...,c-1]; and the number of rounds r.*/
// Output: 2r+4 w-bit round keys stored in the array
// S[0,...,2r+3]

// Assigned constants
P = 0xb7e15163
Q = 0x9e3779b9

S[0] = P

for i = 1 to 2r + 3 do
    S[i] = S[j-1] + Q

A = B = i = j = 0

v = 3 * max{c, 2r+4}
for s = 1 to v do
    A = S[i] = (S[i] + A + B) <<< 3
    B = L[j] = (L[j] + A + B) <<< (A + B)
    i = (i + 1) mod (2r+4)
    j = (j+1) mod c
end for
//End of key schedule
```

2.4.2.3 Encryption Algorithm

RC6 works with four w-bit registers A, B, C, and D, which contain the initial plaintext input, and at the end of the algorithm, the resulting ciphertext. The first byte of a $4 * w$-bit block plaintext or ciphertext is placed in the least significant byte of A, and the final byte is placed in the most significant byte of D. The encryption algorithm can be described as follows:

```
RC6-Encryption (A,B,C,D,r,w,S[0,...,2r+3])
/* The inputs are the 4 w-bit registers: A,B,C, and D; the
number of rounds r; the word size w, and the 2r+4 w-bit
round keys stored in the array S[0,...,2r+3]*/
// Output: ciphertext stored in A, B, C, D

B = B + S[0]
D = D + S[1]
for i = 1 to r do
    t = (B * (2B + 1)) <<< lg w
    u = (D * (2D + 1)) <<< lg w
    A = ((A ⊕ t) <<< u) + S[2i]
    C = ((C ⊕ u) <<< t) = S[2i + 1]
    (A,B,C,D) = (B,C,D,A)
end for
A = A + S[2r + 2]
C = C + S[2r + 3]
//End of encryption algorithm
```

2.4.2.4 Decryption Algorithm

The decryption algorithm can be described as follows:

```
RC6-Decryption (A,B,C,D,r,w,S[0,...,2r+3])
/* The inputs are the 4 w-bit registers: A,B,C and D; the
number of rounds r; the word size w; and the 2r + 4 w-bit round
keys stored in the array S[0,...,2r + 3] */
// Output: plaintext stored in A, B, C, D
C = C + S[2r + 3]
A = A - S[2r + 2]
for i = r downto 1 do
    (A,B,C,D) = (D,A,B,C)
    u = (D * (2D + 1)) <<< lg w
    t = (B * (2B + 1)) <<< lg w
    C = ((C - S[2i + 1])>>> t) ⊕ u
    A = ((A - S[2i]) >>> u) ⊕ t
end for
D = D - S[1]
B = B - S[0]
//End of decryption algorithm
```

The description of RC6 was adapted from [RRSY97], which is available at *http://www.nist.gov/aes*. For information about the design philosophies or analysis, or any additional information about RC6, please refer to [RRSY97], which contains the original specification of RC6.

2.4.3 AES (Rijndael)

The AES candidate, Rijndael, is an iterated block cipher with variable block and key sizes. It was designed by Joan Daemen and Vincent Rijmen from Belgium. The Rijndael homepage is *http://www.esat.kuleuven.ac.be/~rijmen/rijndael*. Rijndael supports both block and key sizes of 128, 192, and 256 bits; however, we will be using a block size of 128 bits for our presentation. The number of rounds that Rijndael employs depends on both the block and key sizes. If the block size is 128 bits and k is the size of the key in bits, then the number of rounds r is $k/32 + 6$, that is, 10, 12, and 14 rounds for key sizes of 128, 192, and 256 bits, respectively.

Rijneal is a byte-oriented cipher. A 128-bit block plaintext is used as the initial state. The state undergoes a number of key-dependent transformations, and the final state is the 128-bit block ciphertext. A state is regarded as a 4×4 matrix $(A_{i,j})$, $i,j \in \{0,1,2,3\}$ of bytes. In the initial state, $A_{0,0}$ is the first byte in a 128-bit block of plaintext, $A_{0,1}$ is the second byte, $A_{1,0}$ is the fifth byte, etc, and $A_{4,3}$ is the final byte of this 128-bit block plaintext. Note that we use the notation $(A_{i,j})$ to represent a 4×4 state matrix that consists of 16 bytes, and $A_{i,j}$ to represent a single element in the state, which consist of 1 byte.

Rijndael uses four elementary operations to transform a state $A = (A_{i,j})$ into a new state $B = (B_{i,j})$. These elementary operations are described as follows:

1. *Byte Substitution* (ByteSub): The byte substitution operation is a non-linear permutation that operates on each of the bytes in the state independently. The operation is equivalent to the multiplication of a 8×8 matrix by the individual bytes, where the bits of the bytes are represented as 8×1 column vectors, followed by the addition of another 8×1 column vector. If we represent the bits in a given byte in the state, as $a_0 a_1 a_2 \ldots a_7$, the byte substitution operation is equivalent to the following operation:

$$
\begin{bmatrix} b_0 \\ b_1 \\ b_2 \\ b_3 \\ b_4 \\ b_5 \\ b_6 \\ b_7 \end{bmatrix} = \begin{bmatrix} 1 & 0 & 0 & 0 & 1 & 1 & 1 & 1 \\ 1 & 1 & 0 & 0 & 0 & 1 & 1 & 1 \\ 1 & 1 & 1 & 0 & 0 & 0 & 1 & 1 \\ 1 & 1 & 1 & 1 & 0 & 0 & 0 & 1 \\ 1 & 1 & 1 & 1 & 1 & 0 & 0 & 0 \\ 0 & 1 & 1 & 1 & 1 & 1 & 0 & 0 \\ 0 & 0 & 1 & 1 & 1 & 1 & 1 & 0 \\ 0 & 0 & 0 & 1 & 1 & 1 & 1 & 1 \end{bmatrix} \begin{bmatrix} a_0 \\ a_1 \\ a_2 \\ a_3 \\ a_4 \\ a_5 \\ a_6 \\ a_7 \end{bmatrix} + \begin{bmatrix} 1 \\ 1 \\ 0 \\ 0 \\ 0 \\ 1 \\ 1 \\ 0 \end{bmatrix}
$$

where $b_0 b_1 \ldots b_7$ is the bit representation of the byte after the byte substitution operation. This operation can be implemented quite efficiently using a 256-byte lookup table or S-box.

2. *Shift row operation* (ShiftRow): This is a cyclic shift of the bytes in a state. The operation can be represented as $B_{i,j} = A_{i,(j+i) \bmod 4}$. Thus, the bytes in the first row are not shifted, the bytes in the second row are shifted one column, the bytes in the third row are shifted two columns, and the bytes in the fourth row are shifted three columns.

3. *Mix column operation* (MixColumn): Each column A_i of a state A is transformed by a linear transformation. The transformation is equivalent to multiplying a 4×4 matrix by the bytes in the individual columns—represented as 4×1 column vectors—of the state. The operation is as follows:

$$
\begin{bmatrix} b_0 \\ b_1 \\ b_2 \\ b_3 \end{bmatrix} = \begin{bmatrix} 02 & 03 & 01 & 01 \\ 01 & 02 & 03 & 01 \\ 01 & 01 & 02 & 03 \\ 03 & 01 & 01 & 02 \end{bmatrix} \begin{bmatrix} a_0 \\ a_1 \\ a_2 \\ a_3 \end{bmatrix}
$$

The a_i's are bytes of a given column in the state, the entries in the 4×4 matrix are hexadecimal values (for example, 02 represents the bit string 00000010), and the b_i's are the bytes in the column after the mix column operation.

4. *Round key addition* (AddRoundKey): For each round, a round key RK is derived from the cipher key by means of the key scheduling function. The length of the round key is the same as the size of the encryption block. The round keys are also represented as 4×4 matrices in a similar fashion as a block of plaintext. In the round

key addition operation, the round key is exclusive-or to the state. Thus, the byte $B_{i,j}$ in the state B that resulted after the round key addition operation can be represented as $B_{i,j} = A_{i,j} \oplus RK_{i,j}$, where $A_{i,j}$ is the byte at the ith row and jth column in the state before the round key addition, and $RK_{i,j}$ is the byte at the ith row and jth column of the round key.

Note that all the elementary operations that Rijndael uses are invertible.

2.4.3.1 Key Schedule

The round keys are derived from the cipher key by means of the key schedule. The key schedule consists of two components: the key expansion and the round key selection. The key schedule can be described as follows: the cipher key is expanded, using a key expansion function, to produce the appropriate number of bits for the round keys. The total number of round key bits required is equal to $N(R + 1)$, where N is the block size and R is the number of rounds. Thus, for 10 rounds using a 128-bit block size, 1408 bits are required. After the key expansion, the 128 most significant bits are used as the round key for the first round, the next 128-bit block of the expanded key for the second round, etc., and finally, the least significant 128 bits are used as the round key for the final round. Let us now take a look at the key expansion function.

2.4.3.2 Key Expansion Function

There are two version of key expansion function: one for cipher keys of length 192 bits or less, and another for key sizes greater than 192 bits. We use the following notation in describing the key expansion function:

- R is the number of rounds.
- N is the block size, in 32-bit words, that the cipher uses.
- K is the cipher key length in 32-bit words.
- SubByte(S) represents the byte substution operation on the state S.
- RotByte (W) represents the operation in which the bytes in a word W are cyclically permuted; for example, an input of a word with bytes (a,b,c,d) would produce (b,c,d,a) as an output.
- $RC[\,]$ is an array which stores 8-bit round constants, which are employed in the computation. $RC[1] = 0x01$, $RC[2] = 0x01$, $RC[3] = 0x04$, $RC[4] = 0x08$, $RC[5] = 0x10$, $RC[6] = 0x20$, $RC[7] = 0x40$, and $RC[8] = 0x80$. Note that the prefix $0x$ indicates that the number is in hexadecimal format.

The key expansion function takes as input two arrays: key[] contains $4K$ bytes of the cipher key bits, and $W[]$ is an $N(R+1)$ 32-bit word array, that will store the expanded key bits that will be used for the round keys. The first K entries of $W[]$ contains the $4K$ bytes of the cipher key. The expanded key bits are outputted in $W[0,\ldots N(R+1)-1]$.

We are now ready to describe the algorithm. For $K \leq 6$, the algorithm is:

```
KeyExpansion(key[0,...,4K - 1], W[0,...,N(R + 1) - 1]
for i = 0 to K - 1 do
    W[i] = (key[4i],key[4i + 1],key[4i + 2], key[4i + 3])
for i = K to N(R + 1) do
    temp = W[i - 1]
    if i mod K = 0 then
        temp = SubByte(RotByte(temp)) ⊕ RC[i/K]
    W[i] = W[i - K] ⊕ temp
// End of key expansion algorithm for K ≤ 6
```

For $K \geq 6$, the algorithm is:

```
KeyExpansion(key[0,...,4K + 1], W[0,...,N(R + 1) - 1])
for i = 0 to K - 1 do
    W[i] = (key[4i],key[4i + 1],key[4i + 2], key[4i + 3])
for i = K to N(R + 1) do
    temp = W[i - 1]
    if i mod K = 0 then
        temp = SubByte(RotByte(temp)) ⊕ RC[i/K]
    if i mod K = 4 then
        temp = SubByte(temp)
    W[i] = W[i - K] ⊕ temp
// End of key expansion algorithm for K ≥ 6
```

2.4.3.3 Rijndael encryption algorithm

The Rijndael encryption algorithm takes as input a state—as defined in the second paragraph of our discussion of Rijndael (Section 2.4.3)—and a cipher key, and takes as output a state that contains the ciphertext. The algorithm can be described as follows:

```
Rijndael-Encryption(state, key[0,...,4K - 1])
// Take as input a state and a K-word cipher key stored in the
// array key[0,...K - 1]

KeyExpansion(key[0,...,K - 1], W[0,...,N(R + 1)- 1])
// The first K words of W[] contain the 4K bytes of the
// key[0,...,K - 1] array
```

```
AddRoundKey(state, W[0,...,3N])
// Add first round key to the state

for i = 0 to R - 2 do      // R is the number of rounds
    ByteSub(state)
    ShiftRow(state)
    MixColumn(state)
    AddRoundKey(state,W[i,...3 + i])
end for

// Final round
ByteSub(state)
ShiftRow(state)
AddRoundKey(state, W[N(R + 1) - 4,...,N(R + 1) - 1])
// End of encryption algorithm
```

2.4.3.4 Rijndael Decryption Algorithm

The decryption algorithm can be described as follows:

```
Rijndael-Decryption(state, key[0,...,4K - 1])
/* Take as input a state containing the ciphertext, and a
K-word cipher key stored in the array key[0,...,K - 1]. */

Inverse_KeyExpansion(key[0,...,K - 1],W[0,...,N(R + 1) - 1])
AddRoundKey(state, W[N(R + 1) - 4,...,N(R + 1) - 1])
for i = R - 2 downto 0 do      // R is the number of rounds
    Inverse_ByteSub(state)
    Inverse_ShiftRow(state)
    Inverse_MixColumn(state)
    AddRoundKey(state,W[i - 3,...,i])
end for

// Final round
Inverse_ByteSub(state)
Inverse_ShiftRow(state)
AddRoundKey(state, W[0,...,3N])
// End of decryption algorithm
```

The `Inverse_KeyExpansion` function can be described as follows: Apply the `KeyExpansion` function, and then apply `Inverse_MixColumn` to all round keys except the first and and the last. The other `Inverse_...`, operations are the inverse of the respective elementary operations.

The description of Rijndael was adapted from [DR99] and [Luc99], which are both available at *http://www.nist.gov/aes*. For information about the design philosophies or analysis or any information related to the design of Rijndael, see [DR99], which contains the original specification of Rijndael.

The C and Java source codes of Rijndael are also presented in Appendices A and B, respectively.

2.4.4 Serpent

Serpent is a 32-round block cipher that operates on a block size of 128 bits of plaintext and produces 128-bit blocks of ciphertext. Serpent employs cipher key of variable sizes up to 256 bits; however, if the keys are smaller than 256 bits, they are padded by adding a 1 bit to the most significant bit end; then an appropriate number of 0's are added so that the final length of the padded key is 256 bits. This cipher was developed by Ross Anderson from Cambridge University, England; Eli Biham from Technion, Haifa, Israel; and Lars Knudsen from the University of Bergen, Norway. Two applications for patent have been filed for Serpent in the United Kingdom. The homepage for Serpent is *http://www.cl.cam.ac.uk/ ~rja14/serpent.html*. The design of Serpent is somewhat similar to that of DES; however, Serpent is believed to be more secure than triple-DES; whereas, its speed is approximately that of DES.

The primitive operations that Serpent utilizes are exclusive-OR, bit rotation, and bit shifting. It also employs two 8×16 permutation tables with integers between 0 and 127, inclusively, and eight S-boxes with 16 entries each—the entries are integers between 0 and 15, inclusively. Let us now take a look at how these operations are utilized in the cipher.

2.4.4.1 Enciphering algorithm

Serpent operates on four 32-bit words. The words are in little-endian byte format; that is, the first byte of the plaintext is the least significant byte of the first word, and the final byte of the 128-bit block of plaintext is the most significant byte of the fourth word. Serpent utilizes a key schedule function that produces 33 128-bit subkeys $\tilde{K}_0, \ldots, \tilde{K}_{32}$ from the cipher key; these subkeys are used to operate on the 128-bit block of data during the 32 rounds of the cipher.

The first step of the enciphering process involves a mixing of the bits of the 128-bit plaintext P, using the permutation table IP. This is followed by 32 rounds of ciphering that involve key mixing operations, passthrough S-boxes, and a linear transformation. In the final step, the intermediate ciphertext is permuted using the permutation table FP. The output from the final permutation FP is the resulting 128-bit block ciphertext.

Both the the initial permutation IP and the final permutation FP are tables with 8 rows and 16 columns, and the entries are integers between 0 and 127, inclusively. The permutation operation can be described as follows: for the permutation $\tilde{X} = IP(X)$ or for $\tilde{X} = FP(X)$, the bit at position i

in $\tilde{X}$, where $i \in \{0,\ldots,127\}$, is determined as follows: look up the value at position i in the respective permutation, let us call this value j; the bit at position j in the 128-bit input $\overset{\downarrow}{X}$, is the bit that will be at position i in the 128-bit output $\tilde{X}$.

The key schedule function takes a variable-length cipher key and pads it—if necessary—to 256 bits. It then produces 33 128-bit subkeys $\tilde{K}_0,\ldots,\tilde{K}_{32}$, which are used to operate on the intermediate ciphertext during the 32 rounds of the cipher. We are now ready to describe the enciphering algorithm. The algorithm can be described as follows:

```
Serpent-Encryption (P, k)
// Input: a 128-bit block plaintext P and a variable-length
// cipher key k

// Pass plaintext through the initial permutation IP
B̃₀ = IP(P)

// The first 31 of the 32 rounds
for i = 0 to 30 do
     B̃ᵢ = IP(B̃)         // Apply the initial permutation
     (X₀,X₁,X₂,X₃) = Sᵢ(B̃ᵢ ⊕ K̃ᵢ)
/* S̃ᵢ is the S-box lookup operation at round i, followed by
   the application IP. K̃ᵢ is the application of IP to the
   subkey Kᵢ, for round i. The 128-bit intermediate ciphertext
   that resulted from the S-box operation is split into four
   words X₀, ..., X₃ and each word operated on separately as
   follows: */
     X₀ = X₀ <<< 13
     X₂ = X₂ <<< 3
     X₁ = X₁ ⊕ X₀ ⊕ X₂
     X₃ = X₃ ⊕ X₂ ⊕ (X₀ << 3)    // << Represents the bit shift
                                 // operation

     X₁ = X₁ <<< 1
     X₃ = X₃ <<< 7
     X₀ = X₀ ⊕ X₁ ⊕ X₃
     X₂ = X₂ ⊕ X₃ ⊕ (X₁ << 7)
     X₀ = X₀ <<< 5
     X₂ = X₂ <<< 22
     Bᵢ₊₁ = (X₀,X₁,X₂,X₃)
end for                          // End of for loop

// The final round
B̃₃₁ = IP(B₃₁)
B̃₃₂ = Sᵢ(B̃₃₁ ⊕ K̃₃₃) ⊕ K̃₃₂

/* Finally, the 128-bit block ciphertext is obtained by
applying the the final permutation FP to B̃₃₂ */
C = FP(B̃₃₂)
// End of enciphering algorithm
```

2.4.4.2 Key Schedule

The key schedule function takes a cipher key of variable length. If the length is less that 256 bits, the key is padded by adding a 1 to the most significant byte end, and then the appropriate number of 0 added to make the length of the padded key 256 bits. The 256-bit key K is split into eight 32-bit words $w_{-8}, \ldots, w_{-1}$ and expanded into 132 32-bit words, as follows:

```
Serpent-Keyschedule(K)
/* Input: a 256-bit key K consisting of eight
   32-bit words w_-8,=,w_-1 */
// Output: 33 128-bit subkeys K̃_i

for i = 0 to 131 do
    w_i = (w_{i-8} ⊕ w_{i-5} ⊕ w_{i-3} ⊕ w_{i-1} ⊕ φ ⊕ i) <<< 11
/* φ is the fractional part of the Golden ratio ( √5 + 1)/2
   or 0x9e3779b9 */

/* The S-boxes are then used to transform the prekeys w_i in
   words k_i of the round key, as follows: */
    (k_0, k_1, k_2, k_3)      = S_3(w_0, w_1, w_2, w_3)
    (k_4, k_5, k_6, k_7)      = S_2(w_4, w_5, w_6, w_7)
    (k_8, k_9, k_10, k_11)    = S_1(w_8, w_9, w_10, w_11)
    (k_12, k_13, k_14, k_15)  = S_0(w_12, w_13, w_14, w_15)
    (k_16, k_17, k_18, k_19)  = S_7(w_16, w_17, w_18, w_19)

    (k_124, k_125, k_126, k_127) = S_4(w_124, w_125, w_126, w_127)
    (k_128, k_129, k_130, k_131) = S_3(w_128, w_129, w_130, w_131)

/* Arrange the 32-bit k_i into groups of four to form the
   33 128-bit subkey. */
for i = 0 to 32 do
    K_i = (k_4i, k_4i+1, k_4i+2, k_4i+3)
    K̃i = IP(Ki)
// End of keyschedule function
```

2.4.4.3 S-boxes

Serpent utilizes eight S-boxes that contains 16 4-bit entries. Each of the 32 rounds of Serpent selects an S-box and makes 32 copies of it and applies the replicated S-box in parallel. The S-box that is selected depends on the round: S_0 is used for round 0, S_1 for round 1,..., S_7 for round 7, then S_0 for round 8, S_1 for round 9, and so on; each S-box is used for four different rounds. For each round, the first 4 bits of the 128-bit input to the S-box are taken as the input to the first replicated copy of the S-box, the next four bits, that is, bits 4 to 7, are inputted to the second copy of the S-box, and so on. The output from each of the replicated S-boxes is the bits in the equivalent position of the resulting intermediate vectors; for example, bits 0 to 3 for the first copy, bits 4 to 7 for the second,..., and bits 125 to 127 for the final copy. The eight S-boxes are as follows:

S_0:	3	8	15	1	10	6	5	11	14	13	4	2	7	0	9	12
S_1:	15	12	2	7	9	0	5	10	1	11	14	8	6	13	3	4
S_2:	8	6	7	9	3	12	10	15	13	1	14	4	0	11	5	2
S_3:	0	15	11	8	12	9	6	3	13	1	2	4	10	7	5	14
S_4:	1	15	8	3	12	0	11	6	2	5	4	10	9	14	7	13
S_5:	15	5	2	11	4	10	9	12	0	3	14	8	13	6	7	1
S_6:	7	2	12	5	8	4	6	11	14	9	1	15	13	3	10	0
S_7:	1	13	15	0	14	8	2	11	7	4	12	10	9	3	5	6

2.4.4.4 Decryption

The decryption process is the reverse of the encryption process, except that the inverse of the S-boxes must be applied in reverse order; and the sub-keys must be applied in reverse order.

This concludes our discussion of Serpent. The description was adopted from [ABK98] which is available at *http://www.nist.gov/aes*. For information about the design philosophies or analysis or for any additional information on Serpent, please refer to [ABK98], which contains the original specifications.

2.4.5 Twofish

Twofish was designed by Bruce Schneier, John Kelsey, Doug Whiting, David Wagner, Chris Hall, and Niels Ferguson. Twofish is unpatented. The home page of Twofish: *http://www.counterpane.com/twofish.html*, states that the source code for this cipher is uncopyrighted and license-free, and it is free for all to use. The source code is available for download at the home page.

Twofish is a 16-round cipher that employs 128-bit block size and accepts variable-length keys of up to 256 bits. This cipher utilizes the following primitive operations: exclusive-OR, addition, bit rotation, and integer multiplication; it also employs four key-dependent 8 × 8 S-boxes. Let us now look at the Twofish encryption algorithm.

2.4.5.1 Twofish Encryption Algorithm

Twofish takes as input plaintext splitted into four 32-bit words registers $P_0, \ldots, P_3$; and N bytes of cipher key k, where N equals to 16, 24 or 32. The plaintext is inputted in the registers in little-endian byte format; that is, the first byte of the plaintext is placed in the least significant byte of P_0, etc. and the last byte is placed in the most significant byte of P_3. The first step of the algorithm involves the expansion of the N-byte cipher key k to 40 32-bit words $K_0, \ldots, K_{39}$, using the key schedule function. The encipher algorithm proceeds as follows:

```
Twofish-Encryption(P_0,P_1,P_2,P_3,k)
/* Input: four plaintext 32-bit words P_0,...,P_3, and N-byte
cipher key k.
Output: four ciphertext 32-bit words */


(K_0,...,K_39) = Key-Schedule(k)
/* The key schedule function produced 40
   32-bit words K_0,...,K_39, from the N-byte cipher key. */


// Plaintext words exclusive-ORed with expanded key words
R_{0,0} = P_0 ⊕ K_0
R_{0,1} = P_1 ⊕ K_1
R_{0,2} = P_2 ⊕ K_2
R_{0,3} = P_3 ⊕ K_3


/* In each of the 16 rounds that follow, the first two words
R_{i,0} and R_{i,1}--where i = 0,...,15--are used as input to a
function F. F also takes the round number r as input.
F produces two words F_{r,0} and F_{r,1}, as output. */
for r = 0 to 15 do
    (F_{r,0},F_{r,1}) = F(R_{r,0},R_{r,1},r)
    R_{r+1,0} = (R_{r,2} ⊕ F_{r,0}) >>> 1
    R_{r+1,1} = (R_{r,3} <<< 1) ⊕ F_{r,1}
    R_{r+1,2} = R_{r,0}
    R_{r+1,3} = R_{r,1}
end for


// The ciphertext words C_i are out-putted next
for i = 0 to 3 do
    C_i = R_{16,(i+2) mod 4} ⊕ K_{i+4}
// End of enciphering algorithm.
```

The four words of the ciphertext are written as 16 bytes $c_0,...,c_{15}$, using the little-endian convention utilized for the plaintext.

2.4.5.2 Function F

The function F takes two 32-bit words R_0 and R_1 and a round number r and produces two 32-bit words F_0 and F_1 as output. F can be described as follows:

```
F(R_0,R_1,r)
/* The first step involves running R_0 through the function g,
which produces another 32-bit word T_0. */
T_0 = g(R_0)
T_1 = g((R_1 <<< 8))
F_0 = (T_0 + T_1 + K_{2r+8}) mod 32
F_1 = (T_0 + 2T_1 + K_{2r+9}) mod 32
// End of F
```

2.4.5.3 Function g

The g function is the heart of Twofish [SKW98]. This function takes a word X, consisting of the bytes $x_0, \ldots, x_3$, and runs each byte through a different key-dependent S-box. The S-boxes take 8 bits of input and produce 8 bits of output. The operation is equivalent to the multiplication of a 4 $\times$ 4 matrix with the column vector containing the bytes of X. The output of g is the bytes in the resulting column vector. The function g can be described as follows:

```
g(X)
/* x_0,...,x_3 are the bytes of the input word X.
Output: the word Y, consisting of the bytes y_0,...,y_3. */
```

$$
\begin{pmatrix} y_0 \\ y_1 \\ y_2 \\ y_3 \end{pmatrix} = \begin{pmatrix} 01 & ef & 5b & 5b \\ 5b & ef & ef & 01 \\ ef & 5b & 01 & ef \\ ef & 01 & ef & 5b \end{pmatrix} \cdot \begin{pmatrix} x_0 \\ x_1 \\ x_2 \\ x_3 \end{pmatrix}
$$

```
// End g
```

The entries in the 4 $\times$ 4 matrix are hexadecimal numbers.

2.4.5.4 Key Schedule

The twofish key schedule function takes as input a cipher key of length $8k$ bytes, where k is equal to 2, 3, or 4, and produces 40 32-bit words of expanded key $K_0, \ldots, K_{39}$, and the four key-dependent S-boxes used in the g function. The input key bytes are first arranged into $2k$ 32-bit words, and then converted into two word vectors V_b and V_a, of length k:

$$
V_a = (W_o, W_2, \ldots, W_{2k-2})
$$
$$
V_b = (W_1, W_3, \ldots, W_{2k-1})
$$

where the W_i's are the words of the cipher key. V_a and V_b are used as inputs to a function h that is utilized in the computation of the expanded key words. A third vector of length k is derived by taking the key bytes in groups of eight, interpreting them as a vectors, and multiplying them by a 4 $\times$ 8 matrix. Each result of 4 bytes is then interpreted as 32-bit words. This can be represented as follows:

$$
\begin{pmatrix} s_{i,0} \\ s_{i,1} \\ s_{i,2} \\ s_{i,3} \end{pmatrix} = \begin{pmatrix} 01 & a4 & 55 & 87 & 5a & 58 & db & 9e \\ a4 & 56 & 82 & f3 & 1e & c6 & 68 & e5 \\ 02 & a1 & fc & c1 & 47 & ae & 3d & 19 \\ a4 & 55 & 87 & 5a & 58 & db & 9e & 03 \end{pmatrix} \cdot \begin{pmatrix} w_{8i} \\ w_{8i+1} \\ w_{8i+2} \\ w_{8i+3} \\ w_{8i+4} \\ w_{8i+5} \\ w_{8i+6} \\ w_{8i+7} \end{pmatrix}
$$

The byte vector $(s_{i,0}, s_{i,1}, s_{i,2}, s_{i,3})$ is considered as a word S_i, where $s_{i,0}$ is the first byte of $S_i, \ldots,$ and $s_{i,3}$ is the last byte. The vector S can be written as: $S = (S_{k-1}, S_{k-2}, \ldots, S_0)$. Note that S lists the words in reverse order. S is used as an input to a function h to derive the key-dependent S-boxes that the function g utilizes. Let us now take a look at the h function.

2.4.5.5 Function h

The function h takes as input a 32-bit word X and a list $L = (L_0, \ldots, L_{k-1})$ of 32-bit words of length k and produces one word as output. The words of the input list L are first split into bytes $l_{i,j}$, such that, for example, $L_0 = l_{0,0} l_{0,1} l_{0,2} l_{0,3}$; $L_1 = l_{1,0} l_{1,1} l_{1,2} l_{1,3}$, etc. Similarly, $X = x_0 x_1 x_2 x_3$. The function then proceeds in eight stages as outlined below.

```
h(X,L)
// Input: a word X and a k length list L = (L₀, ..., L_{k-1})
// Output: a word Z = z₀z₁z₂z₃ where the z_i's are the bytes of Z

// Split the input words into bytes
L = (l_{0,0}l_{0,1}l_{0,2}l_{0,3}, ..., l_{k-1,0}l_{k-1,1}l_{k-1,2}l_{k-1,3})
X = x₀x₁x₂x₃
for i = 0 to 3 do
        Y_{k,i} = x_i
if k = 4, then              /* q₀ and q₁ are fixed permutation that
                                will be described shortly. */

        Y_{3,0} = q₁[Y_{4,0}] ⊕ l_{3,0}
        Y_{3,1} = q₀[Y_{4,1}] ⊕ l_{3,1}
        Y_{3,2} = q₀[Y_{4,2}] ⊕ l_{3,2}
        Y_{3,3} = q₁[Y_{4,3}] ⊕ l_{3,3}

else if k ≤ 3, then
        Y_{2,0} = q₁[Y_{3,0}] ⊕ l_{2,0}
        Y_{2,1} = q₁[Y_{3,1}] ⊕ l_{2,1}
        Y_{2,2} = q₀[Y_{3,2}] ⊕ l_{2,2}
        Y_{2,3} = q₀[Y_{3,3}] ⊕ l_{2,3}

Y₀ = q₁[q₀[q₀[Y_{2,0}] ⊕ l_{1,0}] ⊕ l_{0,0}]
    Y₀ = q₀[q₀[q₁[Y_{2,1}] ⊕ l_{1,1}] ⊕ l_{0,1}]
    Y₀ = q₁[q₁[q₀[Y_{2,2}] ⊕ l_{1,2}] ⊕ l_{0,2}]
    Y₀ = q₀[q₁[q₁[Y_{2,3}] ⊕ l_{1,3}] ⊕ l_{0,3}]
```

$$
\begin{pmatrix} z_0 \\ z_1 \\ z_2 \\ z_3 \end{pmatrix} = \begin{pmatrix} 01 & ef & 5b & 5b \\ 5b & ef & ef & 01 \\ ef & 5b & 01 & ef \\ ef & 01 & ef & 5b \end{pmatrix} \cdot \begin{pmatrix} y_0 \\ y_1 \\ y_2 \\ y_3 \end{pmatrix}
$$

```
// End of h function
```

2.4.5.6 Key-dependent S-Boxes

The S-boxes used in the function g can be defined as follows:

$$g(X) = h(X,S)$$

where S is the word vector that was derived from the cipher key. In other words, for $i = 0$ to 3, the key-dependent S-boxes s_i are formed by mapping the input to g to the output from h.

2.4.5.7 The permutations q_0 and q_1

The permutations q_0 and q_1 are fixed permutations on 8-bit values. They are each constructed from four different 4-bit permutations. For an input value x to the permutations q_0 or q_1, the output value y can be described as shown below. The notation $\lfloor N \rfloor$ represents the "flooring" of a real number, that is, a number with a fractional part. The flooring of a number is the integer part of the number, for example, $\lfloor 4.827 \rfloor = 4$. The permutations are described as follows:

- $a_0, b_0 = \lfloor x/16 \rfloor, x \bmod 16$
- $a_1 = a_0 \oplus b_0$
- $b_1 = a_0 \oplus (b_0 \gg 1) \oplus 8a_0 \bmod 16$
- $a_2, b_2 = t_0[a_1], t_1[b_1]$
- $a_3 = a_2 \oplus b_2$
- $b_3 = a_2 \oplus (b_2 \gg 1) \oplus 8a_2 \bmod 16$
- $a_4, b_4 = t_2[a_3], t_3[b_3]$
- $y = 16b_4 + a_4$

The t_i's are 4-bit S-boxes. For the permutation q_0, the 4-bit S-boxes are:

$t_0 = [8 \quad 1 \quad 7 \quad d \quad 6 \quad f \quad 3 \quad 2 \quad 0 \quad b \quad 9 \quad 5 \quad e \quad c \quad a \quad 4]$
$t_1 = [e \quad c \quad b \quad 8 \quad 1 \quad 2 \quad 3 \quad 5 \quad f \quad 4 \quad a \quad 6 \quad 7 \quad 0 \quad 9 \quad d]$
$t_2 = [b \quad a \quad 5 \quad e \quad 6 \quad d \quad 9 \quad 0 \quad c \quad 8 \quad f \quad 3 \quad 2 \quad 4 \quad 7 \quad 1]$
$t_3 = [d \quad 7 \quad f \quad 4 \quad 1 \quad 2 \quad 6 \quad e \quad 9 \quad b \quad 3 \quad 0 \quad 8 \quad 5 \quad c \quad a]$

The 16 entries in the t_i's are the hexadecimal values outputted for the inputs of $0, \ldots, 15$, listed in consecutive order. Similarly, for the permutation q_1, the 4-bit S-boxes are:

$t_0 = [2 \quad 8 \quad b \quad d \quad f \quad 7 \quad 6 \quad e \quad 3 \quad 1 \quad 9 \quad 4 \quad 0 \quad a \quad c \quad 5]$
$t_1 = [1 \quad e \quad 2 \quad b \quad 4 \quad c \quad 3 \quad 7 \quad 6 \quad d \quad a \quad 5 \quad f \quad 9 \quad 0 \quad 8]$
$t_2 = [4 \quad c \quad 7 \quad 5 \quad 1 \quad 6 \quad 9 \quad a \quad 0 \quad e \quad d \quad 8 \quad 2 \quad b \quad 3 \quad f]$
$t_3 = [b \quad 9 \quad 5 \quad 1 \quad c \quad 3 \quad d \quad e \quad 6 \quad 4 \quad 7 \quad f \quad 2 \quad 0 \quad 8 \quad a]$

2.4.5.8 Expanded Key Words K_j

The words for the expanded key are derived from the function h as follows:

```
c = 2^24 + 2^16 + 2^8 + 2^0      // c is a constant
A_i = h(2ic, V_a)
B_i = (h((2i + 1)c, V_b)) <<< 8
K_2i = (A_i + B_i) mod 2^32
K_2i+1 = ((A_i + 2B_i) mod 2^32) <<< 9
```

This concludes our presentation of the Twofish enciphering process. The decryption algorithm is the reverse of the encryption process. The presentation was adapted from [SKW98], which contains the original specifications of Twofish. [SKW98] is available at *http://www.nist.gov/aes*.

2.4.6 Performance Comparison of the AES Finalists

In this section, we give a brief comparison of the performance of the five AES finalists. The data is adopted from [SW00], which is available at: http://www.nist.gov/aes.

Let us start with a comparison of the setup, encryption, and decryption time for the five ciphers, using keys of length 128, 192, and 256 bits. MARS, RC6 and Serpent's setup, encryption, and decryption times are the same irrespective of the key length; Rijndael takes a longer time for all three variables for longer keys, whereas Twofish takes a longer time to set up longer keys. Table 2-5 summarizes the speed of the ciphers for different key lengths.

2.4.6.1 Software Performance

We now compare the performance of the five AES finalists using 128-, 192, and 256-bit keys in Assembly and C programming languages. The

TABLE 2-5

Speed of AES Finalists for Different Key Lengths

Cipher	Key Setup Time	Encryption/Decryption Time
MARS	Constant	Constant
RC6	Constant	Constant
Rijndael	Increasing	192-bit key: 20% slower than for 128-bit key 256-bit key: 40% slower than for 128-bit key
Serpent	Constant	Constant
Twofish	Increasing	Constant

ciphers that employ multiplication and variable rotation operations extensively, such as MARS and RC6, show marked differences in performance on hardware, such as the Pentium Pro/II/III, PowerPC, Alpha, Ultra-SPARC, and others, that optimize multiplication operations compared to hardware that does not, such as Pentium I and the original SPARC. Therefore, we are going to present two sets of tables: one for the hardware that optimizes multiplication operation, and another for hardware that does not. Tables 2-6 to 2-9 summarize the software performance of the five finalists for the different key sizes. The performances are given in terms of clock cycles; the smaller the clock cycle, the faster is the encryption speed.

2.4.6.2 Memory Requirement of AES Finalists

We conclude our discussion of the AES by looking at the amount of RAM that each of the five finalists requires. The amount of RAM that a cipher requires is important because this dictates whether or not the cipher is suitable for memory-limited 8-bit Smart Cards. At the time of writing, most lower- to medium-priced Smart Card CPUs include from 128 to 256 bytes of on-board RAM. For a cipher to be suitable for implementation on these applications, it typically should require less than 100 bytes of RAM. Table 2-10 summarizes the Smart Card memory requirements of the five finalists.

2.5　Other Symmetric-Key Cryptosystems

In this section, we give brief descriptions of some other symmetric-key cryptosystems that are in widespread use:

1. *Blowfish:* Blowfish is a 16-round block cipher that was developed by Bruce Schneier [Sch93]. Blowfish is unpatented, it has no license requirement, and it is available for use royalty-free. The Blowfish home page is *http://www.counterpane.com*. The source code for this cipher is available for download at *http://www. counterpane.com/blowfish-download.html*. Blowfish uses keys of variable length from 32 to 448 bits to encrypt blocks of 64-bit plaintext into blocks of 64-bit ciphertext. This cipher has a simple structure that makes it easy to implement. Blowfish is faster than DES when implemented on 32-bit microprocessors, and it also is believed to be much more secure, particularly for larger key sizes. The variable-length key allows for varied degrees of security.

TABLE 2-6

Encryption Speed for 128-, 192-, and 256-Bit Keys in Assembly Language on Pentium II Hardware.

Ciphers	Clock cycles		
	128-Bit Key	192-Bit Key	256-Bit Key
MARS	300	300	300
RC6	225	225	225
Rijndael	230	275	330
Serpent	750	750	750
Twofish	250	250	250

TABLE 2-7

Encryption Speed for 128-, 192-, and 256-Bit Keys in Assembly on Pentium I Hardware

Ciphers	Clock cycles		
	128-Bit Key	192-Bit Key	256-Bit Key
MARS	550	550	550
RC6	700	700	700
Rijndael	320	380	450
Serpent	800	800	800
Twofish	290	290	290

TABLE 2-8

Encryption Speed for 128-, 192-, and 256-Bit Keys in C Programming Language on Pentium II Hardware

Ciphers	Clock cycles		
	128-Bit Key	192-Bit Key	256-Bit Key
MARS	380	380	380
RC6	240	240	240
Rijndael	400	520	600
Serpent	750	750	750
Twofish	380	380	380

TABLE 2-9

Encryption Speed for 128-, 192-, and 256-Bit Keys in C Programming Language on Pentium I Hardware

Ciphers	Clock cycles		
	128-Bit Key	192-Bit Key	256-Bit Key
MARS	750	750	7500
RC6	750	7500	750
Rijndael	650	810	980
Serpent	900	900	900
Twofish	420	420	420

TABLE 2-10

Smart Card RAM
Requirements of
the AES Finalists

Ciphers	Smart Card RAM (Bytes)
MARS	100
RC6	210
Rijndael	52
Serpent	50
Twofish	60

2. *CAST-128*: CAST was developed by Carlisle Adams and Stafford
   Tavares. The algorithm is patented by Entrust Technologies; however
   Entrust has made it available free for commercial and noncom-
   mercial use. The Entrust home page is *http://www.entrust.com*.
   There are two variants of CAST: CAST-128 and CAST-256. The
   specifications for both are available as Request For Comments
   (RFC) documentations: RFC 2144 for CAST-128 and RFC 2612 for
   CAST-256. CAST-128 supports variable key length from 40 to 128
   bits; and it encrypts 64-bit blocks of plaintext into 64-bit block
   ciphertext. The cipher utilizes 16 rounds of computations that are
   somewhat similar to those of DES. However, CAST, with a key size
   of 128 bits, encrypts data at a speed that is more than twice that
   of triple DES in software, but it is considered to be somewhat less
   secure than triple DES, with three different keys, and IDEA.
   CAST-256 was accepted as one of 15 candidates for the AES. This
   variant of CAST encrypts 128-bit block plaintext into 128-bit block
   ciphertext. It uses variable key sizes from 128 to 256 bits, in increments of 32 bits. The design of CAST-256 is similar to that of
   CAST-128.

3. *International Data Encryption Algorithm (IDEA):* IDEA was developed by Xuejia Lai and James Massey at the Swiss Institute of
   Technology. The original specifications and later modifications
   are outlined in [LM90] and [LM91], respectively. The algorithm is
   patented; licensing information and the source code for IDEA are
   available at *http://www.ascom.com*. IDEA employs a 128-bit key
   length and operates on 64-bit blocks of plaintext. The algorithm
   proceeds in eight rounds and relies extensively on multiplication
   operations: it employs 32 multiplication operations in total. As
   explained previously, multiplication operations are not as efficient

as other primitive operations. As a result, IDEA is slower than other commonly used 64-bit block ciphers, except triple DES. However, of the commonly used 64-bit block ciphers, only triple DES, with three different keys, is considered to be more secure than IDEA.

4. *RC2:* RC2 was developed by Ronald Rivest [Riv98]. It is protected as a trade secret by RSA Security. RC2 is designed to be easily implemented on 16-bit microprocessors. The algorithm uses a variable-length key of from 8 to 128 bytes and enciphers blocks of 64-bit plaintext into 64-bit blocks of ciphertext.

5. *RC5:* RC5 was developed by Ronald Rivest [Riv94]; a later description is given in [BR96]. RC5, like DES, is suitable for both hardware and software implementation. It is adaptable to processors of different word lengths: the number of bits in the processor's word is one of the inputs to the RC5 algorithm. The RC5 algorithm also has a variable number of rounds, which allows tradeoffs between higher speed and higher security. The algorithm uses a variable length key to encrypt blocks of 32, 64, or 128 bits of plaintext and output blocks of ciphertext of corresponding length.

6. *Skipjack*: Skipjack was developed by the National Security Agency (NSA). It was previously classified, but was declassified in June 1998. Skipjack uses an 80-bit key to encrypt 64-bit block plaintext. The specification of Skipjack [NSA98] is available at *http://csrc. nist.gov/encryption/skipjack-kea.htm*, and the source code for a C implementation is available at *http://jya.com/skipjack.txt*.

This concludes the chapter on symmetric-key cryptosystems. In the next chapter, we discuss public-key cryptosystems.

Public-Key Cryptosystems

Overview of Chapter 3

In this chapter, we discuss the following topics:

Symmetric-key cryptosystems suffer from a major drawback. These ciphers are *symmetric*; that is, the same key is used for encrypting and decrypting the data. Therefore, the sender and receiver of the message need to exchange the "secret" cryptographic key via a secure channel, or use a key exchange algorithm to put in place "shared values" from which the keys can be generated. However, these mechanisms may not be available. *Public-key* cryptosystems address this issue. These ciphers are *asymmetric* systems: the key that is used to decipher the data is different from that which is used to encipher it. The encrypting keys—commonly referred to as the public keys—do not need to be kept secret. This eliminates the need for a secure channel to exchange cryptographic keys.

The ideas on which public-key cryptosystems are based were first published in 1976 by Whitfield Diffie and Martin Hellman [DH76]. These systems are based on the concept of trapdoor one-way functions. One-way functions are functions that are easy to compute but hard to invert, whereas trapdoor one-way functions are one-way functions which can be inverted easily with the knowledge of some additional information; this additional information is referred to as the *trapdoor*.

In this chapter, we discuss the RSA and ElGamal cryptosystems, elliptic curve cryptography, and Diffie-Hellman key exchange. Then we conclude the chapter by giving a comparison of symmetric-key and public-key cryptosystems.

3.1   RSA Cryptosystem

Whitfield Diffie and Martin Hellman put forward the idea of public-key cryptography in 1976 [DH76]; however, they did not propose a practical public-key cryptosystem. Two years after the Diffie-Hellman publication, Ronald Rivest, Adi Shamir, and Len Adlemar developed the first public-key cryptosystem at MIT [RSA78]. Before we describe the RSA cryptosystem, we give a brief overview of some necessary mathematical concepts.

A *group* is an abstract mathematical object that consists of a set of elements, an operator,[1] and some other defining properties. An example of a group is the integer modulo n group under the addition modulo n operation. This group consists of n elements. The group can be represented as $\mathbb{Z}_n = \{0, 1, 2, \ldots, n - 1\}$. For example, consider the group $\mathbb{Z}_{15}$. The elements

---

[1] For the group that we will encounter in our discussion, the operator is either + or *.

of $\mathbb{Z}_{15}$ are $\{0, 1, 2, 3, \ldots, 13, 14\}$. Some examples of computations in this group are as follows:

$$5 + 7 \bmod 15 = 12$$
$$13 + 2 \bmod 15 = 0$$
$$10 + 12 \bmod 15 = 7$$

An element $x \in \mathbb{Z}_n$ has a multiplicative inverse x^{-1} if and only if the greatest common divisor of x and n is 1; that is, gcd $(x, n) = 1$. In other words, x must be relatively prime to n. The inverse of x, if it exists, is such that $x * x^{-1} \bmod n = 1$. Let us look at some examples. The elements in $\mathbb{Z}_{15}$ that have an inverse are those that are relatively prime to 15, that is, 1, 2, 7, 11, 13, and 14. Thus we have $1^{-1} = 1$, $2^{-1} = 8$, $7^{-1} = 13$, $11^{-1} = 11$, $13^{-1} = 7$, and $14^{-1} = 14$. We are now ready to describe the RSA cryptosystem.

The RSA cryptosystem is based on the difficulty of factoring large integers in the $\mathbb{Z}_n$ group. The RSA system can be described as follows:

1. Generate two large primes[2] p and q.

2. Compute the product of the primes $n = pq$.

3. Compute the number of integers that are less than n and relatively prime to n. This is equal to the Euler phi function $\phi(n) = (p - 1)(q - 1)$.

4. Select a random number b such that $1 < b < \phi(n)$ and b is relatively prime to $\phi(n)$, that is, gcd$(b, \phi(n)) = 1$. This condition is necessary to ensure that b has a multiplicative inverse.

5. Compute $a = b - 1 \bmod \phi(n)$.

6. Keep $a, p,$ and q secret and make n and b available to any one who wishes to send you encrypted messages.

3.1.1 The Encryption and Decryption Processes

Plaintext is encrypted in blocks. Each block should be less than the binary representation of n in bits; that is, each block should be less than $\log_2 n$ bits in length. For a block of plaintext x, the public keys (b, n) are used to generate the corresponding block of ciphertext c by computing: $c = x^b \bmod n$. The block of plaintext x can then be generated from the block of ciphertext c by calculating $x = c^a \bmod n$.

---

[2] Prime number are integers that can only be divided by themselves and 1.

3.1.2 Security Factors

The primes p and q should be large enough such that, given their product n, it should be computationally infeasible to factor n without prior knowledge of either p or q. Breaking the RSA cryptosystem is essentially equivalent to factoring n; since, if p and q are known, then $\phi(n)$ can be easily computed; then since a is the multiplicative inverse of $b \bmod \phi(n)$, a can be readily computed as well.

In 1999, a network consisting of 292 computers used the number field sieve[3] to factor a 155-decimal digit (512-bit) prime in 5.2 months; see *http://www.rsasecurity.com/rsalabs/challenges/factoring/rsa155.html* for further detail. For short-term security, it is therefore recommended that n be at least 1024-bits in length. The number of bits in the binary representation of an integer is $\log_2 10$ times the number of decimal digits. Therefore, a 1024-bit number has $1024/\log_2 10 \approx 308$ decimal digits. For long-term security, however, n should be at least a 2048-bit (or 616-decimal-digit) number.

We now turn to the question of how suitably sized primes are generated. Currently, the most practical way of generating a large prime is to use a *pseudorandom number generator* to generate sufficiently large add numbers, and then use a *probabilistic primality testing* algorithm to determine if the number is a prime. A commonly used algorithm that tests for prime is the *Miller-Rabin* primality testing algorithm. This algorithm, along with other probabilistic primality testing algorithms, is outlined in [Sti95].

3.2 ElGamal Cryptosystem

The ElGamal cryptosystem was developed by ElGamal and published in 1985 in [ElG85]. This system is based on the *Discrete Logarithm* problem in a finite field. A *field* is essentially a group[4] with one additional property: every nonzero element in the field has a multiplicative inverse. $\mathbb{Z}_p$, where p is a prime, is an example of a finite field. This field consists of the set of elements $\{0, 1, 2, \ldots, p-1\}$, with the addition modulo p and the multiplication modulo p operators. Another example of a finite field is $\mathbb{Z}_{p*}$. The elements of this field are all relatively prime to p. $\mathbb{Z}_{p*}$ has an additional characteristic: it is a *cyclic* field. In other words, every element $\beta \in \mathbb{Z}_{p*}$

---

[3] The number field sieve is a technique for factoring large numbers. For further detail about this technique, see [BLP93].

[4] See Section 3.1 for the definition of a group.

can be generated using a generator g by raising it to some power a, where $0 \le a \le p - 2$. Let us look at an example. Consider the $\mathbb{Z}_{13*}$ field $\mathbb{Z}_{13*} = \{1,2,3,4,5,6,7,8,9,10,11,12\}$. The generator for this field is 2 because every element in this field can be generated by raising 2 to some power a, where $0 \le a \le p - 2$; that is;

$2^0 \bmod 13 = 1$, $2^1 \bmod 13 = 2$, $2^4 \bmod 13 = 3$, $2^2 \bmod 13 = 4$

$2^9 \bmod 13 = 5$, $2^5 \bmod 13 = 6$, $2^{11} \bmod 13 = 7$, $2^3 \bmod 13 = 8$

$2^8 \bmod 13 = 9$, $2^{10} \bmod 13 = 10$, $2^7 \bmod 13 = 11$, and $2^6 \bmod 13 = 12$

The generator for a field is called the *primitive element* modulo p.

The discrete logarithm problem is applicable to any finite field; however, in this section we restrict our discussion to its application to the $\mathbb{Z}_p$ field. Consider the equation $\beta = g^a \bmod p$, where $\beta \in \mathbb{Z}_{p*}$; if p is carefully chosen, it is considered to be very difficult to compute the values of a given β, g, and p. However, β can be computed quite efficiently if g, a and p are given. In other words, exponentiation modulo p is a one-way function for suitable p.

We now describe the ElGamal system. First, a suitable prime p is chosen such that the discrete logarithm problem is difficult for integers less than p. Then suitable β, g, and a are chosen such that $\beta = g^a \bmod p$. β, g and p are then made public and a kept private.

3.2.1 Encryption and Decryption Processes

To encipher a plaintext x, Alice chooses a secret random integer k such that $k < (p - 1)$; then if e_K is the encryption process, we write:

$$e_K(x,k) = (y_1, y_2)$$

where $y_1 = g^k \bmod p$ and $y_2 = x\beta^k \bmod p$. Note that since the ciphertext depends on the value of k that Alice chooses, a plaintext x can be encrypted into many different ciphertext; therefore, the ElGamal cryptosystem is nondeterministic.

If d_K is the decryption process, we write:

$$d_K(y_1, y_2) = y_2 \, (y_1^a)^{-1} \bmod p$$

In simple terms, a plaintext x is "masked" by multiplying it by β^k; the products y_2 and g^k are then sent to Bob—the holder of the private key. Bob can then use his private key a to compute β^k from g^k. Finally, the plaintext x can be determined by dividing y_2 by the "mask" β^k.

3.2.2   Security Considerations

At the time of writing, the most effective algorithm available for solving the discrete logarithm problem is the number field sieve algorithm. A variation of this algorithm is also used to factor large numbers. The discrete logarithm problem in the Z_{p*} field is considered to be somewhat more difficult than the factoring problem in the Z_n group. However, as in the case of n for the Z_n group for RSA, for reasonable security, the prime p for the Z_{p*} field for the ElGamal cryptosystem should be at least 1024 bits; and 2048 bits for long-term security.

3.3   Elliptic Curve Cryptography

Public-key cryptography is based on problems that can be computed efficiently in one direction but are very hard to inverse, as is the case with the discrete logarithm and the factorization problems. Over the years, researchers have been looking for problems that are considered difficult enough to merit being used as a base for cryptosystems. In 1985, two researchers, Neal Koblitz [Kob87] and Victor Miller [Mil86], independently proposed that elliptic curves can be used as the basis for public-key cryptosystems. Since these findings, elliptic curves have generated considerable interest. The motivation for elliptic curve cryptography (ECC) is the notion that the discrete logarithm problem is much harder for elliptic curves over finite fields[5] compared to that over the Z_p field. Since the discrete logarithm problem is more difficult for elliptic curves, smaller keys can be used for these cryptosystems to provide a similar degree of security compared to other public-key cryptosystems with much larger keys. Smaller keys result in faster encryption or decryption time, bandwidth saving, and in some cases, lower memory requirements.

The operation of public-key ciphers is very computationally intensive, particularly for larger key sizes; therefore, elliptic curve cryptosystems are very attractive because of the high degree of security they provide for key sizes that, in some cases, are less than a tenth of those of other public-key cryptosystems. Although elliptic curve cryptosystems are generally more difficult to implement than other public-key ciphers, it is expected that

---

[5] See Section 3.2 for the definition of a field.

these cryptosystems will experience much more widespread use in the future because of the increased encryption throughput and the other advantages that the smaller keys afford.

Elliptic curves can be defined over any finite fields; however, the fields that are of primary interest for ECC are the Z_p and the *characteristic two finite field* F_{2^m}, for some $m \geq 1$. We will describe the elliptic curve cryptographic scheme over these two finite fields; and we start with elliptic curves over the Z_p field.

3.3.1 Elliptic Curve over Z_p

Before we proceed with the description, we need to introduce another mathematical concept. If a and b are integers, we say that a is *congruent* to b modulo m; that is, $a \equiv b \pmod{m}$, where m is a positive integer if m divides $b - a$.

The elliptic curve $E(Z_p)$ over the field Z_p is the set of solutions or points $P = (x, y)$, for $x, y \in Z_p$ to the equation $y^2 \equiv x^3 + ax + b \pmod{p}$, where $a, b \in Z_p$ are constants, such that $4a^3 + 27b^2 \neq 0 \pmod{p}$, together with the point O, called the *point at infinity*.

Two points $P = (x_1, y_1)$ and $Q = (x_2, y_2)$ on the elliptic curve E can be added together using the following rules: if $x_2 = x_1$ and $y_2 = -y_1$, then $P + Q = O$; otherwise, $P + Q = (x_3, y_3)$ where:

$$x_3 \equiv \lambda^2 - x_1 - x_2 \pmod{p}$$
$$y_3 \equiv \lambda(x_1 - x_3) - y_1 \pmod{p}$$

and

$$\lambda = \begin{cases} \dfrac{y_2 - y_1}{x_2 - x_1} & \text{if } P \neq Q \\[2ex] \dfrac{3x_1^2 + a}{2y_1} & \text{if } P = Q \end{cases}$$

Note also that $P + O = O + P = P$.

The total number of points on an elliptic curve $E(Z_p)$ is denoted as $\#E(Z_p)$. The Hasse theorem states that $\#E(Z_p)$ satisfies the following inequality:

$$p + 1 - 2\sqrt{p} \leq \#E(Z_p) \leq p + 1 + 2\sqrt{p}$$

Cryptographic schemes under elliptic curve cryptography rely on the scalar multiplication of elliptic curve points. The multiplication of an elliptic curve point $P \in E(\mathbb{Z}_p)$ by a scalar n, is the process of adding P to itself n times. For example, $3P = P + P + P$. Scalar multiplication can be done quite efficiently using the addition rules outlined above.

3.3.1.1 Elliptic Curve Domain Parameters over $\mathbb{Z}_p$

Elliptic curve domain parameters over $\mathbb{Z}_p$ specify an elliptic curve E and a base point $P = (x_P, x_P)$ on E. This is necessary in order to precisely define public-key cryptographic schemes based on elliptic curve cryptography. Elliptic curve domain parameters over $\mathbb{Z}_p$ are a sextuple:

$$T = (p, a, b, P, n, h)$$

where p is the prime that defines the field $\mathbb{Z}_p$, the two elements $a, b \in \mathbb{Z}_p$ specify the elliptic curve $E(\mathbb{Z}_p)$ defined by the equation:

$$y^2 \equiv x^3 + ax + b \pmod{p}$$

such that

$$4a^3 + 27b^2 \not\equiv 0 \pmod{p}$$

P is the base point $P = (x_P, y_P)$ on $E(\mathbb{Z}_p)$, n is a prime that is the order[6] of P, and the integer h is the cofactor $h = \#E(\mathbb{Z}_p)/n$.

To avoid some known attacks on ECC, p should be chosen such that p is not equal to the total number of points on the elliptic curve; that is, $p \neq \#E(\mathbb{Z}_p)$, and $p^m \not\equiv 1 \pmod{n}$ for any $1 \leq m \leq 20$. Similarly, the base point $P = (x_P, y_P)$ should be chosen so that the order n is such that $h \leq 4$.

We have covered the necessary mathematical base for ECC over the $\mathbb{Z}_p$ field, and we can proceed to describe the elliptic curve key pairs and outline the actual encryption/decryption process. However, before we proceed, we describe the elliptic curve over the characteristic two field $\mathbb{F}_{2^m}$.

3.3.2 Elliptic Curve over $\mathbb{F}_{2^m}$

Before we describe elliptic curves over $\mathbb{F}_{2^m}$ fields, we need to define the finite field $\mathbb{F}_{2^m}$.

The Finite Field $\mathbb{F}_{2^m}$

The characteristic two finite field $\mathbb{F}_{2^m}$, contains 2^m elements, where m $\geq$ 1. The field $\mathbb{F}_{2^m}$ can be represented as:

$$a_{m-1}x^{m-1} + a_{m-2}x^{m-2} + \cdots + a_1 x + a_0$$

---

[6]The order of a point $P = (x,y)$ is the smallest integer n such that $nP = \mathcal{O}$ (point at infinity).

where the a_i are either 0 or 1; that is $a_i \in \{0,1\}$.

■ Addition is defined over the $\mathbb{F}_{2^m}$ field as follows:

if $a = a_{m-1}x^{m-1} + \cdots + a_0$ and $b = b_{m-1}x^{m-1} + \cdots + b_0$,
such that $a, b \in \mathbb{F}_{2^m}$,

then $a + b = r$, where $r \in \mathbb{F}_{2^m}$ and $r = r_{m-1}x^{m-1} + \cdots + r_0$,
such that $r_i \equiv a_i + b_i \pmod{2}$.

■ Multiplication is defined over $\mathbb{F}_{2^m}$ in terms of an irreducible poly-nomial[7] $f(x)$ of degree m. Recall that the degree of a polynomial is the highest power of the polynomial. Multiplication is defined as follows:

if $a = a_{m-1}x^{m-1} + \cdots + a_0$ and $b = b_{m-1}x^{m-1} + \cdots + b_0$,
such that $a, b \in \mathbb{F}_{2^m}$,

then $a \cdot b = s$, where $s = s_{m-1}x^{m-1} + \cdots + s_0$ is the remainder when the polynomial $a \cdot b$ is divided by an irreducible polynomial $f(x)$ with all coefficient arithmetic performed modulo 2.

■ The additive inverse of $a \in \mathbb{F}_{2^m}$, denoted as $-a$, is the unique solu-tion to the equation $a + x = 0$ in $\mathbb{F}_{2^m}$.

■ The multiplicative inverse of $a \in \mathbb{F}_{2^m}$, such that $a \neq 0$, denoted as a^{-1}, is the unique solution of $a \cdot x = 1$ in $\mathbb{F}_{2^m}$.

Both the additive and the multiplicative inverses can be calculated effi-ciently using the extended Euclidean algorithm; for a description of this algorithm, see [Sti95].

3.3.2.2   Elliptic Curve over $\mathbb{F}_{2^m}$

A non-supersingular[8] elliptic curve $E(\mathbb{F}_{2^m})$ over the field $\mathbb{F}_{2^m}$ is the set of solutions or points $P = (x,y)$, for $x, y \in \mathbb{F}_{2^m}$, to the equation:

$$y^2 + xy = x^3 + ax^2 + b$$

where $a, b \in \mathbb{F}_{2^m}$, and $b \neq 0$; together with an extra point O called the point at infinity.

The following addition rules apply:

---

[7] An irreducible polynomial $f(x)$ is a polynomial that has no factor other than itself, 1 and 0 over the given field.

[8] Supersingular elliptic curves are vulnerable to certain attacks.

1. $O + O = O$.

2. $(x,y) + O = O + (x,y) = (x,y)$ for all $(x,y) \in \mathbb{F}_{2^m}$.

3. $(x,y) + (x, x + y) = O$ for all $(x,y) \in \mathbb{F}_{2^m}$; that is, the negative of the point (x,y) is $-(x,y) = (x, x + y)$.

4. For two points $P = (x_1, y_1)$ and $Q = (x_2, y_2)$ on the elliptic curve E, such that $x_2 \neq x_1$, their sum $P + Q = (x_3, y_3)$ where:

$$x_3 = \lambda^2 + \lambda + x_1 + x_2 + a$$
$$y_3 = \lambda(x_1 + x_3) + x + 3 + y_1$$
$$\lambda \equiv \frac{y_1 + y_2}{x_1 + x_2} \qquad x_3, y_3, \lambda \in \mathbb{F}_{2^m}$$

5. For any point $P = (x, y) \in \mathbb{F}_{2^m}$, such that $x \neq 0$, $P + P = (x_3, y_3)$, where:

$$x_3 = \lambda^2 + \lambda + a$$
$$y_3 = x_1^2 + (\lambda + 1)x_3$$
$$\lambda = x_1 + \frac{y_1}{x_1} \qquad x_3, y_3, \lambda \in \mathbb{F}_{2^m}$$

The total number of points on an elliptic curve $E(\mathbb{F}_{2^m})$ is denoted as $\#E(\mathbb{F}_{2^m})$. Hasse theorem states that $\#E(\mathbb{F}_{2^m})$ satisfies the following inequality:

$$2^m + 1 - 2\sqrt{2^m} \leq \#E(\mathbb{F}_{2^m}) \leq 2^m + 1 + 2\sqrt{2^m}$$

The multiplication of an elliptic curve point $P \in E(\mathbb{F}_{2^m})$ by a scalar n, is the process of adding P to itself n times. As in the case of an elliptic curve over the $\mathbb{Z}_p$, scalar multiplication can be done efficiently for elliptic curve over the $\mathbb{F}_{2^m}$ field, using the above addition rules.

3.3.2.3 Elliptic Curve Domain Parameters over F2m

Elliptic curve domain parameters over $\mathbb{F}_{2^m}$ specify an elliptic curve E and a base point $P = (x_p, x_p)$ on E. This is necessary in order to precisely define public key cryptographic schemes based on elliptic curve cryptography. Elliptic curve domain parameters over $\mathbb{F}_{2^m}$ are a septuple:

$$T = (m, f(x), a, b, P, n, h)$$

where m is the integer that defines the field $\mathbb{F}_{2^m}$, $f(x) \in \mathbb{F}_{2^m}$ is an irreducible polynomial of degree m specifying the representation of $\mathbb{F}_{2^m}$, the two elements $a, b \in \mathbb{F}_{2^m}$ specify an elliptic curve $E(\mathbb{F}_{2^m})$ defined by the equation:

$$y^2 + xy = x^3 + ax^2 + b$$

such that $b \neq 0$, P is a base point $P = (x_p, y_p)$ on $E(\mathbb{F}_{2^m})$, n is a prime that is the order of P, and the integer h is the cofactor $h = \#E(\mathbb{F}_{2^m})/n$.

To avoid some known attacks on ECC, 2^m should be chosen such that p is not equal to the total number of points on the elliptic curve; that is,

$2^m \neq \#E(\mathbb{F}_{2^m})$, and $2^{mB} \not\equiv 1 \pmod{n}$ for any $1 \leq B \leq 20$. Similarly, the base point $P = (x_P, y_P)$ should be chosen so that the order n is such that $h \leq 4$.

We can now proceed with the description of the elliptic curve key pairs.

3.3.3 Elliptic Curve Key Pairs

As stated earlier, elliptic curve cryptography is based on the difficulty of solving the *elliptic curve discrete logarithm problem* (ECDLP). The ECDLP can be stated as follows: given an elliptic curve $E(\mathbb{F}_q)$, where $\mathbb{F}_q$ is the finite field $\mathbb{Z}_p$ or $\mathbb{F}_{2^m}$, a point $P \in E(\mathbb{F}_q)$ of order n, with n being a prime, and a point $Q \in E(\mathbb{F}_q)$ determine the integer k, $1 \leq k \leq n - 1$, such that $Q = kP$. n should be a prime because an algorithm due to Pohlig and Hellman [PH78] reduced the determination of k to the determination of k modulo each of the prime factor of n. Therefore, for maximum security, n should have no factor; that is, n should be a prime.

Let us now look at what constitutes the private and public keys for elliptic curve cryptographic schemes. Given some elliptic curve domain parameters

$$T = (p,a,b,P,n,h) \quad \text{or} \quad (m,f(x),a,b,P,n,h)$$

an elliptic curve key pair (k,Q) associated with T consists of an elliptic curve secret key k (the private key), which is an integer such $1 \leq k \leq n - 1$, and an elliptic curve public key $Q = (x_Q, y_Q)$, which is the point $Q = kP$.

ECC can be adapted to just about any public-key cryptosystem. The actual encryption scheme depends on the cryptosystem to which it is adapted. Later in this chapter, we show how ECC can be adapted to the Diffie-Hellman key exchange, and the Digital Signature Algorithm (DSA).

The description of ECC presented in this section was adapted from [SEC99], which is available at the "The Standard for Efficient Cryptography (SEC)" home page, at http://www.sec.org. [SEC99] contains the specifications for the implementation of public-key cryptographic schemes based on ECC. For additional information about any implementation detail of ECC, [SEC99] is a good source of reference.

3.3.4 Security Considerations

Since the Koblitz and Miller discovery of the virtues of public-key cryptosystems based on ECC in 1985, the ECDLP has received a lot of attention. The best know algorithm to date for the ECDLP is the Pollard-ρ method [PC78], which takes approximately $\sqrt{\Pi n/2}$ steps—n is the elliptic

TABLE 3-1

Computing Power
Required to
Compute the
ECDLP

Size of n (in Bits)	$\sqrt{\Pi\, n/4}$	MIPS Years
160	2^{80}	8.5×10^{11}
184	2^{93}	7.0×10^{15}
234	2^{117}	1.2×10^{23}
354	2^{177}	1.3×10^{41}
426	2^{213}	9.2×10^{51}

curve domain parameter n—and a step is an elliptic curve addition. In 1998, two researchers, Wiener and Zuccherato [WZ99], showed that the Pollard-ρ method can be speeded up by a factor of $\sqrt{2}$, so the expected running time of this algorithm is $\sqrt{\Pi\, n/4}$ steps. Table 3-1, adapted from [SEC99], contains an estimate of million instructions per second (MIPS) years of computing power required to solve the ECDLP on a general curve using the improved Pollard-ρ method. An MIPS year is equivalent to the computational power of a 1-MIPS machine running for 1 year. Table 3-2, adapted from [JM99], shows the computing power required to factor integers using the general number field sieve (NFS).

Let us try and put the data in these tables in perspective: if 1,000,000 computers are available and each is able to execute 1,000,000 MIPS, for a 160-bit n, these computers working in parallel could compute an ECDLP in approximately 0.85 years, that is, 10.2 months. Compare this to a 1024-bit integer, which could be factored using these computers in approximately 0.3 years or 4 months. Note that in this example, even though the size of the integer n is greater than 6 times that of the order n of the base

TABLE 3-2

Computing Power
Required to Factor
Integers Using the
General NFS

Size of n (in Bits)	MIPS Years
512	3×10^{4}
768	2×10^{8}
1024	3×10^{11}
1280	1×10^{14}
1536	3×10^{16}
2048	3×10^{20}

TABLE 3-3

Comparable
Key Sizes

Symmetric-Key Schemes (Key Size in Bits)	ECC-Based Schemes (Size of n in Bits)	RSA/DSA (Modulus Size in Bits)
56	112	512
80	160	1024
112	224	2048
128	256	3072
192	384	7680
256	512	15360

point on the elliptic curve, it took more than twice the time to compute the ECDLP compared to that for factoring the integer.

The computing resources used in the above example are very elaborate; it is very unlikely, for the foreseeable future, that this number of "supercomputers" will be available to dedicate to a single task. Therefore, a 160-bit n for an elliptic curve cryptosystem should provide a good degree of security.

Table 3-3, adapted from [SEC99], gives an approximation of the equivalent key sizes of symmetric-key, ECC-based and RSA/DSA schemes. Note that as the size of n for the ECC-based schemes increases, the ratio of the size of the RSA/DSA modulus to the size of n is much larger. For example, compare $512/112 \simeq 4.5$ with $15360/512 \simeq 30$.

In terms of the differences between the elliptic curve over the $\mathbb{Z}_p$ field and that over the field $\mathbb{F}_{2^m}$, there is not any difference in terms of security; however, the performance of hardware implementations of ECC-based schemes over the $\mathbb{F}_{2^m}$ field is slightly higher. Software implementations over both fields give approximately the same performance.

3.4 Diffie-Hellman Key Exchange

The Diffie-Hellman key exchange was the first published public-key cryptographic scheme. It was published in 1976 in [DH76]. This key exchange protocol is based on the *Discrete Logarithm* problem. See Section 3.2 for a discussion on the discrete logarithm problem over the $\mathbb{Z}_{p*}$ field. If Alice and Bob wish to exchange a secret key over an insecure channel using the Diffie-Hellman key exchange protocol, they would proceed as follows:

1. Alice and Bob decide on a suitable prime p and an integer α, such that α is a primitive root of p; α and p can be made public.

2. Alice chooses a secret integer α_A, computes $y_A = \alpha^{\alpha_A} \bmod p$ and sends y_A to Bob.

3. Bob chooses a secret integer a_B, computes $y_B = \alpha^{a_B} \bmod p$ and sends y_B to Alice. y_A and y_B are referred to as *Diffie-Hellman public values*.

4. Alice generates the secret key K by computing $K = \left(y_B\right)^{a_A} \bmod p$.

5. Bob generates the secret key K by computing $K = \left(y_A\right)^{a_B} \bmod p$.

6. Alice and Bob will generate the identical key K since:

$$K = \left(y_B\right)^{a_A} \bmod p = \left(\alpha^{a_B} \bmod p\right)^{a_A} \bmod p$$

$$= \left(\alpha^{a_B}\right)^{a_A} \bmod p = \alpha^{a_B a_A} \bmod p$$

$$= \left(\alpha^{a_A}\right)^{a_B} \bmod p = \left(a^{a_A} \bmod p\right)^{a_B} \bmod p$$

$$= \left(y_A\right)^{a_B} \bmod p$$

The security of the Diffie-Hellman key exchange is based on the assumption that it is computationally infeasible to compute a_A or a_B from y_A or y_B and α; since this is equivalent to solving the discrete logarithm problem.

3.4.1   Man-in-the-Middle Attack

The Diffie-Hellman Key Exchange is vulnerable to a *man-in-the-middle attack* in which an intruder—let's call her Eve—intercepted messages, modified them, and sent the modified messages to Bob and Alice as illustrated in Figure 3-1. Alice thinks that she is using Bob's y_B to generate the key; but she is actually using Eve's value $y_B{'}$. Similarly, Bob thinks that he is using Alice's y_A to generate the key; whereas, he is actually using Eve's value $y_A{'}$. Hence, the the key that Alice and Bob generate will—unknown to both parties—be shared by Eve. The man-in-the-middle attack can be thwarted by using an authenticated Diffie-Hellman key exchange.

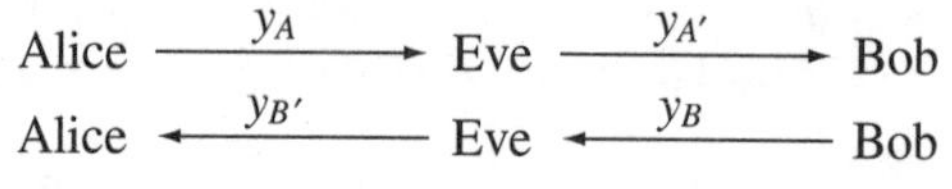

Figure 3-1
Illustration of
Man-in-the-Middle
Attack

$$\text{Alice} \xrightarrow{\quad y_A \quad} \text{Eve} \xrightarrow{\quad y_{A'} \quad} \text{Bob}$$

$$\text{Alice} \xleftarrow{\quad y_{B'} \quad} \text{Eve} \xleftarrow{\quad y_B \quad} \text{Bob}$$

3.4.2 Authenticated Diffie-Hellman Key Exchange

A possible modification to the Diffie-Hellman key exchange that can foil the man-in-the-middle attack is the use of digital signatures[9] to sign and authenticate the integers y_A and y_B that Alice and Bob exchange. This scheme is similar to the Diffie-Hellman exchange, except that Alice signs y_A using a digital signature algorithm and generates the signature $sig(y_A)$; she then sends y_A and $sig(y_A)$ to Bob. Bob can then use Alice's public verification algorithm to determine whether $sig(y_A)$ is indeed Alice's signature for y_A. Similarly, Bob signs y_B and sends both y_B and $sig(y_B)$ to Alice, who will be able to use Bob's public verification algorithm to ascertain whether or not $sig(y_B)$ is Bob's signature for y_B. Both parties will therefore be able to determine whether or not the messages that they received from each other have been tampered with. Thus, Alice or Bob will not be fooled into receiving components for the generation of the key from Eve, thinking that they came from Bob or Alice, respectively.

3.4.3 Security Factors

The Diffie-Hellman key exchange, like the ElGamal cryptosystem, is based on the discrete logarithm problem; therefore, with regard to the size of the modulus p for the field, the same arguments apply. For reasonable security, the prime p should be at least 1024 bits (2048 bits for long-term security). For additional details, see the discussion of the ElGamal cryptosystem in Section 3.2.

3.4.4 Elliptic Curve Diffie-Hellman Key Exchange Scheme

As we mentioned in our discussion of elliptic curve cryptography in Section 3.3, ECC can be adopted to most public-key cryptographic schemes. In this section, we briefly show how ECC can be adopted to the Diffie-Hellman key exchange. For the purpose of our discussion we use an elliptic curve over the $\mathbb{Z}_p$ field; however, an elliptic curve over the $\mathbb{F}_{2^m}$ field could be utilized as well. First, we need to choose an elliptic curve with the elliptic curve domain parameter

$$T = (p, a, b, P, n, h)$$

---

[9] Digital signatures are discussed later in this chapter.

as described in the discussion of the elliptic curve over $\mathbb{Z}_p$ (Section 3.3.1). p is the prime that defines the field $\mathbb{Z}_p$ (we will use a 180-bit prime p as the modulus, that is $p \simeq 2^{180}$, the two elements $a, b \in \mathbb{Z}_p$ specify the elliptic curve $E(\mathbb{Z}_p)$ defined by the equation:

$$y^2 \equiv x^3 + ax + b \ (\text{mod } p)$$

such that

$$4a^3 + 27b^2 \not\equiv 0 \ (\text{mod } p)$$

P is the base point $P = (x_P, y_P)$ on $E(\mathbb{Z}_p)$, n is a prime that is the order of P, and the integer h is the cofactor $h = \#E(\mathbb{Z}_p)/n$. A key exchange between Alice and Bob can be described as follows:

1. Alice selects an integer k_A, such that $1 \le k_A \le n - 1$. This is Alice's private key. Alice then generates a public key $Q_A = k_A P$, which is a point $\left(x_{Q_A}, y_{Q_A}\right)$ on the elliptic curve, and sends it to Bob.

2. Bob similarly selects an integer k_B, such that $1 \le k_B \le n - 1$, that constitutes his private key. Bob then generates a public key $Q_B = k_B P$, which is another point on the elliptic curve, and sends it to Alice.

3. Alice generates the secret key $K = k_A Q_B$, which is a point (x_K, y_K) on the elliptic curve.

4. Bob generates the secret key $K = k_B Q_A$, which is a point (x_K, y_K) on the elliptic curve. The key K that Alice and Bob generated is the same, since

$$k_A Q_B = k_A(k_B P) = k_B(k_A P) = k_B Q_A$$

To break this scheme, an attacker needs to be able to solve the elliptic curve discrete log problem over the $\mathbb{Z}_p$ or $\mathbb{F}_{2^m}$ fields.

The public keys $Q_A = \left(x_{Q_A}, y_{Q_A}\right)$, $Q_B = \left(x_{Q_B}, y_{Q_B}\right)$ and the generated key $K = (x_K, y_K)$ are all points on the elliptic curve. These points need to be converted into binary representation using an appropriate conversion scheme. For an example of a conversion scheme that can be used to encode an elliptic curve point into a binary number, refer to [SEC99], which contains implementation details of the processes involved in deploying elliptic curve cryptography.

3.5 Digital Signature

One of the most important applications of public-key cryptography is digital signatures. What exactly is a digital signature? A *digital signature* is a bit-string or the ASCII representation of a bit-string that binds the electronic data under consideration to a cryptographic private key. Before we discuss digital signatures further, let us talk a little about conventional signatures. We sign important documents to attest to their validity. When we open a bank account, for example, the bank stores our signature. For every transaction request on the account, the signature on the transaction request form is compared with the signature we submitted when we opened the account; a transaction request is granted only if the signatures match. It is not very difficult to forge a conventional signature. This highlights an important difference between digital signatures and conventional signatures: it is computationally infeasible to forge a signature generated by a secure cryptographic digital signature scheme, without possessing the private key that produced the signature.

Since conventional signatures can be forged, people can actually deny that they signed a document in question. However, it is much more difficult to repudiate a digital signature; doing so essentially involves proving that the security of the private key was compromised before the signature was generated. This is because the generation of a digital signature requires the use of a private key; the corresponding public key is used to validate the signature. Therefore, a digital signature has the important quality of *nonrepudiation* because there are schemes such as digital certificates[10] that bind the identity of an entity, that is, a person, an organization, or a system, to a private and public key pair. This makes it rather difficult for a person to disown a digital signature.

It is important to note, however, that unlike conventional signatures, one cannot tell the difference between an original digital signature and a copy of it. For example, a person could create an electronic document authorizing Alice to perform a certain transaction on his or her behalf and digitally sign the document. Alice can generate several copies of this electronic document and unless the original document was timestamped, there is actually no way of differentiating the original document from the copies. Due diligence must therefore be taken when using digital signatures for important legal documents. Important documents should always be timestamped before they are digitally signed. Timestamps can be generated using Network Time Protocol (NTP) applications.

Digital signatures now carry as much weight, if not more, legally, as do conventional signatures. President Bill Clinton passed legislation in the summer of 2000 making digital signatures just as legally binding

---

[10]We will discuss digital certificates in Chapter 5.

in the United States as conventional signatures. A number of European and other nations adopted similar legislation giving legal status to digital signatures.

Digital signature schemes are commonly used in e-mail applications. At the request of a user, the e-mail application digitally signs the composed e-mail and attaches the signature at the end of message. The recipient can then use the sender's cryptographic public key to validate whether or not the message is from him or her, and ascertain if the message has been modified. Security protocols such as IPSec also rely heavily on digital signatures for access control. Let us now look at the mechanism of digital signature schemes.

A digital signature scheme consists of a signing algorithm and a verification algorithm. The signing algorithm utilizes a private cryptographic key to generate the signature. Let us call the signature $sig(m)$ for a message m; the pair $(m, sig(m))$ is then sent to the recipient. The verification algorithm, on the other hand, uses the signatory public keys and takes the pair (m, y) as input and returns true if $y = sig(m)$ and false if $y \neq sig(m)$. The verification algorithm, in essence, decrypts the attached signature using the sender's public key. If the message m has not been modified and it was indeed signed using the private key of the signatory, the decryption output will be identical to m. Digital signatures can therefore be used to detect unauthorized modifications of data and to authenticate the identity of the signatories. Note that unlike public-key encryption algorithms, where public keys are used to encrypt and private keys to decrypt. The opposite occurs for digital signature schemes: private keys generate the signatures and public keys validate them.

Digital Signature Standard

The National Institute of Standards and Technology (NIST) adopted a signature scheme—known as the Digital Signature Algorithm (DSA)—as the Digital Signature Standard (DSS) on December 1994. The DSS specification was revised in 1998 and published as FIPS PUB 186-1 [NIST98] on December 15, 1998. FIPS PUB 186-1 specified that either DSA or RSA signature schemes can be used to generate digital signatures for U.S. agencies. On February 15, 2000, the NIST issued a new standard, FIPS 186-2, for DSS. FIPS 186-2 specifies that in addition to DSA and RSA, the elliptic curve digital signature algorithm (ECDSA) can also be used to generate digital signatures for U.S. agencies. We present all three DSS signature schemes in the following subsections. Let us start with DSA.

Digital Signature Algorithm

DSA is a modification of the the ElGamal signature scheme [ElG85]. As we discussed in Section 3.2, the ElGamal scheme is based on the Discrete Logarithm problem over a finite field. The DSA can be described as follows: let

- p be a prime such that $2^{L-1} < p < 2^L$ for $512 \leq L \leq 1024$ and L is a multiple of 64.

- q be a 160-bit prime that divides $p - 1$.

- $g = h^{(p-1)/q} \bmod p$, where h is any integer with $1 < h < p - 1$, such that $h^{(p-1)/q} \bmod p > 1$; that is, g has order $q \bmod p$.

- $\beta = g^a \bmod p$, where a is a randomly or pseudorandomly generated integer such that $0 < a < q$.

- k be a randomly or pseudorandomly generated integer such that $0 < k < q$.

The values p, q, g, and β are public and a and k are private. A new k should be generated for each signature.

The signature of a message m for a given k can be defined as:

$$sig(m,k) = (y,s)$$

where

$$y = (g^k \bmod p) \bmod q$$
$$s = (k^{-1}(\text{SHA-1}(m) + ay)) \bmod q$$

The SHA-1 hash function[11] is used to reduce the variable-length message m to a 160-bit message digest, which is then signed using the digital signature scheme.

Let $ver(m,y,s)$ be the verification algorithm that takes as input the message m and y and s as defined above. *The verification of a signature* is done by performing the following computations:

$$d_1 = ((\text{SHA-1}(m))s^{-1}) \bmod q$$
$$d_2 = (ys^{-1}) \bmod q$$
$$ver(m,y,s) = \text{true} \Leftrightarrow ((g^{d_1}\beta^{d_2}) \bmod p) \bmod q = y$$

---

[11]We discuss hash functions in the next chapter.

The signature for the message m is valid if and only if $ver(m,y,s)$ returns true. If $ver(m,y,s)$ returns false, then either the message m has been modified or the signature is not that of the signatory.

Security Considerations

As mentioned previously, the DSA is a modification of the ElGamal cryptosystem. They are both based on the discrete logarithm problem over finite fields. Therefore, the security considerations of both cryptography schemes are similar. Hence, as is the case for the ElGamal cryptosystem we discussed in Section 3.2, for short-term security, the prime p for the $\mathbb{Z}_{p^*}$ field should be at least 1024 bits for the DSA scheme and at least 2048 bits for long-term security.

RSA Signature Scheme

The RSA public-key cryptosystem can also be used to generate digital signatures. As we discussed in Section 3.1, the RSA cryptosystem is based on the difficulty of factoring large primes. The RSA signature scheme can be described as follows:

1. Generate two large primes p and q.
2. Compute the product of the primes, $n = pq$.
3. Compute the number of integers that are less than n and relatively prime to n. This is equivalent to the Euler phi function, $\phi(n) = (p - 1)(q - 1)$.
4. Select a random number b such that $1 < b < \phi(n)$ and b is relatively prime to $\phi(n)$, that is, $gcd(b, \phi(n)) = 1$.
5. Compute $a = b^{-1} \bmod \phi(n)$.
6. Make n and b publicly available and keep a, p, and q secret.

The signature $sig(m)$ for a message m is generated by computing the following:

$$sig(m) = (h(m))^a \bmod n$$

where $h(m)$ is the message digest that resulted from hashing the message m with a cryptographic hash function such as SHA-1 or MD5.

The verification algorithm $ver(m,y)$, which takes as input the message m and the signature y, can be defined as:

$$ver(m,y) = \text{true} \Leftrightarrow h(m) \equiv y^b \pmod{n}$$

Anyone can verify a signature because the verification algorithm uses the signatory public keys; however, only the signatory will be able to generate a valid signature since this requires the signatory's private keys.

Security Considerations

As is the case for the RSA cryptosystem, the primes p and q should be large enough that, given their product n, it should be computationally infeasible to factor n without prior knowledge of either p or q. For short-term security, n should be at least 1024 bits; for long-term security, n should be at least 2048 bits.

Elliptic Curve Digital Signature Algorithm

As we discussed previously in Section 3.3, elliptic curve cryptography is based on the difficulty of solving the ECDLP. The ECDLP can be stated as follows: given an elliptic curve $E(\mathbb{F}_q)$, where $\mathbb{F}_q$ is the finite field $\mathbb{Z}_p$ or $\mathbb{F}_{2^m}$, a point $P \in E(\mathbb{F}_q)$ of order n, with n being a prime, and a point $Q \in E(\mathbb{F}_q)$, determine the integer $k, 1 \leq k \leq n - 1$, such that $Q = kP$. See Section 3.3 for the details about these ECC parameters.

The ECDSA is the elliptic curve analogue of DSA. It is the application of the DSA to elliptic curves over finite $\mathbb{Z}_p$ or $\mathbb{F}_{2^m}$ fields. Let us now look at what constitutes the private and public keys for the ECDSA.

Given the following elliptic curve domain parameters:

$$T = (p,a,b,P,n,h) \quad \text{or} \quad T = (m,f(x),a,b,P,n,h)$$

for elliptic curves over the finite $\mathbb{Z}_p$ or $\mathbb{F}_{2^m}$ fields, respectively. An elliptic curve key pair (k,Q) associated with T consists of an elliptic curve secret key k (the private key), which is an integer such that $1 \leq k \leq n - 1$, and an elliptic curve public key $Q = (x_Q, y_Q)$, which is the point $Q = kP$. As discussed in Section 3.3, the elements constituting the elliptic curve domain parameter $T = (p,a,b,P,n,h)$ are defined as follows: p is the prime that defines the field $\mathbb{Z}_p$; the two elements a, $b \in \mathbb{Z}_p$ specify the elliptic curve $E(\mathbb{Z}_p)$ defined by the equation:

$$y^2 \equiv x^3 + ax + b \pmod{p}$$

such that

$$4a^3 + 27b^2 \not\equiv 0 \pmod{p}$$

P is the base point $P = (x_P, y_P)$ on $E(\mathbb{Z}_p)$; n is a prime that is the order of P; and the integer h is the cofactor $h = \#E(\mathbb{Z}_p)/n$, where $\#E(\mathbb{Z}_p)$ is the total number of points on an elliptic curve $E(\mathbb{Z}_p)$.

For the elliptic curve domain parameter $T = (m, f(x), a, b, P, n, h)$, the elements are defined as follows: m is the integer that defines the field F_{2^m}; $f(x) \in F_{2^m}$ is an irreducible polynomial of degree m specifying the representation of F_{2^m}; the two elements a, $b \in F_{2^m}$ specify an elliptic curve $E(F_{2^m})$ defined by the equation:

$$y^2 + xy = x^3 + ax^2 + b$$

such that $b \neq 0$; P is a base point $P = (x_P, y_P)$ on $E(F_{2^m})$; n is a prime that is the order of P; and the integer h is the cofactor $h = \#E(F_{2^m})/n$. See Section 3.3 for further detail.

ECDSA Signature Generation

The ECDSA signature for a message m can be generated as follows:

1. Choose an elliptic curve over the Z_p or F_{2^m} finite fields with domain parameters $T = (p, a, b, P, n, h)$ or $T = (m, f(x), a, b, P, n, h)$, respectively.

2. Select a statistically unique and unpredictable integer k such that for the domain parameter element n, $1 \leq k \leq n - 1$. k is the private key and should be kept secret. Compute the public key $Q = kP$; Q is the point (x_Q, y_Q) on the elliptic curve.

3. Select another statistically unique and unpredictable integer d such that for the domain parameter element n, $1 \leq d \leq n - 1$. Compute $dP = (x_1, y_1)$, which is another point on the elliptic curve.

4. Convert the x coordinate x_1 of the point (x_1, y_1) to an integer $\bar{x}_1$ using a suitable conversion scheme[12], then let $r = \bar{x}_1 \mod n$. If $r = 0$, then go to step 3. If $r = 0$ were to be allowed, the signing equation $s = d^{-1}\{h(m) + kr\} \mod n$ would not involve the private key k. This is a security violation and should not be allowed.

5. Compute $d^{-1} \mod n$.

6. Compute $s = d^{-1}\{h(m) + kr\} \mod n$, where $h(m)$ is the integer value corresponding to the 160-bit SHA-1 message digest $h(m)$ for the message m. We discussed the SHA-1 hash function in Chapter 4.

---

[12]See [SEC99], which contains implementation detail of the processes involved in deploying elliptic curve cryptography, for a conversion scheme that can be used to encode an elliptic curve point into a binary number.

7. If $s = 0$, then go to step 3. If $s = 0$, then $s^{-1} \bmod n$ does not exist; therefore, the signature cannot be validated. See the signature verification procedure below.

8. The signature for the message m is the pair of integers (r,s).

ECDSA Signature Verification

The ECDSA signature (r,s) for a message m can be verified as follows:

1. Given the public key Q and the domain parameter $T = (p,a,b,P,n,h)$ or $T = (m,f(x),a,b,P,n,h)$ for the elliptic curve over the $\mathbb{Z}_p$ or $\mathbb{F}_{2m}$ finite fields, respectively. Verify that r and s are integers between 1 and n. If they are not, the signature is not valid.

2. Generate the SHA-1 message digest $h(m)$ for the message m and convert the resulting 160-bit bit-string to an integer $h(m)$.

3. Compute $u_1 = s^{-1}h(m) \bmod n$ and $u_2 = s^{-1}r \bmod n$.

4. Compute $R = u_1P + u_2Q = (x_R, y_R)$. If $R = 0$, the signature is invalid.

5. Convert the x coordinate x_R for the point (x_R, y_R) on the elliptic curve to an integer x_R, using a suitable conversion scheme, and then let $v = x_R \bmod n$.

6. The signature is valid if and only if $v = r$.

Security Considerations

The ECDSA offers greater security for much smaller key sizes compared to the DSA and the RSA signature schemes. As was allude to in Section 3.3.4, a 160-bit ECDSA key offers equivalent security to a 1024-bit RSA or DSA key. Likewise, a 224-bit ECDSA key offers similar security to a 2048-bit RSA or DSA key. Therefore, ECDSA allows much greater throughput than either the DSA or the RSA signature scheme, due to the reduced overhead associated with the smaller key sizes. See Section 3.3.4 for further detail.

3.6 Symmetric-Key versus Public-Key Cryptosystems

Before we conclude this chapter, we give a brief comparison of symmetric-key and public-key cryptosystems. As was mentioned at the beginning of this chapter, public-key cryptosystems resolve the problem of having to use a secure channel or a key exchange protocol to exchange secrete keys. However, compared to symmetric-key cryptosystems, public-key systems encrypt data much more slowly because public-key cryptosystems usually involve modular exponential calculations involving large integers—which can be very intensive computationally. On the other hand, the computations involved in symmetric-key systems are usually primitive operations such as exclusive-OR of bit strings, which can be done much more quickly. If we compare speed of encryption of RSA using a 1024-bit modulo p, RSA is over 1500 times slower than any of the five AES finalists. As a consequence of this big difference in the speed of encryption of symmetric-key compared to public-key cryptosystems, applications—such as IPSec—that require high throughput almost exclusively use symmetric-key cryptosystems for enciphering of data. On the other hand, digital signature applications as well as other applications that do not necessarily require high throughput mainly utilize public-key cryptosystems.

Hash Functions and MAC

Summary of Chapter 4

In this chapter, we discuss the following topics:

- MD5 Hash Function
- SHA-1 Hash Function
- RIPEMD-160 Hash Function
- Tiger Hash Function
- Comparative Analysis of the Hash Functions
- HMAC Message Authentication Code

A *cryptographic hash function* is an algorithm that takes a message x of any arbitrary length and produces a fixed-length output $h(x)$, called a *message digest* or *fingerprint*. *Hash functions* are used to verify the integrity of messages or files. For example, a message digest can be generated for a binary file and compared with the digest generated for the same file on a secure site or medium; if the file has not been tampered with, the digests will be identical. Another common use of hash functions is with digital signatures: the message to be digitally signed is first hashed and then the fixed-length message digest is run through the digital signature algorithm. We discuss digital signatures in Chapter 5.

If a hash function is to be useful cryptographically, it must be *strongly collision-free*. That is, it should be computationally infeasible to find two messages x and x', such that $x \neq x'$ and $h(x) = h(x')$. In this chapter, we discuss four commonly used hash functions: MD5, SHA-1, RIPEMD-160, and Tiger; we also present an example of a *message authentication codes* (MACs). MACs are similar to hash functions, except that a secret key is required to produce the fixed-length message digest.

4.1   MD5 Hash Function

The MD5 message digest algorithm [Riv92b] was developed by Ronald Rivest at MIT. It is an extension of an earlier version called MD4 [Riv92a]. MD5 takes a message x of arbitrary length and outputs a 128-bit message digest $h(x)$. The MD5 algorithm consists of five steps. A description of these steps follows:

1. *Append padding bits:* The message x is padded by adding a single 1 bit followed by an appropriate number of 0 bits, such that the length of the message $|x| \equiv 448 \bmod 512$. That is, the message is extended so that the length of the padded message is 64 bits less than a multiple of 512. Padded bits are always added, even if the original message is already 64 bits less than a multiple of 512 in length, thus the number of padded bits added is between 1 and 512, inclusively.

2. *Append length:* The 64-bit representation of the length of the original message is appended to the padded message. If the length of the original message is greater than 2^{64}, then the lower-order 64 bits are appended to the message instead. At this point, the message

has a length that is an exact multiple of 512, and consequently it is divisible by 16. Let $M[0 \ 1 \ldots n-1]$ represents the words of the resulting message, where n is divisible by 16.

3. *Initialize MD buffer:* A 128-bit buffer is used to compute the message digest. The buffer can be represented by four 32-bit registers $A, B, C,$ and D. These registers are initialized to the following hexadecimal values:

$$A: 01 \ 23 \ 45 \ 67$$
$$B: 89 \ ab \ cd \ ef$$
$$C: fe \ dc \ ba \ 98$$
$$D: 76 \ 54 \ 32 \ 10$$

The values are stored in *little-endian* byte format, that is, lower-order bytes first.

4. *Process message in 16-word (512-bit) blocks:* Let X represent a 16-word block of the message. If $X[i]$ and $M[i]$ denote the word at index i in the 16-word block and n-word message, respectively, then process the message according to the following algorithm:

```
for i = 0 to n/16 - 1 do
  for j = 0 to 15 do
    set X[j] to M[i * 16 + j]
  end                        /* of loop j */
  A ∧ A = A
  B ∧ B = B
  C ∧ C = C
  D ∧ D = D
  Round1
  Round2
  Round3
  Round4
  A = (A + AA) mod 2³²
  B = (B + BB) mod 2³²
  C = (C + CC) mod 2³²
  D = (D + DD) mod 2³²
end                          /* of loop i */
```

The four rounds indicated in the algorithm utilize four auxiliary functions and a 64-element table $T[1 \ldots 64]$, where $T[i] = 2^{32} \times abs(\sin(i))$, where i is the index in the table and $T[i]$ is an element at index i. Each of the auxiliary functions takes three 32-bit words as input and outputs a 32-bit word. The functions are defined as follows:

$$F(x,y,z) = x \wedge y \vee ((\neg x) \wedge z)$$
$$G(x,y,z) = x \wedge z \vee (y \vee \neg z)$$

$$H(x,y,z) = x \oplus y \oplus z$$
$$I(x,y,z) = y \oplus (x \vee \neg z)$$

where $x \wedge y$ is the bit-wise AND of x and y, $x \vee y$ is the bit-wise OR of x and y, $x \oplus y$ is the bit-wise exclusive-OR of x and y, and $\neg x$ is the bit-wise complement of x.

A description of the four rounds follows:

■ *Round 1:* Let [*abcd k s i*] represent the operation
$a = b + ((a + F(b,c,d) + X[k] + T[i]) <<< s)$, where $Y <<< s$ represents the circular shift of Y by s positions ($0 \le s \le 31$).
Do the following 16 operations:

[*ABCD* 0 7 1] [*DABC* 1 12 2] [*CDAB* 2 17 3] [*BCDA* 3 22 4]
[*ABCD* 4 7 5] [*DABC* 5 12 6] [*CDAB* 6 17 7] [*BCDA* 7 22 8]
[*ABCD* 8 7 9] [*DABC* 9 12 10] [*CDAB* 10 17 11] [*BCDA* 11 22 12]
[*ABCD* 12 7 13] [*DABC* 13 12 14] [*CDAB* 14 17 15] [*BCDA* 15 22 16]

■ *Round 2:* Let [*abcd k s i*] represent the operation
$a = b + ((a + G(b,c,d) + X[k] + T[i]) <<< s)$.
Do the following 16 operations:

[*ABCD* 1 5 17] [*DABC* 6 9 18] [*CDAB* 11 14 19] [*BCDA* 0 20 20]
[*ABCD* 5 5 21] [*DABC* 10 9 22] [*CDAB* 15 14 23] [*BCDA* 4 20 24]
[*ABCD* 9 5 25] [*DABC* 14 9 26] [*CDAB* 3 14 27] [*BCDA* 8 20 28]
[*ABCD* 13 5 29] [*DABC* 2 9 30] [*CDAB* 7 14 31] [*BCDA* 12 20 32]

■ *Round 3:* Let [*abcd k s t*] represent the operation
$a = b + ((a + H(b,c,d) + X[k] + T[i]) <<< s)$.
Do the following 16 operations:

[*ABCD* 5 4 33] [*DABC* 8 11 34] [*CDAB* 11 16 35] [*BCDA* 14 23 36]
[*ABCD* 1 4 37] [*DABC* 4 11 38] [*CDAB* 7 16 39] [*BCDA* 10 23 40]
[*ABCD* 13 4 41] [*DABC* 0 11 42] [*CDAB* 3 16 43] [*BCDA* 6 23 44]
[*ABCD* 9 4 45] [*DABC* 12 11 46] [*CDAB* 15 16 47] [*BCDA* 2 23 48]

■ *Round 4:* Let [*abcd k s t*] represents the operation
$a = b + ((a + I(b,c,d) + X[k] + T[i]) <<< s)$.
Do the following 16 operations.

[*ABCD* 0 6 49] [*DABC* 7 10 50] [*CDAB* 14 15 51] [*BCDA* 5 21 52]
[*ABCD* 12 6 53] [*DABC* 3 10 54] [*CDAB* 10 15 55] [*BCDA* 1 21 56]
[*ABCD* 8 6 57] [*DABC* 15 10 58] [*CDAB* 6 15 59] [*BCDA* 13 21 60]
[*ABCD* 4 6 61] [*DABC* 11 10 62] [*CDAB* 2 15 63] [*BCDA* 9 21 64]

5. *Output:* The 128-bit message digest is the content of the four registers A, B, C, and D appended in little-endian byte format; that is, it starts with the lower byte of A and ends with the higher byte of D.

The computations involved in this algorithm are all primitive operations. Also, the algorithm does not require any large lookup table; as a result, the MD5 algorithm is quite fast on a 32-bit processor. We present the C source code for MD5 in Appendix C.

4.2   Secure Hash Algorithm

The Secure Hash Algorithm (SHA) was developed by NIST and adopted as the Secure Hash Standard in 1993. The revised version of the algorithm, SHA-1, was issued as Federal Information Processing Standards Publication 180-1 (FIPS PUB 180-1) [NIST95] in 1995. SHA-1 takes a message of length < 2^{64} bits and outputs a 160-bit message digest. The design of the SHA-1 algorithm is similar to that of MD5. A description of the five steps involved in the processing of the SHA-1 message digest follows:

1. *Append padding bits:* The message x is padded by adding a single 1 bit followed by an appropriate number of 0 bits, such that the length of the message $|x| \equiv 448 \mod 512$. That is, the message is extended such that the length of the padded message is 64 bits less than a multiple of 512. Padded bits are always added, even if the original message is already 64 bits less than a multiple of 512 in length. Thus, the number of padded bits added is between 1 and 512, inclusively.

2. *Append length:* The 64-bit representation of the length of the original message is appended to the padded message. If the length of the original message is greater than 2^{64}, then the lower-order 64 bits are appended to the message instead. At this point, the message has a length that is an exact multiple of 512, and consequently it is divisible by 16. Let $M[0 \ 1 \dots n-1]$ represent the words of the resulting message, where n is divisible by 16.

3. *Initialize buffers:* The SHA-1 computation uses three buffers: two buffers, each consisting of five 32-bit registers and a sequence of 80 32-bit words; and a single word buffer TEMP. The words of the 80-word sequence are depicted as $W_0, \dots, W_{79}$. The five registers of the first buffer are labeled A, B, C, D, and E; whereas those of the

second buffer are designated $H_0, H_1, H_2, H_3,$ and H_4. $A, B, C, D,$ and E are initialized to the following hexadecimal values:

$$A: 67\ 45\ 23\ 01$$
$$B: ef\ cd\ ab\ 89$$
$$C: 98\ ba\ dc\ fe$$
$$D: 10\ 32\ 54\ 76$$
$$E: c3\ d2\ e1\ f0$$

The initial values of $A, B, C,$ and D are the same as those for the four MD5 registers except that for SHA-1, the values are stored in big-endian byte format, that is, higher byte order first, whereas for MD5 the values are stored in little-endian byte format.

4. *Process message in 16-word (512-bit) blocks:* SHA-1 uses a sequence of logical functions $f_0, f_1, \ldots, f_{79}$. Each of the f_i's takes three 32-bit words as input and outputs a 32-bit word. The f_i's are defined as follows:

$$f_i(x,y,z) = (x \wedge y) \vee (\neg y \wedge z) \qquad (0 \le i \le 19)$$
$$f_i(x,y,z) = x \oplus y \oplus z \qquad (20 \le i \le 39)$$
$$f_i(x,y,z) = (x \wedge y) \vee (x \wedge z) \vee (y \wedge z) \qquad (40 \le i \le 59)$$
$$f_i(x,y,z) = x \oplus y \oplus z \qquad (60 \le i \le 79)$$

SHA-1 also uses a sequence of constant words $K_0, K_1, \ldots, K_{79}$. The hexadecimal values for these words are as follows:

$$K_i = 5a827999 \qquad (0 \le i \le 19)$$
$$K_i = 6ed9eba1 \qquad (20 \le i \le 39)$$
$$K_i = 8f1bbcdc \qquad (40 \le i \le 59)$$
$$K_i = ca62c1d6 \qquad (60 \le i \le 79)$$

Before we proceed, it is necessary to define some terms. $X + Y$ represents the addition of modulo 32 of two bit strings; that is, $X + Y = X + Y \bmod 32$. $S^n(X)$ represents the circular left shift of the bit string X by n bits $(0 \le n \le 32)$ that is, $S^n(X) = (X << n) \vee (X >> 32 - n)$; where $<<$ and $>>$ represent left and right shift, respectively.

Let $M_1, M_2, \ldots, M_n$ (n is an integer divisible by 16) represent 16-word block sequences of the message that resulted from step 2. Process each M_i as follows:

1. Divide M_i into 16 words $W_0, W_1, \ldots W_{15}$, where W_0 is the left-most word.

2. for $t = 16$ to 79 do
   let $W_t = S^1(W_{t-3} \oplus W_{t-8} \oplus W_{t-14} \oplus W_{t-16})$.

3. Let $H_0 = A$, $H_1 = B$, $H_2 = C$, $H_3 = D$, and $H_4 = E$.

4. for $t = 0$ to 79 do

$$TEMP = S^5(H_0) + f_t(H_1, H_2, H_3) + H_4 + W_t + K_t \text{ and}$$
$$H_4 = H_3, \quad H_3 = H_2, \quad H_2 = S^{30}(H_1), \quad H_1 = H_0, \quad H_0 = TEMP.$$

Let $A = A + H_0$, $B = B + H_1$, $C = C + H_2$, $D = D + H_3$, and
$E = E + H_4$

5. *Output:* The 160-bit message digest is the content of five words A, B, C, D, and E appended in big-endian byte format.

SHA-1 executes more slowly than MD5 since more steps are involved in producing the 160-bit SHA-1 message digest compared to the number of steps executed in the processing of the MD5 128-bit message digest. However, SHA-1 is more secure than MD5 because the additional 32 bits in length of the message digest of SHA-1 makes it less susceptable to brute-force attack.

4.3 RIPEMD-160

RIPEMD is a variant of the MD5 hash function. It essentially consists of two parallel versions of MD5. It was developed in the framework of the EU project RIPE (Race Integrity Primitives Evaluation). RIPEMD-160 is a more secure version of RIPEMD. It was developed by Hans Dobbertin, Antoon Bosselaers, and Bart Preneel in 1996. This hash function takes a message of arbitrary length and outputs a 160-bit message digest or fingerprint.

RIPEMD-160 is a five-round iterative hash function that operates on 32-bit words. The message to be hashed is first padded by adding a single 1 bit followed by an appropriate number of 0 bits, such that the length of the message is 64 bits less than a multiple of 512. Padded bits are always added, even if the original message is already 64 bits less than a multiple of 512 in length. Thus, the number of padded bits added is between 1 and 512, inclusively. Next, the 64-bit representation of the length of the original message is appended to the padded message. At this point, the message has a length that is an exact multiple of 512 (16 32-bit words); that is, the padded message consists of t 16 32-bit word blocks, where $t \geq 1$. The algorithm uses five 32-bit registers h_0, h_1, h_2, h_3, and h_4 to store the intermediate and the final digest. The algorithm can be described as follows:

```
RIPEMD-160(m) // Input: Message m of arbitrary length.
// Output: 160-bit message digest.

/* Pad message as described above. t 16 32-bit word blocks
resulted. Each block is denoted X_i[j] with 0 ≤ i ≤ t - 1 and
0 ≤ j ≤ 15 */

// Initialize the five registers
h_0 = 0x67452301    h_1 = 0xefcdab89    h_2 = 0x98badcfe
h_3 = 0x10325436    h_4 = 0xc3d2e1f0

for i = 0 to t - 1 do
    A = h_0     B = h_1    C = h_2    D = h_3    E = h_4
    A' = h_0    B' = h_1   C' = h_2   D' = h_3   E' = h_4
    for j = 0 to 79 do
        /* In this algorithm, + represents additional modulo
        32. The function f(j,x,y,z), the permutations s(j),
        s'(j), r(j) and r'(j) and the constants K(j) and K'(j)
        will be defined shortly. A <<< b represents the cyclic
        shift of A to the left by b positions. */
        T = ((A + f(j,B,C,D) + X_i[r(j)] + K(j)) <<< s(j)) + E
        A = E      E = D      D = C <<< 10      C = B      B = T
        T = ((A' + f(79 - j,B',C',D') + X_i[r'(j)] + K'(j)) <<<
            s'(j)) + E'
        A' = E'    E' = D'    D' = C' <<< 10    C' = B'    B' = T
    // end for
    T = h_1 + C + D'
    h_1 = h_2 + D + E'
    h_2 = h_3 + E + A'
    h_3 = h_4 + A + B'
    h_4 = h_0 + B + C'
    h_0 = T
// end of algorithm
```

The message digest is the content of five registers $h_0, h_1, h_2, h_3,$ and h_4. The function $f(j,x,y,z)$ is defined as follows:

$$f(j,x,y,z) = x \oplus y \oplus z \qquad \text{for } (0 \le j \le 15)$$
$$f(j,x,y,z) = (x \wedge y) \vee (\neg \wedge z) \qquad \text{for } (16 \le j \le 31)$$
$$f(j,x,y,z) = (x \vee \neg y) \oplus z \qquad \text{for } (32 \le j \le 47)$$
$$f(j,x,y,z) = (x \wedge z) \vee (y \wedge \neg z) \qquad \text{for } (48 \le j \le 63)$$
$$f(j,x,y,z) = x \oplus (y \vee \neg z) \qquad \text{for } (64 \le j \le 79)$$

The constants $K(j)$ and $K'(j)$ are indicated below. Note the that $\lfloor X \rfloor$, where X is a real number, is the integer part of X.

$$K(j) = 0x00000000 \qquad \text{for } (0 \le j \le 15)$$

$$K(j) = \lfloor 2^{30} \times \sqrt{2} \rfloor = 0x5a827999 \qquad \text{for } (16 \le j \le 31)$$

$$K(j) = \lfloor 2^{30} \times \sqrt{3} \rfloor = 0x6ed9eba1 \qquad \text{for } (32 \le j \le 47)$$

$$K(j) = \left\lfloor 2^{30} \times \sqrt{5} \right\rfloor = 0x8fabbcdc \qquad \text{for } (48 \le j \le 63)$$

$$K(j) = \left\lfloor 2^{30} \times \sqrt{7} \right\rfloor = 0xa953fd4e \qquad \text{for } (64 \le j \le 79)$$

$$K'(j) = \left\lfloor 2^{30} \times \sqrt[3]{2} \right\rfloor = 0x50a28be6 \qquad \text{for } (0 \le j \le 15)$$

$$K'(j) = \left\lfloor 2^{30} \times \sqrt[3]{3} \right\rfloor = 0x5c4dd124 \qquad \text{for } (16 \le j \le 31)$$

$$K'(j) = \left\lfloor 2^{30} \times \sqrt[3]{5} \right\rfloor = 0x6d703efe3 \qquad \text{for } (32 \le j \le 47)$$

$$K'(j) = \left\lfloor 2^{30} \times \sqrt[3]{7} \right\rfloor = 0x7a6d76e9 \qquad \text{for } (48 \le j \le 63)$$

$$K'(j) = 0x00000000 \qquad \text{for } (64 \le j \le 79)$$

The permutations $r(j)$ and $r'(j)$ are shown below. These permutations are used to select the 32-bit word to operate on during each iteration of the algorithm.

$$r(j) = j \qquad \text{for } (0 \le j \le 15)$$
$$r(16 \ldots 31) = 7,4,13,1,10,6,15,3,12,0,9,5,2,14,11,8$$
$$r(32 \ldots 47) = 3,10,14,4,9,15,8,1,2,7,0,6,13,11,5,12$$
$$r(48 \ldots 63) = 1,9,11,10,0,8,12,4,13,3,7,15,14,5,6,2$$
$$r(64 \ldots 79) = 4,0,5,9,7,12,2,10,14,1,3,8,11,6,15,13$$
$$r'(0 \ldots 15) = 5,14,7,0,9,2,11,4,13,6,15,8,1,10,3,12$$
$$r'(16 \ldots 31) = 6,11,3,7,0,13,5,10,14,15,8,12,4,9,1,2$$
$$r'(32 \ldots 47) = 15,5,1,3,7,14,6,9,11,8,12,2,10,0,4,13$$
$$r'(48 \ldots 63) = 8,6,4,1,3,11,15,0,5,12,2,13,9,7,10,14$$
$$r'(64 \ldots 79) = 12,15,10,4,1,5,8,7,6,2,13,14,0,3,9,11$$

The permutations $s(j)$ and $s'(j)$ are shown below. These permutations indicate the number of positions a given 32-bit word should to be shifted to the left.

$$s(0 \ldots 15) = 11,14,15,12,5,8,7,9,11,13,14,15,6,7,9,8$$
$$s(16 \ldots 31) = 7,6,8,13,11,9,7,15,7,12,15,9,11,7,13,12$$
$$s(32 \ldots 47) = 11,13,6,7,14,9,13,15,14,8,13,6,5,12,7,5$$
$$s(48 \ldots 63) = 11,12,14,15,14,15,9,8,9,14,5,6,8,6,5,12$$
$$s(64 \ldots 79) = 9,15,5,11,6,8,13,12,5,12,13,14,11,8,5,6$$
$$s'(0 \ldots 15) = 8,9,9,11,13,15,15,5,7,7,8,11,14,14,12,6$$
$$s'(16 \ldots 31) = 9,13,15,7,12,8,9,11,7,7,12,7,6,15,13,11$$
$$s'(32 \ldots 47) = 9,7,15,11,8,6,6,14,12,13,5,14,13,13,7,5$$
$$s'(48 \ldots 63) = 15,5,8,11,14,14,6,14,6,9,12,9,12,5,15,8$$
$$s'(64 \ldots 79) = 8,5,12,9,12,5,14,6,8,13,6,5,15,13,11,11$$

Later in this chapter, we compare the security and the performance of RiPEMD-160 with the other hash functions we presented. For information on the design philosophies or for any other detail about RIPEMD-160, refer to [DBP96], which contains the original specifications of this hash function. A full description of RIPEMD-160, along with source code for the C implementation, also is available at *http://www.esat.kuleuven.ac.be/~bosselae/ripemd160.html*.

4.4 Tiger

The Tiger hash function was designed by Ross Anderson of Cambridge University, England, and Eli Biham of Technion, Haifa, Israel. Anderson and Biham are two of the three designers of Serpent, one of the five AES finalists. Tiger, unlike the other hash functions we discussed, was designed to run quickly and efficiently on 64-bit processors.

Tiger takes as input a message of arbitrary length and outputs a 192-bit message digest. For compatibility with other hash functions, the first 160 or 128 bits of the output can be used as the message digest. These variants of Tiger are referred to as Tiger/160 and Tiger/128, respectively. Tiger with the full 192 bits of output is also called Tiger/192.

In Tiger, all the computations are on 64-bit words in little-endian byte format. Three 64-bit registers A, B, and C are used to stored the intermediate hash value. These registers are initialized as follows:

$$A = 0x0123456789abcdef$$
$$B = 0xfedcba9876543210$$
$$C = 0xf096a5b4c3b2e187$$

The message to be hashed is padded similarly to the padding scheme for the other hash functions we have discussed. That is, a single 1 bit, followed by an appropriate number of 0 bits, such that the length of the message is 64 bits less than a multiple of 512. Padded bits are always added, even if the original message is already 64 bits less than a multiple of 512 in length. Next, the 64-bit representation of the length of the original message is appended to the padded message. The resulting message has a length that is an exact multiple of 512. Each successive 512-bit block of the padded message is divided into eight 64-bit words $x_0, x_1, \ldots, x_7$, and the following computations performed:

$$A' = A$$
$$B' = B$$
$$C' = C$$

```
pass(A,B,C,5)
key_schedule
pass(C,A,B,7)
key_schedule
pass(B,C,A,9)
A = A ⊕ A′
B = B - B′
C = C + C′
```

where pass(a,b,c,n) is the following operations:

$$\text{round}(a,b,c,x_0,n)$$
$$\text{round}(b,c,a,x_1,n)$$
$$\text{round}(c,a,b,x_2,n)$$
$$\text{round}(a,b,c,x_3,n)$$
$$\text{round}(b,c,a,x_4,n)$$
$$\text{round}(c,a,b,x_5,n)$$
$$\text{round}(a,b,c,x_6,n)$$
$$\text{round}(b,c,a,x_7,n)$$

where round(a,b,c,x,n) is the following operations:

$$c = c \oplus x$$
$$a = a - (t_1[c_0] \oplus t_2[c_2] \oplus t_3[c_4] \oplus t_4[c_6])$$
$$b = b + (t_4[c_1] \oplus t_3[c_3] \oplus t_2[c_5] \oplus t_1[c_7])$$
$$b = b * n$$

where c_i is the ith byte of the 64-bit word c, $0 \le i \le 7$; and t_1, t_2, t_3, and t_4 are the four S-boxes. The S-boxes each consist of 256 64-bit bit strings. If the value of the byte c_i is y, such that $0 \le y \le 255$, then $t_m[y]$, for $1 \le m \le 4$, is the yth index into the 256-element lookup table.

```
key_schedule is:
```
$$x_0 = x_0 - (x_7 \oplus \text{0xa5a5a5a5a5a5a5a5})$$
$$x_1 = x_1 \oplus x_0$$
$$x_2 = x_2 + x_1$$
$$x_3 = x_3 - (x_2 \oplus (\sim x_1 << 19))$$
$$x_4 = x_4 \oplus x_3$$
$$x_5 = x_5 + x_4$$
$$x_6 = x_6 - (x_5 \oplus (\sim x_4 >> 23))$$
$$x_7 = x_7 \oplus x_6$$
$$x_0 = x_0 + x_7$$
$$x_1 = x_1 - (x_0 \oplus (\sim x_7 << 19))$$
$$x_2 = x_2 \oplus x_1$$
$$x_3 = x_3 + x_2$$
$$x_4 = x_4 - (x_3 \oplus (\sim x_2 >> 23))$$
$$x_5 = x_5 \oplus x_4$$
$$x_6 = x_6 + x_{50}$$
$$x_7 = x_7 - (x_6 \oplus \text{0x0123456789abcdef})$$

$\sim x$ represents the bit-wise complement of x, and $x \ll s$ and $x \gg s$ represent the logic shift of the bit string x to the left and right, respectively, by s positions. At the end of the execution of the algorithm, the 192-bit digest is contained in the three registers A, B and C, stored in little-endian byte format.

A complete description of Tiger along with the source code for the C implementation is available at the designers' home pages at: *http://www. cs.technion.ac.il/~biham* and *http://www.cl.cam.ac.uk/users/rja14*.

4.5 Comparative Analysis

In this section we give a brief comparative analysis of the hash functions we discussed in this chapter. Of the four hash functions MD5, SHA-1, RIPEMD-160, and Tiger, Tiger is believed to be the most secure by virtue of the larger message digest. Tiger produces a 192-bit digest, compared to 160 bits for SHA-1 and RIPEMD-160, and 128 bits for MD5. SHA-1 and RIPEMD-160 offer approximately the same degree of security, whereas MD5 is considered to be the least secure of the four. Table 4-1 summarizes the assumed number of messages that are required in order to find a collision for the respective hash function.

With respect to the performance of these hash functions, Tiger, unlike MD5, SHA-1, and RIPEMD-160, was designed to run efficiently on 64-bit processors; on 64-bit processors, Tiger is approximately 2.8 times faster than RIPEMD-160, 2.5 times faster than SHA-1, and approximately the same speed as MD5. On 32-bit processors, MD5 is the fastest of the four; it is approximately 3 times faster than RIPEMD-160 and approximately 2.8 times faster than SHA-1 and Tiger.

TABLE 4-1

Approximate Number of Messages Required to Find Collision for the Respective Hash Function

Hash Function	Approximate Number of Messages Required to Find Collision
MD5	$2^{64} \simeq 1.8 \times 10^{19}$
SHA-1	$2^{80} \simeq 1.2 \times 10^{24}$
RIPEMD-160	$2^{80} \simeq 1.2 \times 10^{24}$
Tiger	$2^{96} \simeq 8.0 \times 10^{28}$

4.6 HMAC

Message authentication codes (MACs) are similar to hash functions, except that a secret key is required to produce the message digest. MACs are typically used to validate information transmitted between two parties that share a secret key. HMACs are algorithms that perform message authentication using cryptographic hash functions. HMACs can be used in combination with any iterated cryptographic hash function such as MD5, SHA-1, RIPEMD-160, Tiger, or any other hash function, without modification of the hash function. A brief description of HMACs follows:

Let H denotes a cryptographic hash function,

K denotes a secret key,

B represents the byte length of the block that is used to compute the message digest (64 bytes for MD5 and SHA-1),

L denotes the byte length of the message digest,

ipad represents the byte $0x36$ repeated B times, and

opad represents the byte $0x5c$ repeated B times.

K can be of any length up to B bytes; however, it is recommended that K be not shorter than L in length. Applications that use keys with length greater than B need to hash the key using H and then use the resulting L-byte string as the actual key to the HMAC algorithm.

To compute HMACs of a data "text" do the following:

1. Append zeroes to the end of K to create a B byte string.

2. Exclusive-OR the B-byte string obtained from step 1 with ipad.

3. Append the data stream "text" to the B-byte string resulting from step 2.

4. Apply H to the bit string generated in step 3.

5. Exclusive-OR the B-byte bit string generated in step 1 with opad.

6. Append the message digest that resulted from step 4 to the B-byte string that resulted from step 5.

7. Apply H to the bit sting generated in step 6 and output the result.

The above can be represented as $H(K \oplus, H(K \oplus ipad, text))$

The security of HMAC depends on the hash function H that is used. If H is strongly collision-free, then the HMAC will also be strongly collision-free. For further discussion on the security and design of HMAC refer to [KBC97], which contains the original specifications of HMAC.

This concludes our discussion of hash functions and message authentication code. We discuss Public Key Infrastructure in the next chapter.

CHAPTER **5**

Public-Key Infrastructure

Overview of Chapter 5

In this chapter we discuss the following topics:

In our discussion of public-key cryptography in Chapter 3, we highlighted the fact unlike symmetric-key cryptosystems, the decryption or the signing keys for public-key cryptosystems are different from the encryption or—for digital signature schemes—the verification keys. This attribute of public-key cryptography has made it very attractive for application in various security protocols, particularly those that do not necessarily require very high throughput. The widespread use of public-key cryptographic applications has made it necessary to have mechanisms in place that manage and distribute public keys. The set of hardware, software, personnel, policies, and procedures required to create, manage, store, distribute, and revoke public keys is referred to as the *public-key infrastructure* (PKI).

There are a number of issues involved in the development of an infrastructure for managing and distributing public keys. The most important is trust. A very relevant question is: how can one tell that a public key belongs to Alice and not to Eve? This question brings us to a very important PKI entity: digital certificate. A *digital certificate* is an electronic data that binds a public key to an individual, organization, system, or entity. There are two main certificate formats: X.509 and PGP. We highlight the difference between these certificate formats later in this chapter. The common theme of these certificates is that they give credence to a person or entity claiming to own a public key. Digital certificates, apart from the fact that they actually contain public keys that are typically used to encrypt data or validate signatures, are also used for authentication and authorization; that is, for access control. An example of the use of certificates for authentication is IPSec VPN. This is particularly important for client hosts with dynamic IP addresses. In configuring a VPN link for these client machines, the VPN administrator issues a digital certificate to the client. The client can then use this certificate to authenticate itself to peers with which it needs to establish VPN connections on a given network.

Let us return to the issue of trust. We mentioned that a digital certificate binds the identity of a person or entity to a public key. This brings up another pertinent question: how can one attest to the authenticity of a certificate? This necessitates another important PKI entity: a certificate authority (CA). A *certificate authority* is an entity (an organization or a person) that is trusted by one or more users to create, assign, and manage public-key certificates. A CA is required to digitally sign a certificate to attest to its validity. Therefore, a user can be satisfied that a certificate is valid if the CA's signature and the owner's signature, contained in the certificate, are valid, and in addition, neither the owner's certificate nor the CA's certificate has been revoked. X.509 defines a mechanism for certificate revocation. This method involves each CA periodically issuing a digitally signed data structure called a *certificate revocation list* (CRL). A CRL is a timestamped list identifying revoked certificates that were issued by a CA. Each list is made freely available in a public repository. Each certificate in a CRL is identified by its serial number. Therefore, a user or a certificate-using system can check if a certificate has been revoked by querying a recently issued CRL for the serial number of the certificate; if the serial number is on a CRL, the certificate should be rejected. Note, however, that the X.509 method of identifying revoked certificates is not foolproof. A germane question is: how recent should "recently issued" be? Recently issued, is usually interpreted as the most recently issued. A CA issues CRLs at regular time intervals. This time interval depends on the organization's policy, and it may be weekly, daily, or hourly. When a CA revokes a certificate, the serial number for this certificate appears on the next CRL that the CA issues. For example, if an organization issues a CRL on a Monday of each week and the CA revoked a certificate on a Tuesday, this certificate will not appear on a CRL until the next CRL is issued the following Monday. Meanwhile, a user might be likely to accept the unknowingly revoked certificate as valid because it had not appeared on a CRL. The Online Certificate Status Protocol (OCSP) was designed to address this issue. We discuss the OCSP later in this chapter. Before we proceed to give further detail on the X.509 certificate format, we need to define two other important PKI terms:

- *Registration authority (RA):* An RA is an entity that is given the responsibility of performing some of the administrative tasks associated with registering a subject. These tasks include confirming the identity of the subject and validating that the subject is entitled to have the values requested in the certificate.
- *Root CA:* A root CA is a CA that is at the top of the CA hierarchy.

5.1   X.509 Certificates

X.509 is an international standard recommended by ITU-T. X.509 defines a widely accepted basis for the PKI, which includes data formats and procedures related to the distribution of cryptographic public keys via digital certificates signed by CAs. The first version of X.509 was published in 1988. X.509 v3, the version that we will be discussing, has been in use since 1996.

X.509 was originally designed to support the X.500 directory: the ITU-T Recommendation X.500 [X.500]. X.500 is an electronic directory. An electronic directory is a specialized database that is optimized for reading, searching, and browsing and is tuned to give a quick response to high volume lookup or search operations. Directories contain descriptive, attribute-based information, and they usually support sophisticated filtering capabilities. The entries in an X.500 directory are arranged in a hierarchical tree-like structure called the *directory information tree* (DIT). Each node in the tree has one parent—except the root node—and any number of children (see Figure 5-1). Each node—except the root node—is assigned a *relative distinguished name* (RDN). Table 5-1 shows some of the more commonly used X.500 attributes.

An entry in an X.500 directory is reference by its *distinguished name* (DN). A DN is a globally unique name that is constructed by taking the RDN of the entry and concatenating the RDN of the ancestor entries. For example, in Figure 5-1, the DN for the entry with RDN Carlton Davis is

Figure 5-1
X.500 Directory
Information Tree

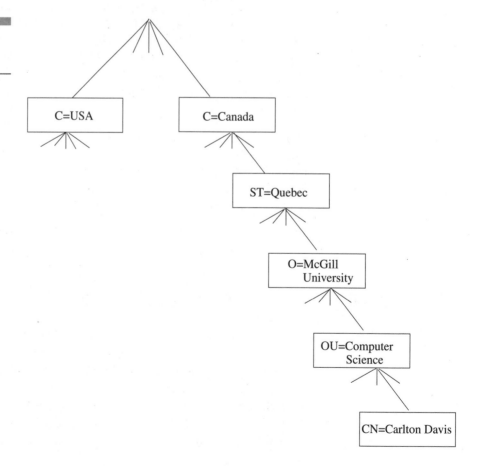

TABLE 5-1	C	Country
Some Commonly Used X.500 Attributes	ST	State or Province
	L	Locality
	STREET	Street Address
	DC	Domain Component
	O	Organization
	OU	Organization Unit
	CN	Common Name
	UID	User ID

"CN=Carlton Davis, OU=Computer Science, O=McGill University, ST=Quebec, C=Canada."

The ITU-T Recommendation X.509 was created to support the authentication of entries in an X.500 directory. X.509 defines the data formats and procedures related to the distribution of certificates digitally signed by CAs; X.509, however, does not include a profile to specify the support requirements for many of the actual data structures of subfields within a certificate. The Internet Engineering Task Force (IETF) formed a working group in October 1995 called PKIX [Public-Key Infrastructure (X.509)]. PKIX was mandated to deliver a profile for the Internet PKI of X.509 v3 and v2 CRLs. PKIX has developed and proposed a number of protocols for the distribution and management of X.509 certificates. We discuss some of these protocols in the remaining portions of this chapter.

5.1.1 X.509 Certificate Format

The X.509 standard defines the information and the format of the information that can go into a certificate. X.509 certificates contain the following data:

- *Version:* This defines which version of X.509 applies to the certificate, which ultimately affects the type and format of the information the certificate contains.

- *Serial number:* The serial number is a unique integer that is assigned to a certificate. It is used to distinguish the certificate from other certificates issued by the CA.

- *Signature:* This field contains the algorithm identifier for the digital signature algorithm that the CA uses to sign the certificate.

- *Issuer:* This field contains the DN of the entity that signed and issued the certificate. This is normally a CA.

- *Validity Period:* A certificate is valid for only a limited period of time. The certificate validity period is the time interval during which the certificate is valid. This field represents a sequence of two dates: the date on which the certificate validity period begins (notBefore), and the date on which it ends (notAfter).

- *Subject:* This field contains the DN of the entity associated with the public key stored in the subject public-key Info field of the certificate.

- *Subject public-key info:* This field contains the public key associated with the subject, as well as the algorithm identifier for the cryptographic algorithm with which the key is used.

- *Issuer unique identifiers:* This is an optional field. It contains a unique identifier of the issuer, usually the CA. It is included in certificates to handle the possibility of reuse of an issuer name over time. The PKIX profile stipulates that names should not be reused for different entities and that Internet certificates conforming to the PKIX profile should not contain this field.

- *Subject unique identifiers:* This is another optional field. It contains a unique identifier of the subject. It is included in certificates to handle the possibility of reuse of a subject name over time. The PKIX profile [HFPS99] stipulates that subject names should not be reused for different entities and that Internet certificates conforming to the PKIX profile should not contain this field.

- *Extension:* X.509 v3 supports the notion of extension. Extensions provide a method for associating additional attributes with users or public keys. X.509 v3 allows the use of private extensions to carry information that is unique to the subject. The extension field contains a sequence of one or more certificate extensions, along with a designation of whether each extension is critical or noncritical. We discuss extensions later in this chapter.

- *Signature value*: This field contains the digital signature of the CA that issued it. The digital signature is generated by inputting all data contained in the certificate—excluding the signature value field—along with the CA's private key, to the digital signature algorithm identified in the Signature field. The output from the algorithm is encoded as a bit-string and placed in the Signature Value field.

The data in a certificate are encoded using two related standards called ASN.1/DER. *Abstract Syntax Notation 1* (ASN.1) [X.208] describes the data structure for the certificate components, and the ASN.1 *Distinguished Encoding Rule* (DER) defines how the data should be stored and transferred. The description of ASN.1 is beyond the scope of this book; however, to give a flavor of this encoding format, we include the ASN.1 syntax for the data structures of the certificate components we discussed above. The ASN.1 syntax for an X.509 certificate is shown below; for an explanation of ASN.1 syntax, see [X.208]:

```
Certificate ::= SEQUENCE {
        tbsCertificate TBSCertificate,
        signatureAlgorithm AlgorithmIdentifier,
        signatureValue BIT STRING }


TBSCertificate ::= SEQUENCE {
        version            [0]  EXPLICIT Version DEFAULT v1,
        serialNumber            CertificateSerialNumber,
        signature               AlgorithmIdentifier,
        issuer                  Name,
        validity                Validity,
        subject                 Name,
        subjectPublicKeyInfo SubjectPublicKeyInfo,
        issuerUniqueID [1]      IMPLICIT UniqueIdentifier
                                OPTIONAL,
                                --If present, version shall be v2
                                  or v3
        subjectUniqueID [2]     IMPLICIT UniqueIdentifier
                                OPTIONAL,
                                --If present, version shall be v2
                                  or v3
        extensions         [3]  EXPLICIT Extensions OPTIONAL
                                --If present, version shall be v3
        }

Version  ::=  INTEGER  { v1(0), v2(1), v3(2) }


CertificateSerialNumber ::= INTEGER


Validity ::= SEQUENCE {
    notBefore       Time,
    notAfter        Time }

Time ::= CHOICE {
    utcTime         UTCTime,
    generalTime     GeneralizedTime }


UniqueIdentifier  ::=  BIT STRING
```

```
SubjectPublicKeyInfo ::= SEQUENCE {
    algorithm           AlgorithmIdentifier,
    subjectPublicKey    BIT STRING }

Extensions ::=   SEQUENCE SIZE (1..MAX) OF Extension

Extension ::=    SEQUENCE {
    extnID        OBJECT IDENTIFIER,
    critical      BOOLEAN DEFAULT FALSE,
    extnValue     OCTET STRING }

AlgorithmIdentifier  ::=  SEQUENCE {
    algorithm               OBJECT IDENTIFIER,
    parameters              ANY DEFINED BY algorithm
                            OPTIONAL }

Name ::= CHOICE {
    RDNSequence }

RDNSequence ::= SEQUENCE OF RelativeDistinguishedName

RelativeDistinguishedName ::=
  SET OF AttributeTypeAndValue

AttributeTypeAndValue ::= SEQUENCE {
  type      AttributeType,
  value     AttributeValue }

AttributeType ::= OBJECT IDENTIFIER

AttributeValue ::= ANY DEFINED BY AttributeType

DirectoryString ::= CHOICE {
        teletexString           TeletexString (SIZE
                                (1..MAX)),
        printableString         PrintableString
                                (SIZE (1..MAX)),
        universalString         UniversalString
                                (SIZE (1..MAX)),
        utf8String              UTF8String (SIZE (1.. MAX)),
        bmpString               BMPString (SIZE (1..MAX)) }
```

5.1.2 X.509 Extensions

As mentioned previously, X.509 v3 defined the notion of extensions, which provide a method for associating additional attributes with users or public keys. Each extension in a certificate is designated as either critical or noncritical. The PKIX profile stipulated that a certificate must reject a certificate if it encounters a critical extension it does not recognize, whereas a system can ignore a noncritical extension that it does not recognize. Therefore, care should be taken in designating extensions as critical. Let us now take a look at the standard extensions that X.509 v3 defined.

Authority Key Identifier

The Authority Key Identifier extension is used when an issuer of a certificate has multiple signing keys. This extension provides a means of identifying the public key corresponding to the private key that was used to sign the certificate. The data structure for this extension has three fields:

- keyIdentifier: A bit-string that identifies the public key corresponding to the private key that the issuer used to sign the certificate.
- authorityCertIssuer: The name of the entity that issued the certificate that contained the public key the extension wishes to identify.
- authorityCertSerialNumber: The serial number of the certificate that contained the public key the extension identifies.

The PKIX profile recommended that the Authority Key Identifier extension should be supported by all compliant X.509 certificates and when used, it must not be designated as critical.

Subject Key Identifier

This extension provides a means of identifying certificates that contain a particular public key. Consider, for example, the situation in which a certificate-using system has multiple certificates from multiple CAs. The Subject Key Identifier provides a means to quickly identify the set of certificates containing a particular public key. The data structure for this extension has one field:

- keyIdentifier: A bit-string that identifies the public key corresponding to the private key the issuer used to sign the certificate.

According to the PKIX profile, this certificate should be supported by all X.509 certificates implementation, and it must not be marked as critical.

Key Usage

The Key Usage extension defines the purpose for which the key contained in the certificate should be used. This extension is typically utilized to restrict the use of a public key for encryption, or for signature verification only. Some public-key encryption algorithms, RSA, for example, can be used both for enciphering and as a signature scheme. If a CA wishes to place a restriction on the key contained in a certificate that it issued, this extension provides the means to do so. In order to enforce the stipulation of this extension, if it is included in a certificate, it must be designated critical. The data structure for this extension consists of nine fields. These fields are all boolean variables: they are set either to true or false. Each variable is assigned a bit in a 9-bit bit-string; a bit representing a variable is set when the variable is true. A description of these variables follows:

- `digitalSignature`: This variable is set to true if the key within the certificate is to be used with a digital signature scheme.

- `nonRepudiation`: When the bit corresponding to this variable is set, it asserts that the subject's public key enclosed in the certificate can be employed to verify digital signatures used to provide nonrepudiation services, which protects against the signing entity falsely denying signing a datum.

- `keyEncipherment`: The `keyEncipherment` bit is set when the public key contained in the certificate is used for key transport. For example, if the key in a certificate is designated to encrypt sessions that are used to transport private keys, then the Key Usage extension will likely be included in the certificate, and the `keyEncryption` bit will typically be set. This variable is mainly applicable to key management protocols or applications.

- `keyAgreement`: This variable asserts that the key enclosed in the certificate is used for key agreement negotiation; that is, the key is intended to be used to encrypt key agreement negotiation sessions for key management protocols or applications.

- `keyCertSign`: This variable should only be set for Key Usage extension within a CA certificate. It indicates that the public key enclosed in the certificate should be used for the verification of signatures on certificates.

- `cRLSign`: When this variable is set, it indicates that the key is intended to be used to verify signatures on revocation information, such as a CRL.

- `encipherOnly`: This bit has no meaning in the absence of the `keyAgreement` bit. However, when both the `keyAgreement` and the `encipherOnly` bits are set, this asserts that the public key enclosed in the certificate should only be used to encrypt data while performing key agreement negotiations.

- `decipherOnly`: This bit has no meaning in the absence of the `keyAgreement` bit. However, when both the `keyAgreement` and the `encipherOnly` bits are set, this asserts that the public key enclosed in the certificate should only be used to decrypt data while performing key agreement negotiations.

Private Key Usage Period

This extension is one of the X.509 standard extensions; the PKIX profile, however, recommends against the use of this extension. The Private Key Usage Period extension allows certificate issuers to specify a different validation period for the private key than that for the certificate. The data structure for this extension consists of two optional fields: `notBefore` and `notAfter`. The former specifies the date for the beginning of the validation period, and the latter specifies the date for the end of the validation period.

Certificate Policies

The Certificate Policies extension is used to indicate the terms under which a certificate is issued and the policies that should govern the use of the certificate. The data structure for this extension consists of one or more sequences of policy information terms, each consisting of an object identifier (OID). If this extension is designated critical, a certificate-processing system is expected to reject the certificate if it is unable to interpret any of the policy information terms.

Policy Mapping

The Policy Mapping extension is used to convey to the issuing CA's users which policies associated with the subject CA are comparable to the policy they accept. This extension is typically used only in CA certificates. It lists one or more pairs of OIDs; each pair includes an issuer domain policy and a subject domain policy. The pairing indicates that the issuing CA considers the subject CA's domain policy to be equivalent to the issuing CA's domain policy. This extension, when used, should be marked noncritical.

Subject Alternative Name

This extension allows additional identities—such as e-mail addresses, IP addresses, DNS names (for example, micah.pgp.com), or URIs—to be bound to the subject of the certificate. The name forms for this extension can be locally designated; that is, an organization can choose whatever descriptive attributes it wishes to add to the identity of a subject. If the Subject field of the certificate is empty, this extension should be marked critical. If the Subject field, however, is nonempty, the CA may designate the Subject Alternative Name extension as noncritical.

Issuer Alternative Name

The Issuer Alternative Name extension is similar to the Subject Alternative Name, except that it binds the additional identities to the issuer of the certificate (usually a CA), rather than to the subject of the certificate. The PKIX profile stipulates that when this extension is present, it should be marked noncritical.

Basic Constraints

The Basic Constraints extension identifies whether the subject of the certificate is a CA, and if so, it specifies the depth of the certification path through this CA. The data structure for this extension consists of two fields:

- `cA`: A boolean variable that indicates if the subject is a CA.
- `pathLenConstraint`: An integer that is greater than or equal to zero. It specifies the maximum number of CA certificates that can follow this certificate in a certification path. Zero indicates that no other CA certificate should follow in the certification path. If the `pathLenConstraint` variable is absent, there is no limit to the number of CA certificates allowed in the certification path. We discuss certification path later in this chapter.

The PKIX profile stipulates that the Basic Constraints extension should only appear in a CA certificate, and it must appear as a critical extension in all CA certificates.

Name Constraints

The Name Constraints extension specifies a name space within which all subject names in the subsequent certificates in the certification path must be located. This extension is only applicable to CA certificates.

Policy Constraints

The Policy Constraints extension can be used to put restrictions on path validation for certificates issued to CAs. The policy constraints have two forms: prohibition of policy mapping (we presented the Policy Mapping extension earlier in this section) or the requirement that each certificate in the path contains an acceptable policy identifier. This extension has two fields:

■ `requireExplicitPolicy`: This is an optional variable that takes an integer value that is greater than or equal to zero. If this field is present, it indicates that subsequent certificates shall include a Certificate Policies extension or any other policy extension with an acceptable policy identifier. The value of this variable specifies the number of additional certificates that may appear in the path before an explicit policy is required.

■ `inhibitPolicyMapping`: This is an optional variable that like the `requireExplicitPolicy` variable, takes an integer value that is greater than or equal to zero. If this variable is present in the Policy Constraints extension data structure, it indicates the number of additional certificates that may appear in the certification validation path before policy mapping is no longer permitted.

The Policy Constraints extension may be designated critical or noncritical.

Extended Key Usage Field

The Extended Key Usage Field extension indicates one or more purposes for which the key contained in the certificate can be used. This extension can be utilized in addition to or in place of the Key Usage extension. The PKIX profile defined five key usage purposes. Below, we present the variables that are used to describe these purposes:

■ `id-kp-serverAuth`: This variable indicates that the public key contained in the certificate should be used for activities related to transport layer security (TLS) web server authentication. These activities include verification of digital signatures, encryption of private keys, or encryption of data during a key agreement negotiation.

■ `id-kp-clientAuth`: The public key should be used for activities related to TLS web client authentication. These activities can be either verification of digital signatures or encryption of data during a key agreement negotiation.

■ `id-kp-codeSigning`: This variable indicates that the public key enclosed in the certificate should be restricted to verifying digital signatures on downloadable executable code.

■ `id-kp-emailProtection`: The public key should be used for activities related to e-mail protection. These activities include verification of digital signatures used to provide nonrepudiation services, which protects against the signing entity falsely denying signing a datum; encryption of private keys, encryption of data during key agreement negotiation sessions.

- `id-kp-timeStamping`: This variable indicates that the public key contained in the certificate should be used for the purpose of verifying signatures on signed timestamped data.

This extension, at the discretion of the certificate issuer, may be designated critical or noncritical.

CRL Distribution Points

The CRL Distribution Points extension identifies how CRL information can be obtained. This extension consists of the following variables:

- `distributionPoint`: This is an optional variable that consists of two fields:
  - `full name`: the name assigned to the distribution point.
  - `nameRelativeToCRLIssuer`: The RDN of the organization of the issuer of the certificate.
- `reasons`: This is another optional variable that consists of one or more of the following seven boolean variables:
  - `unused`: The private key associated with the public key enclosed in the certificate has been unused for a period greater than the organization's policy allows.
  - `keyCompromise`: The private key associated with the public key enclosed in the certificate has been compromised.
  - `cACompromise`: The CA's private key that was utilized to sign certificates the CA issued, has been compromised.
  - `affiliationChanged`: The subject to whom the certificate belonged is no longer with the organization.
  - `cessationOfOperation`: The subject to whom the certificate belonged no longer performs the role that gives him or her entitlement to the usage of the cryptographic key pair in question.
  - `certificateHold`: The certificate is on hold.
- `cRLIssuer`: This is an optional field that contains the name of the entity that issued the CRL.

The PKIX profile stipulated that this extension should be noncritical.

Authority Information Access

The Authority Information Access extension is not one of the standard X.509 v3 extensions; it was defined by PKIX. This extension indicates how to access CA information and services for the issuer of the certificate that the extension appears. Information and service may include online validation services and CA validation data. The data structure for this extension consists of the following variables:

- accessMethod: The protocol (e.g., HTTP, SSL) that should be employed for accessing the information or services.
- accessLocation: The location of the services or information; this is typically a URI (e.g., a web page, or an FTP site).

This extension can be included in a subject or a CA certificate, but it must be marked noncritical.

This concludes our discussion of X.509 certificate extensions. Before we proceed to discuss CRL and the CRL extension format, we discuss a special type of certificate referred to as a qualified certificate.

5.1.3   Qualified Certificates

A *qualified certificate* is a certificate whose primary purpose is to identify a person with high level of assurance in public nonrepudiation services. Qualified certificates, unlike other X.509 certificates, are only issued to living human beings. These certificates were proposed in an effort to satisfy certain legislative requirements for some European countries with regard to digital certificates. The format of these certificates is similar to that of other X.509 certificates, except that the structure of the Subject and the Issuer fields is different. The certificate extensions for qualified certificates are also different. Let us take a look at the format of the Issuer and Subject fields; following this, we present some certificate extensions for qualified certificates.

Issuer

Unlike the Issuer field in other X.509 certificates—which typically contains the name of the CA that issued the certificate—in qualified certificates, the Issuer field contains the officially registered name of the organization responsible for issuing the certificate. The organization name is specified using an appropriate subset of the following attributes: DC (domain component), C (country name), ST (state or province), O (organization), L (locality name), and S (serial number). For example, if a PGP security CA at the corporate headquarter at Santa Clara, California, issued a qualified certificate to anyone, the Issuer field of this certificate would likely have the following DN (distinguished name): C=US, ST=California, O=PGP Security, L=Santa Clara.

Subject

The Subject field of qualified certificates, unlike that of other X.509 certificates, must contain the DN of a living human being to whom the certificate is issued. The DN should consist of an appropriate subset of the following attributes: C (country name), CN (common name), SN (surname name), givenName (given name), pseudonym (pseudonym), serialNumber (serial number) O (organization), OU (organizational unit), ST (state or province), L (locality name), and postalAddress (postal address). To illustrate with an example, if PGP security issued a qualified certificate to Kevin Campbell, the subject field would have the DN: C=US, CN=Kevin Campbell, SN=Campbell, GN=Kevin, O=PGP Security, OU=Sales Engineer, ST=Georgia, L=Tucker.

Most of the attributes are self-explanatory; three of them, however, are less clear; we define these attributes below:

- *Common name:* This attribute is a name of the subject in the format that is preferred by the subject or one preferred by the CA. The name can include pseudonyms or nicknames.
- *Pseudonym:* This attribute is typically a name, other than the registered name, that the subject carries.
- *Serial number:* This attribute is used to differentiate between names where the subject field would otherwise be identical. It contains a number or a code assigned by a CA or an identifier assigned by a government or civil authority.

5.1.4 Qualified Certificate Extensions

The Qualified Certificates Profile Specification [SPBN00] defines five extensions for use with qualified certificates. We describe these extensions below.

Subject Directory Attributes

The Subject Directory Attributes extension contains additional attributes that can be used as compliment to present information that may be useful about the subject, but are not part of the DN of the subject. These attributes are listed below in their ASN.1 format:

- title
- dateOfBirth

- placeOfBirth
- gender
- countryOfCitizenship
- countryOfResidence

Other locally defined attributes can also be used as well.

Certificate Policies

The Certificate Policies extension contains the policy information needed to validate the certificate. The data structure for this extension consists of one or more sequences of policy information terms, each consisting of an OID. The Certificate Policies extension may be marked critical.

Key Usage

The Key Usage extension for qualified certificates is similar to that of other X.509 certificates. It defines the purpose for which the key contained in the certificate should be used. This extension is typically used to restrict the use of a public key for encryption, or for signature verification only. The data structure for this extension consists of nine fields. These fields are all boolean variables: they are set either to true or false. Each variable is assigned a bit in a 9-bit bit-string; a bit representing a variable is set when the variable is true. A description of these variables follows:

- digitalSignature: This variable is set to true if the key within the certificate is used with a digital signature scheme.
- nonRepudiation: When the bit corresponding to this variable is set, it asserts that the subject's public key enclosed in the certificate can be utilized to verify digital signatures used to provide nonrepudiation services, which protects against the signing entity falsely denying signing a datum.
- keyEncipherment: The keyEncipherment bit is set when the public key contained in the certificate is used for key transport. For example, if the key in a certificate is designated to encrypt sessions that are used to transport private keys, then the Key Usage extension likely will be included in the certificate, and the keyEncryption bit typically will be set. This variable is applicable mainly to key management protocols or applications.
- keyAgreement: This variable asserts that the key enclosed in the certificate is used for key agreement negotiation; that is, the key is

intended to be used to encrypt key agreement negotiation sessions for key management protocols or applications.

■ keyCertSign: This variable should only be set for the Key Usage extension within a CA certificate. It indicates that the public key enclosed in the certificate should be used for the verification of signatures on certificates.

■ cRLSign: When this variable is set, it indicates that the key is intended to be used to verify signatures on revocation information, such as a CRL.

■ encipherOnly: This bit has no meaning in the absence of the keyAgreement bit. However, when both the keyAgreement and the encipherOnly bits are set, this asserts that the public key enclosed in the certificate only should be used to encrypt data while performing key agreement negotiations.

■ decipherOnly: This bit has no meaning in the absence of the keyAgreement bit. However, when both the keyAgreement and the enciperOnly bits are set, this indicates that the public key enclosed in the certificate only should be used to decrypt data while performing key agreement negotiations.

It is important to note that for qualified certificates, if the nonRepudiation bit is set, none of the other bits should be set. In other words, if the nonRepudiation variable is set to false, any appropriate combination of the other variables can be set to true; if however, the nonRepudiation variable is set to true, all the other variables have to be false.

Biometric Information

The Biometric Information extension provides a means for the authentication of biometric information, such as a retina scan. This extension stores the biometric information in the form of a hash of the biometric template. It does not store the actual biometric information; however, it may include a URI pointing to the location where the biometric information can be located. The data structure for this extension consists of the following fields:

■ typeOBiometricData: This variable consists of an object identifier that defines the type (picture, handwritten signature, etc.) of biometric data.

■ hashAlgorithm: This is an object identifier that identifies the cryptographic hash algorithm that is used to generate the hash of the biometric data.

- `biometricDataHash`: This field contains the message digest of the biometric data outputted from the hash function specified by the `hashAlgorithm` variable.
- `sourceDataUri`: This is an optional field that stores the URI that points to the actual biometric information.

This extension should not be marked critical.

Qualified Certificate Statement

The Qualified Certificate Statement extension provides defined statements related to the qualified certificate. It typically includes a statement by the issuer of the certificate indicating that the certificate is a qualified certificate issued in accordance with a particular legal system. This extension may be designated critical or noncritical.

5.1.5   Certificate Revocation List

We mentioned previously in this chapter that there needs to be a way for certificate-processing systems to ascertain whether or not a certificate has been revoked. The Internet X.509 Public Key Infrastructure (PKIX) working group specified two methodologies for checking the status of X.509 certificates: the use of CRL or Online Certificate Status Protocol (OCSP) applications. We start our discussion by presenting the format of CRLs. OSCP is discussed in Section 5.1.8.

The PKIX profile uses the X.509 v2 CRL format. X.509 v2 consists of the following fields:

- `version`: This is an optional field that contains the version of the X.509 CRL being used.
- `issuer`: The issuer field stores the DN of the issuer of the CRL.
- `thisUpdate`: Indicates the date and time that this update was issued.
- `nextUpdate`: The date and time that the next update will be issued.
- `revokedCertificates`: This field contains a sequence of data structures that consists of the following variables:
  - `userCertificate`: This variable stores the serial number of the revoked certificate.

- revocationDate: The date and time that the certificate was revoked.
- crlEntryExtensions: This is an optional field that contains the version number of the CRL Entry extensions (we discuss CRL Entry extensions shortly) contained in the CRL.
- crlExtension: This is an optional field that contains the version number of the CRL extensions the certificate employed.

■ signatureAlgorithm: The signatureAlgorithm field contains the algorithm identifier for the signature scheme the CA used to sign the CRL.

■ signatureValue: This field stores the bit-string for the signature computed over all the fields of the CRL—except the signatureValue field—using the signature scheme specified in the signatureAlgorithm field.

5.1.6   CRL Extensions

The CRL extensions provide methods of associating additional attributes with CRLs. As is the case with certificate extensions, CRL extensions can be designated critical or noncritical. If a certificate-processing system encounters a CRL extension it does not recognize and the extension is marked critical, the system is required to reject the CRL. If the CRL is marked noncritical, the system will still process the CRL, even if it does not recognize the extension. Therefore, care should be taken in designating CRL critical. Let us now look at some of the standard X.509 v2 CRL extensions.

Authority Key Identifier

The Authority Key Identifier extension provides a means of identifying the public key that corresponds to the private key that a CA utilized to sign a CRL. This extension is particularly useful when a CA has multiple signing keys. The data structure for this extension has three fields:

■ keyIdentifier: A bit-string that identifies the public key corresponding to the private key the CA used to sign the CRL.

■ authorityCertIssuer: The name of the entity that issued the certificate that contained the public key the extension wishes to identify.

■ authorityCertSerialNumber: The serial number of the certificate that contained the public key the extension identifies.

The PKIX profile recommended that the Authority Key Identifier extension should be included in all compliant X.509 v2 CRLs.

CRL Number

The CRL Number extension consists of a monotonically increasing sequence of number for each CRL issued by a CA. It provides the means for easily ascertaining when a particular CRL supersedes another CRL. PKIX stipulated that all conforming CRLs should contain this CRL extension, and it should be marked noncritical.

Delta CRL Indicator

The Delta CRL Indicator extension is issued along with a base CRL (a complete CRL). It identifies the changes on the current CRL compared to the last issued CRL. The extension can save on the processing of particularly large CRLs, in that it highlights the difference between the previously issued and current CRLs. The data structure for this extension consists of one field:

- `BaseCRLNumber`: The sequence number of the base CRL that is issued along with the delta-CRL.

This CRL extension should be marked critical; moreover, if the difference between the value of the delta-CRL `BaseCRLNumber` and the value of the last processed delta-CRL `BaseCRLNumber` is greater than or less than 1, the delta-CRL should be rejected. Similarly, if a delta-CRL is issued without a complete CRL, it should be rejected as well.

Issuing Distribution Point

The Issuing Distribution Point extension identifies the CRL distribution point for the CRL in question. It also indicates whether the CRL covers for CA certificate only, end-entity (non-CA certificate) only, or a combination of the two. This CRL extension is a critical extension; however, certificates conforming to the PKIX standard are not required to support this extension. The data structure for this extension consists of the following fields:

- `distributionPoint`: This is an optional field that contains the distributing point (usually a URI).
- `onlyContainsUserCerts`: This is a boolean variable that is set to true if the CRL only contains revoked end-entity certificates, and is set to false otherwise.

- onlyContainsCACerts: This is a boolean variable that is set to true if the CRL only contains revoked CA certificates, and is set to false otherwise.
- indirectCRL: A boolean variable that is set to false if the CRL is not issued directly by the CA, and is set to true otherwise.

5.1.7   CRL Entry Extensions

CRL entry extensions provide a method for associating additional attributes to CRL entries. Let us now take a look at these CRL entry extensions.

Reason Code

The Reason Code CRL entry extension identifies the reason for the revocation of the certificate. The data structure for this extension consists of the following fields:

- keyCompromise: The private key associated with the revoked certificate has been compromised.
- cACompromise: The CA's private key that was utilized to sign the revoked certificate has been compromised.
- affiliationChanged: The subject to whom the revoked certificate belonged is no longer with the organization.
- cessationOfOperation: The subject to whom the revoked certificate belonged no longer performs the role that gives him or her the entitlement to the use of the certificate in question.
- certificateHold: The revoked certificate is on hold.
- removeFromCRL: The revoked certificate has been removed from subsequent CRLs.

This CRL entry extension should be marked noncritical.

Hold Instruction Code

The Hold Instruction Code is a CRL entry extension that provides information about the action that should be taken when a certificate that has been placed on hold is encountered. This extension should be marked noncritical.

Invalidity Date

This noncritical CRL entry extension indicates the known or suspected date when the private key associated with the revoked certificate was assumed to be compromised.

Certificate Issuer

The Certificate Issuer CRL entry extension identifies the certificate issuer associated with an entry in an indirect CRL. An indirect CRL is a CRL that contains certificates other than those issued by the CA in question. The data structure for this extension consists of one field:

- `certificateIssuer`: This is the DN of the entity that issued the certificate.

This extension, when present, should be designated critical.

5.1.8 Online Certificate Status Protocol

As mentioned previously, a CA typically issues CRLs at regular time intervals. This time interval depends on the organization's policy, and it may be weekly, daily, or hourly. When a CA revokes a certificate, the serial number for this certificate appears on the next CRL that the CA issues. We used the example in which an organization issues a CRL on a Monday of each week and the CA revoked a certificate on a Tuesday; the revoked certificate will not appear on a CRL until the next CRL is issued the following Monday. In the meantime, a user likely can accept the unknowingly revoked certificate as valid because it had not appeared on a CRL. The OCSP attempts to address this issue. The OCSP was designed to enable applications to determine the revocation state of a certificate in a more timely manner than is possible with CRLs. Let us look at how this protocol operates.

In order to use the OCSP, a certificate-handling system needs to have the OCSP client application installed. When the system needs to check the revocation status of a certificate, it issues a status request to an OCSP responder, and suspends acceptance of the certificate until it receives a response from the responder. A status request consists of the following fields:

- `version`: This is the version number of the OCSP protocol that the OCSP client is using.

- `requestorName`: This is an optional variable that stores the DN of the entity that issued the status request.

- `requestList`: This variable consists of a sequence of requests. Each request consists of the following variables:
  - `hashAlgorithm`: The algorithm identifier for the hash function that is used to generate the hash of the DN of the issuer of the certificate whose status is requested, as well as the hash of the issuer's public key corresponding to the private key used to sign the certificate.

- `issuerNameHash`: This variable stores the hash or the message digest generated by hashing the DN of the certificate issuer, using the hash function specified in the `hashAlgorithm` field.
- `issuerKeyHash`: This field contains the message digest generated by hashing the public key of the issuer of the certificate, using the hash function specified in the `hashAlgorithm` field. It is used along with the `issuerNameHash` variable to distinguished between CAs that may have an identical DN. Though undesirable, it is possible that two CAs may choose the same name; however, it is very unlikely that two CAs—without intentionally desiring to do so—will generate the same key.
- `serialNumber`: This variable stores the serial number of the certificate whose status is requested.
- `singleRequestExtensions`: This is an option variable that outlines the extensions the certificate contains.

■ `signatureAlgorithm`: This is an optional variable that identifies the digital signature algorithm that the requester utilized to sign the status request message.

■ `signature`: This is another optional variable that contains the digital signature computed over the status request message using the algorithm specified in the `signatureAlgorithm` field.

■ `certs`: This optional variable consists of a sequence of the actual certificates whose statuses are requested.

When an OCSP responder receives a status request, it ascertains:

1. If the message is well formed. If the answer is no, the OCSP produces an error message; otherwise, it proceeds to step 2.

2. If the responder is configured to provide the requested service, it proceeds to step 3; otherwise, it returns an error message to the OCSP client.

3. If the request contains the information needed by the OCSP, it returns a definitive response; otherwise, it returns an error message to the OCSP client.

A definitive response must be digitally signed, and the key used to sign the response must belong to the CA that issued the certificate in question, a trusted responder whose public key is trusted by the requester, or an authorized responder who holds a specially marked certificate, issued directly by the CA, indicating that the responder is authorized by the CA to issue OCSP responses for that CA. A definitive response message consists of the following fields:

- `version`: This is the version number of the OCSP protocol that the OCSP responder is using.

- `responderID`: This variable contains the DN or the message digest of the public key of the responder entity.

- `producedAt`: Stores the time and date when the response was generated.

- `responses`: This field contains a sequence of `singleResponse` (the response for the individual requests). The `singleResponse` variable consists of the following fields:
  - `hashAlgorithm`: The algorithm identifier for the hash function that is used to generate the hash of the DN of the issuer of the certificate whose status was requested, as well as the hash of the issuer's public key corresponding to the private key used to sign the certificate.
  - `issuerNameHash`: This variable stores the hash or the message digest generated by hashing the DN of the certificate issuer, using the hash function specified in the `hashAlgorithm` field.
  - `issuerKeyHash`: This field contains the message digest generated by hashing the public key of the issuer of the certificate, using the hash function specified in the `hashAlgorithm` field.
  - `serialNumber`: This variable stores the serial number of the certificate whose status was requested.
  - `certStatus`: Indicates the status of a certificate. The PKIX OCSP profile [OCSP99] defined three possibilities:
    * `good`: This indicates that the certificate is not revoked at the time that the request was issued; however, it does not necessarily mean that the certificate was ever issued, nor that its validation period has not expired. A status of `good` simply implies that the certificate is not on the responder list of revoked certificates.
    * `revoked`: This variable indicates that the certificate has been revoked. When it is present, it also has a field that displays the date and time when the certificate was revoked. Optionally, it can also present the reason why the certificate was revoked.
    * `unknown`: This variable indicates that the responder does not know about the certificate being requested.
  - `thisUpdate`: This variable specifies the time at which the status being indicated is known to be correct.
  - `nextUpdate`: This indicates the time at which newer information will be available on the certificate.

— `singleExtensions`: This is an optional variable that indicates the OCSP extensions that are contained in the `singleResponse`.

■ `responseExtensions`: This is another optional variable that specifies the OCSP extensions that the response contains.

■ `signatureAlgorithm`: This variable identifies the digital signature algorithm that the responder employed to sign the response message.

■ `signature`: This variable contains the digital signature computed over the response message using the algorithm specified in the `signatureAlgorithm` field.

■ `certs`: This optional variable consists of a sequence of the actual certificates whose statuses are requested.

Before we discuss the signed response acceptance for the OCSP client, let us look at some of the standard OCSP extensions.

OCSP Extensions

OCSP defined the following extensions:

■ *Nonce:* The nonce is a bit-string that is used to cryptographically bind a request and response to prevent replay attacks. The nonce is included in one of the `requestExtensions` variables in status request messages, and in the response, the nonce is included in the `responseExtension` variable.

■ *CRL References:* This extension indicates the CRL on which a revoked or on-hold certificate is found.

■ *Acceptable Response Types:* This extension specifies the object identifier of the kind of response it understands.

■ *Service Locator:* The Service Locator extension is applicable when an OCSP server receives a request and routes it to the OCSP server that is known to be authoritative for the particular certificate. This extension typically contains the DN for the issuer of the certificate and a locator (for example, a URI) for the OCSP server.

Signed Response Acceptance Requirements

Before an OCSP client accepts a signed response as valid, the client is required to do the following:

1. Verify that the certificate identified in a received response corresponds to that submitted in the corresponding request.

2. Ascertain if the signature on the response is valid.

3. Confirm that the identity of the signer matches the intended recipient of the status request.

4. Verify that the signer is currently authorized to sign responses.

5. Ascertain whether the time being indicated in the `thisUpdate` variable is sufficiently recent.

6. When available, determine if the time being indicated in the `nextUpdate` field is greater than the current time.

The client will accept the signed response only if the results of these queries are all positive.

5.1.9 X.509 Trust Model

We have spent most of this chapter discussing the framework of X.509 certificates. We have presented the format of X.509 certificates and the certificate extensions and the format of the CRL and the CRL extensions. We have also looked at an alternative to CRL, the OCSP.

Let us now take a look at the X.509 trust model. A trust model is a set of rules that certificate-handling systems use to determine if certificates are valid. X.509 uses *hierarchical* trust, in which is inherited. Figure 5-2 illustrates an example of this trust model.

Figure 5-2
Hierarchical Trust
Model

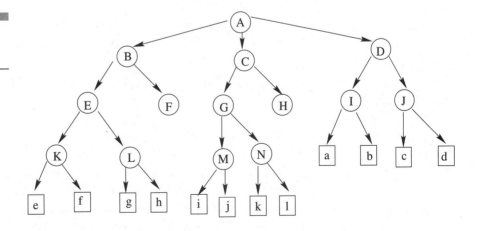

□ Represents an end user   ○ Represents a CA

In the example in Figure 5-2, A is the root CA. A is at the top of the hierarchical structure; therefore, this certificate needs to be created before any of the other certificates. Also, unlike any of the other certificates in the hierarchical structure, A's certificate will be self-signed; that is, it will be signed by the private key associated with the public key the certificate contains. Furthermore, since A has the highest level of trust, no other certificates are required to validate it. To validate A's certificate, an entity would—at a minimum—do the following, not necessarily in the order shown. For each of the steps, if the test fails, the entity rejects the certificate; it proceeds to the next step only if the test succeeds.

1. Verify that it supports the X.509 version identified in the `version` field of the certificate.

2. Check the DN shown in the `issuer` and the `subject` fields of the certificate and verify that the DN in both fields corresponds to that of A.

3. Verify that the current date is greater than the date in the `notBefore` field and less than that in the `notAfter` field.

4. Ensure that the certificate does not contain any critical extension that the entity or the system cannot process; if it does, the certificate should be rejected.

5. Use the public key contained in the certificate and the digital signature algorithm specified in the `signature` field of the certificate to ascertain if the signature value in the `signature value` field is valid.

6. Query a recently issued CRL or an OCSP responder and ensure that the certificate has not been revoked. If the certificate has been revoked, reject it.

Very stringent security requirements should be associated with the private key for the root CA, because if the root CA key is compromised, all of the CA and end-user certificates that are in the hierarchical path to the root CA would need to be revoked, along with the root CA certificate. The length of the root CA private key should be at least 2048 bits; and for signature generation, a hash function with at least a 160-bit message digest (for example SHA-1, RIPEMD-160, or Tiger) should be used. In general, the higher in the hierarchy the CA, the greater are the security requirements that should be associated with the private key of the CA in question, since if a CA key is compromised, all of the certificates that this CA issued, along with all those that were issued by the CAs that are in the path to this CA, would need to be revoked as well.

Let us return to our discussion of Figure 5-2. The root CA issued CA certificates to B, C, and D; they in turn issued other CA certificates, and some of the recipients issued CA certificates and others issued end-user certificates. To validate any of the certificates—except the root CA—the certificate-handling entity is required to ascertain not just if the certificate in question is valid, but rather the system or the entity needs to check every certificate in the path to the root CA and ensure that each is valid. For example, to validate k's certificate, the certificate-handling entity needs to first verify that k's certificate is valid, obtain N's CA certificate and ensure that it is valid, and then similarly validate the certificates for G, C, and A. At a minimum, to validate k's certificate, a certificate-handling system accomplishes each of the following steps. If the test fails, the system rejects the certificate; it proceeds to the next step only if the test succeeded.

1. Verify that the certificate supports the X.509 version identified in the `version` field of the certificate.

2. Check the DN shown in the `subject` field of the certificate and ensure it corresponds to that of the subject to whom the certificate belongs. If the certificate is a root CA, check to ensure that both the DNs in the `subject` and `issuer` fields correspond to that of the root CA entity.

3. Verify that the current date is greater than the date in the `notBefore` field and less than that in the `notAfter` field for the certificate in question.

4. Ensure that the certificate under consideration does not contain any critical extension that the system cannot process.

5. Use the public key contained in the certificate and the digital signature algorithm specified in the `signature` field of the certificate to ascertain if the signature value in the `signature value` field is valid.

6. Query a recently issued CRL or an OCSP responder and ensure that the certificate has not been revoked.

7. If the certificate is not a root CA certificate, then acquire, by a suitable mean, the CA certificate whose `subject` field corresponds to the DN in the `issuer` field of the certificate in question. Repeat steps 1 to 7 for this CA certificate.

8. Accept k's certificate as valid only if the tests in steps 1 to 7 were successful for it, along with all the other certificates in the path to the root CA.

Figure 5-3 illustrates what is called a *cross-certification* between certain CAs. In the example shown in this figure, C and D could be separate organizations, for example, a vendor and a client that have a mutual trust relationship, or they could be different groups within a given organization. The same holds for L and M. A typical situation where cross-certification may be necessary to expedite business transactions is in the case in which two business partners need to access resources that are on each other's service networks via VPN links. If the VPN applications use X.509 certificate–based authentication, both organizations need to issue certificates to the entities from the other organizations that will connect to their network. For example, to allow entities that are under the CA L VPN access to M's network, M would issue a CA certificate to L, and L would then issue end-user certificates to the entities on its network that need to access M's network. Similarly, L would issue a CA certificate to M, and M would in like manner issue end-user certificates to the entities under its control that need to access L's network. When an entity from either network initiates a VPN connection to the other network, the cross-certified certificate will be use to authenticate the initiator to the other communicating peer.

Much care should be taken before cross-certification is put in place, because cross-certification can result in security compromises. For example, if C and D have a cross-certification agreement and D issued a CA certificate to C, and if C issues certificates to other business partners, unless

Figure 5-3

Hierarchical Trust
Model With Cross-
Certification

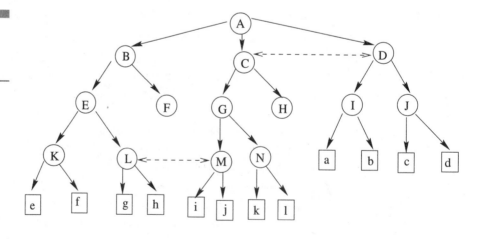

D has very stringent access policies—for example, where certificates are accepted based on the content of selected fields, such as the DN in the subject field of the certificate—these business partners of C may be able to establish VPN links to D's network although D had not intended for them to do so. Figure 5-4 illustrates another example of the risk that is associated with cross-certification.

In this example, B and C are two CAs from different business units within an organization. B and C have a cross-certification agreement; therefore, entities under both CAs can access certain resources on these CAs' networks. B has a cross-certification agreement with H; one of B's clients. H issued CA certificates to I, J, and K and they in turn issued end-user certificates as shown in Figure 5-4. Unless the network/security administrator for C's network takes much care in setting up access policies, a certificate that H, or any of the CAs under H, issued can be used to gain access to C's network. For example, if the entity b wishes to establish a VPN link with a system on C's network, the system likely can accept b's certificate if the validation path from b to A, as indicated by the bold lines, is followed. Owing to the risk associated with cross-certification, other arrangements should be pursued—such as issuing of end-user certificates to entities from other organizations, rather than issuing CA certificates—before cross-certification is considered.

Figure 5-4
Risk Associated with
Cross-Certification

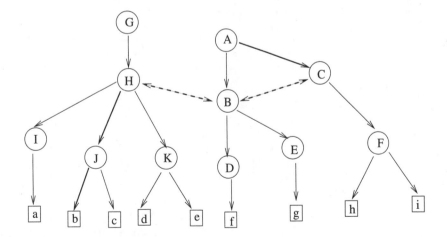

☐ Represents an end-user certificate   ◯ Represents a CA certificate

5.2 PGP Certificates

Pretty good privacy (PGP) is an e-mail encryption application that was created by Phil Zimmermann and published as free software in 1991. Five years after the publication of PGP, its creator formed a company called PGP Inc., which was acquired by Network Associates in December 1997. PGP has evolved much over the years, and it has become the most widely used e-mail and file encryption software in the world. Much of this evolution can be attributed to the work done at Network Associates (http://www.nai.com). Since acquiring PGP Inc., Network Associates has added a number of additional functionalities to and has made numerous enhancements to PGP. As a consequence of the widespread use of PGP, the IETF formed a work group whose focus is to provide an open specification for PGP. This open specification is called OpenPGP. The OpenPGP specification outlined the PGP message format, standards, cryptographic algorithms, and other pertinent issues; see RFC 2440 [CDFT98] for further detail on OpenPGP. PGP has a number of different components; however, we focus our discussion on PGP certificates.

5.2.1 PGP Certificate Format

PGP certificates have a much simpler format than X.509 certificates. PGP certificates have the following fields:

- `Identifier`: This field contains the identity of the entity to which the public key contained in the certificate belongs. The identity is usually in the form of a name followed by an e-mail address enclosed in a pair of brackets. The name can be a DN, the registered name of the entity, an alias, or a pseudonym. For example, the `Identifier` field could contain the following: Davis, Carlton `<cdavis@pgp.com>`

- `Key Info`: This field contains the public key of the entity identified in the `Identifier` field. A PGP key is contained in what is called a *keyring*. Keyrings can be nested together; in other words a single keyring can contain several PGP keys. Each key on a keyring has the following information associated with it.
  - *ID:* This a unique hexadecimal number that is used to identify the key.
  - *Type:* This stores the information with regard to the cryptographic algorithm that the key requires. Examples of key types are DSA, RSA, and Diffie-Hellman keys.

- *Size:* This is the size of the key in bits.
- *Created:* The date the key was generated.
- *Expires:* The date the key will expire.
- *Fingerprint:* The fingerprint or message digest of the PGP public key.
- *Trust attribute:* PGP has four inherent trust attributes; these attributes are:
  * *Completely trusted:* This attribute is assigned to keys that are fully trusted. When the private key associated with a public key that has a completely trusted attribute is used to sign a PGP key, the signed key is implicitly trusted.
  * *Marginally trusted:* Marginally trusted keys are only partially trusted. More than one marginally trusted key is required to sign a PGP key if this key is to be trusted implicitly.
  * *Untrusted:* This attribute is assigned to keys that are not trusted.
  * *Unknown:* This attribute is assigned to keys whose trust attribute is not known. These keys are treated similarly to untrusted keys.
- *Signatures:* This field stores the signatures that vouch for the PGP key. Unlike X.509 certificates, which can only contain one signature, a PGP keyring or certificate can contain several signatures.
- *Revokers:* This is an optional field that contains the identity or identities of the entity or entities, respectively, that are allowed to revoked a given PGP key. Normally, only the entity that has access to the private key that is associated with a given public key can revoke this key since the revoke request for the key in question needs to be signed with the associated private key. The revokers field stores the identity or identities of the entity or entities, respectively, whose private keys can be used to revoke a given key.
- *Key status:* This field indicates the status (revoked, valid, invalid, etc.) of the key.

5.2.2   Revocation of PGP Certificates

One of the ways that PGP certificates differ from X.509 certificates is in regard to the issue of key revocation. To revoke a X.509 key, one simply needs to add the serial number of the certificate, along with other pertinent information about the certificate, to a CRL and have the CA that issued the certificate sign the CRL; alternatively, one could put the information about the revoked certificate on an OCSP responder and have the CA that issued the certificate sign the information. However, for PGP certificates, the request to revoke a key needs to be signed with the private key associated with the key in question; if revokers are specified, the private keys of the revokers are used to generate the signature instead. In other words, a X.509 certificate ultimately can be revoked only by the CA that issued it, whereas a PGP certificate can be revoked only by the subject of the certificate, or other entities that the subject authorized to do so when the key was created.

Another difference between X.509 and PGP certificates is that PGP does not publish a CRL. Typically, all PGP certificates—valid or revoked—are placed on a certificate server. If Alice revoked her key, she sends the revoked certificate along with her new certificate to a certificate server. When a user attempts to upload Alice's certificate from the certificate server, both the revoked and the new certificate will be displayed. Therefore, the user will be informed that Alice's previous certificate has been revoked and she has a new certificate. The drawback to this method of circulating revoked certificate information is that users that have revoked certificates on their keyrings, unless they update their keyring from the certificate server, will not be informed about the certificate's revocation unless the revocation information is communicated to them via other means, that is, through word of mouth or other offline mediums.

5.2.3   PGP Trust Model

PGP has a more flexible trust model compared to that of X.509. As mentioned earlier in this chapter, the X.509 trust model uses a hierarchical trust, in which trust is inherited. PGP, however, supports two forms of trust model: a *cumulative* trust model, which is commonly referred to as a *web of trust,* and a hierarchical trust.

Web of Trust

Figure 5-5 illustrates an example of a web of trust. In this figure, A through I are PGP certificate holders; B trusts A and A trusts D; therefore, B will automatically trust D. Similarly, C trusts B and D, B trusts A, and D trusts E; consequently, C will inherently trust E and A. The term *web of trust* is applicable because with the trust scheme illustrated in Figure 5-5, eventually there will be a large number of trusted entities that will be implicitly trusted by a given PGP certificate holder, owing to the fact they are trusted by entities that this given PGP certificate holder trusts.

In this trust model, a certificate is considered valid if it is signed by a trusted individual who has a valid certificate, or if it is signed by a set of cumulatively trusted individuals whose certificates are all valid. In this model, each PGP certificate holder is essentially his or her own CA. This PGP certificate holder is therefore responsible for determining the degree of trust that he or she allots to each certificate holder.

The flexibility of this scheme has made it very popular for individuals who desire to exchange e-mails or other electronic data securely; however, it has been less readily embraced by organizations that require a high degree of PKI security. The problem associated with the web of trust scheme is that it only takes one "bad apple" to cause the whole trust scheme to be compromised. For example, if a PGP certificate holder, knowingly or unknowingly, assigns a high degree of trust to a certificate that belongs to an untrustworthy entity, and this untrustworthy entity

Figure 5-5
An Example of a
Web of Trust

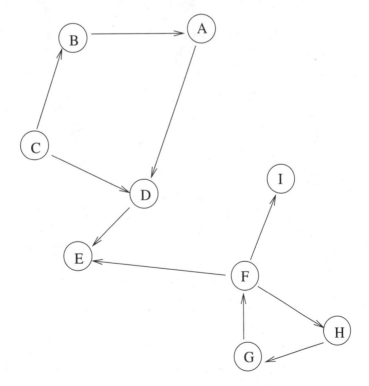

introduced other untrustworthy entities, eventually the entire web of certificates could be compromised. Hierarchical trust schemes are much less prone to this degree of compromised because these schemes effectively collapse trust into a single root entity. Hence, if an untrustworthy entity is incorporated into a hierarchical trust model, only that part of the hierarchical tree that contains the untrustworthy entity will be affected, rather that the entire tree. In the light of this, PGP offers a hierarchical trust model that can be used as an alternative to a web of trust. We present this trust model next.

PGP Hierarchical Trust Model

Figure 5-6 illustrates an example of a PGP hierarchical trust model. In this scheme, the meta-introducer is equivalent to a root CA. The meta-introducer can introduce any number of trusted introducers—whose role is equivalent to that of a CA—and the trusted introducers each can in turn introduce any number of PGP certificate holders. A certificate is trusted only if it is signed by one or more trusted introducers or by a meta-introducer. This allows a more structured validation mechanism. It limits the entities that can vouch for PGP keys to those that are appointed by the meta-introducer. Therefore, there is greater accountability associated with these introducers; if any of them err in their duties and a branch of the tree

Figure 5-6

An Example of a PGP Hierarchical Trust Model

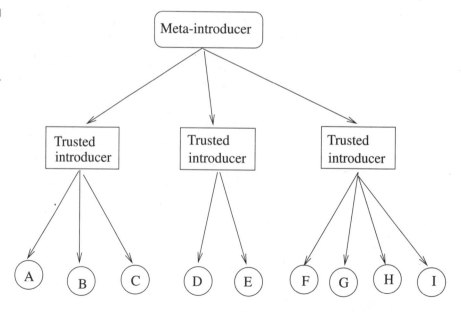

is compromised, the delinquent introducer can easily be identified. This trust model has been embraced more readily by corporations than the web of trust scheme.

5.3   Other PKI Issues

There are several other PKI issues that are too numerous to address in a single chapter. There are, in fact, entire books on the subject of PKI. An important PKI issue is the storage and retrieval of certificates. We address this issue in the next chapter when we discuss the Lightweight Directory Access Protocol (LDAP), the de facto protocol that is used to access X.500-like directories. Before we conclude this chapter however, we briefly discuss a few other issues that are relevant to PKI. We will start with key recovery.

Key Recovery

Key recovery is one of PKI's hotly debated issues. Let us consider the scenario in which a disgruntled employee quits his or her job, but before quitting, he or she encrypt important information that the company needs and then deleted the decryption key. What policies should an organization put in place to avoid, or to be able to recover from such eventualities?

Key recovery—whether through the frequent use of schedule backups of all symmetric, private, and public keys or through other key recovery techniques—is seen as a possible solution. However, there are objections to key recovery that the opponents of this scheme have argued very effectively. For example, consider the issue of *nonrepudiation*. Nonrepudiation is the term that is used to describe the situation in which one cannot successfully deny digitally signing a document, if the document was in fact signed by this individual. Nonrepudiation, in its true form, is not possible if an administrator is able to recover a user signing key, whether through restoration from backup mediums or through any other means. It stands to reason that if nonrepudiation is desired, only the owner of a signing key should be able to recover or restore it.

Private keys, in general typically are used for both decryption and digital signing. Hence, if an organization desires nonrepudiation, its policies should dictate that only the entity to whom a private key belongs should be able to recover or restore it. Decryption of data requires the private key that is associated with the public key used to encrypt the data if a public-key cryptographic algorithm was used for the encryption. Consequently, key recovery may not be a viable option. A more favorable option that allows a corporation to recover data encrypted by its employees is through the use of additional decryption keys.

Additional Decryption Keys

To recover from eventualities such as those mentioned above, in which an employee encrypts important data that an organization needs, and loses access— intentionally or unintentionally—to the decryption key, the organization can opt for a policy whereby all data its employees encrypt using its encryption applications must be encrypted to, in addition to the employee's key, an additional decryption key (ADK).

When one encrypts data, whether using a symmetric-key or public-key cryptographic algorithm, the data can be encrypted to more than one key. If a symmetric-key algorithm is used, the ciphertext outputted from the algorithm for the given plaintext will be different for each of the keys and the decryption of a given ciphertext requires the identical key that was used to produce the ciphertext. Similarly, data can be encrypted to different public keys simultaneously using public-key cryptographic algorithms. The important thing is that, for each ciphertext, the private key corresponding to the public key used to encrypt the data is required to decrypt it. An ADK is an additional key—symmetric key for symmetric-key ciphers, or public key for public-key cryptoschemes—to which data is encrypted. The data can consequently be decrypted using this key, when the need arises.

The use of additional decryption keys is only associated with encryption, and not with the signing of data; hence, ADK has no bearing on non-repudiation. Therefore, the use of ADK is a viable means of ensuring that corporations will be able to decrypt important data encrypted by their employees if the employees' keys are not available.

Key Reconstruction

For security reasons, most encryption applications force users to associate a pass phrase with the use of their decryption or signing keys. If a user encrypts data and forgets the pass phrase that is required to utilize the decryption key, she will not be able to recover the data unless the key can be reconstructed. There are a number of approaches to key reconstruction. Network Associates' PGP encryption and VPN client software uses a very elegant methodology. This methodology involves tagging each private or symmetric key with a set of user-defined questions and associated answers.

The tagged key is then sent to a key reconstruction server. If a user forgets her pass phrase, provided she can access the reconstruction server using a suitable access protocol such as LDAP and supply a given number of the questions and associated answers that were used to tag the key, the key reconstruction server will allow her to assign a new pass phrase to her key, and if necessary, download the key with the associated new pass phrase to her workstation.

Another key reconstruction technique that merits mentioning is the "m of n" split-key reconstruction. This is another key reconstruction technique that Network Associates implemented in its PGP e-Business Server encryption software for enterprises. This technique allows the assigning of reconstruction privileges to n different private or symmetric keys, when a private or symmetric key is generated. If the pass phrase for the generated key is forgotten, then any m of the n private keys can be used to reconstruct the key and allow a new pass phrase to be assigned to it. The idea here is that no single entity can reconstruct a key. The reconstruction requires at least m entities, where $m > 1$. This requirement adds a certain amount of security in that a collaborative effort is required.

Lightweight Directory Access Protocol

Overview of Chapter 6

In this chapter, we cover the following topics:

- X.500 Directory
- An Overview of Lightweight Directory Access Protocol (LDAP)
- LDAP/X.500 Attribute Types
- LDAP URL Format

Lightweight Directory Access Protocol (LDAP) is a protocol for accessing directory services over TCP/IP networks. Directories are specialized databases that are optimized for reading, searching, and browsing. They are tuned to give quick response to high volumes of queries. Directory services play an important role in helping users to locate resources—such as digital certificates, printers, e-mail addresses, telephone numbers, and other pertinent information—on a network. Directory service often is seen as the center of a distributed system, in which a single directory service supports numerous applications and utilities; Figure 6-1 illustrates such an example.

6.1 X.500 Directory

X.500 is a standard recommended by the ITU that defines the protocol and information model for a directory service that is independent of computing applications and network platforms. The X.500 standard was first released in 1988 and updated in 1993 and 1997. The X.500 directory architecture uses a client-server model. The data are arranged in a hierarchical tree-like structure, called a *directory information tree* (DIT). Each node except the root node in the tree has one parent and any number of children.

Figure 6-1
Directory Service:
The Center of a
Distributed System

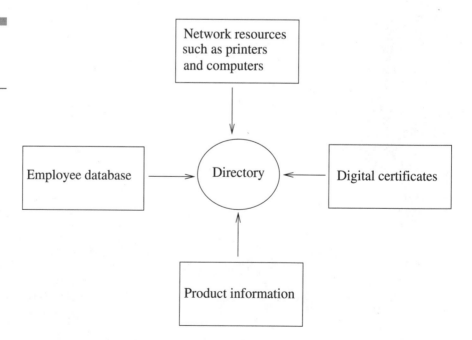

Each node except the root node is assigned an RDN. Figure 6-2 illustrates an example of a DIT. A DIT is distributed among server agents, referred to as *directory system agents* (DSAs). The directory client, called the *directory user agent* (DUA), provides the standardized functionalities that support the users in searching or browsing the DIT and retrieving directory information. A DUA queries DSAs using the *Directory Access Protocol* (DAP). DSAs collaborate to provide directory service to a DUA in such a way that the end-user can access information in the directory without knowing the exact location of that specific piece of information. The *Directory System Protocol* (DSP) controls the interaction between DSAs.

An entry in an X.500 directory is referenced by its DN. A DN is a globally unique name that is constructed by taking the RDN of the entry and concatenating the RDNs of the ancestor entries. For example, in Figure 6-2, the DN for the entry with RDN Carlton Davis, is C=US, O=NAI, OU=PGP, CN=Carlton Davis. Users can search or browse a directory using any supported attributes. We present some of the supported LDAP/X.500 attributes later in this chapter.

As an example, let us consider a VPN client using an X.509 certificate for authentication at a security gateway. The client sends the certificate to the security gateway. In the process of validating the certificate, the gateway, via a DUA, issues a request to a DSA to search for and retrieve

Figure 6-2
An X.500 Directory
Information Tree

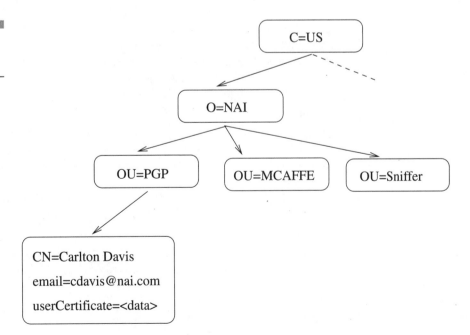

the certificate that is associated with the DN in the Issuer[1] field of the client's certificate. If the certificate exists, the DSA will retrieve it; if the record containing the certificate is not located on this DSA, the DSA will collaborate with other DSAs to locate and retrieve the certificate and send it to the security gateway.

X.500 directories are very versatile, feature rich, but complex entities. The DAP, the protocol that DUA utilizes to query or update DSAs, is based on the OSI seven-layered network architecture, and therefore it has high associated overhead. Figure 6-3 shows the layers in the OSI reference model. Recall that the TCP/IP protocol stack has only four layers: the Session and the Presentation layers are not part of the TCP/IP reference model. The two extra layers in the OSI network architecture not only add complexity to protocols that utilize this model, but they also require greater processor resources.

The complexity and the high overhead associated with the use of X.500 DAP have impeded its widespread use. LDAP is a simpler, less resource-intensive protocol that was developed as an alternative to DAP.

6.2   Overview of LDAP

LDAP was developed by the University of Michigan. At the beginning, LDAP was essentially a TCP/IP-based version of DAP. The first version of LDAP was published in July 1993 as RFC 1487. LDAP version 3, the version we will be discussing, was published in December 1997 as a series of RFCs (RFC 2251–2256). LDAP was originally developed as a simplified protocol for accessing X.500 directory services; however, LDAP evolved and has become, not just the de facto protocol for accessing directory services over TCP/IP networks, but a stand-alone directory as well. LDAP essentially took the best features of X.500 and built on them. LDAP clients can query and update X.500 DSAs, LDAP servers, and even some proprietary directory servers.

LDAP servers utilize the X.500 DIT structure. Entries in the DIT consist of a set of attributes. An *attribute* is a type with one or more associated values. The attribute type dictates whether there can be more than one value of an attribute of that type in an entry, the syntax to which the values must conform, the sorts of matching that can be performed on values

---

[1] We discussed the format of X.509 in Chapter 5.

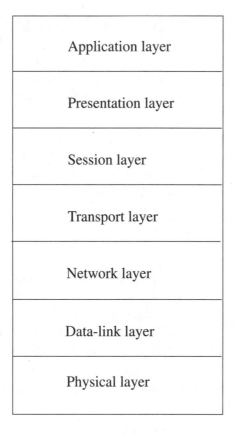

Figure 6-3
The OSI Reference
Model

| Application layer |
| Presentation layer |
| Session layer |
| Transport layer |
| Network layer |
| Data-link layer |
| Physical layer |

of that attribute, and other functions. We present some of the LDAP/X.500 attribute types later in this chapter.

Each entry in a DIT must have an object class attribute. An *object class attribute* is of the type `objectClass`; these attributes partly determine the permitted attributes on an entry. The values of the `objectClass` attribute can be modified by clients; however, the attribute cannot be removed from an entry.

A *schema* is the collection of attribute type definitions, object class definitions, and other information that a server uses to determine the operations (add, modify, etc.) that should be permitted on an entry, and how to match a filter or attribute value against the attributes of an entry in compare operations. The schema definition for LDAP is outlined in RFC 2252.

We present an overview of some of the X.500 attributes LDAP supports later in this chapter. It is noteworthy to mention that LDAP also supports the use of self-defined attributes; that is, one can create an attribute if none of the existing ones suffice in qualifying an entity.

6.3   LDAP/X.500 Attribute Types

The attributes' descriptors can be written in either upper- or lower-case letters; however, we will conform to the description given in RFC 2256 [Wah97] and represent them as they appeared in this document.

objectClass

The objectClass is present in every entry in an LDAP or X.500 DIT. The values of this attribute describe the kind of object the entry represents. Some of the object classes LDAPv3 supports are as follows:

- top: One of the two base object classes from which all others are derived.

- alias: The other base object class.

- country: This object class tags an entry as a country. The attribute c (the two-letter ISO 3166 country code) must be included in any entry with the country object class. The description attribute is another attribute that can be used with this object class. We describe the attributes mentioned in this section a little later on.

- locality: The locality object class identifies an object as a locality. The attributes that can define this entry are street, st, l, and description.

- organization: All entries that are identified as an organization object class must contains the attribute o (the attribute descriptor for organization). Other possible attributes for this object class are userPassword, businessCategory, registeredAddress, destinationIndicator, telephoneNumber, facsimileTelephoneNumber, street, postOfficeBox, postalCode, postalAddress, physicalDeliveryOfficeName, st, l, and description.

- organizationalUnit: Every entry that is defined as an organizationalUnit object class must have the ou (organization unit) attribute. Additionally, the following attributes can also be used to define this object class: userPassword, businessCategory, registeredAddress, destinationIndicator, telephoneNumber, facsimileTelephoneNumber, street, postOfficeBox, postalCode, postalAddress, physicalDeliveryOfficeName, st, l, and description.

- person: All entries that are tagged as a person object class must contain either the cn (common name) or the sn (surname) attribute. Other possible attributes are userPassword, telephoneNumber, and description.

- organizationalPerson: This object class identifies an entry as a person belonging to an organization. Some of the attributes that can be used with this object class are title, registeredAddress, destinationIndicator, and telephoneNumber.

- organizationalRole: This object class identifies an entry in a DIT as being a role of an organization. Every entry with this object class tag must include the cn attribute. Some of the other possible attributes are registeredAddress, destinationIndicator, telephoneNumber, facsimileTelephoneNumber, street, postOfficeBox, postalCode, postalAddress, physicalDeliveryOfficeName, ou, st, l, and description.

- residentialPerson: The residentialPerson object class identifies an entry as being a person that belong to a particular residence. Every entry with this object class must contain the l (locality) attribute. The following attributes can also be used: businessCategory, registeredAddress, destinationIndicator, telephoneNumber, facsimileTelephoneNumber, street, postOfficeBox, postalCode, postalAddress, and physicalDeliveryOfficeName.

- device: Identifies an entry as being a device. All DIT entries with this object class must include the cn attribute. Some of the other possible attributes are serialNumber, owner, ou, o, l, and description.

- strongAuthenticationUser: This object class identifies an entry that contains a certificate. The userCertificate attribute must be included in all entries tagged with this object class.

- certificationAuthority: Entries defined with this object class indicate that the entries contain pertinent CA information. Every entry with this tag must contain the certificateRevocationList or cACertificate attribute.

- userSecurityInformation: Indicates that an entry contains user security information such as a cryptographic algorithm identifier. An attribute for this object class is supportedAlgorithms.

■ cRLDistributionPoint: Identifies an entry that contains information related to a CRL distribution point. Entries with this object class tag must contain the cn attribute. Other possible attributes for this object class include certificateRevocationList and deltaRevocationList.

Let us consider an example to illustrate how an entry could be added to the DIT of an LDAP server. Suppose one wants to use an LDAP client with a command line interface to add information pertaining to a person to an LDAP directory. This could be done as follows: first, enter the information in a file. For example, the following information could be entered:

```
dn: cn=Mike McKinzie, o=PGP, ou=SE, c=US
cn: Mike McKinze
mail: mike@pgp.com
objectClass: person
```

What is this information saying? First, the distinguished name (dn) of the entry is indicated; each DIT entry must have a dn. A dn is a unique name that is constructed by taking the rdn (relative distinguished name) of the entry and concatenating the rdn of the ancestor entries. Next, the attributes the entry contains and their values are indicated. Lastly, the entry is identified as a person object class; i.e., it contains information about a person.

The LDAP directory can then be updated with this entry by executing the following command:

```
ldapadd -D "cn=admin, o=PGP, c=US" -w secret_password <
FILENAME
```

ldapadd is the command for adding entries to directory DIT. The -D option followed by the dn indicates that the client should bind to the LDAP directory, using the UID of the user indicated in the dn. The -w option indicates the password that should be used for authentication with the directory server. Finally, < FILENAME denotes that the content of the file FILENAME should be inputted to the command.

One can then confirm that the directory was updated with the new information by executing the command:

```
ldapsearch -b "o=PGP, c=US" "(cn=Mike McKinzie)"
```

This command should return:

```
dn: cn=Mike McKinzie, o=PGP, ou=SE, c=US
cn: Mike McKinze
mail: mike@pgp.com
objectClass: person
```

If we want to add a telephone number to this entry we can accomplish this by executing the following command:

```
ldapmodify -D "cn=admin, o=PGP, c=US" -w secret_password
<ENTER>
dn: cn=Mike McKinzie, o=PGP, ou=SE, c=US
telephoneNumber: 408-999-9999
<CTRL D>
```

where <ENTER> represents a carriage return, and <CTRL D> represents the pressing of the CTRL and D keys simultaneously.

If one tries to update this entry by adding, for example, an ou (organization unit) attribute, this operation would not be allowed because the person object class cannot contain an ou attribute. Similarly, if one tries to add the following entry for a device:

```
dn: owner=Billy Bob, o=PGP, ou=SE, c=US
ou: SE
l: Santa Clara
owner: Billy Bob
serialNumber: 99999
description: SE laptop
objectClass: device
```

the operation will not be successful because the cn attribute is absent and an entry belonging to the device object class must contain the cn attribute.

Let us now return to the description of the LDAP/X.500 attributes.

aliasedObjectName

The aliasedObjectName attribute is used by the directory service if the entry containing this attribute is an alias.

cn

This is the common name of the entity the attribute defines. A common name can be a registered name, a preferred name, or a pseudonym.

sn

This attribute contains the family name of a person.

serialNumber

The serial number of a device is stored in this attribute.

c

This attribute contains a two-letter ISO 3166 country code.

l

This attribute stores the name of a locality, such as a city, county, or other geographic region.

st

This attribute contains the full name of a state or province.

street

The `street` attribute stores the physical address of the object to which the entry corresponds.

o

This attribute contains the name of an organization.

ou

This attribute stores the name of an organizational unit.

title

This attribute contains the title, such as Chief Technology Officer, of individuals in their organizational context. It does not include titles that are independent of the individuals' job functions. The `personalTitle` attribute is used for these titles.

description

This attribute contains a human-readable description of the entity it qualifies.

businessCategory

This attribute describes the kind of business performed by an organization.

postalAddress

The `postalAddress` attribute contains the full postal address of the entity it represents.

postalCode

This attribute contains the postal code of the entity is represents.

postOfficeBox

This is the post office box of the entity.

physicalDeliveryOfficeName

This attribute contains the address of the office to which physical delivery, such as packages, for the entity it represents should be made.

telephoneNumber

This attribute stores the telephone number of an entity.

facsimileTelephoneNumber

This attribute contains the fax number of an entity.

registeredAddress

This attribute stores the address of an entity to which personal deliveries can be made.

destinationIndicator

This attribute is used for the telegram service.

owner

This attribute stores information about the owner of the entity it represents.

userPassword

This attribute holds a user password.

userCertificate

This attribute holds a user certificate. The certificate should be stored and requested in binary form.

cACertificate

This attribute holds a CA certificate. The certificate should be stored and requested in binary form.

certificateRevocationList

This attribute holds a CRL. The CRL should be stored and requested in binary form.

givenName

The givenName attribute is used to hold the part of individuals' names that is not their surname or middle name.

initials

The initials attribute holds the initials of some or all of a person's name, but not the surname.

enhancedSearchGuide

This attribute is for use by X.500 clients in constructing search filters.

houseIdentifier

This attribute is used to identify a building within a location.

supportedAlgorithms

This attribute holds the object identifier for cryptographic algorithms that the entity to which it belongs supports. It should be stored and requested in binary form.

deltaRevocationList

This attribute stores a delta CRL. A delta CRL is a CRL that only contains information that is different from the previously issued CRL[2]. This attribute should be stored and requested in binary form.

The presentation of the attribute types was adapted from RFC 2256 [Wah97]; for further detail about any LDAP/X.500 attributes, see [Wah97].

Before we conclude this chapter, we would like to give a brief overview of the LDAP URL format.

---

[2] See Chapter 5 for further detail on CRLs.

6.4 LDAP URL Format

A large portion of the access to LDAP directories is done through the LDAP URL. Therefore, it is necessary to outline the LDAP URL format, and for us to elaborate a bit on how LDAP URLs are resolved. The presentation is adapted from RFC 2255 [HS97].

An LDAP URL begins with the protocol prefix `ldap` and is defined by the following grammar. In the syntax given, characters inclosed in `" "` should be imputed verbatim in the URL; for the descriptors enclosed in `[ ]`, the actual values of the descriptors should be entered in the URL. For example, `[hostport]` could be keyserver.pgp.com or keyserver.pgp.com:7777, the latter indicating the port to which the connection should be made on the LDAP server.

```
ldapurl = scheme "://" [hostport] ["/"[dn ["?" [attributes] ["?"
          [scope] ["?" [filter] ["?" extensions]]]]]]
```

- scheme: `"ldap"`

- hostport: A host (an IP address or a DNS host name) optionally followed by `":"` and the port to which the connection is to be made. A port number needs to be specified if the port that LDAP services are running on, on the LDAP server, is not TCP port 389, the default port for LDAP.

- dn: An X.500 distinguished name. It identifies the base object of the LDAP search.

- attributes: One or more attributes construct. The attributes construct is used to indicate which attributes should be returned from the entry or entries. If no attributes construct is included in the URL, this is equivalent to requesting all user attributes of the entry or entries. We give some examples of attributes construct, later.

- scope: The scope construct is used to specify the scope of the search to perform in the given LDAP server. The allowable scopes are base for a base object search, one for a one-level search, or sub for a subtree search. If scope is omitted from the URL, a scope of base is assumed.

- filter: These are LDAP search filters that are defined by the following grammar, adapted from RFC 2254 [How97]:

```
filter       = "(" filtercomp ")"
filtercomp   = and / or / not / item
and          = "&" filterlist
or           = "|" filterlist
not          = "!" filter
filterlist   = 1*filter
item         = simple / present / substring / extensible
simple       = attr filtertype value
filtertype   = equal / approx / greater / less
equal        = "="
approx       = "~="
greater      = ">="
less         = "<="
extensible   = attr [":dn"] [":" matchingrule] ":=" value
             / [":dn"] ":" matchingrule ":=" value
present      = attr "=*"
substring    = attr "=" [initial] any [final]
initial      = value
any          = "*" *(value "*")
final        = value
attr         = Attributed descriptor
matchingrule = A printable representation of an object
               identifier.
value        = The value of the attribute.
```

We present some examples of search filters momentarily.

- **extensions:** The extensions construct provides the LDAP URL with a mechanism for treating LDAP extensions. This essentially allows the capabilities of the URL to be extended in the future. Extensions are lists of type=value pairs—separated by commas. Each type=value pair is a separate extension. An extension prefixed with a ! character (ASCII 33) is critical, whereas an extension not prefixed with a ! character is noncritical. If a client does not support an extension that is designated as critical, the client will not process the URL; however, if an unsupported extension is marked as noncritical, the client will ignore the extension and process the URL.

Before we conclude this chapter, let us look at some example of LDAP URLs:

```
ldap://ldap.europe.keys.pgp.com:11370/ou=PGP,o=NAI,c=US
```

The above URL corresponds to a base object search of the ou=PGP, o=NAI, c=US entry—using no filter, that is, requesting all attributes—on the LDAP server running on port 11370 of the machine with DNS name ldap.europe.keys.pgp.com.

The next URL performs a search that is similar to the previous one, except that only the `telephoneNumber` attribute, that is, the telephone number associated with the entry, is returned:

```
ldap://ldap.europe.keys.pgp.com:11370/ou=pgp,o=NAI,
        c=US?telephoneNumber
```

The final example does a subtree search of all the entries under the `o=NAI`, `c=US` branch of the DIT—on the LDAP server, running on the default LDAP port (389), on the host with DNS name pgpkeyserver.pgp.com—for any entry with a common name of `Carlton Davis`, retrieving only the `userCertificate` attribute:

```
ldap://pgpkeyserver.pgp.com/o=NAI,c=US?userCertificate?
        sub?(cn=Carlton Davis)
```

IP Security Architecture

In this chapter, we discuss the following topics:

- What IPSec Does
- How IPSec Works
- Security Association
- Security Association Databases
  - Security Policy Database
  - Security Association Database

In the previous six chapters, our presentation was centered on the following subjects:

- TCP/IP protocol architecture
- Symmetric-key and public-key cryptographic algorithms, digital signature schemes, hash functions, and message authentication code
- Public-key infrastructure (PKI)
- Lightweight Directory Access Protocol (LDAP)

Each of these topics is relevant to a discourse on IPSec. In covering these subject areas in the depth that we did, we laid the foundation for a sound discussion on the actual IPSec protocols. We start by first giving an overview of IPSec.

7.1 What IPSec Does

IP packets are inherently insecure. It is relatively easy to forge IP addresses, modify the contents of IP packets, replay old content, and inspect the content of packets in transit. Therefore, there is no guarantee that an IP datagram originated from the source it claims to originate from, that it will get to the intended destination, or that the contents have not been modified or examined by a third party while it was in transit from the source to the destination.

In Chapter 1, in our presentation on the IP protocol, we mentioned briefly how the 16-bit header checksum is utilized in an effort to validate the integrity of an IP header. To illustrate how relatively easy it is to forge an IP header, let us take a more detailed look at how an IP header checksum is calculated and used to rudimentarily ascertain the integrity of an IP header. Figure 7-1 is the figure we presented in Chapter 1, illustrating an IPv4 header.

The IP header checksum is calculated over the IP header only. It does not include the data field since all the transport protocols (TCP, UDP, ICMP, and IGMP) have a checksum in their header to check their data. To compute the checksum for an outgoing datagram, the 16-bit checksum field is first set to zero, and then the one's complement sum of the header is computed; that is, the entire IP header, excluding the data field, is considered as a sequence 16-bit words, and the one's complement sum of these 16-bit sequences is computed and stored in the checksum field.

Figure 7-1
IPv4 Datagram

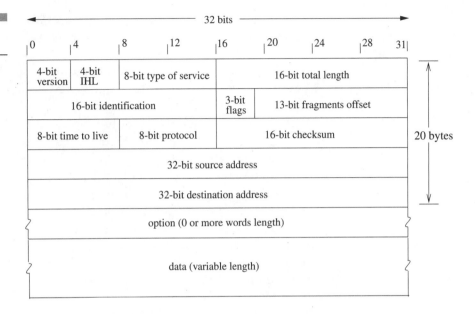

When an IP datagram is received, the receiver calculates the 16-bit one's complement sum of the header. Since the receiver's calculated checksum included the checksum stored by the sender, if the IP header has not been modified, the checksum the receiver computes will be zero. If the receiver's checksum is not zero, the datagram will be discarded. Let us illustrate the calculation of an IP header checksum with an example.

In our example, a computer cracker—we'll call him cracker Joe—is operating from home on a machine that is connected to the Internet via DSL. Assume that the IP address of his machine is 64.143.185.5. (This is a randomly chosen IP address, no malicious intent was intended by choosing this IP address. At the time of writing, an `nslookup` on this IP address indicated that it was either unassigned or it was assigned to a machine that is behind a firewall.) Let us say that Cracker Joe wants to stage a denial of service (d.o.s) attack at the machine hosting the webserver *www.victim.com*. d.o.s attacks are exploits that render a machine unusable until it is rebooted. Assume that the IP address for this machine is 126.30.17.52. Cracker Joe desires to cover his path; that is, he does not want the attack trail to be traceable back to his machine. Cracker Joe did a search on the web and found the source code for a program that launches d.o.s. attacks. He also found another program that is able to intercept IP datagrams immediately after they leave the TCP/IP stack, modify their contents, and replay the modified datagrams. We will construct an IP datagram and illustrate by way of an example how this program could modify this datagram and replay it.

The first 4 bits of an IP datagram are the version field (see Figure 7-1). Since we are talking about an IPv4 datagram, the version number is 4. The 4-bit binary equivalent of 4 is 0100.

The next field, the IHL (Internet header length) field, is the length of the header in 32-bit words. The minimum value is 5 words (20 bytes), which is the case when no options are present; the maximum value is 15 words (60 bytes), which applies when the options field is 40 bytes. We will assume that there are no options. Therefore, the value of the IHL field is 5; the 4-bit binary number for 5 is 0101.

Next, the 8-bit type of service (TOS) field, is set to zero, since there are no special TOS requirements; thus, the value for the TOS field is 00000000.

The next field is a 16-bit field that stores the total length of the IP datagram, including the data field. In our example, we assume that Cracker Joe is launching a SYN flood attack. In Chapter 1, in our presentation on the TCP protocol, we explained how a three-way handshake is necessary to establish a TCP connection. We recapitulated the information we presented with regard to the initiation of a TCP connection. TCP uses a 32-bit sequence number to uniquely identify each datagram segment that a host transmits. The first sequence number, the initial sequence number (ISN), that a host employs during a TCP session must be randomly generated. The sequence number of the remaining data fragment will be the ISN plus the segment sequence. For example, the first data segment will have sequence number ISN+1 and the second, ISN+2, etc. Note that the fragment with the ISN as the sequence number contains no actual TCP data because the connection has not yet been established. During a TCP session, a host uses the sequence numbers associated with the datagram segments it received from its communicating peer for a number of important functions, such as to reassemble the data fragments and to perform flow control. Therefore, the peer needs to inform the other peer about the ISN it generated for the session, before the TCP connection can be established. The steps involved in exchanging the ISNs are illustrated below (in the illustration, A is the initiator of the TCP session and B is the other peer):

```
1) A --> B:   SYN bit set; sequence no. field contains A's ISN.
2) A <-- B:   SYN and ACK bits set; sequence no. field contains
              B's ISN. Acknowledge no. field contains A's ISN.
3) A --> B:   ACK bit set; Acknowledge no. field contains B's
              ISN.
```

The above is referred to as the three-way handshake. A TCP connection is established only if the three-way handshake is successful.

In a SYN flood attack, the host perpetrating the attack—let us call this host A—floods the victim host B with a large number of TCP connection request packets with the SYN bit set, with no accompanying acknowledgment. If the victim host has not been configured correctly so that it is protected from these kinds of attacks, it will attempt to reply to each of the packets it received as indicated in step 2 of the three-way handshake illustrated above. Meanwhile, there will be no acknowledgment from the perpetrating host; as a result, the victim host will be kept waiting for acknowledgments until the time it has been configured to wait for an acknowledgment expires. If there are enough of these connection requests from A, soon all of B's resources will be used up in responding to these SYN packets, and B will be incapacitated until it is rebooted.

The length of a SYN packet, a TCP packet with the SYN bit set, is 20 bytes. A SYN packet has no data and, typically, no options—Figure 7-2 is the figure illustrating the TCP header that we presented in Chapter 1—therefore, the total length of an IP datagram encapsulating a SYN packet is 20 + 20 = 40 bytes. The 16-bit binary equivalent of 40 is 0000000000101000.

The next field is the 16-bit identification field. The identification field allows a host to determine which datagram a newly arrived fragment

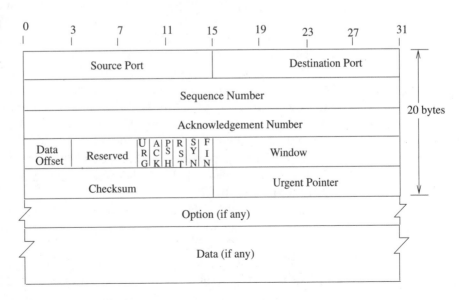

Figure 7-2
TCP Header Format

belongs to. Each datagram has a unique identification number, and each fragment of a datagram has the same identification number. We give this field a 16-bit binary value of 0001110001010100.

For the 3-bit flags field, only 2 of the 3 bits are used. The first of the 2 bits, called the DF (don't fragment) bit, indicates whether or not the IP datagram should be fragmented. If this bit is set, it indicates that the datagram should not be fragmented. In our example, we set the DF bit because we do not want the datagram to be fragmented. The second of the 2 bits, is called the MF (more fragment) bit. It indicates when the last fragment of a datagram arrives. Since the DF bit is set, this bit must be unset. Therefore, the binary value for the 3-bit flag is 100.

The next field, the 13-bit fragment offset field, tells where in the current datagram this fragment belongs. Because the datagram is not fragmented, this 13-bit field will be 0, i.e., 0000000000000.

The 8-bit time-to-live (TTL) field is used to limit the lifetime of a datagram, thus preventing the datagram from looping infinitely within a network segment. The TTL field is set to a default value by the source. Each router that the datagram passes through decrements the TTL value by 1. When a router decrements the TTL value, it recalculates the header checksum and replaces the old checksum with the new value. For the purpose of our example, we will set the TTL field to 12. The 8-bit binary equivalent of 12 is 00001100.

The next field is the 8-bit protocol field. It indicates which transport protocol is used for the data encapsulated within the IP datagram. The packet is a TCP packet; therefore, the protocol number is 6. The 8-bit binary equivalent is 00000110.

The 16-bit checksum field must be set to 0, i.e., 0000000000000000.

The source IP address is the IP address of Cracker Joe's machine, that is, 64.143.185.5. The binary equivalent of this IP address can be computed by calculating the 8-bit binary number for each byte of the IP address and then concatenating the binary numbers. Thus, for this IP address, the binary equivalent of the first byte is 01000000, the second byte is 10001111, the third byte is 10111001, and the last byte is 00000101. The 32-bit representation of this IP address is therefore 01000000 10001111 10111001 00000101.

The destination address is the IP address of *www.victim.com*, which we assume to be 126.30.17.52; the binary equivalent is 01111110 00011110 00010001 00110100.

Table 7-1 shows the binary value we assigned to each field.

The next step involves arranging these values in 16-bit sequences, and summing the sequences. This information is shown in Table 7-2.

TABLE 7-1

Summary of
Binary Values
for the Fields

Field	Binary Values
Version	0100
Header length	0101
TOS	00000000
total length	0000000000101000
identification	0001110001010100
3-bit flag	100
fragment offset	0000000000000
TTL	00001100
protocol	00000110
checksum	0000000000000000
source IP address	01000000 10001111 10111001 00000101
destination IP address	01111110 00011110 00010001 00110100

As indicated in Table 7-2, the 16-bit calculated sum is 1011 1100 0010 0100. The one's complement of this sum is 0100 1101 1101 1011. Thus, for our example, the binary value 0100 1101 0011 1011 would be placed in the header checksum field.

TABLE 7-2

Summation of the
16-bit Sequences

16-bit Sequences	Fields Composing the Sequence
0100 0101 0000 0000	Values from version, IHL, and TOS fields
0000 0000 0010 1000	16-bit total length field
0001 1100 0101 0100	16-bit identification field
1000 0000 0000 0000	Flags and fragmentation offset fields
0000 1100 0000 0110	TTL and protocol fields
0000 0000 0000 0000	Checksum field
0100 0000 1000 1111	First 2 bytes of source IP address
1011 1001 0000 0101	Last 2 bytes of source IP address
0111 1110 0001 1110	First 2 bytes of destination IP address
0001 0001 0011 0100	Last 2 bytes of destination IP address
1011 1100 0010 0100	16-bit calculated sum

TABLE 7-3

Summation of the
16-bit Sequences at
the Receiving Host

16-bit Sequences	Fields Composing the Sequence
0100 0101 0000 0000	Values from version, IHL, and TOS fields
0000 0000 0010 1000	16-bit total length field
0001 1100 0101 0100	16-bit identification field
1000 0000 0000 0000	Flags and fragmentation offset fields
0000 1100 0000 0110	TTL and protocol fields
0100 0011 1101 1011	Checksum field
0100 0000 1000 1111	First 2 bytes of source IP address
1011 1001 0000 0101	Last 2 bytes of source IP address
0111 1110 0001 1110	First 2 bytes of destination IP address
0001 0001 0011 0100	Last 2 bytes of destination IP address
1111 1111 1111 1111	16-bit calculated sum

When the datagram reaches the destination host, the checksum is recomputed as shown in Table 7-3.

In actuality, the TTL field likely would have been changed; however, since a new checksum is calculated each time that the TTL value is decremented, the effect will be canceled out. We are using the checksum that was calculated by the source host, rather than that calculated by an intermediate router; therefore, we need to use the original TTL value.

As indicated in Table 7-3, the computed 16-bit sum at the receiver's end consists of all 1 bits. The complement of this bit-string is a bit-string consisting of 16 zeros. Therefore, the datagram will be accepted by the receiving host as authentic.

The point is that if a datagram is intercepted, modified, and then sent to its intended destination, provided that the header checksum is recalculated correctly after the changes to the desired fields are made, the receiving host likely will not detect that the datagram has been tampered with. We illustrate this by returning to our example involving cracker Joe.

Cracker Joe executed a d.o.s. attack on the machine hosting the *www. victim.com* web server; in order to cover his tracks, he used a spoofing software to capture the packets that are used to launch the d.o.s attack—immediately after they left the TCP/IP stack—and then changed the source destination field, recalculated the header checksum, and relayed the packets to their intended destination. Let us assume that Cracker

Joe wanted the administrator of the *www.victim.com* machine to think that the d.o.s packets originated from a machine with the IP address 161.69.3.155. Therefore, cracker Joe configures his spoofing software to replace the source IP address of the packets that are used to attack the victim computer with 10100001 01000101 00000011 10011011, which is the 32-bit binary equivalent of 161.69.3.155. The new checksum value is as shown in the summation of the 16-bit sequences in Table 7-4.

The new header checksum is the one's complement of 1110 0111 0111 0000, which is 0001 1000 1000 1111. This 16-bit value is placed in the checksum field. When the datagram with the spoofed source IP address arrives at the victim host, it will calculate the one's complement checksum, which will be zero. The summation is shown in Table 7-5.

The one's complement of 1111 1111 1111 1111 is a 16-bit zero string. Therefore, the victim host will accept the packet as being authentic, whereas, as we indicated, the source IP address was in fact spoofed.

The spoofing of IP addresses—particularly when a connection is not required between the spoofed host and the destination host—can be done quite easily using software that is freely available on the Internet. Changing a field in an IP datagram is quite trivial; calculation of the header checksum requires more effort. However, RFC 1071 [BBP88] outlines how it can be done efficiently; this RFC even includes C source code for calculating IP checksums.

TABLE 7-4

Summation of the 16-bit Sequences After the Modification of Destination IP Address

16-bit Sequences	Fields Composing the Sequence
0100 0101 0000 0000	Values from version, IHL, and TOS fields
0000 0000 0010 1000	16-bit total length field
0001 1100 0101 0100	16-bit identification field
1000 0000 0000 0000	Flags and fragmentation offset fields
0000 1100 0000 0110	TTL and protocol fields
0000 0000 0000 0000	Checksum field
1010 0001 0100 0101	First 2 bytes of source IP address
0000 0011 1001 1011	Last 2 bytes of source IP address
0111 1110 0001 1110	First 2 bytes of destination IP address
0001 0001 0011 0100	Last 2 bytes of destination IP address
1110 0111 0111 0000	16-bit calculated sum

TABLE 7-5

Summation of the
16-bit Sequences
for the Modified
Datagram at the
Receiving Host

16-bit Sequences	Fields Composing the Sequence
0100 0101 0000 0000	Values from version, IHL, and TOS fields
0000 0000 0010 1000	16-bit total length field
0001 1100 0101 0100	16-bit identification field
1000 0000 0000 0000	Flags and fragmentation offset fields
0000 1100 0000 0110	TTL and protocol fields
0001 1000 1000 1111	Checksum field
1010 0001 0100 0101	First 2 bytes of source IP address
0000 0011 1001 1011	Last 2 bytes of source IP address
0111 1110 0001 1110	First 2 bytes of destination IP address
0001 0001 0011 0100	Last 2 bytes of destination IP address
1111 1111 1111 1111	16-bit calculated sum

If a connection is desired between the spoofed host and the victim host, much more effort is required since the perpetuation of these types of exploits involves predicting the ISN of the SYN packet used to initiate the connection from the host that is being spoofed. However, this has not been much of an impediment to crackers, who over the years have fine-tuned different techniques for predicting ISNs and consequently routinely spoofed IP addresses.

IPSec was designed to prevent the spoofing of IP addresses, prevent any form of tampering with and replaying of IP datagrams, and provide confidentiality and other security services for IP datagrams. IPSec offers these services at the network layer—the layer in the TCP/IP protocol stack that contains the IP protocol. The security that IPSec affords is provided via combinations of cryptographic protocols and security mechanisms. IPSec enables systems to select required security protocols, choose the cryptographic algorithms that are desired to be used with the selected protocols, and generate and put in place any cryptographic keys that are necessary to provide the requested services.

The security services that IPSec affords include access control to network elements, data origin authentication, connectionless integrity for protocols such as UDP that offer connectionless services, detection and rejection of replayed packets, use of encryption to provide data confidentiality, and limited traffic flow confidentiality. Since the IPSec services are offered at the network layer—layer 2 of the TCP/IP protocol stack—these services can be used by any of the upper-layer protocols such as TCP, UDP, ICMP, and IGMP or any application layer protocol.

7.2 How IPSec Works

IPSec is designed to provide high-quality, interoperable cryptographic-based security for IPv4 and IPv6 datagrams. IPSec achieves these objectives by using two traffic security protocols: authentication header (AH) and encapsulating security payload (ESP), and through the use of cryptographic-key management procedures and protocols such as Internet Key Exchange (IKE) protocol.

The IP AH protocol provides data origin authentication, connectionless integrity, and an optional anti-replay service. The ESP protocol provides data confidentiality, limited traffic flow confidentiality, connectionless integrity, data origin authentication, and anti-replay service. There are two modes of operation of both AH and ESP: transport mode and tunnel mode. We explain these modes of operation, as they apply to AH and ESP, in the next two chapters. The IKE protocol is used to negotiate the cryptographic algorithm choices to be utilized by AH and ESP, and put in place the necessary cryptographic keys that the algorithms require. AH, ESP, and IKE protocols are discussed in more detail in later chapters.

The protocols that IPSec utilizes are designed to be algorithm independent. The choice of algorithms is specified in the Security Policy Database (SPD). The available choice of cryptographic algorithms depends on the IPSec implementation; however, a standard set of default algorithms are specified by IPSec to ensure interoperability on the global Internet.

IPSec allows the user or administrator of a system or a network to control the granularity at which the security service is offered. For example, an organization's policy might specify that data traffic that originated from certain subnets should be protected with both AH and ESP and that the encryption should be done with triple-DES with three different keys. On the other hand, the policy might specify that data traffic from another site should be protected with only ESP and that this traffic should be afforded encryption with AES (Advanced Encryption Standard). IPSec is able to differentiate between the security services it offers to different data traffic by the use of security association (SA).

7.3   Security Association

The concept of SA is fundamental to IPSec. The two protocols that IPSec uses—AH and ESP—both use SA, and a principal function of the IKE protocol, the key management protocol that IPSec uses, is the establishment and maintenance of SA. SA is an agreement between communicating peers on factors such as the IPSec protocol, mode of operation of the protocols (transport mode or tunnel mode), cryptographic algorithms, cryptographic keys, and lifetime of the keys that will be used to protect the traffic between them. If both AH and ESP are desired for protecting the traffic between two peers, then two sets of SAs are required: an SA for AH and one for ESP. SAs that define tunnel mode operation for AH or ESP are called tunnel mode SAs, whereas those that define transport mode are called transport mode SAs. Security associations are simplex (that is, they are unidirectional); therefore, separate SAs are required for outbound and inbound traffic. The term SA bundle is used to describe a set of SAs that are to be applied to data originated from or destined to a given host.

SAs are negotiated between the communicating peers via key management protocols such as IKE. When the negotiation of an SA completes, both peers store the SA parameters in their security association databases (SADs). One of the parameters of an SA is its lifetime, which takes the form of a time interval or a count of the number of bytes to which IPSec protocol will be applied for the SA in question. When the lifetime of an SA expires, this SA is either replaced by a new SA or is terminated. When the SA terminates, its entry is deleted from the SAD.

SAs are uniquely identified by a triplet consisting of a security parameter index (SPI), a destination IP address for outbound SAs or a source IP address for inbound SAs, and a specified protocol (example AH or ESP). The SPI is a unique 32-bit integer that is generated and used as a unique identifier of an SA. It is transported in the AH and ESP headers. Therefore, the recipient of the IPSec datagram can readily identify the SPI and use it along with the source or destination IP address and the protocol to search the SAD to ascertain the SA or SA bundle that is associated with the datagram.

7.4   Security Association Databases

There are two databases that are necessary for the processing of IPSec traffic: security policy database (SPD) and SAD. SPD specifies the policies that are to be applied to the traffic destined to or originated from a given host or network. SAD contains the active SA parameters. For both SPD and SAD, separate inbound and outbound databases are required.

7.4.1 Security Policy Database

The IPSec protocol mandates that the SPD must be consulted during the processing of all traffic, whether the traffic is inbound or outbound. The SPD contains an order list of policy entries. Each entry is specified by the use of one or more selectors. The selectors that IPSec currently allows are:

- *Destination IP address:* The destination IP address can be a 32-bit IPv4 or a 128-bit IPv6 address. The address can be a host IP address, a broadcast, unicast, anycast, a multicast group, a range of addresses, address plus netmask, or wild card address. The destination IP address is obtained from the *destination IP address* field of the AH, ESP, or—if IPSec is not applied to the packet— IP header.

- *Source IP address:* The source IP address, like the destination IP address, can be a 32-bit IPv4 or a 128-bit IPv6 address. This address, similarly, can be a host IP address, a broadcast, unicast, anycast, a multicast group, a range of addresses, address plus netmask, or wild card address. The destination IP address is obtained from the *source IP address* field of the AH, ESP or IP header.

- *Transport layer protocol:* The transport layer protocol is obtained from the IPv4 *protocol* or the IPv6 *next header fields.*

- *System name:* The system name can be a fully qualified DNS name, or e-mail address, such as bert.cs.mcgill.ca, or an X.500 DN, for example, *cn=bert,ou=Computer Science,o=McGill University, st=Quebec,c=Canada.* Refer to the discussion on the X.500 directory in Chapter 5 for detail on DNs.

- *User ID:* The user ID can be a fully qualified DNS user name such as *foo@cs.mcgill.ca* or an X.500 DN.

Each entry in the SPD consists of one or more selectors, an indication of whether the packets that match the selectors in the the entry should be discarded, be subjected to IPSec processing, or not be subjected to IPSec processing. If the packets are to be subjected to IPSec processing, the entry must also contain a pointer to an SA specification that details the IPSec protocols, modes, and cryptographic algorithms to be applied to the packets matching this policy entry.

The first entry with selectors matching those corresponding to the traffic under consideration will be applied. If no matching entry is found, the packets for the traffic under consideration will be discarded. Therefore, the entries in the SPD should be ordered according to the desired preference of application.

The entries in the SPD determine the granularity with which the traffic is processed. For example, the policies could specify that IPSec service corresponding to a given SA or SA bundle should be applied to all traffic to or from any source or destination, or the policy could specify the application of different SAs or SA bundles based on specified selectors. The SPD plays a very important role in the control of the flow of all traffic through an IPSec system.

7.4.2 Security Association Database

The SAD contains the active SA entries. Each SA entry is indexed by a triplet consisting of an SPI, a source or destination IP address, and an IPSec protocol. In addition, an SAD entry consists of the following fields:

- *Sequence number counter:* This is a 32-bit integer that is used to generate the sequence number field in AH or ESP headers.

- *Sequence counter overflow:* This is a flag indicating whether the overflow of the sequence number counter should be audited and the transmission of additional traffic be blocked for the given SA.

- *Anti-replay window:* A 32-bit counter and a bit-map that are used to ascertain whether an inbound AH or ESP packet is a replay.

- AH authentication cryptographic algorithm and the required key.

- ESP authentication cryptographic algorithm and the required key.

- ESP encryption algorithm, key, initial vector (IV), and IV mode. We discussed the IV and IV modes of operation in Section 2.3.

- *IPSec protocol mode:* This field indicates which IPSec protocol mode (transport, tunnel, or wild card) should be applied to AH and ESP traffic.

- *Path maximum transfer unit (PMTU):* Any observed PMTU and aging variables. The PMTU is the maximum size of an IP datagram that will be allowed to pass through a given network path on route from a source to a destination host, without being subjected to fragmentation.

■ *Lifetime of the SA:* This field contains the time interval within which a SA must be replaced by a new SA or be terminated, plus an indication of whether the SA should be replaced or terminated when it expires. The lifetime of a SA takes two forms: a time interval or a byte count that represents the number of bytes that IPSec protocols have been applied to. The parameter that expires first takes precedence.

Separate SADs are kept for inbound and outbound IPSec processing. For inbound or outbound traffic, the respective SADs are searched for selectors matching the SPI, the source or destination IP address, and the IPSec protocol, extracted from the packet header. If a matching entry is found, the parameters for this SA are compared with the appropriate fields in the AH or ESP headers. If the header fields correspond with the SA parameters in the database, the packet is processed. However, if there are any discrepancies, the packet is discarded. If no SA entry matches the selectors, the packet is discarded if it is an inbound packet. However, if the packet is outbound, a new SA or SA bundle will be created and entered in the outbound SAD.

A SA lifetime has two kinds of limits: a soft limit and a hard limit. When the soft limit is reached, the communicating peers must renegotiate a new SA to replace the existing one. However, the existing SA is not deleted from the database until the hard limit expires. Unlike the SPD, the entries in the SAD are not ordered. Nonetheless, as is the case with SPD lookups, the first matching SA entry that is found in the SAD is used for the IPSec processing of the packets that are associated with the given SA.

In the following three chapters, we give detailed descriptions of the three IPSec protocols, AH, ESP and IKE, and explain how they interoperate to secure IP traffic.

Authentication Header

In this chapter, we discuss the following topics:

- Authentication Header (AH) Format
- AH Modes of Operation
  - AH Transport Mode
  - AH Tunnel Mode
- Integrity Check Value Computation
- AH Processing
  - Outbound Processing
  - Inbound Processing

The IP protocol is inherently insecure. The authentication mechanism that is used to provide integrity for the IP datagrams is rather primitive. The IP header checksum field was intended to guarantee the integrity of IP datagrams. As we discussed in the Chapter 7, the checksum is computed by setting the checksum field to 0, calculating the 16-bit one's complement sum of the IP header, and storing the result in the checksum field. When the destination host receives the packet, it computes the 16-bit one's complement sum of the IP header. If none of the IP header fields have been modified, the destination host's one's complement sum should all be 0 bits since it involves the source's one's complement sum. The datagram is discarded if the receiver's one's complement sum is not all 0 bits. This provides very little security, however, since the IP header fields can easily be modified and the original checksum replaced with a new value that reflects the changes. A receiving host is not likely to detect when a datagram has been tampered with, provided the new checksum for the modified datagram was calculated correctly.

The Authentication Header (AH) protocol was designed to improve the security of IP datagrams. The AH Protocol provides connectionless integrity, data origin authentication, and an anti-replay protection service. However, AH does not provide any confidential services: it does not encrypt the packets it protects. AH's role is to provide strong cryptographic authentication for IP traffic to ensure that packets that are tampered with will be detected. AH uses cryptographic message authentication (MAC) codes to authenticate the IP datagram. An MAC is an algorithm that takes a message of any arbitrary length, and a cryptographic key, and produces a fixed-length output, called a message digest or fingerprint. MACs differ from hash functions in that a cryptographic key is required to generate the message digest for MACs; whereas, hash functions have no key requirement. The most commonly used MAC is HMAC. HMAC can be used in combination with any iterated cryptographic hash function (such as MD5, SHA-1, RIPEMD-160, or Tiger) without any modification of the hash function. See Chapter 4 for further details on hash functions and MACs.

The key requirement for the generation of the message digest of an IP datagram necessitates that the IPSec communicating peers share cryptographic keys. It is assumed to be computationally infeasible for one to produce a message digest that is identical to that produced for a given datum imputed to an MAC if the keys used are not identical. Hence, only the communicating peers that share the secret key are able to generate identical authentication data for a given message, using a predefined MAC. We will elaborate further on the generation of the authentication data for AH; before we do, let us look at the AH format.

8.1   Authentication Header Format

AH consists of five fixed-length fields and a variable-length authentication data field. Figure 8-1 shows the relative position of these fields in an AH. A description of these fields follows:

- *Next header:* This is an 8-bit field that identifies the next payload after the AH. For example, if an ESP header follows the AH, this field will contain the value 50, whereas if another AH follows the AH in question, the value in this field would be 51. RFC 1700 [IANA00] contains information regarding the assigned IP protocol numbers.

- *Payload length:* This 8-bit field contains the length of an AH in 32-bit words minus 2. Why minus 2? AH is essentially an IPv6 extension header; see Section 1.2.2 for the discussion of IPv6 datagrams. RFC 1883 [DH95], the specification for IPv6, specified that the header extension length for IPv6 extension headers should be calculated by first subtracting one 64-bit word from the header length—measured in 64-bit words. Since the payload length is measured in 32-bit words, two 32-bit words—the equivalent of one 64-bit word—are subtracted from the total authentication header length.

- *Reserved:* This 16-bit field is reserved for future use. The specification for AH, (RFC 2402) [KA98], stipulated that this field should be set to zero.

- *Security parameter index* (SPI): The SPI is a 32-bit integer that is used in combination with the source or destination address and

Figure 8-1
Authentication
Header Format

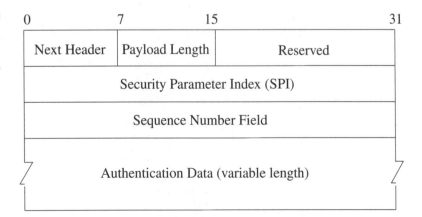

0	7	15	31
Next Header	Payload Length	Reserved	

Security Parameter Index (SPI)

Sequence Number Field

Authentication Data (variable length)

the IPSec protocol (AH or ESP) to uniquely identify the security association (SA) for the traffic to which a datagram belongs. As discussed previously in Section 7.3, SA is an agreement between communicating peers on factors such as the IPSec protocol, mode of operation of the protocols, cryptographic algorithms, cryptographic keys, and lifetime of the keys that will be used to protect the traffic between them. With regard to the integer value for SPI field, the range of integers from 1 to 255 is reserved by the Internet Assigned Number Authority (IANA) for future use; zero is reserved for local and implementation-specific use. Therefore, the current valid SPI values are between 256 and $2^{32} - 1$, inclusively.

- *Sequence number:* This field contains a 32-bit unsigned integer that serves as a monotonically increasing counter. The sender and receiver's sequence number counters are initialized to 0 when the SA is established. The peers increase their sequence number by 1 for every packet they send using a given SA. The sequence number is used to prevent the replay of packets, that is, the situation in which datagrams are captured by an intruder and retransmitted. The AH specification mandated that the sender must always transmit the sequence number to the receiver; the receiver, however, can choose to disable the anti-replay feature, and in so doing, it ignores the sequence number field in datagrams associated with incoming traffic. If anti-replay is enabled on the receiver host, it uses a sliding receiving window to detect duplicated packets. The specifics of a sliding window vary with different IPSec implementations; however, in general, a sliding window has the functionalities indicated below. The window size should be a minimum of 32 bits. The right edge of the window represents the highest validated sequence number value received on the given SA. Packets that have sequence numbers that are less than the left edge of the window should be rejected. Packets with sequence number values that are within the window should be checked against a list of received packets within the window. If the packets fall within the window, and they are new, or if the sequence number values of the packets are greater than the right edge of the sliding window and less than 2^{32}, then the receiver host proceeds to the computation of the authentication data. Sequence number values are not allowed to be recycled for a given SA; therefore, a new SA and consequently new keys must be negotiated prior to the transmission of 2^{32} packets on a given SA.

- *Authentication data:* This is a variable-length field that contains the authentication data, referred to as the integrity check value

(ICV), for the datagram. For IPv4 datagrams, the value of this field must be an integral multiple of 32, whereas for IPv6 datagrams it must be an integral multiple of 64. The algorithm utilized for the generation of the ICV is specified by the SA. The choice of available algorithms for the computation of the ICV differs with different IPSec implementations; to ensure interoperability, however, the AH protocol specification mandated at least two MACs, HMAC-MD5 and HMAC-SHA-1, be implemented in all IPSec implementations. If the length of the ICV is not an integral multiple of 32 for IPv4 datagrams and an integral multiple of 64 for IPv6 datagrams, padding bits must be added to acquire the desired length for the ICV.

8.2 AH Modes of Operation

The location of the AH header depends on the mode of operation of AH. There are two modes of operations: *transport mode* and *tunnel mode*. We discuss these modes of operations in the following two subsections. AH can be applied in a nested fashion through the use of tunnel mode, applied in combination with ESP, or applied alone.

8.2.1 AH Transport Mode

In transport mode, AH is inserted after the IP header but before any transport layer protocol, or before any other IPSec protocol header. Thus, for IPv4 in transport mode AH is inserted after the variable-length option field. Figure 8-2 illustrates the position of AH relative to other header fields for transport mode.

Note that AH authenticates the entire IP header. Therefore, there are limitations to the use of AH in transport mode. Figure 8-3 illustrates a case in which AH transport mode authentication cannot be employed. In this figure, host A has a private IP address. As we discussed in Chapter 1, private IP addresses are addresses in the range 10.0.0.0–10.255.255.255, 172.16.0.0–172.31.255.255, and 192.168.0.0–192.168.255.255. These addresses are nonroutable: routers on public networks typically do not route packets with private IP addresses. In order for hosts with any of these addresses to communicate with peers that are external to their network, the traffic destined to the external peers needs to pass through an NAT (network address translation) gateway before leaving the source network. NAT gateways replace the private IP address in the source address fields

Figure 8-2

AH Relative to Other
IPv4 Header Fields in
Transport Mode

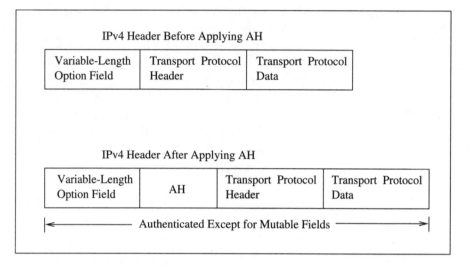

IPv4 Header Before Applying AH

Variable-Length Option Field	Transport Protocol Header	Transport Protocol Data

IPv4 Header After Applying AH

Variable-Length Option Field	AH	Transport Protocol Header	Transport Protocol Data

|←———— Authenticated Except for Mutable Fields ————→|

Figure 8-3

A Scenario in Which
AH Transport Mode
Authentication Is
Not Suitable

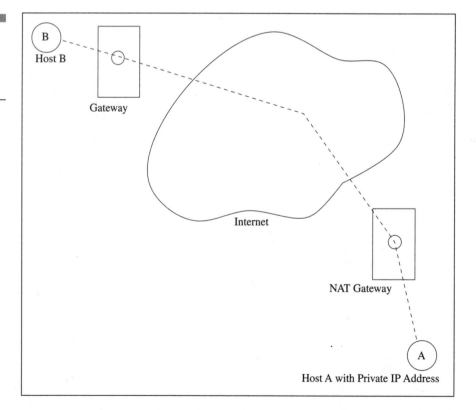

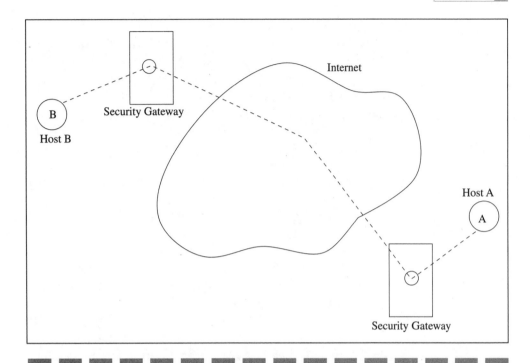

Figure 8-4 *Another Situation in Which AH Transport Mode Authentication Is Not Suitable*

of headers in outbound packets with an assigned public IP address, recompute the checksum, and forward the packets to their intended destinations.

If AH authentication is enabled on both host A and host B, when the packets arrive at host B, the AH integrity check will fail because the ICV[1] that B computes will be different from that which host A computed, owing to the fact that the NAT gateway modified the source address fields of the datagrams.

Figure 8-4 shows another example of a topology in which AH transport mode authentication would also fail. In this example, host A has a public IP address; however, it is behind a security gateway. One of the roles of the security gateway is to conceal the IP addresses of the machines it protects. In so doing, like the NAT gateway, the security gateway replaces the source address fields of headers in outbound packets, with its public IP address, recomputes the checksum, and forwards the packets to their destinations.

Therefore, as in the scenario with the NAT gateway we discussed, if AH transport mode authentication is enabled on both host A and host B, the

---

[1]The ICV is the authentication data that are used for verifying the integrity of a datagram. We will show how they are computed, later in this chapter.

authentication of traffic between these hosts will fail because the ICV that the hosts compute will be different owing to the fact that the source security gate changed the source address fields in the packets headers.

If AH transport mode authentication is desired for either of the scenarios we presented, the authentication needs to be performed on the gateways. In other words, AH transport mode authentication needs to be enabled on the gateways. In so doing, the gateway for the source host computes an ICV for each datagram after it modified the source address fields. The gateway for the destination host will be able to successfully perform AH transport mode authentication for IPSec traffic from the source gateway, provided that the traffic has not been tampered with. It should be noted, however, that the protection offered to the traffic in this solution is incomplete: there is no protection for the traffic while it is on route from a host to its gateway, or from a gateway to a host behind it. ESP can be employed to provide the additional security; we discuss ESP in the next chapter. Let us now look at the placement of AH headers for transport mode with IPv6 datagrams.

The option field in IP headers was eliminated from IPv6. Options, in this version of IP, are treated as separate headers, called extension headers. Extension headers are inserted after the IP header. This feature speeds up packet processing in that, except for the hop-by-hop[2] extension header, which contains routing information that routers need to examine, the extension headers are not examined or processed by any intermediate node on the path from the source to the destination. They are only processed by the destination host.

In transport mode, for IPv6, the AH is inserted after the hop-by-hop, routing, and fragmentation extension headers; the destination options extension headers can be placed before or after the AH header. If the destination option header is to be processed by the first destination that appears in the IPv6 destination address field, plus subsequent destinations listed in the routing header, it should be processed immediately after the processing of the hop-by-hop options header and consequently should be placed before the AH. However, if the destination options header is to be processed only by the destination host, it can be placed after the AH. Figure 8.5 illustrates the position of the AH header relative to the other IPv6 extension headers in transport mode.

As in the case of IPv4 datagrams, AH authenticates the entire IPv6 header; therefore, all of the limitations that we discussed with regard to the application of AH transport mode authentication to IPv4 traffic apply to IPv6 traffic as well.

---

[2]See Chapter 1 for further details on IPv6 extension headers.

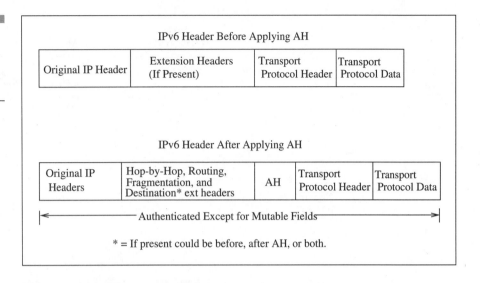

Figure 8-5
AH Relative to Other
IPv6 Extension
Headers in
Transport Mode

8.2.2 AH Tunnel Mode

In tunnel mode AH is inserted before the original IP header and a new IP header is inserted in front of the AH. This is illustrated diagrammatically for IPv4 datagrams in Figure 8-6. For IPv6 datagrams, in addition to the new IP header, the extension headers present in the original IPv6

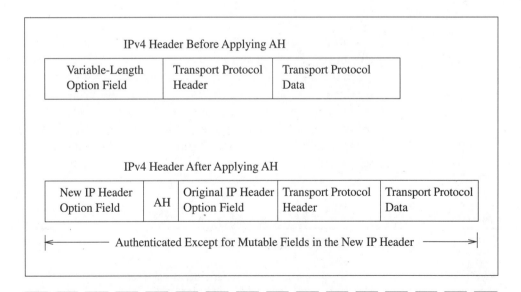

Figure 8-6   AH Relative to Other IPv4 Header Fields in Tunnel Mode

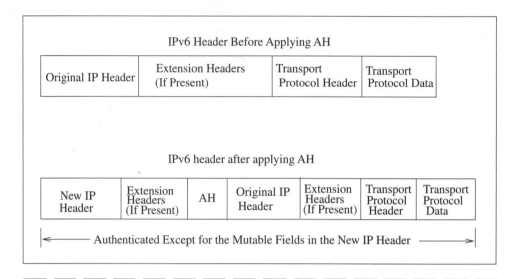

Figure 8-7 *AH Relative to Other IPv6 Extension Headers in Tunnel Mode*

datagram are also inserted before the AH. Figure 8-7 illustrates this information for IPv6 datagrams.

Tunnel mode is more useful when employed with ESP; ESP encrypts IP datagrams. In order for routers to route packets to their destination, they need certain information in the IP header. The new IP headers inserted on the packets are accessible by routers, but the inner IP headers are protected.

As in the case with transport mode, AH in tunnel mode authenticates the entire IP datagram, including the new IP header. The limitations we discussed for AH in transport mode are therefore applicable to AH in tunnel mode as well. If AH tunnel mode authentication is to be utilized for traffic between peers that are behind security gateways, or peers that operate in NAT environment, as in the case for AH transport mode authentication, the authentication needs to be done at the gateway to the peers, rather than at the peers. See Section 8.2.1 for further details.

8.3 Integrity Check Value Computation

The ICV is the authentication data that AH or ESP use to verify the integrity of IP datagrams. The ICV for a datagram is generated using a MAC; we discussed MACs in Section 4.6. A secret cryptographic key is necessary for the generation of MACs. IPSec communicating peers need to be able to generate ICVs to validate the integrity of datagrams exchanged between the peers; consequently, the secret key needs to be shared by both communicating peers. Before IPSec peers can exchange data, they need to negotiate a SA. A SA is an agreement between IPSec communication peers on the choice of parameters such as the cryptographic algorithm that will be used to authenticate the traffic, or for ESP, encrypt the traffic; the cryptographic key that will be used for the given cryptographic algorithm; the IPSec protocol (AH or ESP); the mode of operation of the protocol; and the lifetime of the SA. We discuss IKE—the IPSec protocol that negotiates SAs—in a later chapter.

When a SA is established between two communicating peers, they will have all the requirements to compute the ICVs for datagrams they exchange. ICVs are computed over the entire IP header; however, the mutable fields—the fields that are likely to change while the datagram is on route from the source to the destination—are set to zero prior to the computation of the ICV. We present the mutable and immutable fields below, first for IPv4 datagrams, and then for IPv6 datagrams.

Mutable IPv4 Header Fields

- *Type of service:* the 8-bit type of service (TOS) field indicates the traffic requirement of the datagram in terms of the combination of delay, throughput, and reliability. IP does not consider this field mutable; however, IPSec treats it as mutable because some routers are known to change the value of this field.

- *Flags:* There are three flag bits in an IP header. The first is the DF (do not fragment) bit, when set indicates that the datagram should not be fragmented. The second is the MF (more fragment) bit. When set, this bit indicates that the last fragment of a datagram has arrived. The final bit of the 3-bit flag is reserved for future use. This field is excluded from ICV computation because intermediate routers may set the DF bit, even if the source has not set it.

- *Fragment offset:* This 13-bit field indicates where in the current datagram a fragment belongs. AH is applied only to nonfragmented IP packets; therefore, this field must be set to zero prior to the ICV computation.

- *TTL:* This 8-bit field is used to limit the lifetime of a datagram, thus preventing the datagram from looping infinitely within a network segment. The TTL value is decremented by each router that the packet passes through. The destination host cannot predict the TTL value; therefore, it is not included in the ICV computation.

■ *Header checksun:* This 16-bit field stores the IP header checksum. If any part of the IP header field changes, the value for the checksum changes; hence, the checksum value must be made zero prior to the ICV computation.

■ *Options:* The variable-length options field carries optional information about a datagram, such as the security and handling restrictions. This field is rarely used and is usually ignored by most routers. Therefore, most IPSec implementations do not include the options field in the computation of ICV.

Immutable IPv4 Header Fields

■ Version

■ IHL (Internet header length)

■ Total length

■ Identification

■ Protocol

■ Source address

■ Destination address

■ Data (the encapsulated transport protocol header and data)
  See Chapter 1 for details on these fields.

Mutable IPv6 header fields

■ *Priority:* This 4-bit IPv6 field indicates the quality of service that a packet requires. This field may be changed by intermediate routers; therefore, it is not included in the ICV computation.

■ *Flow label:* The 24-bit flow label field is an experimental field. It is ignored by most applications; consequently the IPSec specification mandated that it should be set to zero prior to the calculation of the ICV.

■ *Hop limit:* The hop limit field is the same as the IPv4 TTL field. It is decremented by each intermediate router on the path from the source to the destination of a datagram.

The hop-by-hop and destination options' extension headers contain a bit indicating whether the option might change during transit. These extension headers can be designated mutable or immutable by setting or unsetting these bits. The hop-by-hop extension header is used to carry optional routing information that must be examined by every node on the path from the source to the destination of the datagram. The destination option extension header carries optional information that needs to be examined only by the destination nodes.

Immutable IPv6 header fields

- Version
- Payload length
- Next header
- Source address
- Destination address

Mutable but predicatable

The routing extension header is characterized as mutable but predictable. This extension header is used by the IPv6 source to list one or more intermediate gateways through which a packet should pass on its way from the source to the destination. The address fields within the routing extension header can be rearranged during transit from the source to the destination; however the contents of the packet as it will appear at the destination host are known to the sender and all the intermediate nodes. Therefore, the sender is expected to order the address fields so that they appear as they will at the destination host and then include this extension header in the ICV computation.

The fragmentation extension header, if it exists, is not seen by IPSec since fragmentation occurs after outbound IPSec processing and reassembly occurs before inbound IPSec processing. Therefore, this extension header is not considered in the computation of the ICV.

Integrity check values

After the mutable fields of the IP and the extension headers for IPv6 are set to zero, the entire IP and the extension headers are taken as a bit string and imputed to the MAC, which uses the designated cryptographic key to generate the ICV. It should be noted that for tunnel mode, the mutable fields for the inner IP header are not set to zero because only the mutable fields of the outer IP header should be modified while a datagram is in transit from its source to its destination.

The length of the ICV depends on the MAC algorithm utilized. For example, for HMAC-MD5, the ICV is 128 bits, whereas it is 160 bits for HMAC-SHA1 or HMAC-RIPEMD-160.

If a MAC algorithm is used that results in an ICV whose value is not an integral multiple of 32 for IPv4 datagrams and 64 for IPv6 datagrams, padded bits are added so that the ICV becomes an integral multiple of these integers.

After the ICV is computed and padded, if necessary, it is placed in the authentication data field and the datagram is then sent to its destination.

8.4   AH Processing

The final topic that we address in this chapter is the processing of AH traffic. Some of the specifics may vary with different IPSec implementations; however, according to the the specification for AH, each implementation is expected to follow the general scheme outlined below

Outbound Processing

When an IPSec implementation receives an outbound packet from the IP stack, it uses the relevant selectors (destination IP address, port, transport protocol, etc.) to search the security policy database (SPD) and ascertain what policy is applicable to the traffic. If IPSec processing is required and a SA or SA bundle has already been established with the destination host, the SPD entry that matches the selectors in the packet will point to the appropriate SA bundle in the outbound SAD. If a SA has not been established, the IPSec implementation will call on IKE to negotiate a SA and link it to the SPD entry. The SA is then used to process the packet as follows:

1. It generates or increments the sequence number value: The sequence number is used to prevent replay of previously transmitted packets. When a new SA is established, the sender initializes its sequence number counter to zero. For each packet that the sender transmits, it increases the sequence number by 1 and inserts the resulting value of the sequence number counter into the `sequence number` field of the AH header.
2. It calculates ICV as described previously.
3. It forwards the packet to its destination.

Inbound Processing

If the MF bit is set when a datagram arrives at an IPSec destination node, this is an indication that other fragments are yet to arrive. The IPSec application therefore waits until a fragment arrives with a sequence number that is similar to the previous ones, with the MF bit not set. It then reassembles the IP fragments and performs the following steps:

1. It uses the SPI, destination IP address, and IPSec protocol in the IP header (outer IP header if in tunnel mode) to look up the SA for the traffic that the datagram is associated with in the inbound SAD. If the lookup fails, it drops the packet and logs the event. The amount of information enter in the log entry typically depends on the IPSec implementation. However, at a minimum, the time, the IP address of the source node, and the reason for dropping the packet should be recorded.

2. It uses the SA found in step 1 to do the IPSec processing. This involves first checking to determine whether the selectors in the IP header (inner header if in tunnel mode) match those in SA. If the selectors do not match, the application drops the packet and audits the event. If the selectors match, the IPSec application keeps track of the SA and the order in which it is applied relative to the others and repeats steps 1 and 2 until a transport layer protocol is encountered, or for IPv6, a non-IPSec extension header.

3. It uses the selectors in the packet to find a policy in the inbound SPD whose selectors match those of the packet.

4. It checks whether the SAs found in steps 1 and 2 match the policy specified in step 3. If the check fails, it repeats steps 4 and 5 until all policy entries have been checked, or until the check succeeds.

5. If antireplay is enabled, it uses the antireplay window of the SA, as described earlier in the chapter, to determine if the packet is a replay. If the packet is a replay, it should be dropped and the event audited.

6. it uses the MAC algorithm specified by the SA or SA bundle to calculate the ICV for the packet and compares it with the value stored in the authentication data field. If the two values differ, then it discards the packet and audits the event.

At the end of these steps, if the packet has not been discarded, it is then passed up the IP stack to the transport layer protocol or is forwarded to the designated node.

Encapsulating Security Payload

In this chapter, we discuss the following topics:

- Encapsulating Security Payload (ESP) Format
- ESP Modes of Operation
  - ESP Transport Mode
  - ESP Tunnel Mode
- ESP Processing
  - Outbound Processing
  - Inbound Processing

As is the case with the authentication header (AH), the encapsulating security payload (ESP) is designed to improve the security of the Internet Protocol (IP). ESP provides data confidentiality, data origin authentication, connectionless integrity, antireplay service, and limited traffic flow confidentiality. In essence, ESP offers similar services to those provided by AH, plus two additional services: data confidentiality and a limited traffic flow confidentiality. The confidentiality service is afforded by the use of a cryptographic algorithm to encrypt relevant portions of the IP datagram. Traffic flow confidentiality is provided by the confidentiality service in tunnel mode; we discuss the mode of operation for ESP later in the chapter.

The cryptographic algorithms that ESP uses to encrypt datagrams are exclusively symmetric-key cryptosystems. Public-key cryptographic algorithms involve computationally intensive modular exponentiation of large integers of magnitude greater than 300 decimal digits, whereas symmetric-key ciphers utilize mainly primitive operations (exclusive-OR, bitwise AND, bit rotation, etc.) that are executed very efficiently in both hardware and software. As a result, symmetric-key cryptosystems give significantly greater encryption/decryption throughput compared to that of public-key cryptosystems.

ESP provides authentication service by the use of message authentication codes (MACs). MACs are similar to cryptographic hash functions except that a key is required to generate the message digest. For further detail about MACs, refer to Chapter 4.

The choice of encryption and authentication algorithms varies with different IPSec implementations; however, in order to ensure interoperability, the ESP specification RFC 2406 [KA98] stipulates mandatory algorithms that each implementation must support. At the time of writing, the mandatory-to-implement encryption algorithms were DES in CBC[1] mode and the NULL encryption algorithm, whereas the authentication algorithms were HMAC-MD5, HMAC-SHA-1, and the NULL authentication algorithm. The NULL encryption and authentication algorithms are options for no encryption and no authentication respectively. The NULL algorithm options are mandatory because ESP confidentiality and authentication services are optional. However, it is important to note that the NULL encryption and the NULL authentication algorithms cannot be utilized simultaneously; in other words, if ESP is employed, its confidentiality or its authentication or both must be utilized. DES is a weak encryption algorithm and is rarely used for VPN solutions. It is expected

---

[1] We discuss the mode of operation of block ciphers in Section 2.3.3.

that revisions of RFC 2406 will replace DES as a mandatory-to-implement algorithm with AES. Other common choices of encryption algorithms are CAST-128 and IDEA; we discussed these ciphers in Chapter 2.

ESP can be applied alone, in a nested fashion, or in combination with AH. In this chapter, we discuss the format of ESP packets, the modes of operation of ESP, and the processing of ESP packets.

9.1   ESP Packet Format

ESP packets consist of four fixed-length fields and three variable-length fields. Figure 9-1 shows the packet format for this protocol. A description of the fields follows:

■ *Security parameter index (SPI):* The SPI is a 32-bit integer that is used in combination with the source or destination address and the IPSec protocol (ESP or AH) to uniquely identify the security association (SA) for the traffic to which a datagram belongs. A SA is an agreement between IPSec communicating peers on entities such as the encryption algorithm that will be used to provide ESP confidentiality service, the authentication algorithm, the crypto-graphic keys, the mode of operation of the IPSec protocol, and the lifetime of the SA; see Section 7.3 for further details on SA. The range of numbers from 1 to 255 is reserved by IANA for future use, and 0 is reserved for local and implementation-specific use. Therefore, the current valid SPI values are between 256 and $2^{32} - 1$. This field is similar to the AH SPI field.

Figure 9-1
ESP Packet Format

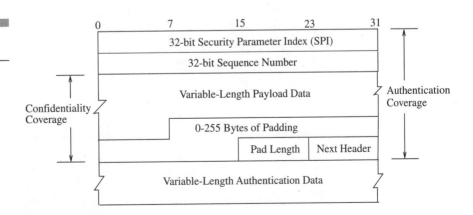

■ *Sequence number:* As is the case for the AH, this field contains a 32-bit unsigned integer that serves as a monotonically increasing counter. The sender's and receiver's sequence number counters are initialized to 0 when the SA is established. The sender consequently increases its sequence number by 1 for every packet it sends using a given SA. The sequence number is used to prevent intruders from capturing and resending previously transmitted datagrams. Sequence number values are not allowed to be recycled for a given SA; therefore, a new SA and consequently new keys must be negotiated prior to the transmission of 2^{32} packets on a given SA. It is mandatory that the sender transmit the sequence number to the receiver; however, the receiver can choose to disable the antireplay feature, and in so doing, ignore the sequence number field in datagrams associated with incoming traffic. If antireplay is enabled on the receiver host, it uses a sliding receiving window to detect duplicated packets. The specifics of a sliding window vary with different IPSec implementations. In general, the window size should be a minimum of 32 bits. The right edge of the window represents the highest validated sequence number value received on the given SA. Packets that have sequence numbers that are less than the left edge of the window should be rejected. Packets with sequence number values that are within the window should be checked against a list of received packets within the window. If the packets fall within the window, and they are new, or if the sequence number values of the packets are greater than the right edge of the sliding window and less than 2^{32}, the receiver node continues with the processing of the packet. If not, it drops the packet and audits the event.

■ *Payload data:* This is a variable-length field that contains the actual payload data (that is, the ciphertext for the encrypted portion of the datagram) if the confidentiality service is utilized. This field is mandatory so it is present whether or not the SA in question requires the confidentiality service. If the encryption algorithm employed requires an initial vector (IV), the IV is transported in the payload data field, and the specification for the algorithm needs to specify the length of the IV and its location in the payload data field. We explained the use of the IV with block ciphers in Section 2.3.3; in brief, initial vectors are employed with block ciphers in certain modes of operation to ensure that the ciphertext resulting from plaintexts that are similar in the first few bytes—for example, the header of IP datagrams—are different. The length of the payload data field in bits must be an integer multiple of 8.

■ *Padding:* This field contains the padding bits—if any—that are utilized by the encryption algorithm, or that are used to align the pad length (see Figure 9-1) field so that it begins at the third byte within the 4-byte word. The length of this field can be between 0 and 255 bytes.

■ *Pad length:* The pad length field is a 8-bit field that indicates the number of padding bytes in the padding field. The valid values for this field are integers between 0 and 255.

■ *Next header:* This is an 8-bit field that identifies the type of data encapsulated in the payload. It may indicate an IPv6 extension header or a transport layer protocol. For example, a value of 6 indicates that the payload contains TCP data. IANA is the group that is responsible for assigning IP Protocol numbers. The IANA home page is http://www.iana.org.

■ *Authentication data:* This is a variable-length field that contains the ICV, which, as indicated by Figure 9-1, is calculated over the length of the ESP packet minus the authentication data field. The actual length of this field depends on the authentication algorithm employed; for example, if HMAC-MD5 is utilized, the length of the authentication data field will be 128 bits, whereas if HMAC-SHA-1 or HMAC-RIPEMD-160 is used, it will be 160 bits. The authentication data field is optional, and it is included only if ESP authentication service is required for the given SA.

9.2   ESP Modes

As is the case with AH, the location of the ESP in the packet depends on the mode of operation of ESP. There are two modes of operations: *transport mode* and *tunnel mode*.

9.2.1   ESP Transport Mode

In transport mode, ESP is inserted after the IP header and any options it contains but before any transport layer protocol, or before any IPSec protocol that has already been applied. So, for IPv4 in transport mode, ESP is inserted after the variable-length options field. Figure 9-2 shows the position of ESP in transport mode relative to other header fields. In this diagram, the ESP header field consists of the SPI and sequence number fields, whereas the ESP trailer field consists of the padding, pad length, and next header fields. The portions of the datagram that are encrypted or authenticated are indicated in the diagram. If confidentiality service is required, the SPI and the sequence number fields are not encrypted because the receiver node utilizes these fields to identify the SA that should be used to process the datagram and to identify replayed packets if antireplay is enabled, respectively. Similarly, the authentication data field, if present, is not encrypted because if a given SA requires ESP authentication service, the destination host uses this field to verify the integrity of the datagram before it is processed.

For IPv6 datagrams, ESP is inserted after the hop-by-hop, routing, and fragmentation extension headers; the destination options extension header can be placed before or after the ESP header. If the destination option header is to be processed by the first destination that appears in the IPv6 destination address field, plus subsequent destinations listed in the routing header, it should should be placed before ESP. However, if it is to be processed only by the destination node, it can be placed after ESP. Figure 9-3 illustrates the position of the ESP relative to the other IPv6 extension headers for the transport mode of operation.

It is important to note that for ESP authentication service, unlike that for AH, the entire IP datagram is not authenticated; consequently, ESP

Figure 9-2
ESP Relative to Other IPv4 Header Fields in Transport Mode

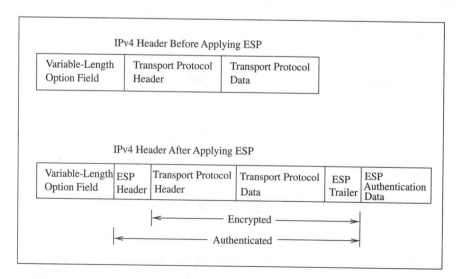

Figure 9-3
ESP Relative to
Other IPv6 Extension
Headers in
Transport Mode

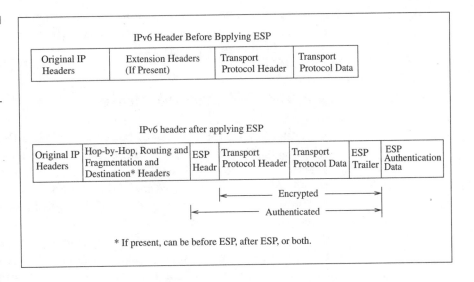

IPv6 Header Before Bpplying ESP

Original IP Headers	Extension Headers (If Present)	Transport Protocol Header	Transport Protocol Data

IPv6 header after applying ESP

Original IP Headers	Hop-by-Hop, Routing and Fragmentation and Destination* Headers	ESP Headr	Transport Protocol Header	Transport Protocol Data	ESP Trailer	ESP Authentication Data

←——— Encrypted ———→
←——————— Authenticated ———————→

* If present, can be before ESP, after ESP, or both.

transport mode does not suffer from any of the limitations discussed in Section 8.2.1. The communication between hosts with ambiguous (or private) IP addresses (via the Internet) or that between hosts behind secure gateways can be secured with ESP authentication service because the source and destination IP address fields and other fields in the IP header are not authenticated. Therefore, NAT and security gateways can change relevant IP header fields in a datagram and, provided that the header checksum[2] is recomputed correctly after the modification and none of the ESP header fields are modified, the destination node will successfully authenticate the datagram.

This degree of flexibility that the ESP authentication service offers, however, accounts for its weakness. Apart from the ESP header, any of the IP header fields can be modified while a datagram is in transit from the source node to the destination and, provided that the header checksum is recomputed correctly after the modification (if the SA in question only uses ESP authentication and confidentiality services), the destination host will not detect the modification. ESP transport mode authentication service, therefore, offers less security than that provided by the AH transport mode. Hence, if a high degree of security is needed and the communicating peers have public IP addresses, AH authentication service should be utilized instead of or in conjunction with ESP transport mode authentication service.

---

[2]We discussed the computation of the IP header checksum in Chapter 7; see this chapter for further details.

It is noteworthy to mention that ESP in transport mode does not offer any traffic flow confidentiality service since the source and destination IP address fields are not encrypted.

9.2.2 ESP Tunnel Mode

In tunnel mode, ESP is inserted before the original IP header, and a new IP header is inserted in front of the ESP header. This is illustrated diagrammatically for IPv4 in Figure 9-4. For IPv6 datagrams, in addition to the new IP header, the extension headers present in the original IPv6 datagram are also inserted in front of the ESP header. Figure 9-5 illustrates this for IPv6 datagrams.

The inner IP header carries the true source (the node that generated the packet) and the final destination address. The outer source and destination IP header fields can carry the source and destination nodes' security gateways, respectively. Consequently, the source addresses in the inner and outer IP headers may be different. The same holds for the destination address.

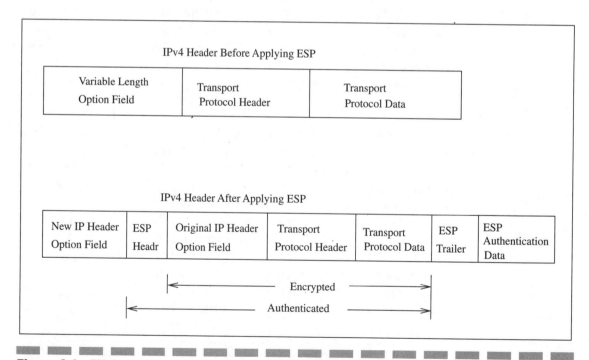

Figure 9-4 ESP Relative to Other IPv4 Header Fields in Tunnel Mode

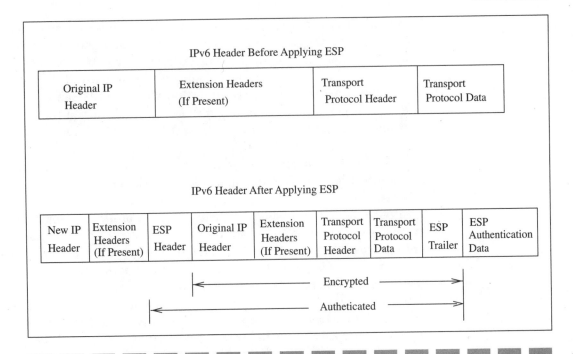

Figure 9-5   ESP Relative to Other IPv6 Extension Headers in Tunnel Mode

As is the case for transport mode, the ESP header field consists of the SPI and sequence number fields, whereas the ESP trailer field consists of the padding, pad length, and next header fields. The portions of the IPv4 and IPv6 datagrams that are encrypted or authenticated are indicated in Figures 9-4 and 9-5, respectively. The ESP header and trailer fields are not encrypted because these fields contain information the destination nodes need to identify the SA for the traffic that the datagrams are a part of or information that might be necessary to process the datagrams prior to them being encrypted.

Note that for the tunnel mode authentication and confidentiality services the entire inner IP header is authenticated and encrypted. However, the outer IP header is neither authenticated nor encrypted. It is not encrypted because routers need the information in it to route the packet. It is not authenticated because if it were, it would suffer from the same limitations, discussed in Sections 8.2.1 and 8.2.2, that are associated with AH authentication service. That is, if the outer IP header were authenticated, ESP tunnel mode authentication service, like that of AH, would not be able to authenticate end-to-end traffic between hosts that are behind

NAT or security gateways that modify the source or destination address fields of packets they forward. The modifications that gateways make to the packets would cause the authentication to fail at the receiver host.

It is important to note that ESP tunnel mode authentication and confidentiality services offer more security than those of ESP transport mode since the former, unlike the latter, authenticate and encrypt the original IP header. However, tunnel mode services utilize more bandwidth than transport mode services because an extra IP header is inserted on datagrams that are protected by tunnel mode services. Therefore, if bandwidth utilization is a big concern, transport mode services might be more suitable.

Although ESP tunnel mode authentication theoretically does not offer as much security as either AH transport or tunnel mode authentication—since it does not authenticate the outer IP header—the security it offers is nonetheless adequate because it is the information in the inner IP header that is used to process the packet.

It is also noteworthy to mention that ESP tunnel mode confidentiality service, particularly when implemented on security gateways, provides confidentiality service for the traffic flow, in that the inner IP header—which contains the IP address from which the packet originated—is encrypted.

9.3 ESP Processing

Let us now look at what is involved in processing packets that are protected with ESP service. The details of processing procedures may vary with different implementations of IPSec; however, in general, the procedure is as outlined below.

9.3.1 Outbound Processing

When an IPSec implementation receives an outbound packet, it uses the relevant selectors (destination IP address and port, transport protocol, etc.) to search the security policy database (SPD) and ascertain what policy is applicable to the traffic. If IPSec processing is required and a SA or SA bundle has already been established, the SPD entry that matches the selectors in the packet will point to the appropriate SA in the security association database (SAD). If a SA has not been established, the IPSec implementation will employ the IKE (Internet key exchange) protocol to negotiate a SA and link it to the SPD entry. The SA is then used to process the packet as follows:

1. *Generate or increment sequence number:* The sequence number is used to prevent replay of previously transmitted packets. When a new SA is established, the sender initializes its sequence number counter to zero. For each packet that the sender transmits, it increases the sequence number by 1 and inserts the resulting value of the sequence number counter into the sequence number field of the ESP packet.

2. *Encryption of the packet:* If the traffic requires confidentiality services, the SA will specify the encryption algorithm to be used. The available choices of encryption algorithms depend on the IPSec implementation; however, as mentioned previously, only symmetric-key cryptosystems are currently used because of the slow execution speed of public-key cryptosystems compared to symmetric-key ciphers. When the encryption algorithm requires an initial vector (IV), as is the case with DES in CBC,[3] the IV is carried in the first few bytes of the payload data field. When encryption service is required, the packet must be encrypted before the calculation of the integrity check value (ICV).

3. *Calculate the integrity check value:* If the SA for the packet stipulates that ESP authentication service should be applied, the ICV is calculated using the values in all the fields of the ESP header except the authentication data field, which will ultimately store the computed ICV. The SA for the packet specifies the message authentication code (MAC) algorithm that should be used to generate the ICV. The available choices of authentication algorithms vary with different IPSec implementations. However, for interoperability, the ESP specification stipulated that all implementations must support HMAC-MD5 and HMAC-SHA-1. The authentication algorithms require cryptographic keys to generate the ICV. The IKE protocol is responsible for negotiating and establishing necessary cryptographic keys and other SA parameters. We discuss IKE in later chapters.

4. *Fragmentation:* If fragmentation is required, the maximum transfer unit (MTU) of the path from the packet's source to its destination is discovered by suitable means[4] The packet is then broken into the appropriate sizes and sent to the destination node.

---

[3]We discussed the modes of block ciphers in Section 2.3.3.
[4]For details on path MTU discovery, see RFC 1191.

9.3.2   Inbound Processing

When a packet arrives at an IPSec host or security gateway, if the more fragment (MF) bit is set this is an indication that there are other fragments that are yet to arrive. The IPSec application waits until a fragment arrives with a sequence number that is similar to the previous ones, and has the MF bit not set. It then reassembles the IP fragments and performs the following steps:

1. It uses the destination IP address and IPSec protocol in the IP header (outer IP header if in tunnel mode) and the SPI in the ESP header to look up the SA for the packet in the inbound SAD. If the lookup fails, it drops the packet and audits the event.

2. It uses the SA found in step 1 to process the ESP packet. This involves first checking to determine whether the selectors in the IP headers (inner header if tunnel mode) match those in the SA. If the selectors do not match, the application drops the packet and audits the event. If the selectors match, the IPSec application keeps track of the SA and the order in which it is applied relative to the others, and continues to do steps 1 and 2 until it encounters a transport layer protocol—for IPv4 datagrams, or a non-IPSec extension header—for IPv6 datagrams.

3. It uses the selectors in the packet to find a policy in the inbound SPD whose selectors match those of the packet.

4. It checks whether the SAs found in steps 1 and 2 match the policy specified in step 3. If the check fails, it repeats steps 4 and 5 until all policy entries have been checked or until the check succeeds.

5. If anti-replay is enabled, it uses the anti-replay window of the SA—as discussed earlier in the chapter—to determine if the packet is a replay. If the packet is a replay, it drops the packet and audits the event.

6. If the SA stipulates that authentication service is required, the authentication algorithm and the private key specified by the SA bundle are used to calculate the ICV for the packet and compare it with the value stored in the ESP authentication data field. If the two values differ, the packet is discarded and the event audited.

7. If the SA indicates the confidentiality service is required, the cryptographic algorithm and the key that the SA specifies are utilized to decrypt the packet. Decryption processes are, in general, quite CPU- and memory-intensive. If the IPSec system is allowed to

perform unnecessary decryption or encryption of packets, then the system will be vulnerable to denial of service attack. Consequently, when decryption or encryption is required, this service is applied only after the packet has been successfully authenticated.

At the end of these steps, if the packet have not been discarded, it is then passed to the transport layer protocol or is forwarded to the node indicated in the destination IP address field.

ISAKMP

Overview of Chapter 10

In this chapter, we discuss the following topics:

- ISAKMP Header Format
- ISAKMP Payload Formats
- ISAKMP Negotiation Phases
- ISAKMP Exchange Types

The Internet Security Association Key Management Protocol (ISAKMP) defines procedures and packet formats to negotiate, establish, modify, and delete SAs. ISAKMP provides a common framework for the format of SA attributes and the methodologies for negotiating, modifying, and deleting SAs that different key exchange protocols can use. ISAKMP was designed to be key exchange independent; it is not bound to any specific key exchange protocol, nor is it bound to any particular cryptographic algorithm, key generation technique, or authentication mechanism.

ISAKMP provides networking elements with the ability to present—in an authenticated and protected manner—to communicating peers the functionalities they support for agreement on common security attributes. ISAKMP messages can be transmitted via the UDP or TCP transport protocol. UDP and TCP port 500 have been reserved for ISAKMP by IANA (Internet Assigned Number Authority), the organization that is responsible for assigning protocol numbers and other assigned services.

The information ISAKMP peers exchange is transmitted in what are called *payloads*. At the time of writing, ISAKMP had defined 13 payloads. These payloads provide modular building blocks for constructing ISAKMP messages. We present all 13 ISAKMP payloads in this chapter. The presentation is adapted from RFC 2408 [MSST98], which contains the original specification of ISAKMP. Before we proceed with a description of the payload types, let us look at the ISAKMP header format.

10.1   ISAKMP Header Format

ISAKMP messages consist of a fixed-length header followed by a variable number of payloads. The fixed-length header contains the necessary information for the protocol to maintain state and process the payloads. The ISAKMP header format is illustrated in Figure 10-1. A description of the ISAKMP header fields follows:

- *Initiator Cookie:* This field contains a unique 8-byte (64-bit) bitstring that is generated by the initiator of the ISAKMP exchanges. It is used as an anticlogging protection agent; it helps the communicating peers to ascertain whether or not a particular message originated from the other peer. If the initiator determines that the cookie in the Responder Cookie field does not match the cookie it previously received from the responder, it discards the message; similarly, if the responder ascertains that the Initiator Cookie field

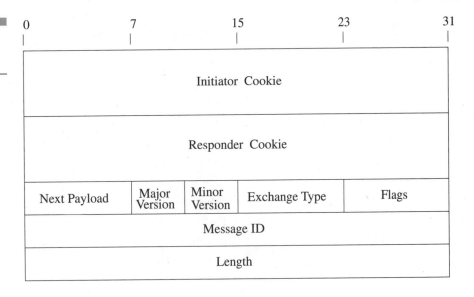

Figure 10-1
ISAKMP Header
Format

does not match the cookie it previously received from the initiator, it drops the message without any further processing. This mechanism provides protection against denial of service attacks. The method of generating the cookies varies with different implementations of ISAKMP; however, the protocol specifies that the cookies, whether those of the initiator or responder, should be generated using secret information that is unique to the respective ISAKMP communicating hosts, and it should not be possible to determine the secret information from the cookie. In addition, the cookie for each SA should be unique. A possible method of generating cookies is to perform a hash—using MD5, SHA-1, or any supported hash function—of the concatenation of the source and destination address, UDP source and destination ports, a locally generated secret random number, and the current date and time. The first 64 bits of the message digest are then selected as the cookie.

- *Responder Cookie:* This field contains the responder's 8-byte cookie. The attributes of this cookie are similar to those of the initiator's cookie.

- *Next Payload:* This is an 8-bit field that indicates the first payload in the message. Table 10-1 shows the payloads that ISAKMP currently defines and the value that is assigned to each payload.

TABLE 10-1

Assigned Values for
ISAKMP Payloads

Next Payload Type	Assigned Value
None	0
Security Association	1
Proposal	2
Transform	3
Key Exchange	4
Identification	5
Certificate	6
Certificate Request	7
Hash	8
Signature	9
Nonce	10
Notification	11
Delete	12
Vendor	13
RESERVED	14–127
Private Use	128–255

■ *Major Version:* This 4-bit field indicates the major version of the ISAKMP protocol in use. The specification for ISAKMP stipulates that an ISAKMP implementation should not accept packets with a major version or minor version that is larger than its own.

■ *Minor Version:* This 4-bit field contains the protocol's minor version number.

■ *Exchange Type:* This 8-bit field indicates the type of exchange of which the message is comprised. Table 10-2 shows the exchange types that ISAKMP currently defines.

■ *Flag:* This 8-bit field indicates specific options that are set for ISAKMP exchanges. The first 3 bits of this field are currently used, and the others are set to zero before transmission. A description of these flag bits follows:

1. *Encryption bit:* This is the least significant of the flag bits. When it is set to 1, all payloads following the header are encrypted using the encryption algorithm specified in the ISAKMP SA. However, when this bit is set to zero, the payload is not encrypted.

TABLE 10-2

ISAKMP Exchange
Types and Assigned
Values

Exchange Type	Assigned Value
NONE	0
Base	1
Identity Protection	2
Authentication Only	3
Aggressive	4
Informational	5
ISAKMP Future Use	6–31
DOI Specific Use	32–239
Private Use	240–255

2. *Commit bit:* This is the second bit of the Flag field. It is used to ensure that encrypted data are not received before the establishment of the SA is completed. When this bit is set to 1, the communicating peer that did not set the bit must wait until it receives an information exchange containing a notify payload with the CONNECTED Notify message from the peer that set the commit bit.

3. *Authentication only bit:* This is the third bit of the flag bits. It allows the transmission of information with an integrity check using the authentication algorithm specified in the SA, but with no encryption.

■ *Message ID:* This is a 4-byte field that contains a random value generated by the initiator of the phase 2 negotiation (we discuss ISAKMP exchange phases later in this chapter). It serves as a unique message identifier that is used to identify the protocol state during phase 2 negotiations.

■ *Length:* This is a 4-byte field that indicates the length of the total message (header plus payloads) in bytes.

10.2   ISAKMP Payloads Formats

Let us now take a look at the formats of the different ISAKMP payloads. We start with the generic payload header.

10.2.1 Generic Payload Header

Each ISAKMP payload begins with a generic header. The generic payload header clearly defines the boundaries of the payload and consequently allows the chaining of different payloads. Figure 10-2 illustrates the generic payload header. A description of the generic payload header fields follows:

■ *Next Payload:* This 8-bit field identifies the payload type that follows the payload in question. If the current payload is the last payload of the message, the Next Payload field will be set to zero.

■ *RESERVED:* This field is unused and it is set to zero.

■ *Payload Length:* This field contains the length in bytes of the current payload including the generic payload header. This is a 2-byte field.

10.2.2 Data Attributes

Data attributes are data structures that can be used to represent SA attributes. SA attributes are used to pass miscellaneous values or information between ISAKMP peers. For example, information about encapsulation mode (transport or tunnel mode) is transmitted to ISAKMP peers using data attributes. The format for data attributes provides flexibility for the representation of many different types of information. Data attributes are not ISAKMP payloads; however, they can be contained within ISAKMP payloads (as will be seen when we discuss the transform payload), and there can be multiple data attributes within a payload. Figure 10-3 illustrates the format of data attributes. A description of the data attribute fields follows:

■ *Attribute Type:* This is a 16-bit field. It contains a unique identifier of the attribute type. Table 10-3 shows the SA attribute types defined at the time of writing. The number of supported attributes

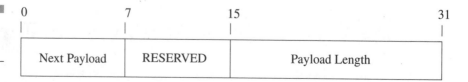

Figure 10-2
Generic Payload
Header Format

0	7	15	31
Next Payload	RESERVED	Payload Length	

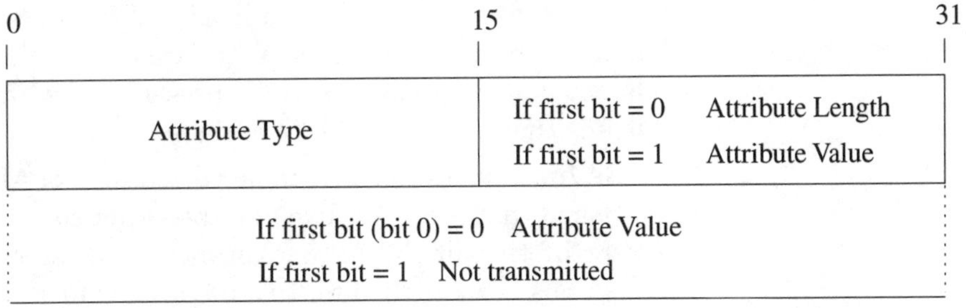

Figure 10-3
Data Attributes

0	15	31
Attribute Type	If first bit = 0 Attribute Length	
	If first bit = 1 Attribute Value	

If first bit (bit 0) = 0   Attribute Value
If first bit = 1   Not transmitted

typically depends on the IPSec implementation; however, for inter-operability the IPSec ISAKMP DOI specification (RFC 2407) stipulates that all implementation must support the following three attributes:

SA Life Type

SA Life Duration

Authentication Algorithm

The most significant (MS) bit of the Attribute Type field (bit 0 in Figure 10-3) dictates whether the data attribute is of fixed or variable length. If the MS bit is zero, the attribute type will be of variable length and the data attribute will have three fields: Attribute Type, Attribute Length, and Attribute Value. If the MS bit is 1, the attribute type will be of fixed length and the data attribute will have only two fields: Attribute Type and Attribute Value.

TABLE 10-3

SA Attribute Types

Class	Value	Length
SA Life Type	1	Fixed
SA Life Duration	2	Variable
Group Description	3	Fixed
Encapsulation Mode	4	Fixed
Authentication Algorithm	5	Fixed
Key Length	6	Fixed
Key Rounds	7	Fixed
Compress Dictionary Size	8	Fixed
Compress Private Algorithm	9	Variable

Let us take a more detailed look at Table 10-3. The first column contains the attribute class. At the time of writing not all of these classes had assigned values. We present below the attribute classes that had class values assigned.

SA life type: Recall that in our discussion of AH and ESP we mentioned that there are two variables that can be used to measure the lifetime of an SA: time duration and the number of bytes the SA has been applied to. Two life type values have therefore been defined. They are:

—RESERVED   0

—Seconds   1

—Kilobytes   2

Let us look at an example. Suppose a host needs to convey to an ISAKMP peer that it desires a given SA to be terminated 10,800 seconds (3 hours) after it has been established. The peer would send two data attributes within a transform payload (we discuss the transform payload later in the chapter). The MS bit of the first data attribute would have a 1, indicating that it is a fixed-length attribute with only two fields: Data Type and Data Value. The first field would have the bit-string 1000000000000001, and the second field would have the 16-bit binary equivalent of 1, that is, 0000000000000001, indicating that the SA lifetime should be measured in seconds. The second data attribute would have a 1 in the MS bit and a value of 2 in the remaining 15 bits of the Attribute Type field, that is, 000000000000010, indicating that this is an SA Life Duration class. The Attribute Value field of this data attribute would then contain the binary equivalent of 10,800, that is, 0010101000110000.

Encapsulation mode: This is the mode of operation, AH or ESP. The assigned values are:

—RESERVED   0

—Tunnel   1

—Transport   2

Authentication algorithm: This indicates that the algorithm is to be used to provide integrity protection. The values for the algorithms are shown in Table 10-4. The number of supported algorithms depends on the the IPSec implementation; however, each IPSec-compliant implementation must support HMAC-MD5 and HMAC-SHA.

TABLE 10-4

Authentication
Algorithm Values

Name	Description	Value
RESERVED	Unused	0
HMAC-MD5	Described in Chapter 4	1
HMAC-SHA	HMAC-SHA-1 authentication algorithm	2
DES-MAC	DES used as an authentication algorithm	3
KPDK	Addressed in RFC 2407	4
HMAC-SHA2-256	HMAC-SHA2 with a 256-bit message digest	5
HMAC-SHA2-384	HMAC-SHA2 with a 384-bit message digest	6
HMAC-SHA2-512	HMAC-SHA2 with a 512-bit message digest	7
HMAC-RIPEMD	HMAC-RIPEMD-160 (discussed in Chapter 4)	8

- *Attribute Length:* This 16-bit field contains the length in bytes of the Attribute Value field. This field is present only if the MS bit of the data attribute is zero.
- *Attribute Value:* This field is of fixed length (16-bit) if the MS bit is 1, and of variable length otherwise.

10.2.3   Security Association Payload

The security association payload is used to negotiate the SA and to indicate the DOI (Domain of Interpretation) under which the negotiation takes place. A DOI defines payload formats, exchange types, and conventions for naming relevant information (cryptographic algorithms, modes, etc.). RFC 2407 [Pip98] outlined the DOI for ISAKMP. The format of the security association payload depends on the applicable DOI. Figure 10-4 illustrates the format of this payload for the IPSec DOI. A description of the fields in the security association payload follows.

- *Next Payload:* The Next Payload field identifies the payload type of the next payload in the message. A value of zero in this 8-bit field indicates that the payload under consideration is the last payload in the message.
- *RESERVED:* The RESERVED field is unused. This 8-bit field must be set to zero.
- *Payload Length:* This 16-bit field contains the length in bytes of the current payload, including the generic payload header.

Figure 10-4

Security Association
Payload Format

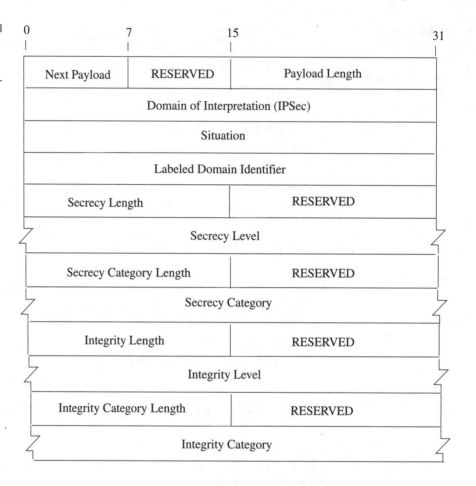

- *DOI:* This 32-bit field contains a 4-byte unsigned integer which identifies the DOI under which the negotiation is taking place. For IPSec DOIs, the value in this field is 1. This field is mandatory for all SA payloads.

- *Situation:* This 32-bit field identifies the situation under which the negotiation is taking place. A situation, in this context, is the information that will be used to determine the required security service. RFC 2407 [Pip98] defined three situations for the IPSec DOI; we present a brief description of these situations below:

  SIT_IDENTITY_ONLY: This situation type is assigned a value of 1. It specifies that the SA will be identified by source identity information present in an associated identification payload. We discuss the identification payload shortly.

SIT_SECRECY: The assigned number for this situation type is 2. The SIT_SECRECY type indicates that the SA is being negotiated in an environment that requires labeled secrecy.

SIT_INTEGRITY: The SIT_INTEGRITY type is assigned a value of 4. It indicates that the SA is being negotiated in an environment that requires labeled integrity.

- *Labeled Domain Identifier:* This is a 32-bit field. It contains an IANA-assigned number that is used to interpret the secrecy and integrity information.

- *Secrecy Length:* this 16-bit field specifies the length in bytes of the secrecy level identifier, excluding padding bits.

- *RESERVED:* The 16-bit RESERVED fields are unused and must be set to zero.

- *Secrecy Level:* This variable-length field indicates the secrecy level required. The IPSec DOI document (RFC 2407) stipulated that this field must be padded with zeros to align on the next 32-bit boundary.

- *Secrecy Category Length:* This 16-bit field specifies the length in bits of the secrecy category bitmap, excluding the pad bits.

- *Secrecy Category:* This variable-length field contains a bitmap that is used to designate required secrecy categories. If necessary, the bitmap must be padded with zeros to align on the next 32-bit boundary.

- *Integrity Length:* This 16-bit field indicates the length in bytes of the integrity level identifier, excluding pad bits.

- *Integrity Level:* This variable-length field specifies the integrity level required. The integrity level must be padded with zeros to align on the next 32-bit boundary.

- *Integrity Category Length:* This 16-bit field specifies the length in bits of the integrity category bitmap, excluding the pad bits.

- *Integrity Category:* This variable-length field contains a bitmap that is used to designate required integrity categories. If necessary, the bitmap must be padded with zeros to align on the next 32-bit boundary.

10.2.4   Proposal Payload

The proposal payload contains information used during SA negotiations. This payload provides the framework for the initiator of the ISAKMP exchange to present to the recipient the preferred security protocols and associated security mechanisms desired for the SA being negotiated. The proposal payload is illustrated in Figure 10-5. Let us now look at the fields that comprise the proposal payload.

- *Next Payload:* This 8-bit field identifies the payload type of the next payload in the message. This field can only contain the value 2, indicating that another proposal payload follows, or zero, indicating that this is the last payload in the message.

- *RESERVED:* This 8-bit field is unused and must be set to zero.

- *Payload Length:* This 16-bit field contains the length in bytes of the entire proposal payload, including the generic payload header, the proposal payload, and all the transform payloads associated with this payload.

- *Proposal Number:* This 8-bit field contains the identification number of the proposal for the current payload. The proposal number allows the peers that are involved in the SA establishment negotiation to present preferences to their communicating peers in the form of logical AND or OR operations. For example, if the initiator of the exchange wishes to inform the other peer that it desires a combined protection suite consisting of ESP encryption with Triple-DES and authentication with HMAC-SHA-1 and AH authentication with HMAC-MD5, it would send a message that contains three proposal payloads, each with the same proposal number. However, if the peer needs to transmit the information that it requires with either ESP authentication with HMAC-MD5 or AH authentication with HMAC-SHA-1, it would send a message

Figure 10-5
Proposal Payload Format

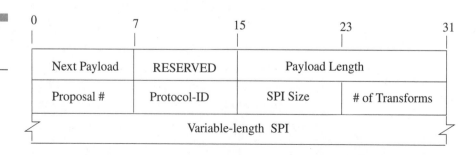

TABLE 10-5

IPSec Protocol
Identifiers

Protocol Identifier	Description	Value
RESERVED	Unassigned	0
PROTO_ISAKMP	Protocol identifier for ISAKMP	1
PROTO_IPSEC_AH	Protocol identifier for AH	2
PROTO_IPSEC_ESP	Protocol identifier for ESP	3
PROTO_IPCOMP	Protocol identifier for IP compression	4

consisting of two proposal payloads, each with monotonically increasing proposal numbers. The proposal number here indicates the order of preference of the proposals: the greater the preference, the smaller the proposal number.

■ *Protocol ID:* This 8-bit field contains the protocol identifier. At the time of writing, the protocol identifiers and the assigned values, as outlined by RFC 2407, the IPSec DOI document, are indicated in Table 10-5.

■ *SPI Size:* Contains the length in bytes of the SPI (security parameter index) of the protocol specified by the Protocol-ID field. If the protocol is ISAKMP, the SPI is the initiator-responder cookie pair. The length of this field is 8 bits.

■ *Number of Transforms:* This 8-bit field gives the number of transforms for the proposal. Each of the transforms specified is embodied in a transform payload. We discuss the transform payload shortly.

■ *SPI:* This is a variable-length field that contains the source node SPI.

10.2.5   Transform Payload

The transform payload provides the framework for the initiating peer to present different security mechanisms for a given protocol during the negotiation to establish a SA. The proposal payload identifies a protocol for which services are being negotiated. The transform payload allows the initiating peer to present the supported transform or mode of operation of the proposed protocol. Figure 10-6 illustrates the format of the transform payload. A description of the transform payload fields follows:

- *Next Payload:* The 8-bit Next Payload field identifies the payload type that follows the current payload. This field will either contains the value 3 or zero. If another transform payload follows the current transform payload, the value in this field will be 3; however, if the current transform payload is the last one for the proposed protocol, the value in this field will be zero.

- *RESERVED:* Reserved for future use. The value of this 8-bit field must be zero.

- *Payload Length:* Contains the length of the current payload (including the generic payload header, transform values, and all SA attributes) in bytes. The length of the Payload Length field is 16 bits.

- *Transform Number:* This 8-bit field identifies the transform number for the current payload. If there are more than one transforms for the proposed protocol, each transform will be embodied in a transform payload and each transform is identified by a monotonically increasing number. The transforms are ordered according to the initiating peer's preference: the most desired transform has the lowest transform number.

- *Transform ID:* This 8-bit field specifies the transform identifier for the proposed protocol. If the protocol being used to protect the communication between the peers is ISAKMP—as is the case for ISAKMP phase 1 negotiation (we discuss ISAKMP phases later in the chapter)—the transform identifiers and assigned values are:

    RESERVED: The assigned value is zero, and this value is reserved for future use.

    KEY_IKE: Identifies the IKE (Internet Key Exchange) protocol. The assigned value is 1. We discuss IKE in the next chapter.

Figure 10-6
Transform Payload Format

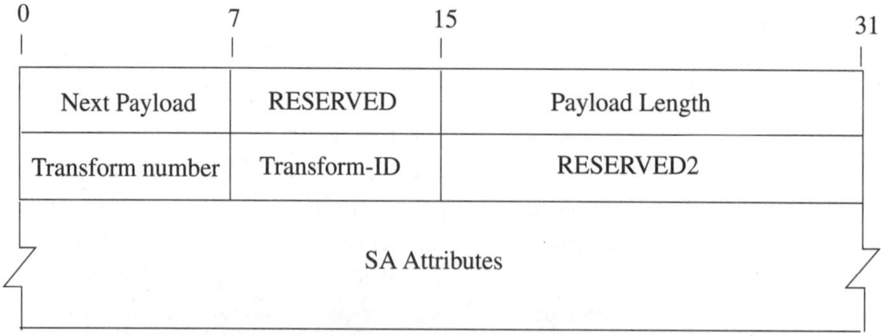

0	7	15	31
Next Payload	RESERVED	Payload Length	
Transform number	Transform-ID	RESERVED2	
SA Attributes			

TABLE 10-6

AH Transform
Identifiers

Transform ID	Description	Value
RESERVED	Unused	0–1
AH_MD5	Any generic MAC (message authentication code) using MD5	2
AH_SHA	Any generic MAC using the SHA-1 authentication algorithm	3
AH_DES	A DES used as an authentication algorithm	4
AH_SHA2-256	A generic MAC using SHA-2 with a 256-bit message digest	5
AH_SHA2-384	A generic MAC using SHA-2 with a 384-bit message digest	6
AH_SHA2-512	A generic MAC using SHA-2 with a 512-bit message digest	7
AH_RIPEMD	A generic MAC using RIPEMD-160 (discussed in Chapter 4)	8

Tables 10-6, 10-7 and 10-8 present the transform identifiers and the assigned values for AH, ESP, and the IP Compression protocol (IPComp). The transform identifiers presented in these tables are the ones defined at the time of writing. New transform identifiers are periodically defined and added to the lists. For updated lists of the ISAKMP IPSEC transform identifiers see the IANA home page (http://www.iana.org).

TABLE 10-7

ESP Transform
Identifiers

Transform ID	Description	Value
Reserved	Unused	0
ESP_DES_IV64	DES in CBC mode with a 64-bit IV (presented in Chapter 2)	1
ESP_DES	DES in CBC mode	2
ESP_3DES	Triple DES	3
ESP_RC5	RC5 cipher (outlined in RFC 2451)	4
ESP_IDEA	IDEA (discussed in Chapter 2)	5
ESP_CAST	CAST-128 (presented in Chapter 2)	6
ESP_BLOWFISH	Blowfish cipher (presented in Chapter 2)	7
ESP_3IDEA	Triple-IDEA	8
ESP_DES_IV32	DES in CBC mode with a 32-bit IV	9
ESP_RC4	A stream cipher developed by a RSA team	10
ESP_NULL	No confidentiality service	11
ESP_AES	AES (Rijndael); presented in Chapter 2	12

Transform ID	Description	Value
RESERVED	Unused	0
IPCOMP_OUI	A proprietary compression algorithm	1
IPCOMP_DEFLATE	IPCom using DEFLATE compression algorithm (Chapter 12)	2
IPCOMP_LZS	IPCom using LZS compression algorithm (Chapter 12)	3

- *RESERVED2:* This 16-bit field is unused and is set to zero.
- *SA Attributes:* This variable-length field contains the SA attributes for the transform specified by the Transform ID field. SA attributes are used to pass miscellaneous values such as mode of operation (tunnel or transport mode) between ISAKMP communicating peers. We presented the SA attribute types earlier in Table 10-3.

10.2.6 Key Exchange Payload

The key exchange payload is used to transport key exchange data. This payload is not restricted to any particular key exchange protocol; it can be used to transport key exchange data for any of the commonly used key exchange protocols. Figure 10-7 illustrates the key exchange payload format. We give a description of the fields of this payload below:

- *Next Payload:* This 8-bit field identifies the payload type of the next payload in the message. A value of zero in this field indicates that the payload under consideration is the last payload in the message.
- *RESERVED:* This 8-bit field is unused and must be set to zero.

Figure 10-7
Key Exchange
Payload Format

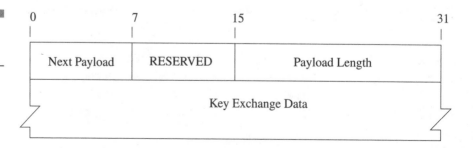

- *Payload Length:* This 16-bit field contains the length in bytes of the current payload, including the generic payload header.
- *Key Exchange Data:* This field is of variable length and contains the data required to generate a session key. The DOI for the respective key exchange specifies the format and the interpretation of the data in this field.

10.2.7   Identification Payload

The identification payload allows communicating peers to exchange identity information. The information contained in this payload is used to ascertain the identities of the initiator of the SA negotiation. The responder uses the identity information to determine the security policy that should be applied for the SA. Figure 10-8 illustrates the format of this payload. The Next Payload, RESERVED and Payload Length fields are similar to those of the payload previously discussed. A description of the other fields follows:

- *ID Type:* The value of this 8-bit field describes the identity information found in the Identification Data field.
- *Protocol ID:* The value of this 8-bit field specifies an IP protocol ID, example UDP (a value of 17), or TCP (a value of 6). A value of zero indicates that this field should be ignored.
- *Port:* This 16-bit field specifies an associated port. A value of zero indicates that the port should be ignored.
- *Identification Data:* This variable-length field contains identification information specified by the ID Type field. Table 10-9 lists the assigned values for the identification type.

Figure 10-8
Identification
Payload Format

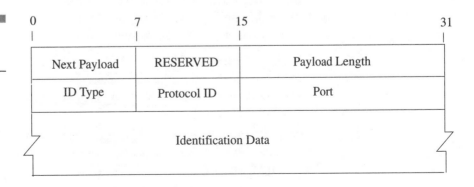

TABLE 10-9

Identification Type
Values for the
Identification
Payload

ID Type	Description	Value
RESERVED	Unused	0
ID_IPV4_ADDR	A single 4-byte IPv4 address	1
ID_FQDN	A fully-qualified domain name string, e.g., bert.cs.mcgill.ca	2
ID_USER_FQDN	A fully-qualified username string, e.g., luc@bert.cs.mcgill.ca	3
ID_IPV4_ADDR_SUBNET	An IPv4 address followed by a 4-byte subnet mask, e.g., 132.206.50.12 255.255.255.0	4
ID_IPV6_ADDR	A single 16-byte IPv6 address	5
ID_IPV6_ADDR_SUBNET	An IPv6 address followed by a 16-bit subnet mask	6
ID_IPV4_ADDR_RANGE	A range of IPv4 addresses, 132.206.50.1 132.206.50.254	7
ID_IPV6_ADDR_RANGE	A range of IPv6 addresses	8
ID_DER_ASN1_DN	Binary DER encoding of an ASN.1 X.500 DN (discussed in Chapter 5)	9
ID_DER_ASN1_GN	Binary DER encoding of an ASN.1 X.500 generalName (discussed in Chapter 5)	10
ID_KEY_ID	Byte stream used to pass vendor-specific information	11

10.2.8 Certificate Payload

The certificate payload allows communicating peers to exchange certificates or certificate-related material using the ISAKMP protocol. Figure 10-9 illustrates the format of this payload. The Next Payload, RESERVED, and Payload Length fields are similar to those of the payloads previously discussed. We describe the other fields below:

■ *Certificate Encoding:* This 8-bit field identifies the kind of certificate or certificate-related information the Certificate Data field contains. Table 10-10 indicates the assigned values for the different certificate types.

■ *Certificate Data:* This variable-length field contains the actual certificate data for the certificate type specified in the Certificate Encoding field.

Figure 10-9
Certificate
Payload Format

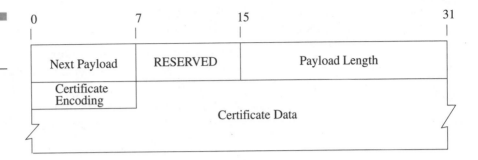

Let us take a brief look at the different certificate types in Table 10-10.

■ *None:* A value of zero in the Certificate Encoding field indicates that certificate payload does not contain any certificate-related data.

■ *PKCS #7* (Public Key Cryptography Standards #7): The Cryptographic Message Syntax Standard is a standard developed by RSA Laboratories. This standard describes a general syntax for data that may have cryptography applied to it. PKCS #7 is commonly used for wrapping and transporting digital certificates, cryptographic keys, digital signatures, and other cryptographic data. RFC 2315 [Kal98] contains the specifications for PKCS #7.

TABLE 10-10

Certificate Types
and Assigned
Values

Certificate Type	Assigned Value
NONE	0
PKCS #7 wrapped X.509 certificate	1
PGP certificate	2
DNS signed key	3
X.509 certificate–Signature	4
X.509 certificate–Key Exchange	5
Kerberos tokens	6
CRL (certificate revocation list)	7
ARL (authority revocation list)	8
SPKI certificate	9
X.509 certificate–Attribute	10
RESERVED	11–255

- *PGP certificate:* Developed by Phil Zimmermann and PGP Inc. For detail about this certificate format refer to Chapter 5.

- *DNS signed key:* Used by DNS (domain name service) systems with DNSSec (domain name system security extensions). DNSSec provides security to DNS by offering data integrity and authentication to security-aware resolvers and applications via the use of cryptographic digital signatures. The specification for DNSSec is outlined in RFC 2535 [Eas99].

- *X.509 certificates* The most commonly used digital certificates. We discuss this certificate format in Chapter 5.

- *Kerberos:* A security protocol that provides a mechanism for verifying the identities of workstation users and network servers on open networks. A Kerberos token is a data structure that grants the bearer permission to access an object or service protected by the Kerberos protocol. RFC 1510 [KN93] contains the specifications of Kerberos.

- *CRL (certificate revocation list):* A time-stamped list identifying revoked certificates that were issued by a CA (certificate authority). We discuss CRLs in Chapter 5.

- *ARL (authority revocation list):* Similar to a CRL, except that an ARL is signed by a designated authority rather than by the CA that issued the certificates.

- *SPKI certificates:* Digital certificates whose main purpose is authorization rather than authentication. RFC 2693 [EFLR99] outlines the theory of SPKI certificates.

- *X.509 certificate attributes:* Data structures that include additional information in X.509 certificates. We discuss X.509 attributes in Chapter 5.

10.2.9 Certificate Request Payload

The certificate request payload provides the capability for communicating peers to request certificates using ISAKMP. The responder of a certificate request payload, if it supports certificates, is required to transmit the requested certificate using the certificate payload. If more than one certificates are required, the equivalent number of certificate request payloads should be sent. Figure 10-10 shows the format of the certificate request payload. The fields in this payload are as follows:

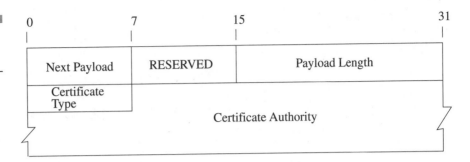

Figure 10-10
Certificate Request
Payload Format

- *Next Payload:* This 8-bit field identifies the payload type of the next payload in the ISAKMP message. If the payload under consideration is the last payload in the message, the value in this field must be zero.

- *RESERVED:* This 8-bit field is unused and is set to zero.

- *Payload Length:* This 16-bit field contains the length of the current payload, including the generic payload header, in bytes.

- *Certificate Type:* The Certificate Type field is an 8-bit field. It contains an encoding of the type of payload requested. Table 10-10 indicates the supported certificate types and the value assigned to each type.

- *Certificate Authority:* This is a variable-length optional field. If desired, it contains an encoding of an acceptable CA for the type of certificate requested. For example, if an X.509 certificate is required, this field would typically contain the DN (distinguished name) (we present the definition and examples of DNs in Chapter 5) encoding of the issuer name of the X.509 CA acceptable to the sender of the certificate request payload. If the sender of this payload has no particular preference with regard to the CA of the requested certificate, the Certificate Authority field is omitted.

10.2.10 Hash Payload

The hash payload contains the data generated by the hash function selected during the SA negotiation. The data in this payload are typically used to verify the integrity of other data contained in the ISAKMP message or for authentication of the identity of the negotiating entities. Figure 10-11 illustrates the format of the hash payload. The Next Payload,

Figure 10-11

Hash Payload Format

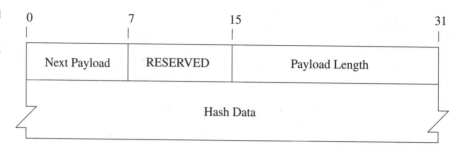

RESERVED, and Payload Length fields are similar to those of the payloads previously discussed. The variable-length Hash Data field contains the message digest that resulted from the application of the hash function to the input data.

10.2.11 Signature Payload

The signature payload contains the data generated by the signature function negotiated for the SA; it is used to verify the integrity of the data in an ISAKMP message and may be used for nonrepudiation services. The format of this payload is illustrated in Figure 10-12. The Next Payload, RESERVED, and Payload Length fields are similar to those of the payloads we previously discussed. The variable-length Signature Data field contains the signature data that resulted from the signing of the ISAKMP message using the digital signature algorithm negotiated for the SA.

10.2.12 Nonce Payload

The nonce payload contains random data that are used to protect the exchange data against replay attacks. If nonce (random data) is used by

Figure 10-12

Signature Payload Format

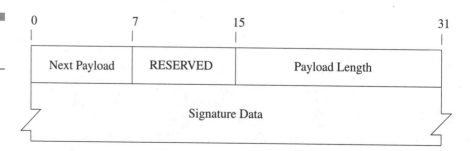

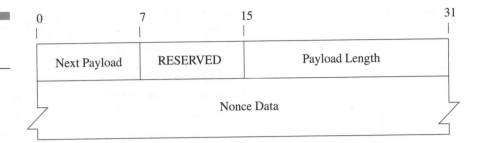

Figure 10-13
Nonce Payload
Format

a given key exchange protocol, the utilization of the nonce payload is dictated by the key exchange mechanism. The nonce may be transmitted as part of the key exchange data of the key exchange payload, or it may be transmitted separately using the nonce payload. Figure 10-13 illustrates the format of this payload. The field that is unique to this payload is the Nonce Data field. This is a variable-length field that contains the random data generated by the entity that is sending the message.

10.2.13 Notification Payload

The notification payload is used to transmit informational data such as error conditions to an ISAKMP peer. Figure 10-14 illustrates the format of this payload. A description of the fields that are unique to this payload follows:

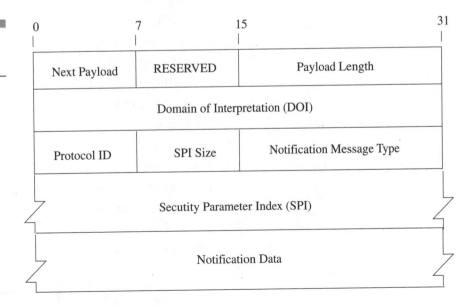

Figure 10-14
Notification Payload
Format

TABLE 10-11

Notification
Messages:
Error Types

Errors	Value
INVALID-PAYLOAD-TYPE	1
DOI-NOT-SUPPORTED	2
SITUATION-NOT-SUPPORTED	3
INVALID-COOKIE	4
INVALID-MAJOR-VERSION	5
INVALID-MINOR-VERSION	6
INVALID-EXCHANGE-TYPE	7
INVALID-FLAGS	8
INVALID-MESSAGE-ID	9
INVALID-PROTOCOL-ID	10
INVALID-SPI	11
INVALID-TRANSFORM-ID	12
ATTRIBUTES-NOT-SUPPORTED	13
NO-PROPOSAL-CHOSEN	14
BAD-PROPOSAL-SYNTAX	15
PAYLOAD-MALFORMED	16
INVALID-KEY-INFORMATION	17
INVALID-ID-INFORMATION	18
INVALID-CERT-ENCODING	19
INVALID-CERTIFICATE	20
CERT-TYPE-UNSUPPORTED	21
INVALID-CERT-AUTHORITY	22
INVALID-HASH-INFORMATION	23
AUTHENTICATION-FAILED	24
INVALID-SIGNATURE	25
ADDRESS-NOTIFICATION	26
NOTIFY-SA-LIFETIME	27
CERTIFICATE-UNAVAILABLE	28
UNSUPPORTED-EXCHANGE-TYPE	29
UNEQUAL-PAYLOAD-LENGTHS	30
RESERVED (for future use)	31–8191
Private (for private use)	8192–16,383

TABLE 10-12

Notification
Messages:
Status Types

Status	Value
CONNECTED	16,384
RESERVED (for future use)	16,385–24,575
DOI-specific codes	24,576–32,767
Private (for private use)	32,768–40,959
RESERVED (for future use)	40,960–65,535

- *DOI (Domain of Interpretation):* This 32-bit field identifies the DOI under which the notification is taking place.
- *Protocol ID:* This 8-bit field specifies the protocol identifier for the current notification. We presented the assigned values for the protocol identifiers earlier in Section 10.2.4.
- *SPI Size:* This is another 8-bit field. It contains the length in bytes of the SPI for the protocol identified in the Protocol ID field. If the protocol identified in the Protocol ID field is ISAKMP, the initiator and responder cookie pair from the ISAKMP header is the ISAKMP SPI and the value in the SPI Size field will be zero since the size of the SPI is irrelevant in this case.
- *Notify Message Type:* This 16-bit field specifies the notification message types. Tables 10-11 and 10-12 present the values assigned to the different message types.
- *SPI (Security Parameter Index):* This variable-length field contains the receiving entity's SPI. The SPI Size field indicates the length of this field.
- *Notification Data:* This is an optional variable-length field that is used to transmit informational or error data in addition to the notification message types shown in Tables 10-11 and 10-12. The values for this field are DOI-specific.

10.2.14   Delete Payload

ISAKMP entities utilize the delete payload to inform peers that a given SA for a particular IPSec protocol (ISAKMP, AH, or ESP) has been moved from their SAD (security association database). It is important to note that the information in this payload is not a request for the responder to delete

Figure 10-15
Delete Payload
Format

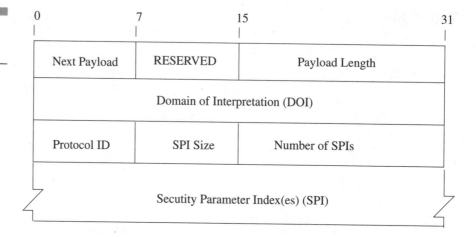

an SA, but an advisory from the initiator to the responder. If the responder chooses to ignore the advisory, the next message from the responder to the initiator using the given SA will fail. An acknowledge to a delete payload is not required. Figure 10-15 indicates the format of this payload. A description of the fields that are unique to this payload follows:

- *DOI:* This 32-bit field identifies the DOI under which the deletion is being performed. Recall that a DOI defines payload formats, exchange types, and conventions for naming relevant information.
- *Protocol ID:* Identifies the protocol (ISAKMP, AH, or ESP) for which the SA is deleted. The protocol IDs are presented in Table 10-5. This is a 8-bit field.
- *SPI Size:* This 8-bit field indicates the length of the SPI bytes, as defined by the Protocol ID field.
- *Number of SPIs:* This 16-bit field specifies the number of SPIs contained in the payload.
- *Security Parameter Indexes (SPIs):* This variable-length field contains the SPIs for the deleted SA. The length of this field depends on the values contained in the SPI Size and the Number of SPIs fields.

10.2.15 Vendor ID Payload

A vendor ID payload is used to pass vendor-defined constants. This payload allows vendors to experiment with new features while maintaining

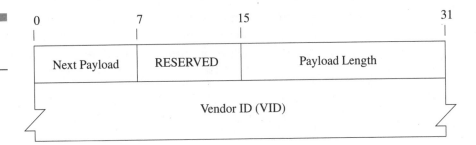

Figure 10-16
Vendor ID Payload
Format

backward compatibility. Figure 10-16 illustrates the format of this payload. The Next Payload, RESERVED, and Payload Length fields of the vendor ID payload are similar to those of the other payloads we discussed. The Vendor ID field is a variable-length field that contains a hash of the vendor ID string.

10.3   ISAKMP Negotiation Phases

ISAKMP offers two phases of negotiation: phase 1 and phase 2. Negotiation during each phase is accomplished using ISAKMP-defined exchanges, or exchanges defined for a key exchange protocol, such as Internet Key Exchange (IKE) protocol; we discuss ISAKMP exchange types later in the chapter, and IKE in the next chapter.

Phase 1 Negotiation
In this phase, two ISAKMP communicating peers establish an ISAKMP SA, which essentially is an agreement on how further negotiation traffic between the peers will be protected. This ISAKMP SA is then used to protect the negotiation of SAs for other protocols, such as ESP or AH.

Phase 2 Negotiation
This phase is used to establish SAs for other security services, such as AH or ESP. A single phase 1 SA can be used to establish many phase 2 SAs.

10.4   ISAKMP Exchange Types

At the time of writing ISAKMP defined five exchange types. Exchanges specify the type and ordering of ISAKMP payloads within ISAKMP messages during communication between peers. The exchange types differ in that they provide varying degrees of protection for the information they transmit. There are also differences in the overhead cost of each exchange type. We present a description of the five exchange types below. Before we proceed, let us look at some notations that we utilize to describe the ISAKMP exchange types.

Notations

HDR: An ISAKMP header, as described in Section 10.1.

SA: A security association payload (Section 10.2.3) with one or more proposal and transform payloads.

KE: A key exchange payload (Section 10.2.6).

HASH: A hash payload (Section 10.2.10).

SIG: A signature payload (Section 10.2.11).

AUTH: A generic authentication mechanism, such as a scheme utilizing the content of a hash or signature payload.

IDi: An identity payload (as described in Section 10.2.7) for an ISAKMP initiator.

IDr: An identity payload for an ISAKMP responder.

NONCE: A nonce payload (Section 10.2.12).

*: Indicates that the payloads after the ISAKMP header are encrypted.

→: Signifies initiator to responder communication.

←: Signifies responder to initiator communication.

10.4.1 Base Exchange

Base exchange is designed to allow key exchange and authentication related information to be transmitted together. The combination of these data into one message reduces bandwidth utilization at the expense of not providing identity protection. Identity protection is not provided because the identities are exchanged before a common shared secret is established; consequently, encryption of the identity information is not possible. Figure 10-17 illustrates an example of a base exchange. Figure 10-17 can be interpreted as follows:

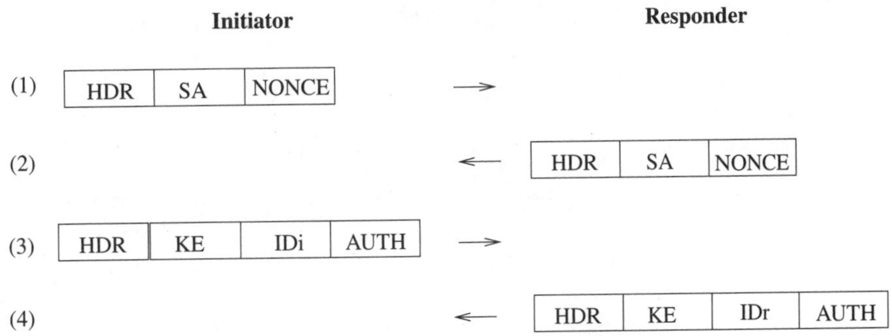

Figure 10-17
Base Exchange

Message 1: The initiator sends a proposal that is based on its security policy. For the purpose of conciseness, we represent the security association proposal as a single SA payload. The security association payload, as represented in Figure 10-17, is accompanied by one or more proposal payloads, which in turn is accompanied by one or more transform payloads. The nonce payload that is transmitted as part of the initiator's message is used to guarantee liveness and protect against replay attacks. Note that the ISAKMP header must be transmitted at the beginning of all ISAKMP messages.

Message 2: The responder indicates that it accepts a given proposal by sending a security association payload accompanied by a single transform payload and by either a single proposal payload or more than two or three proposal payloads with identical proposal numbers. If the responder chooses not to accept any of the initiator security proposals, it would consequently send a message containing the ISAKMP header and a notification payload indicating the reason for the rejection of the proposals. Tables 10-11 and 10-12 show the defined notification messages.

Messages 3 and 4: In messages 3 and 4 the initiator and responder verify the identity of the other peer and exchange identification information and keying material that is used to derive the common shared secret from which encryption and authentication keys are generated. The exchange is protected by an agreed-upon authentication function, typically a digital signature algorithm. Note that all of these messages are transmitted in clear text; therefore the identity information (Table 10-9 lists the defined identification type) is not protected in base exchange.

10.4.2   Identity Protection Exchange

Identity protection exchange differs from base exchange in that it separates key exchange information from the identity and authentication information. In so doing, this exchange provides protection for the identity of the communicating peers at the expense of two additional messages. Figure 10-18 illustrates the identity protection exchange and can be interpreted as follows:

- *Message 1:* The initiator sends the a security association payload accompanied by one or more proposal and transform payloads.

- *Message 2:* The responder indicates that it accepts one of the initiator's proposals by sending a security association payload accompanied by a single transform payload and by either a single proposal payload or more than two or three proposal payloads with identical proposal numbers.

- *Messages 3 and 4:* The initiator and responder exchange keying material and random data that are used to derive to a shared common secret from which encryption and authentication keys are generated.

- *Messages 5 and 6:* The initiator and responder verify the identity of the other peer and exchange identification information and the results of the agreed-upon authentication function. The information transmitted in these messages is encrypted using the secret key generated from the keying material exchanged in messages 3 and 4. Therefore, the identity information of the communicating peers is protected during this exchange.

Figure 10-18

Identity Protection
Exchange

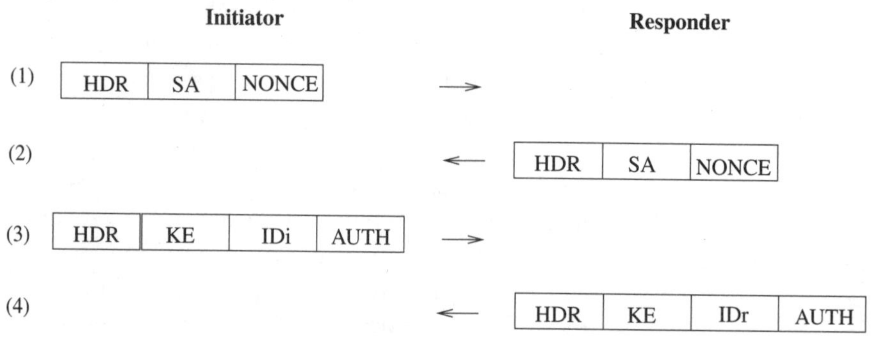

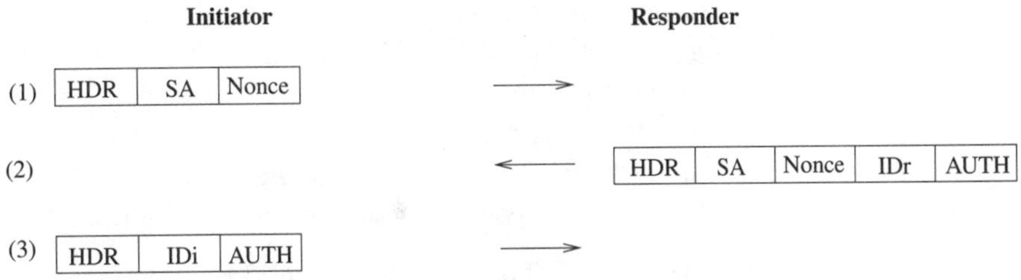

Figure 10-19
Authentication Only
Exchange

	Initiator	Responder

(1) | HDR | SA | Nonce | ⟶

(2)   ⟵ | HDR | SA | Nonce | IDr | AUTH |

(3) | HDR | IDi | AUTH | ⟶

10.4.3 Authentication Only Exchange

The authentication only exchange allows authentication information to be exchanged without the computational expense of generating keys. In phase 1 negotiations, the information transmitted during an authentication only exchange is not encrypted. However, this exchange can proceed under phase 2 negotiations, in which case the messages exchanged will be encrypted. Figure 10-19 illustrates the authentication only exchange and can be interpreted as follows:

■ *Message 1:* The initiator sends a proposal that is based on its security policy. The security association payload is accompanied by the appropriate number of proposal and transform payloads.

■ *Message 2:* In this message the responder indicates the protection suite it accepts by sending a security association payload along with proposal and transform payloads. In addition, the responder sends its identity information and the results of the application of the authentication function.

■ *Message 3:* The initiator verifies the identity of the responder and then transmits its identity information and the results of the authentication function. When the responder receives this message, it verifies the initiator's identity and establishes the SA.

10.4.4 Aggressive Exchange

Aggressive exchange was designed to be used for ISAKMP negotiations in which identity protection of the communicating peers is not required. This exchange allows the SA, key exchange, and authentication-related payloads to be transmitted together. Combining these payloads into one message reduces the number of roundtrips at the expense of not providing protection for the identity of the communicating peers. Aggressive exchange is similar to base exchange, in that both exchanges do not provide identity protection; however, unlike base exchange, which utilizes four messages, Aggressive Exchange uses only three. Figure 10-20 illustrates the aggressive exchange and can be interpreted as follows:

- *Message 1:* The initiator sends the responder a security association payload accompanied by a single transform payload and a single proposal payload, or two or three proposal payloads with identical proposal numbers. In aggressive exchange only one proposal is offered; the responder has the choice of accepting or rejecting this offer. In addition to the SA data, identity information and keying material are also transmitted.

- *Message 2:* The responder verifies the initiator's identity information and then indicates that it accepts the proposal by sending an SA payload along with its identity information and keying material. This message is transmitted under the protection of the agreed-upon authentication function. If the responder chooses not to accept the initiator's proposal, it would send a notification payload informing the initiator why it chose not to accept the proposal.

- *Message 3:* The initiator verifies the responder's identity and then sends the result of the application of the agreed-upon authentication function. This message, in effect, authenticates the initiator and provides a proof of its participation in the exchange. This message is encrypted using the key generated from the keying material exchanged in the first two messages. Note, however, that the messages containing the identity information of the peers are not encrypted; consequently, unlike the identity protection exchange, aggressive exchange does not provide identity protection for the communicating peers.

Figure 10-20

Aggressive Exchange

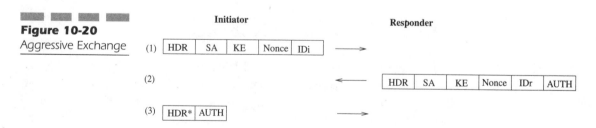

10.4.5 Informational Exchange

Before we conclude this chapter, let us take a brief look at the final ISAKMP exchange: the informational exchange. This exchange provides the means of sending a one-way transmission of information that can be used for security association management. Figure 10-21 illustrates an example of an informational exchange. In Message 1 the initiator or responder sends the other peer a message with a notification or a delete payload. No response is necessary for informational exchanges.

Figure 10-21
Informational
Exchange

		Initiator		Responder
(1)		HDR*	N/D	→

11

Internet Key Exchange

Overview of Chapter 11

In this chapter, we discuss the following topics:

- Exchange Phases
  - Phase 1 Exchange
  - Phase 2 Exchange
- Exchange Modes
  - Main Mode
  - Aggressive Mode
  - Quick Mode
  - New Group Mode
- Generation of Keying Material
- Oakley Groups
- Mode Config
- DHCP Configuration of IPSec Tunnel Mode in IPv4
- XAuth
- Hybrid Auth

Internet Key Exchange (IKE) is a protocol that is used to negotiate and provide authenticated keying materials in a protected manner for security associations (SAs). IKE is a hybrid protocol that utilizes relevant parts of three different protocols: Internet Security Association and Key Management Protocol (ISAKMP) [MSST98], Oakley Key Determination Protocol [Orm98], and SKEME [Kra96]. IKE differs from ISAKMP in that it actually defines a key exchange, whereas ISAKMP merely provides a generic framework for key exchange that can be used by any key exchange protocol.

IKE provides keying material for IPSec peers, from which encryption and authentication keys are generated. IKE also utilizes ISAKMP to negotiate SAs for the other IPSec protocols (AH and ESP). The focus of this chapter is to show how IKE provides these security services. The presentation is adapted from RFC 2409 [HC98].

11.1   Exchange Phases

IKE presents different exchanges in modes that operate in one of two ISAKMP negotiation phases.

Phase 1 Exchange

In this phase, two ISAKMP communicating peers establish an ISAKMP SA. Recall that a SA is essentially an agreement on how further negotiation traffic between the peers will be protected. This ISAKMP SA is then used to protect the negotiation of SAs for other protocols, such as ESP or AH.

Phase 2 Exchange

This phase is used to establish SAs for other security services, such as AH or ESP. A single phase 1 SA can be used to establish multiple phase 2 SAs.

11.2   Exchange Modes

At the time of writing, IKE defined four possible modes of exchange: main mode, aggressive mode, quick mode, and new group mode. The first three negotiate SAs, and the fourth negotiates groups for Diffie-Hellman exchanges. SA or group offers take the form of transform payloads encapsulated in proposal payloads that are encapsulated in security association payloads. These exchange modes will be discussed further in subsequent subsections. However, before this discussion, it is necessary to explain some notation that are employed throughout this chapter.

Notation

HDR: An ISAKMP header whose exchange type is the mode. HDR* indicates that the payloads following the ISAKMP headers are encrypted.

SA: A Security Association Payload with one or more proposal payloads.

KE: A key exchange payload.

IDx: The identification payload where x is either ii, which stands for ISAKMP initiator, or ir, signifying ISAKMP responder.

HASH: The hash payload.

SIG: The signature payload. The data to be signed are exchange-specific.

AUTH: A generic authentication mechanism such as SIG or HASH.

CERT: The certificate payload.

Nx: The nonce payload for x where x is either i or r for ISAKMP initiator and responder, respectively.

<P>_b: The body of the payload <P>, that is, the payload without the ISAKMP generic header.

Ck-I: The initiator cookie from the ISAKMP header.

Ck-R: The responder cookie from the ISAKMP header.

$g_i{}^x$: The initiator's public Diffie-Hellman value.

$g_r{}^x$: The responder's public Diffie-Hellman value.

prf(key,msg): A pseudo-random function—such as HMAC—with key key and input message msg.

SKEYSTR: A key string derived from secret keying material known only to the communicating peers.

SKEYSTR_e: The keying material used by ISAKMP to protect the confidentiality of its messages.

SKEYSTR_a: The keying material used by ISAKMP to authenticate its messages.

SKEYSTR_2: The keying material used to generate keys for non-ISAKMP SAs during phase 2 negotiation.

<x>y: Indicates that x is encrypted using the key y.

—>: Denotes initiator to responder communication.

<—: Denotes responder to initiator communication.

x|y: Denotes that x is concatenated with y.

[x]: Indicates that x is optional.

11.2.1 Main Mode

Main mode is an adaptation of the ISAKMP identity protection exchange discussed in Section 10.4.2. It involves an authenticated Diffie-Hellman key exchange. It is used to negotiate phase 1 ISAKMP SAs. This exchange mode was designed to separate key exchange information from identity and authentication information. The separation of this information provides protection for the identity information; the identity information is exchanged under the protection of the previously generated Diffie-Hellman shared secret. This occurs at the expense of three additional messages. The defined identity information is shown in Table 10-9. Figure 11-1 illustrates an example of a main mode exchange.

■ *Message 1:* The initiator sends the responder an SA Payload that encapsulates proposal payloads, which in turn encapsulate transform payloads.

Figure 11-1

Example of a Main Mode Exchange

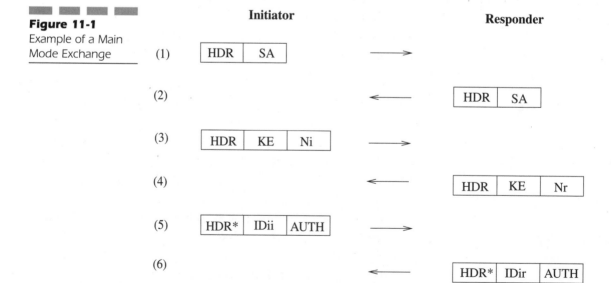

- *Message 2:* The responder sends an SA payload that indicates the proposal it accepted for the SA being negotiated.

- *Messages 3 and 4:* The initiator and responder exchange Diffie-Hellman public values[1] and auxiliary data, such as nonces, which are necessary to compute the common shared secret used to generate the encryption and authentication keys.

- *Messages 5 and 6:* The initiator and responder exchange identification data and authenticate the Diffie-Hellman exchange. The information transmitted during these two messages is encrypted using the secret key generated from the keying material exchanged in messages 3 and 4; consequently, the identity information is protected. Note that the ISAKMP header is included in all messages.

11.2.2 Aggressive Mode

Aggressive mode is an implementation of the ISAKMP aggressive mode exchange discussed in Section 10.4.4. It is used to negotiate ISAKMP phase 1 SAs where the protection of identity information is not required. This exchange mode allows the SA-, key exchange–, and authentication-related payloads to be transmitted together. Combining these payloads into one message reduces the number of round trips at the expense of not providing protection for the identity information. Figure 11-2 shows an example of an aggressive mode exchange.

- *Message 1:* The initiator sends the responder an SA payload that contains a single proposal payload encapsulating a transform pay-

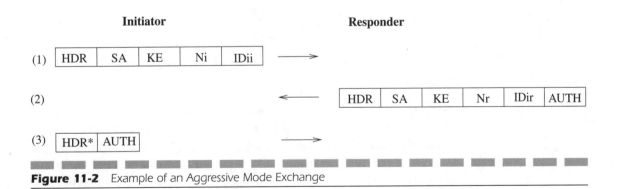

Figure 11-2 Example of an Aggressive Mode Exchange

---

[1]Section 3.4 explains the derivation of Diffie-Hellman public values.

load. In aggressive mode, only one proposal with a single transform is offered; the responder has the choice of accepting or rejecting this offer. The Diffie-Hellman public value, required random data, and identity information are also transmitted in the first message.

■ *Message 2:* If responder accepts the initiator's proposal, it sends an SA payload encapsulating the proposal payload containing the proposal and transform the initiator proposed. It also transmits the Diffie-Hellman public value, required random data, and identity information as part of this message. This message is transmitted under the protection of the agreed-upon authentication function.

■ *Message 3:* The initiator sends the result of the application of the agreed-upon authentication function. This message, in effect, authenticates the initiator and provides a proof of its participation in the exchange. The message is encrypted using the key generated from the keying material exchanged in the first two messages. Note, however, that the messages containing the identity information are not encrypted; consequently, unlike the main mode, aggressive mode does not provide identity protection.

11.2.3   Quick Mode

Quick mode is used to negotiate phase 2 SAs under the protection of the negotiated Phase 1 ISAKMP SA. All of the payloads in a quick mode exchange are encrypted. Quick mode exchange can be described as shown below.

```
Initiator                          Responder

(1) HDR*, HASH(1), SA, Ni
      [KE], [IDi, IDr]    —>
(2)                       <— HDR*, HASH(2), SA, Nr
                                [KE], [IDi, IDr]
(3) HDR*, HASH(3)         —>
```

■ *Message 1:* The initiator sends a hash, an SA (which encapsulates one or more proposal payloads, which in turn encapsulate one or more transform payloads) a nonce payload, optional key exchange material, and identification information to the responder. If perfect forwarded secrecy (PFS) is required, then key exchange material must be included in this message. The term *perfect forwarded secrecy* is used to describe the phenomenon in which the derivation of the keying material is such that if a single key is comprised, this will not affect the security of the data protected by other keys. The hash payload contains the message digest—using the negotiated pseudo-random function (prf) of the Message ID (MsgID) from the ISAKMP header, concatenated with the entire message that follows the hash payload, including all payload headers. That is,

```
HASH(1) = prf(SKEYSTR_a, MsgID|SA|Ni[|KE][|IDi|IDr])
```

The generation of the keying materials (SKEYSTR or SKEYSTR_*) is discussed below.

- *Message 2:* The payloads in this message are similar to those in message 1. The fingerprint contained in hash2 is generated like that for hash1, except that the initiator's nonce Ni minus the payload header is added after MsgID but before the complete message:

```
HASH(2) = prf(SKEYSTR_a, MsgID|Ni_b|SA|Nr[|KE][|IDi|IDr])
```

- *Message 3:* This message is used to authenticate the previous exchanges and consists of only the ISAKMP header and a hash payload. The message digest in the hash payload is generated using as input a byte of 0 concatenated with MsgID, followed by the initiator's nonce minus the payload header, followed by the responder's nonce minus the payload header. That is,

```
HASH(1) = prf(SKEYSTR_a, 0|MsgID|Ni_b|Nr_b)
```

If PFS is required, then a KE payload is included in Messages 1 and 2. The new keying material (NewKEYSTR) can be defined as:

```
NewKEYSTR = prf(SKEYSTR_d, g^xy|protocol|SPI|Ni_b|Ni_r)
```

where g^{xy} is the Diffie-Hellman shared secret exchanged in the KE payload, and protocol and SPI are obtained from the Protocol-ID and SPI fields, respectively, of the proposal payload encapsulated in the SA payload. When PFS is not required, the KE payload is not exchanged in quick mode messages. In this case, the new keying material can be defined as:

```
NewKEYSTR = prf(SKEYSTR_d, protocol|SPI|Ni_b|Ni_r)
```

11.2.4   New Group Mode

The new group mode (NGM) is used to negotiate a new group for Diffie-Hellman key exchange. NGM is carried out under the protection of ISAKMP phase 1 exchange. The message exchange in this exchange mode is shown below.

```
Initiator                  Responder

(1) HDR*, HASH(1), SA   ─→
(2)                        <── HDR*, HASH(2), SA
```

where

```
HASH(1) = prf(SKEYSTR_a, MsgID|SA)
and HASH(1) = prf(SKEYSTR_a, MsgID|SA)
```

The proposal payloads encapsulated within the SA payload specify the characteristics of the groups.

11.3   Generation of Keying Material

We discussed the generation of keying material for quick mode exchanges; however, we have not yet discussed how keying material is generated for main and aggressive mode exchanges. At the time of writing, three methods of authentication were allowed for both main mode and aggressive mode exchanges: digital signature, public-key encryption, and preshared key. The value of SKEYSTR depends on the method of authentication.

1. For digital signature:
   ```
   SKEYSTR = prf(Ni_b|Nr_b,gxy)
   ```

2. For public-key encryption:
   ```
   SKEYSTR = prf(Hash(Ni_b|Nr_b, CK-I|Ck-R))
   ```

3. For preshared keys:
   ```
   SKEYSTR = prf(preshared-key, Ni_b|Nr_b)
   ```

Both main mode and aggressive mode exchanges generate three groups of authenticated keying materials. These keying materials are derived similarly for both exchange modes and they are transported in the Key Exchange Data field of the KE payload. The derivations are as follows:

```
SKEYSTR_2 = prf(SKEYSTR, gˣʸ|Ck-I|Ck-R|0)
SKEYSTR_a = prf(SKEYSTR, SKEYSTR_d|gˣʸ|Ck-I|Ck-R|1)
SKEYSTR_e = prf(SKEYSTR, SKEYSTR_a|gˣʸ|Ck-I|Ck-R|2)
```

The values 0, 1, and 2 in the above expressions are the 1-byte representations of these values. The exchanges are authenticated by the generation of HASH_i and HASH_r by the initiator and the responder, respectively, of the exchanges, where

```
HASH_i = prf(SKEYSTR, g^x_i|g^x_r|Ck-I|Ck-R|SAi_b|IDii_b)
HASH_r = prf(SKEYSTR, g^x_r|g^x_i|Ck-R|Ck-I|SAi_b|IDir_b)
```

The necessary keys for encryption, digital signature, and message authentication code (MAC) algorithms are derived from the keying materials in an algorithmic-specific manner.

11.4 Oakley Groups

The IKE protocol allows negotiation of the group for Diffie-Hellman exchange. We discussed Diffie-Hellman key exchange in Section 3.4. The original specification of IKE [HC98] defined four groups that originated from the Oakley protocol. In addition, an Internet Draft defined several other groups; however, at the time of writing only one of them has been assigned a group ID. We present a brief description of the groups with assigned group IDs.

First Oakley Group

This group is a modular exponentiation group (MODP) and it is the default group for both the Oakley and IKE protocols. The assigned group ID is 1. The prime is $2^{768} - 2^{704} - 1 + 2^{64} * \{[2^{638}\pi] + 149686\}$. The generator is 2. This is a 768-bit group. The hexadecimal value is:

```
FFFFFFFF FFFFFFFF C90FDAA2 2168C234 C4C6628B 80DC1CD1
29024E08 8A67CC74 020BBEA6 3B139B22 514A0879 8E3404DD
EF9519B3 CD3A431B 302B0A6D F25F1437 4FE1356D 6D51C245
E485B576 625E7EC6 F44C42E9 A63A3620 FFFFFFFF FFFFFFFF
```

Second Oakley Group

The second group is also an MODP and it is assigned a group ID of 2. The prime is: $2^{1024} - 2^{960} - 1 + 2^{64} * \{[2^{894}\pi] + 129093\}$. The generator is 2. This is a 1024-bit group. The hexadecimal value is:

```
FFFFFFFF FFFFFFFF C90FDAA2 2168C234 C4C6628B 80DC1CD1
29024E08 8A67CC74 020BBEA6 3B139B22 514A0879 8E3404DD
EF9519B3 CD3A431B 302B0A6D F25F1437 4FE1356D 6D51C245
E485B576 625E7EC6 F44C42E9 A637ED6B 0BFF5CB6 F406B7ED
EE386BFB 5A899FA5 AE9F2411 7C4B1FE6 49286651 ECE65381
FFFFFFFF FFFFFFFF
```

Third Oakley Group

This is an elliptic curve group defined over the Galois field GF[2^{155}]. This group has a group ID of 3. We discussed elliptic curve cryptography in Section 3.3. The field size is 155 and the irreducible polynomial for the field is $u^{155} + u^{62} + 1$. The equation for the elliptic curve is $y^2 + xy = x^3 + ax^2 + b$. The other characteristics are as follows:

Group prime/irreducible polynomial: 0x0800000000000000000000000 04000000000000001

Group generator 1: 0x7b

Group curve A: 0x0

Group curve B: 0x07338f

Group order: 0X0800000000000000000057db5698537193aef944

When this group is used, the data in the Key Exchange Data field of the KE payload is the value of x from the solution (x,y), the point on the curve chosen by taking the randomly secret K_a*P, where $*$ is the repetition of the group addition and double operations, and P is the point on the curve with x coordinate equal to generator 1 and the y coordinate determined from the equation of the elliptic curve.

Fourth Oakley Group

This is an elliptic curve group defined over the Galois field GF[2^{185}] and has a group ID 4. The field size is 185. The irreducible polynomial for the field is $u^{185} + u^{69} + 1$. The equation for the elliptic curve is $y^2 + xy = x^3 + ax^2 + b$. Other characteristics are as follows:

Group prime/irreducible polynomial: 0x02000000000000000000000 000000002000000000000000001

Group generator 1: 0x18

Group curve A: 0x0

Group curve B: 0x1ee9

Group order: 0X01ffffffffffffffffffffffffdbf2f889b73e48417 5f94ebc

When this group is used, the data in the Key Exchange Data field of the KE payload is generated as for the Third Oakley group.

1536-bit MODP Group

The Diffie-Hellman groups that we presented so far (the two MODP groups of sizes 768 and 1024 bits, and the two elliptic curve groups of sizes

155 and 185 bits) all have strengths that are equivalent to symmetric keys of length 70–80 bits. With the rapid rate of increase in processing power, for adequate security larger group sizes have become a necessity. An Internet Draft [KK00] has proposed several new MODP groups of sizes from 1536–8192 bits.

The 1536-bit group has strength that is equivalent to 128-bit symmetric keys. The assigned group ID is 5. The prime is: $2^{1536} - 2^{1472} - 1 + 2^{64} *$ $\{[2^{1406}\pi] + 741804\}$. The generator is 2 and its hexadecimal value is:

```
FFFFFFFF FFFFFFFF C90FDAA2 2168C234 C4C6628B 80DC1CD1
29024E08 8A67CC74 020BBEA6 3B139B22 514A0879 8E3404DD
EF9519B3 CD3A431B 302B0A6D F25F1437 4FE1356D 6D51C245
E485B576 625E7EC6 F44C42E9 A637ED6B 0BFF5CB6 F406B7ED
EE386BFB 5A899FA5 AE9F2411 7C4B1FE6 49286651 ECE45B3D
C2007CB8 A163BF05 98DA4836 1C55D39A 69163FA8 FD24CF5F
83655D23 DCA3AD96 1C62F356 208552BB 9ED52907 7096966D
670C354E 4ABC9804 F1746C08 CA237327 FFFFFFFF FFFFFFFF
```

For information about the larger groups see [KK00].

11.5 Mode Config

For security reasons most system, network, or security administrators configure their systems (mail servers, NetBios name servers (WINS), internal DNS servers) such that access to these systems is limited to hosts with IP addresses that are internal to the network in question. For example, if an organization has a block of class C addresses in the range 132.206.50.1–132.206.50.254, the important internal system resources would typically be configured to restrict access to nodes with IP addresses 132.206.50.*. For dial-up access from remote sites to the organization network, the remote access servers are configured to assign IP addresses that are internal to the network; in so doing, the dial-up client machines— although they are physically removed from the organization's internal network—are still recognized as internal machines because the PPP (Point-to-Point Protocol) server issued them internal IP addresses when the PPP connections are established.

The earlier implementations of IPSec VPN suffered from a big limitation in that they did not provide the configuration flexibility outlined in the paragraph above. Internal IP address had to be manually assigned to each user given access to a corporate network. Imagine a large organization with over 1000 users requiring remote VPN access to the corporate network; the VPN gateway to the corporate network had to be configured by manually assigning internal IP address to each of the users allowed access. This could be a quite tedious task.

The IETF (Internet Engineering Task Force) proposal known as the ISAKMP configuration method [DP00], commonly referred to as mode config, or *virtual identity*, provides a solution for this issue. Mode config allows IPSec VPN peers to exchange configuration items securely during security association negotiations. Mode config solves the problem outlined above in that it allows a pool of IP addresses that are internal to the network to be assigned on the VPN gateway. When a remote VPN client connects to the corporate network in question, the VPN gateway issues it an internal IP address, thus allowing this remote client to be recognized as an internal host. The solution that mode config provides differs from that of previous IPSec VPN implementations in that, rather than manually assigning an internal IP address for each user that requires VPN access, a pool of IP addresses—typically a range of IP addresses, or an IP address followed by a netmask—is assigned, and each remote client is automatically issued an address from the pool. Other pertinent information, such as IP addresses for internal DNS servers, NetBios (WINS) servers, DHCP servers, etc., can also be requested and issued via mode config. Let us take a closer look at how mode config provides these services. The presentation is adapted from Mode Config Internet Draft [DH00].

11.5.1   Configuration Method Payload and Exchange

The ISAKMP configuration method defined a new ISAKMP payload and a new exchange type. This is in addition to the 13 ISAKMP payloads and the 5 ISAKMP exchange types we presented in Chapter 10.

Attribute Payload

The ISAKMP configuration method defined a new payload called the attribute payload. This payload is utilized to carry attributes and transaction messages. Recall that attributes are used to pass miscellaneous values or information between IPSec peers. Figure 11-3 illustrates the format of this payload. A description of the fields follows:

- `Next Payload`: This 8-bit field identifies the payload type of the next payload in the message. If the current payload is the last payload in the message, the value in this field will be 0. The payload type for the attribute payload has a value of 14.

Figure 11-3
Attribute Payload
Format

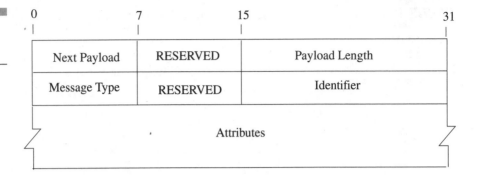

0	7	15	31
Next Payload	RESERVED	Payload Length	
Message Type	RESERVED	Identifier	
Attributes			

- RESERVED: The 8-bit RESERVED fields are unused and must be set to 0.

- Payload Length: This 16-bit field contains the length in bytes of the current payload, including the generic payload header and all attributes.

- Message Type: This 8-bit field specifies the type of message the attributes represent. Table 11-1 shows the value assigned to each of the configuration message types.

- Identifier: This 16-bit field carries an identifier that is used to reference a configuration transaction within the individual message.

- Attributes: This is variable-length field. It carries zero or more ISAKMP data attributes; we described ISAKMP data attributes in Section 10.2.2. The attribute types defined for the attribute payload are listed in Table 11-2. Note that all the defined attributes types in Table 11-2 are of variable length.

TABLE 11-1

Configuration
Message Types

Types	Description	Value
RESERVED	Unused	0
ISAKMP_CFG_REQUEST	A request for configuration (CFG) info	1
ISAKMP_CFG_REPLY	A reply to a CFG message	2
ISAKMP_CFG_SET	Pushes CFG info to a peer	3
ISAKMP_CFG_ACK	Acknowledgment of acceptance of CFG info	4
Reserved	For future use	5–127
Reserved	For private use	128–255

TABLE 11-2

Attribute Types for
the Attribute
Payload

Attribute	Description	Value
RESERVED	Unused	0
INTERNAL_IP4_ADDRESS	An internal IPv4 address	1
INTERNAL_IP4_NETMASK	The internal network IPv4 netmask	2
INTERNAL_IP4_DNS	IPv4 address for an internal DNS server	3
INTERNAL_IP4_NBNS	IPv4 address for an internal NetBios name server (WINS)	4
INTERNAL_ADDRESS_EXPIRY	The number of seconds before the IP address is expired	5
INTERNAL_IP4_DHCP	IPv4 address for an internal DHCP server	6
APPLICATION_VERSION	Version of application info of IPSec host	7
INTERNAL_IP6_ADDRESS	An internal IPv6 address	8
INTERNAL_IP6_NETMASK	The internal network IPv6 netmask	9
INTERNAL_IP6_DNS	IPv6 address for an internal DNS server	10
INTERNAL_IP6_NBNS	IPv6 address for an internal NetBios name server (WINS)	11
INTERNAL_IP6_DHCP	IPv6 address for an internal DHCP server	12
INTERNAL_IP4_SUBNET	The protected subnetwork that the VPN gateway protects. This attribute is made up of two fields: an IPv4 address and an IPv4 netmask	13
SUPPORTED_ATTRIBUTES	Information about supported attributes	14
INTERNAL_IP4_SUBNET	The protected subnetwork that the VPN gateway protects. This attribute is made up of two fields: an IPv6 address and an IPv6 netmask	15
Reserved	For future use	16–16,383

Transaction Exchange

The ISAKMP configuration method defined a new ISAKMP exchange type called the transaction exchange. It is assigned an exchange type value of 6. This exchange is typically employed after ISAKMP phase 1 negotiations; therefore, the messages are encrypted using encryption keys generated from common shared secret computed during ISAKMP phase 1 negotiations. Figure 11-4 illustrates an example of a transaction exchange.

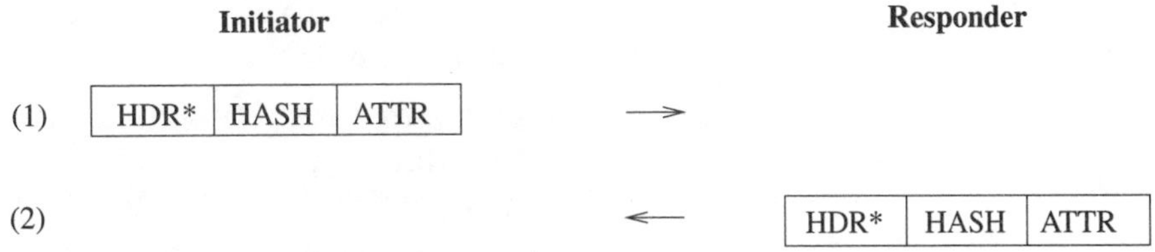

Figure 11-4
Illustration of a
Transaction
Exchange

Initiator Responder

(1) | HDR* | HASH | ATTR | $\longrightarrow$

(2) $\longleftarrow$ | HDR* | HASH | ATTR |

Figure 11-4
Illustration of a
Transaction
Exchange

For both messages in Figure 11-4, HDR* is the generic ISAKMP header. The * indicates that all the payloads following the ISAKMP header are encrypted. The HASH payload contains the pseudo-random function (prf) output, using SKEYSTR_a as the key and the M-ID (ISAKMP header message ID), concatenated with all the payloads after the HASH payload. That is, the hash for this exchange is:

```
HASH = prf(SKEYSTR_a, M-ID|ATTR)
```

Note that only one attribute payload can be present in a transaction exchange.

11.6 DHCP Configuration of IPSec Tunnel Mode in IPv4

DHCP configuration of IPSec tunnel mode in IPv4 (DHCP mode config) has been proposed as an alternative to mode config. This proposal leverages the feature-rich Dynamic Host Configuration Protocol (DHCP) RFC 2131 [Dro97] for configuring remote IPSec hosts and allowing them to appear as if they are physically on a given local network. The reasons for the advancement of DHCP mode config over mode config are as follows:

■ This proposal does not require an extension to IKE. The IPSec working group is very wary about extending any of the IPSec protocols. The group's caution is based on sound security principles because previous experience has shown that if a protocol is allowed to be extended, there will likely be numerous proposals for extending it; for each extension that is allowed, there will likely be a potential for new security compromises to the protocol. Therefore, proposals that address limitations in a given protocol by leveraging other protocols that have proven to be reliable and secure are often considered more desirable than proposals that require extension of the protocol in question.

■ DHCP mode config affords more configuration features than mode config supports, according to the specification in [DH00]. For example, with DHCP, a client can indicate a preference for a particular IP pool; configuration options can be assigned based on the remote host operating system, user groups or other requirements; and special treatment can be allowed for various hardware types. DHCP is very feature-rich; it has had a number of enhancements over the years, and it is far superior to mode config in terms of the richness of its configuration features.

■ The leveraging of DHCP for remote IPSec host configuration allows integration with existing IP address management facilities.

■ With DHCP mode config, fail-over can be achieved more smoothly. DHCP servers typically do not reside on the same machine as the IPSec gateway; therefore, if the IPSec gateway fails, the remote host configuration information will still be intact and available— since it is kept on a separate machine—when the fail-over IPSec gateway takes over.

DHCP mode config does have some limitations when it is compared with mode config:

■ DHCP mode config, as specified by the Internet Draft [PAKG00], is restricted to tunnel mode, whereas mode config supports both tunnel and transport mode.

■ DHCP mode config is limited to IPv4. Mode config, on the other hand, supports both IPv4 and IPv6.

11.6.1   Description of DHCP mode config

The entities that are involved are a DHCP server, an edge device (typically an IPSec security gateway), and a remote host. The remote host needs two interfaces:

1. An interface to connect to the Internet (the Internet interface)

2. A virtual interface to connect to the intranet (intranet interface)

The DHCP server and the edge device normally will not reside on the same machine. The edge device will act as a DHCP relay and relay packets between the DHCP server and the remote host.

The configuration event begins with the remote host intranet interface generating a DHCPDISCOVER message in an attempt to locate a DHCP server on the intranet. Figure 11-5 illustrates the general format of a DHCP message. A description of the fields follows:

- op: Message op code; that is, the message type.
- htype: Hardware address type; that is, value assigned by IANA.
- hlen: Hardware address length.
- hops: Client sets to zero; optionally used by relay agents when booting via a relay agent.

Figure 11-5
Format of a DHCP Message

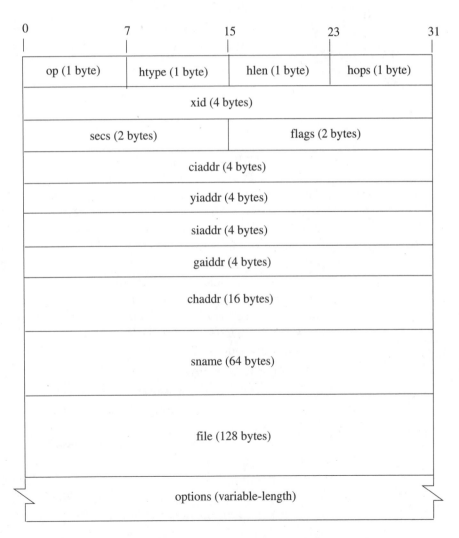

- `xid`: Transaction ID; this is a random number chosen by the client. It is used by the client and the server to associate messages and responses between the DHCP server and client.
- `secs`: The number of seconds since the acquisition or renewal of the address by the DHCP client. The client fills in this field.
- `flags`: Flags.
- `ciaddr`: Client IP address. Only filled in if client is in BOUND, RENEW, or REBINDING state.
- `yiaddr`: Your (client) IP address.
- `siaddr`: IP address of the next server to use in bootstrap. It is returned in DHCPOFFER and DHCPACK messages by the DHCP server.
- `giaddr`: VPN server IP address; used in booting via relay agents.
- `chaddr`: Client hardware address; should be unique.
- `sname`: Optional server host name; it should be a null terminated string.
- `file`: Boot file name; it should be a null terminated string. For DHCPDISCOVER messages, it should be a generic name or null; for DHCPOFFER messages, it should be a fully qualified directory path name.
- `options`: Optional parameters field.

In order to deliver the DHCPDISCOVER message from the intranet interface of the remote host to the edge device, an IKE phase 1 SA is established between the Internet interface of the remote host and the edge device. A phase 2 quick mode DHCP SA tunnel mode SA is then established. In the first message of the quick mode exchange, the client sends an identification payload with the IP address 0.0.0.0 in the Identification Data field, and UDP port 68 in the Port field, that is, 0.0.0.0/UDP/port 68. The edge device then sends an identification payload in the message it returns to the client containing the address of its Internet interface/UDP/port 67. The DHCP SA tunnel mode SA should be established at the end of the quick mode exchange. The remaining process can be described as follows:

1. The initial DHCP message (DHCPDISCOVER or DHCPREQUEST) is then tunneled to the edge device using the tunnel mode SA. When the edge device receives the message, it inserts its IP address in the giaddr field and forwards the message to one or more DHCP servers on the intranet.

2. The DHCP server sends a DHCPOFFER message with the offer of configuration parameters to the edge device, which then forwards it to the Internet interface of the remote client.

3. When the Internet interface of the remote client receives the DHCPOFFER message, it forwards it to the intranet interface after IPSec processing. The intranet interface then responds by generating a DHCPREQUEST message, which is tunneled to the edge device using the DHCP SA.

4. The edge device relays the message to the DHCP server, which replies with a DHCPACK (acknowledgment) or a DHCPNAK (disagreement), which the edge device forwards to the Internet interface of the remote client via the DHCP SA.

5. The remote client then forwards the DHCPACK or DHCPNAK message to its intranet interface after IPSec processing. At this point the intranet interface should be configured; the configuration information is gleaned from the DHCP messages exchanged. The Internet interface can then establish a new IPSec tunnel mode SA with the edge device. The IP address that the client sends to the edge device during the new quick mode exchange will be the IP address of the intranet interface, that is, the IP address obtained from the DHCP server. Consequently, the remote client—although it is physically at a remote location—is nonetheless recognized as an internal host. All subsequent messages exchanged between the remote client and the edge device will be sent via the new SA.

11.7 XAuth

IPSec ISAKMP and IKE protocols provide device-level authentication; however, at the time of writing they do not afford user-level authentication. There are two principal methods for authenticating IPSec VPN connections: digital certificates and preshared secrets. Digital certificate authentication offers much more security than preshared secrets, but it requires deployment of a public-key infrastructure (PKI), which can be quite complex and expensive, particularly for large-scale deployment. Preshared secret authentication is simple. It essentially involves storing identical passwords on the IPSec communicating peers; the passwords are used to authenticate the peers. The preshared secret method of authentication, though it is much less secure than that of digital certificates, because there is no additional cost associated with its use, is nonetheless utilized extensively.

For ease of deployment and management of VPN solutions for users who need to access corporate networks from remote sites (from homes, hotel rooms, or other remote locations), some corporations resort to assigning a single preshared password for authenticating the VPN connections for their users. The problem with this approach is that when a password is shared by several individuals, the likelihood that it will be compromised increases significantly. Anyone with the password has a free VPN access to the corporate network; therefore, the use of preshared secret authentication for remote VPN access—particularly when this "secret" is shared by a large group—is a cause for concern.

XAuth affords an extension to IKE that leverages legacy authentication mechanisms—such as RADIUS, SecurID, and one-time password (OTP)—that are widely deployed to provide user-level authentication. XAuth allows a two-factor authentication: first the device, that is, the user desktop, is authenticated using digital certificate or preshared secret authentication, and then the user is authenticated using a legacy unidirectional authentication system, such as RADIUS, SecurID, or OTP. Both levels of authentication must be successful in order for a VPN link to be established. Let us take a closer look at how XAuth allows corporations to leverage existing remote access authentication mechanisms to add an extra layer of security for remote access VPN links. The presentation is adapted from XAuth Internet Draft [BP00].

11.7.1 Details of XAuth Authentication Mechanism

IKE allows IPSec peers to set up secure sessions utilizing a bidirectional authentication method using either digital certificates or preshared secrets. The authentication is bidirectional since the initiator and the responding peers both authenticate each other. IKE however, according to the specification in RFC 2409 [HC98], does not afford unidirectional authentication where the authentication is done only by one of the peers. XAuth, by extending the mode config protocol [DP00] (discussed in Section 11.5.1), allows legacy unidirectional authentication information to be carried from one peer to another. XAuth works as follows:

- The peers inform each other as to whether or not they support compatible versions of XAuth. This is done during the IKE phase 1 SA negotiation. The edge device—typically a security gateway or network access server—sends the remote IPSec host a vendor ID payload as part of the first message it sends during a main mode or aggressive mode exchange. The Vendor ID field of the vendor ID payload contains an 8-byte hexadecimal value. We discussed the vendor ID payload in Section 10.2.15. Upon receiving the vendor ID payload, if the remote host supports a compatible version of

XAuth, it returns the vendor ID payload in the next IKE message it sends to the edge device. If it does not support a compatible version of XAuth, it sends a notification payload instead. The peers are informed that they support compatible versions of XAuth when they both received a vendor ID payload with the Vendor ID field containing the identical 8-byte hexadecimal value. If either peer receives an IKE message with a notification payload after sending the vendor ID payload, the SA negotiation will terminate due to lack of compatibility of the protocols.

■ The edge device notifies a remote peer that an XAuth exchange will follow the phase 1 exchange. The edge device accomplishes this by sending the remote peer a data attribute encapsulated in a transform payload with the next IKE phase 1 message it sends the remote peer. The data attribute carries information about the authentication method. XAuth defined new authentication methods. Table 11-3 lists these authentication methods and the assigned values.

TABLE 11-3

XAuth
Authentication
Methods

Authentication Method	Description	Value
XAUTHInitPreShared	Indicates that the remote host requires the edge device to authenticate itself with XAuth and preshared secrets	65,001
XAUTHRespPreShared	The edge device requires XAuth and preshared secret authentication	65,002
XAUTHInitDSS	The remote host requires XAuth and DSS signature scheme authentication	65,003
XAUTHRespDSS	The edge device requires XAuth and DSS signature scheme authentication	65,004
XAUTHInitRSA	The remote host requires XAuth and RSA signature scheme authentication	65,005
XAUTHRespRSA	The edge device requires XAuth and RSA signature scheme authentication	65,006
XAUTHInitRSAEncryption	The remote host requires XAuth and RSA encryption for authentication	65,007
XAUTHRespRSAEncryption	The edge device requires XAuth and RSA encryption for authentication	65,008
XAUTHInitRSARevisedEncryption	The remote host requires XAuth and revised encryption with RSA algorithm for authentication	65,009
XAUTHRespRSARevisedEncryption	The edge device requires XAuth and revised encryption with RSA algorithm for authentication	65,010

TABLE 11-4

XAuth Attribute
Types for the
Attribute Payload

Authentication Method	Description	Value
XAUTH-TYPE	The type of extended authentication requested; Table 11-5 lists the authentication types and the assigned values	16,520
XAUTH-USER-NAME	Unique identifier of a user (login name, e-mail, or X.500 DN)	16,521
XAUTH-USER-PASSWORD	The user's password	16,522
XAUTH-PASSCODE	A token card's pass code	16,523
XAUTH-MESSAGE	A textual message containing a challenge or an instruction from an edge device to an IPSec host	16,524
XAUTH-CHALLENGE	A challenge string sent from the edge device to the IPSec remote host for it to include in its calculation of a password	16,525
XAUTH-DOMAIN	The domain to be authenticated in	16,526
XAUTH-STATUS	A variable that is used to indicate authentication success (OK=1) or failure (FAIL=0)	16,527
XAUTH-NEXT-PIN	A variable indicating that the edge device is requesting that the user choose a new pin number	16,528
XAUTH-ANSWER	A variable-length ASCII string used to send input to the edge device	16,529

■ Immediately after the completion of the IKE phase 1 exchange, the edge device initiates a transaction exchange to transmit the XAuth authentication data; see Section 11.5.1 for details on transaction exchange. XAuth defined some new attribute types for the attribute payload utilized in the transaction exchange. Table 11-4 lists these attributes and the assigned values. Note that all the attributes in Table 11-4 are variable-length ASCII strings except

TABLE 11-5

XAuth
Authentication
Types

Authentication Method	Description	Value
Generic	Any generic authentication mechanism	0
RADUS-CHAP	An authentication method defined in RFC 2138	1
OTP	One-time password system (RFC 1938)	2
S/KEY	One-time password system (RFC 1760)	2
Reserved	For future use	4–32,767
Reserved	For private use	32,768–65,535

the XAUTH-TYPE and the XAUTH-STATUS attributes, which have fixed-length integer values. At the end of the transaction exchange, provided that the phase 1 negotiation prior to the transaction exchange, and the XAuth authentication both completed successfully, other security associations (e.g., SA for AH and/or ESP) that might be necessary to establish the VPN link are negotiated using quick mode or new group mode exchange.

11.8 Hybrid Auth

As mentioned previously in our discussion of XAuth, IKE as specified by RFC 2409 [HC98] allows two forms of bidirectional authentication: the digital certificate and preshared secret methods of authentication. We alluded to the fact earlier that digital certificate authentication offers much more security than preshared secret. However, the use of digital certificates requires the deployment of a PKI solution. A large-scale deployment of a PKI solution can be a quite expensive and technically challenging venture.

The alternative bidirectional authentication method, the use of preshared secret, does not offer the desired level of security, particularly for remote connections to a corporate network. Hybrid Auth provides an extension to IKE that allows existing legacy unidirectional authentication mechanisms—such as RADIUS (RFC 2138), TACACS (RFC 1492), one-time password (RFC 1938), and other proprietary systems, such as SecurID—to be used to authenticate remote users, whereas edge devices (security gateways or routers) are authenticated with digital certificates. Hybrid Auth discourages the use of preshared secrets for authentication. Therefore, it requires a limited PKI deployment. The cost of a PKI solution is usually based on the number of certificates issued. Thus, there can be a considerable difference in cost if certificates are issued only to network servers, edge devices, and, if need be, to selected users, and existing legacy authentication systems are used to authenticate users requiring remote VPN access to a corporate network. Hybrid Auth differs from XAuth in two ways:

1. Hybrid Auth provides a single-fold asymmetric authentication for edge devices and remote users. The edge device authenticates itself to the remote host using digital certificates, whereas the remote user authenticates to the edge device using legacy authentication mechanisms such as OTP, SecurID, RADIUS, TACACS, etc. XAuth, on the other hand, allows a two-fold authentication method. First, there is the bidirectional authentication, in which both the edge

device and the remote host authenticate each other using digital certificates or preshared secrets. Next, there is a unidirectional authentication mechanism in which the remote user authenticates to the edge device using a legacy authentication system.

2. Hybrid Auth requires a limited deployment of PKI, whereas XAuth does not. Hybrid Auth requires digital certificates for the authentication of edge devices; however, for XAuth, preshared secrets can be used.

Let us take a closer look at how Hybrid Auth provides the security services it offers; the presentation is adapted from Hybrid Auth Internet-Draft [LSZ00].

11.8.1   Details of Hybrid Auth Authentication Mechanism

The Hybrid Auth authentication scheme is similar to the XAuth scheme we outlined in Section 11.7.1, except that the authentication during the phase 1 exchange is one-directional; that is, only the edge device is authenticated during the phase 1 exchange. As is the case for the XAuth scheme, a transaction exchange is initiated immediately after the completion of the phase 1 exchange. The transaction exchange is use to transmit the authentication data for the unidirectional legacy authentication mechanism. Either of the peers can initiate the phase 1 SA negotiation; however, only the edge device can initiate the transaction exchange.

Since the authentication during the phase 1 SA negotiation is unidirectional for Hybrid Auth, there needs to be a slight modification of the phase 1 exchanges, both for main mode and aggressive mode. The changes are as follows:

- *For main mode:* If we assume that the remote client is the initiator of the phase 1 SA negotiation in message 5 of the main mode exchange, since the remote host does not send a digital signature to the edge device, the AUTH payload, which typically represents a signature payload, should be replaced by a hash payload (HASH). The hash payload contains the hash of the data that would have otherwise been signed. Figure 11-6 illustrates the modified main mode exchange.

- *For aggressive mode:* For illustration purposes, let us assume that the initiator is the edge device. In this case message 2 will not contain a digital signature; thus, the signature payload (AUTH) should be replaced with a hash payload, which will contain the

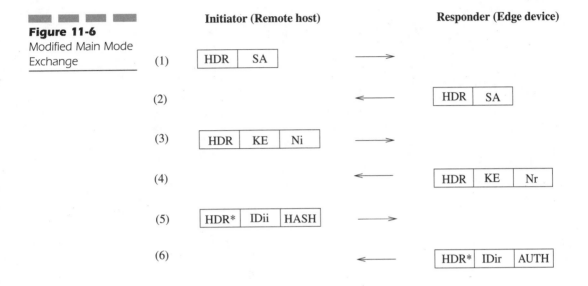

Figure 11-6
Modified Main Mode
Exchange

hash of the data that would have otherwise been signed. Figure 11-7 illustrates the modified aggressive mode exchange.

Immediately after the completion of the phase 1 SA negotiation, a transaction exchange is initiated by the edge device. The transaction exchange is used to transmit the legacy authentication system's authentication data. The transaction exchange is secured by the phase 1 SA and it is similar to that outlined for XAuth.

At the end of the transaction exchange, provided it completed successfully, other security associations (SA for AH and/or ESP) that might be necessary to establish the VPN connection are negotiated using quick mode or new group mode exchange.

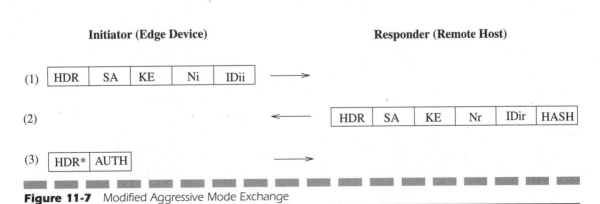

Figure 11-7 Modified Aggressive Mode Exchange

IP Compression

Overview of Chapter 12

We discuss the following topics in this chapter:

- Important Considerations for the Use of IPComp
- Compressed IP Datagram Header Structure
  – IPv4 Header Modification
  – IPv6 Header Modification
- IPComp Association

In our discussion of AH and ESP in Chapters 8 and 9, we alluded to the fact that the application of these protocols to IP traffic can result in a considerable increase in the sizes of IP datagrams transmitted. For example, the application of a single ESP header to an IPv4 datagram in tunnel mode can result in an increase in the size of the datagram in excess of 300 bytes. Moreover, ESP or AH can be nested with itself or with each other, so there can be multiple ESP and/or AH headers in a given datagram. The extra data traffic associated with the use of IPSec can be a problem in terms of communication performance, particularly on network links where bandwidth utilization is of concern.

The IP Compression protocol (IPComp) offers a solution to this issue. IPComp reduces the sizes of IP datagrams, and in so doing, it increases the communication performance between communicating peers. IPComp, however, is not a general panacea for congested communication links. In fact, the application of IPComp to IP datagrams can result in an increase rather than a reduction in the sizes of the datagrams. Our goals for this chapter are to present IPComp and give some guidelines for its utilization. The presentation is adapted from RFCs 2393 [SMPT98], 2394 [Per98], and 2395 [FM98].

12.1   Important Considerations for the Use of IPComp

IPComp employs different compression algorithms to reduce the size of IP datagrams. Two of the more commonly used compression algorithms are DEFLATE and LZS. DEFLATE is described in RFC 1951; it is the compression algorithm that the popular compression programs, gzip and pkzip, employ. The specification for LZS is outlined in the American National Standards Institute (ANSI) document ANSI X3.241-1994. LZS is patented by Hi/fn, Inc.; however, licenses for reference implementations are available at no cost for IPSec and a few other protocols.

IPComp utilizes compression algorithms to compress outbound IP datagrams and decompress inbound datagrams. These compression algorithms possess the important characteristic of having a lossless compression/decompression process. In other words, when an IP datagram is compressed, the decompression of the compressed datagram produces the datagram in its original form without any loss of data.

Compression algorithms compress data by encoding the data using special encoding techniques such as Huffman encoding[1] and removing redundant or duplicate codes, thus rendering the data more random. Therefore, compression is least effective on random data. In fact, compression of random data can actually result in an increase in the size of the data rather than a reduction.

Encrypted data are typically very random so attempting to compress encrypted data can be counterproductive. The same holds for data that result from the application of a hash function or a message authentication code (MAC). Consequently, if compression of outbound IP datagrams is required, it must be done before any IPSec processing, such as the application of ESP or AH, and before any fragmentation of the datagrams. In addition, for IPv6, the compression of outbound IP datagrams must be done before the addition of either a hop-by-hop option header or a routing header. Recall that the hop-by-hop extension header is used to carry optional routing information that must be examined by every node on the path from the packet's source to its destination; whereas, the routing header is used by the IPv6 source to list one or more intermediate gateways through which a packet should pass on its way from the source to the destination. Intermediate routers on the path from the source to the destination need the information contained in these extension headers to route the packets; therefore, these fields should not be compressed.

Similarly, for compressed inbound datagrams, decompression must be done after the IP fragments have been assembled and after all IPSec processing, such as authentication and/or decryption.

During the application of IPComp, it is important that each IP datagram be compressed and decompressed by itself without any relation with other datagrams. This is necessary since datagrams may arrive at their destination out of order, or they may not arrive at all.

Small IP payloads are likely to expand rather than be reduced after the application of IPComp. Therefore, a numeric threshold should be set for the application of IPComp in which IP payloads that are smaller than this minimum value should not be compressed. The recommended threshold for DEFLATE and LZS compression algorithms is 90 bytes. It likely will be counterproductive to attempt to compress IP datagrams with payloads—the datagram minus the IP header—that are smaller than 90 bytes.

The compression process can be quite CPU-intensive. Since some data are not compressible, implementations of IPComp should involve an adap-

---

[1]See RFC 1951.

tive algorithm to avoid performance degradation. For example, if the compression of i consecutive IP datagrams for a given data traffic fails, the next j IP datagrams should be sent without attempting compression. If the next k datagrams also fail to compress, the next $j+n$ should be sent without attempting compression. Once a datagram compresses successfully, then the normal process of IPComp restarts. The values of the integers i, j, k, and n are implementation-specific and should be chosen based on the variation that gives the best performance enhancement.

12.2   Compressed IP Datagram Header Structure

For both IPv4 and IPv6, no portion of the IP header or the IP header options is compressed. Intermediate routers on the path from a packet's source to its destination need the information in the IP header to route the packet to its final destination. Hence, compression is applied after the IP header, that is, to the transport layer protocol (TCP, UDP, ICMP, or IGMP) of the IP datagram. For IPv6, the compression is applied starting at the first IP Header Option field that does not carry information that must be examined and processed by intermediate nodes on the packet's delivery path—if the datagram contains such an IP Header Option field—and continues to the transport layer protocol of the IP datagram.

An IPComp header is inserted immediately before the compressed payload. Figure 12-1 illustrates the format of an IPComp header. A description of the fields follows:

- Next Header: This 8-bit field contains the IPv4 Protocol field or the IPv6 Next Header field of the original IP header.

- Flags: This 8-bit field is unused; it is reserved for future use and must be set to zero.

- Compression Parameter Index (CPI): This 16-bit field stores the value of the IPComp transform identifier. The values of the assigned transform identifiers for IPComp are presented in Table

Figure 12-1
IPComp Header
Structure

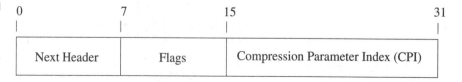

0	7	15	31
Next Header	Flags	Compression Parameter Index (CPI)	

10-8. The values are stored in network byte order; that is, the lower-order bytes are transmitted first. The values can be categorized as follows:

– 0–63 define well-known compression algorithms.
– 64–255 are reserved for future use.
– 256–61,439 are negotiated between the two nodes in definition of IPCom SA; we discuss IPComp SA below.
– 61,440–65,535 are for private use among mutually consenting peers.

12.2.1 IPv4 Header Modification

After the insertion of the IPComp header to an IPv4 datagram, some of the IPv4 header fields are modified before the datagram is transmitted. Figures 12-2 and 12-3 show an IPv4 datagram before and after the application of IPComp.

The IPv4 header fields that require modification after the application IPComp are as follows:

■ `Total Length`: The content in this field is changed to the value representing the length of the entire capsulated IP datagram, in bytes, including the IP header, the IPComp header, and the compressed payload.

Figure 12-2
An IPv4 Datagram Before Application of IPComp

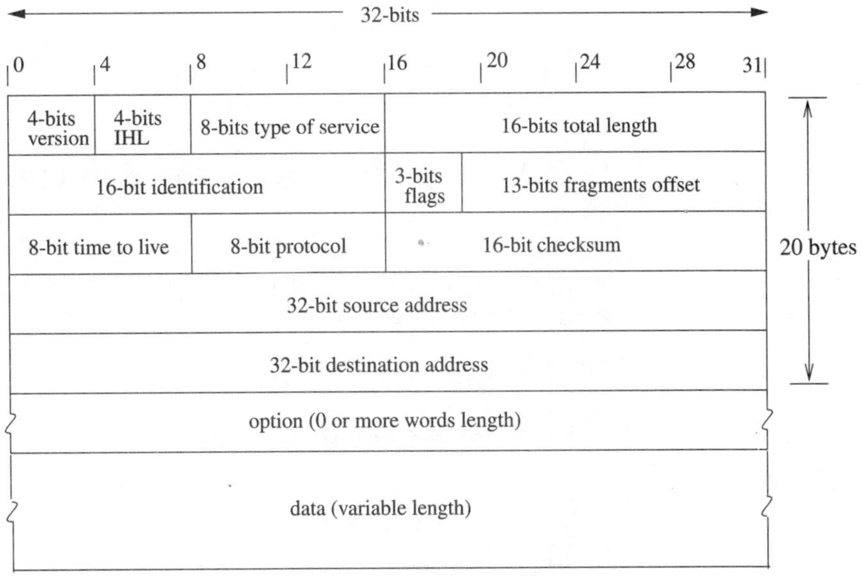

Figure 12-3
An IPv4 Datagram
After Application
of IPComp

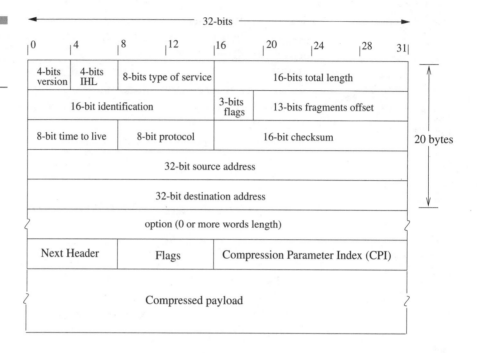

- `Protocol`: The content of the protocol field is changed to 108; thus indicating that the encapsulated data are a compressed payload.
- `Checksum`: The checksum is recalculated to reflect the changes to the datagram.

All the other IPv4 header fields are kept unchanged.

12.2.2 IPv6 Header Modification

Figures 12-4 and 12-5 show an IPv6 datagram before and after the application of IPComp. The following IPv6 header fields are modified after the application of IPComp:

- `Payload Length`: The value representing the total length of the IP payload in bytes—that is, the entire IP datagram minus the IPv6 header—is inserted in this field.
- `Next Header`: The `Next Header` field is set to a value of 108, indicating that the encapsulated data are a compressed payload.

All other IPv6 header fields are kept unchanged.

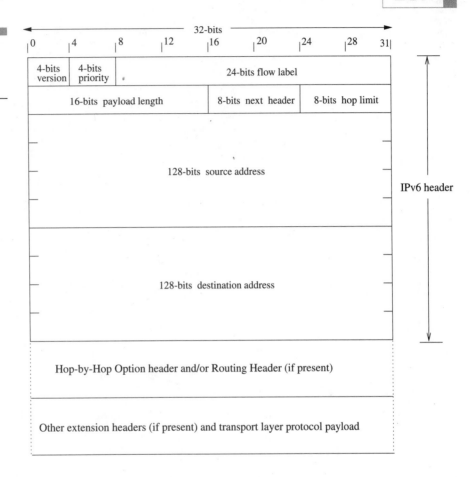

Figure 12-4
An IPv6 Datagram
Before Application
of IPComp

12.3   IPComp Association

In order for IPSec communicating peers to utilize IPComp, it is necessary that they establish an IPComp association (IPCA) between them. The IPCA includes all the required information for the operation of IPComp: the mode of operation, the compression algorithm to be used, and any required parameter for the selected algorithm. The IPComp mode of operation is either a node-to-node policy, in which IPComp is applied to every IP packet between the nodes, or a transport layer protocol–based policy, in which IPComp is applied only to selected transport layer protocols.

An IPCA can be asymmetric in that the peers can opt for compression of the IP traffic in one direction only. Similarly, one compression algo-

Figure 12-5
An IPv6 Datagram
After Application
of IPComp

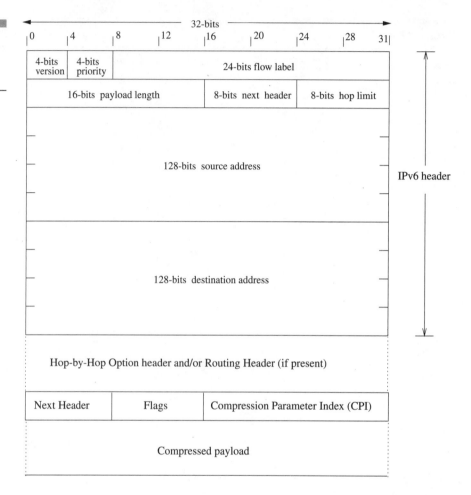

rithm can be used in one direction and a different algorithm in the other direction. The default algorithm for IPComp is no IPComp compression.

An IPCA can be established by dynamic negotiations or by manual configuration. Manual configuration might be suitable for the deployment of a small number of IPSec hosts; however, for larger deployments, dynamic negotiations are more suitable. Dynamic negotiations employ IKE quick mode exchange to negotiate the IPCA. For details on IKE quick mode exchange, refer to Section 11.2.3.

VPN Solutions

Overview of Chapter 13

In this chapter, we discuss the following topics:

- Scenarios for VPN Utilization
  - Interconnecting Branch Offices
  - Interconnecting Different Organizations' Intranets
  - Secure Remote Access via DSL or Other Broadband Alternatives
- Choosing a VPN Solution
- A VPN Configuration Case Study
  - Configuration of the PKI Server
  - Configuration of the VPN Gateway
  - Configuration of the VPN Client

In the previous chapters, we examined the technological components of IPSec and studied the cryptographic algorithms that help secure this protocol. In this chapter, we illustrate how IPSec security services can be utilized to provide VPN solutions. We start by presenting some scenarios for which VPN solutions are ideal; following this, we give some tips regarding the important features that one should look for in a VPN solution; and then we conclude by presenting a case study involving the configuration of a VPN client to a gateway using PKI for authentication. Before we proceed, we define some terms that we have used but have not yet formally defined.

Notation

- *VPN:* For the purpose of our discussion, virtual private networks (VPNs) are secure communication channels that offer data protection via the use of strong cryptographic authentication and/or encryption algorithms. VPN consists of computers (IPSec enabled servers or workstations) and communication links; optionally, VPN can also involve routers, switches, and security gateways.

- *Security gateway:* A security gateway is an access point to a network. A security gateway often includes a firewall (see next entry), and it provides access control, thus allowing only authorized traffic to transverse the network it protects.

- *Firewall:* A firewall is a packet filtering entity that examines the protocol headers of packets and either accepts the packets and forwards them to the destination hosts, or rejects them, depending on how the selectors in the packets headers—source and destination IP address, Transport or Application Layer protocols, source and destination ports, etc.—match the firewall access control rules.

13.1   Scenarios for VPN Utilization

In this section, we present some scenarios in which VPN provides ideal solutions. The emphasis will be on showing how VPN can be used to secure data traffic, often at considerably less cost than other security infrastructures.

13.1.1   Interconnecting Branch Offices

Let us consider a company that has a number of branch offices located at different geographical locations. For example, let us assume that the company has offices in Asia, Europe, and North America. To interconnect these offices, the corporation basically has two choices: utilize private network infrastructures or VPN. Let us consider the options for the former: the company will need to either lease dedicated communication channels from telecommunication providers, set up satellite data feeds, or install trans-Atlantic data channels. The cost of even the most cost-effective implementation of any of these options is much more prohibitive than a VPN solution, considering that each of these options involves the purchasing or leasing of additional equipment—network cables and supporting infrastructures—plus the high associated maintenance costs. However, a VPN solution typically involves the purchasing of the VPN software and the necessary licenses and perhaps a few additional computers and providing the necessary training for the network or security administrators who will administer the VPN.

Figure 13-1 illustrates an example of how the branch offices of an enterprise can be interconnected via VPN using the Internet as a backbone network. Each branch office has a security gateway that provides an interface with the Internet and the corporation's internal network. The security gateways are configured to enforce the access control policies of the respective branch offices. There are a number of security service options that can be employed when a host on any of the corporation's intranets wishes to

Figure 13-1

VPN Interconnecting Branch Offices Using the Internet as a Backbone Network

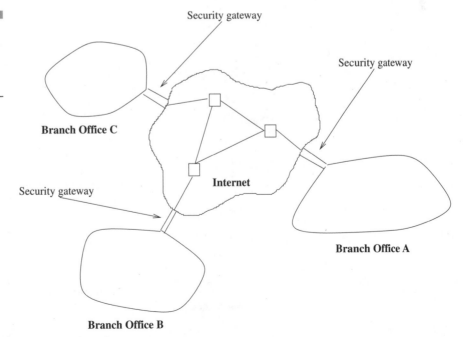

communicate with a entity on the intranet of another branch office. We examine below the option that offers the greatest level of security.

End-to-End Authentication and Encryption

This option is employed when a high degree of security for the data traffic is required and the internal network cannot be fully trusted. Employing this option, a host negotiates a security association (SA) with a peer on the intranet of another branch office. The SA will specify the security services required (AH and/or ESP), the mode of operation of these services, and the required authentication and encryption algorithms. Internet Key Exchange (IKE) protocol will then generate and put in place the necessary encryption and authentication keys on the communicating peers.

Figure 13-2 illustrates a typical end-to-end secure tunnel connecting communicating peers on the internal network of two branch offices. In this scenario, since there is a security gateway on the intranet of both branch offices, the hosts typically will negotiate the transport mode for the authentication and encryption services that will be applied to the traffic they will exchange. As explained in Chapters 8 and 9, the transport mode of operation for AH or ESP protects the data that the upper layer protocols encapsulate, but this mode of operation does not protect the IP header. However,

Figure 13-2

Secure End-to-End Tunnel Connecting Communicating Peers on Internal Networks of Two Branch Offices

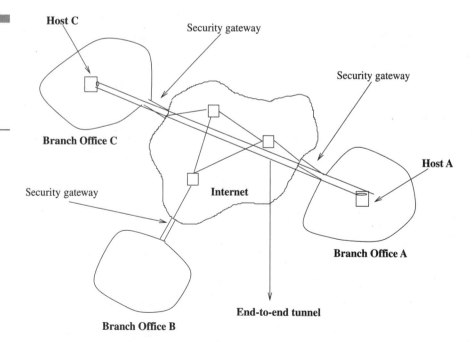

when the packet from host A—destined for host C—is forwarded to branch office A's security gateway, it will typically negotiate an SA with the destination host's security gateway, which will involve the tunnel mode of operation for the required security services. The ESP tunnel mode confidentiality service protects both the data and the identity of the sending entity (host A in our example) while the packet is in transit from one security gateway to the next via the Internet.

When the packet arrives at branch office C's security gateway, it will check its security policy database to determine if it should accept the packet. If the packet should be given access, the security gateway will then consult its SA database to ascertain the SA for the traffic, and then authenticate the packet using the authentication algorithm that the SA specifies. If the authentication succeeds, it forwards the packet to the intended destination—host C.

When host C receives the packet it consults its SA database to identifies the SA that is applicable to the packet, and then authenticates the packet to ensure that it has not been modified while it was in transit from the security gateway. Finally, if the authentication succeeds, Host C accepts the packet process it based on the negotiated SA for the traffic. For details about the processing of IPSec traffic, see Chapters 8, 9, and 12.

The end-to-end tunnel provides both authentication and confidentiality services. The traffic is authenticated with a strong cryptographic authentication algorithm; therefore, the probability of it been spoofed is very small. Similarly, the traffic is encrypted with a strong cryptographic algorithm; therefore, it is very unlikely for its confidentiality to be compromised, even though it is transmitted via the public Internet. Another important point to note is that the identities of the machines on the internal networks are protected via the use of ESP tunnel mode by the security gateways. This protection suite is quite comprehensive, and considering that it can be achieved with a fraction of the cost for that of private network infrastructures, it certainly merits exploration.

13.1.2 Interconnecting Different Organizations' Intranets

There are situations in which it might be necessary for an organization to give restrictive access to other organizations to its intranet. Consider, for example, a supplier who wishes to give clients access to its database servers that contain relevant information the clients might wish to access. The end-to-end authentication encryption scenario explained in the previous section can be adapted to this situation as well. In this case, the supplier's security gateway is configured to accept packets from the domains of its clients, provided that the destination hosts are the entities to which specific access has been given. Apart from addressing issues that might need to be resolved if the companies are using private (globally ambiguous) IP addresses, most of the information presented in the previous example applies to this scenario as well.

13.1.3   Securing Remote Access via DSL or Other Broadband Alternatives

The utilization of DSL (digital subscriber line) and other broadband alternatives to connect home users to the Internet has increased dramatically since the beginning of the 21st century. Many corporations have given their employees access to their corporate networks via the use of broadband[1] as opposed to slow conventional dial-up access. Unlike dial-up access to an intranet, broadband connection to an intranet via the Internet is not secure. The traffic for dial-up access travels from the home or roaming user machines via a telephone line directly to dial-up access servers on the respective intranet; the dial-up access servers then route the traffic to destination hosts on the intranet. Thus, the traffic exchanged between a home user machine and hosts on a given intranet is confined to private telephone lines. On the other hand, for broadband connection via the Internet the traffic exchanged by the home users' machines and a given intranet travels via the public Internet.

This is another scenario for which VPN provides ideal solutions. The data traffic under consideration can be secure using a VPN solution in a manner similar to that discussed in Section 13.1.2; however, there are a few differences:

■ There are typically no security gateways on the client side—we use the term client to refer to a home or roaming user machine.

■ For the scenario discussed in Section 13.1.2, the VPN peers likely have static IP addresses; therefore, source IP addresses can be used to configure access control. For remote clients, however, the IP addresses are likely to be dynamic so they are usually not known beforehand; hence, access control for remote clients to a

---

[1]For the purposes of our discussion we use the term broadband to encompass DSL and other broadband alternatives.

corporate network typically cannot be based on the IP addresses of the clients.

How then can access control be configured for remote clients if their IP addresses cannot be used to determine whether or not they should be given access to a corporate network? PKI provides the most secure solution. Digital certificates can be issued to the clients. The security gateways on the corporate network can then be configured to give access only to clients with valid certificates issued by a given certificate authority (CA).

If the corporation has not yet deployed a PKI but has in place a remote access authentication system such as SecurID, RADIUS, or others; XAuth is another viable alternative. Passwords can be issued to the remote clients. In establishing a VPN connection to a security gateway, the remote clients present the issued password to the security gateway for device-level authentication. In addition to the device-level authentication, a user-level authentication is required—using the given remote access authentication system—before the connection is established. Therefore, the remote access authentication system can be used for access control.

13.2   Choosing a VPN Solution

VPN solutions are generally categorized as VPN servers (or concentrators) and VPN clients. VPN server applications are typically deployed on security gateways, whereas VPN client applications are installed on hosts that are not gateways. A typical VPN deployment usually involves installation of both VPN servers and clients. However, for the purposes of our discussion, we use the term *VPN solution* for either a combination of VPN server and client applications, or the server or client application, separately.

Selecting an appropriate VPN solution can be a daunting task. Marketing information on VPN applications often does not address some of the important parameters that should be considered in selecting a VPN solution. Our aim is to arm you with the knowledge that will allow you to ask your VPN vendors or potential vendors probing questions that will proverbially "blow away smoke screens" and divulge meaningful information from the vendors that will enable you to choose the VPN solution that is right—in terms of security and flexibility—for you or your corporation. Below is a list of 10 important features that merit consideration in choosing a VPN solution and some suggestions as to what one should look for with regard to these features.

1. *Method of authentication:* One of the first criteria that one should look for in a VPN solution is the method of authentication. PKIs from the major PKI vendors as well as other X.509-compliant PKIs should be supported. At the time of writing, some of the major PKI vendors were Verisign (*http://www.verisign.com*); Entrust (*http://www.entrust.com*); Xcert (*http://www.xcert.com*), which has been acquired by RSA Security (*http://www.rsasecurity.com*); Baltimore Technologies (*http://www.baltimore.com*); iPlanet (*http://www.iplanet.com*); and Microsoft.

If a PKI is not deployed, the alternative is authentication via preshared secrets. One should be mindful, however, that the security that preshared secrets offer is rather limited, especially if the passwords that are utilized to establish the VPN links are shared by a group of individuals.

If the corporation has remote access authentication systems deployed—such as SecurID, TACACS, RADIUS, one-time password systems, or others—it would be a good idea to find a solution that supports XAuth and Hybrid Auth with the given remote access authentication system that the corporation has in place. XAuth provides a twofold authentication: authentication of the machine using digital certificates or preshared secrets, and authentication of the user using legacy authentication systems. Hybrid Auth, on the other hand, allows asymmetric authentication in which remote VPN clients authenticate to VPN gateways using legacy authentication systems but the gateways authenticate to the remote client using digital certificates. Therefore, Hybrid Auth requires a limited deployment of PKIs, whereas XAuth does not. See Sections 11.7 and 11.8 for further information on XAuth and Hybrid Auth, respectively.

2. *Support for configuration via DHCP or Mode config:* It is essential that configuration via DHCP or Mode config be supported. If a VPN solution does not support either, it will be very tedious to configure, particularly for large-scale deployment. Of the two choices, configuration via DHCP is more desirable because it provides greater configuration features, and it leverages a mature protocol rather than extending IKE. For further details on configuration via DHCP and Mode config, see Sections 11.6 and 11.5, respectively.

3. *Supported encryption algorithms:* For encryption algorithms, at a minimum, AES should be supported; for interoperability with older VPN implementations, triple-DES support is also desirable. AES supports key sizes of 128, 192, and 256 bits; however, not all implementations support all three key sizes. AES with a 128-bit key is secure for most VPN traffic; however, for traffic with a medium or high security requirement, 192- or 256-bit keys should be used. If a high degree of flexibility is desired for the

VPN solution, one that supports all three key sizes for AES is more desirable. See Chapter 2 for details on AES and other cryptographic algorithms.

4. *Supported authentication algorithms:* The specification for IPSec stipulates that all IPSec implementations should support MD5 and SHA-1 hash functions with the message authentication code HMAC. SHA-1 is the more secure of the two hash functions by virtue of the fact that it produces a 160-bit message digest, versus a 128-bit digest for MD5. However, MD5 is faster so, if speed as opposed to added security is the concern—as is the case for dial-up or DSL links—MD5 might be the more prudent choice. In either case, both hash functions should be supported. For a high security requirement, a VPN solution that supports Tiger with a 192-bit message digest might be desirable. We discussed hash functions and message authentication codes in Chapter 4.

5. *Diffie-Hellman groups:* IKE employs Diffie-Hellman key exchange in ISAKMP phase 1 SA negotiations to establish common shared secrets for IPSec peers from which encryption and authentication keys are generated. The security of a Diffie-Hellman key exchange depends on the size of the Diffie-Hellman group it utilizes. Since phase 1 SAs are used to protect the negotiation of phase 2 (quick mode and new group mode) SAs, the overall security of the IPSec services, to a large extent, depends on the security of the Diffie-Hellman key exchange, the security of which ultimately depends on the size of the Diffie-Hellman group utilized. Therefore, it is paramount that a VPN solution supports adequately secure Diffie-Hellman groups. The security of the first four Diffie-Hellman groups (see Section 11.4 for information on these groups) is equivalent to that of a symmetric key of length between 70 and 80 bits. Considering that the minimum key size for AES is 128 bits, the security of the first groups may not be adequate. Support for group 5 or above, with a size of at least 1536 bits, should be sought.

6. *Supported IP compression algorithms:* Ideally, both DEFLATE and LZS compression algorithms should be supported. However, it is not critical that both algorithms be supported since an IPComp security association (IPCA) can be asymmetric; that is, for a given IPCA, the peers can use different compression algorithms. A VPN solution should nonetheless support at least one of these compression algorithms. As a word of caution, it can be counterproductive to use IP compression algorithms that are implemented badly. We mentioned in Chapter 12 that implementations of IPComp should involve adaptive algorithms to avoid degradation in performance resulting from attempts to compress incompressible data; if an appropriate adaptive algorithm is not implemented as part of an

IPComp implementation, enabling IPComp can result in a decrease in throughput rather than an increase. See Chapter 12 for further details on IPComp.

7. *Exchange modes:* IKE, according to the specification in RFC 2409, supports two modes of exchange for phase 1 SA negotiation: main mode or aggressive mode. The primary difference between them is that main mode offers protection for the identification information exchange during a phase 1 SA negotiation—the defined identification types are listed in Table 10-9—whereas aggressive mode exchange does not. Main mode protects the identification information at the expense of three additional messages from each of the negotiating peers. Considering that a single phase 1 SA can be used to protect multiple phase 2 SAs, the three additional round trip messages are worth having the identification information protected. However, aggressive mode is easier to implement than main mode; as a result, unfortunately, some VPN implementations only support aggressive mode for phase 1 SA negotiation. For interoperability with these VPN applications, aggressive mode exchange is required. Therefore, ideal VPN solutions usually support both main and aggressive modes for phase 1 SA negotiations. In addition, quick mode and new group mode exchanges should be supported for phase 2 SA negotiations.

8. *AH and ESP mode of operation:* Most VPN implementations support both transport and tunnel mode for AH and ESP. Some implementations allow one to explicitly select the desired mode of operation for these protocols, whereas others make the selection intuitively based on selected parameters. Each choice has its merits. Deciding between these two methodologies is often a matter of personal preference.

9. *Ease of deployment:* Another important consideration is the relative ease of deploying the VPN solutions. This should be of interest particularly for solutions that offer similar technological features. Some questions worth considering are: Can the deployment be automated? How easily can changes be made after the deployment? How readily can policies be enforced? For example, can features be "locked down" such that unauthorized users are unable to modify policies? An appropriate VPN solution should address these concerns in a meaningful way.

10. *Availability of a compatible distributed or personal firewall:* When a remote host establishes a VPN connection to a corporate network, if the remote host is compromised, the attacker will have free access to the corporate network via the compromised remote client. Therefore, it is important that steps be taken to protect the clients that are allowed to establish remote VPN links to the corporate network. Installing a personal firewall on the remote hosts, or alternatively, a distributed firewall that can be managed from a central location on the corporate network, are solutions that merit consideration. An ideal VPN solution should therefore allow the integration of personal and distributed firewalls for the protection of established VPN links.

13.3   A VPN Configuration Case Study

We conclude our presentation by presenting a case study involving the configuration of a VPN link between a Gauntlet firewall VPN server and a PGP VPN client using NetTools PKI for authentication. The applications involved are products of Network Associates Inc. (NAI). Gauntlet is one of the most secure and flexible firewalls and VPN gateways on the market today. The PGP VPN client evolved from the popular PGP (Pretty Good Privacy) file and e-mail encryption software. NetTools PKI is an Xcert PKI application licensed to NAI. Our aim for this case study is to illustrate some of the steps that are involved in configuring PKI servers, VPN gateways, and VPN clients to provide X.509 certificate authenticated VPN solutions. The configuration details differ for different PKI and VPN applications; however, some of the underlying principles are similar. The processes involved in configuring the VPN link are as follows:

1. Configuration of the PKI server

2. Configuration of the VPN gateway

3. Configuration of the VPN client

13.3.1   Configuration of the PKI Server

There are several steps involved in the configuration of a PKI server, and the steps and the format of the information required vary with different PKI solutions. However, the underlying principles are simular. For our presentation, we focus on five steps that are relevant to our discussion; they are as follows:

1. Input general configuration information

2. Creation of the root certificate authority (CA) certificate

3. Administrative CA certificate generation

4. Generation of the enrollment and administration web server certificates

5. Creation of an administrative client certificate

General Configuration Information

Figure 13-3 shows a screen shot of the web form with the information required for the general configuration of the PKI server. Let us take a look at each of the fields of this figure:

■ Webmaster E-mail Address: The NetTools PKI server uses a web browser as the interface. This field contains the e-mail address of the administrator for the web browser.

■ Name of Server Host: The fully qualified domain name of the machine on which the PKI server is installed.

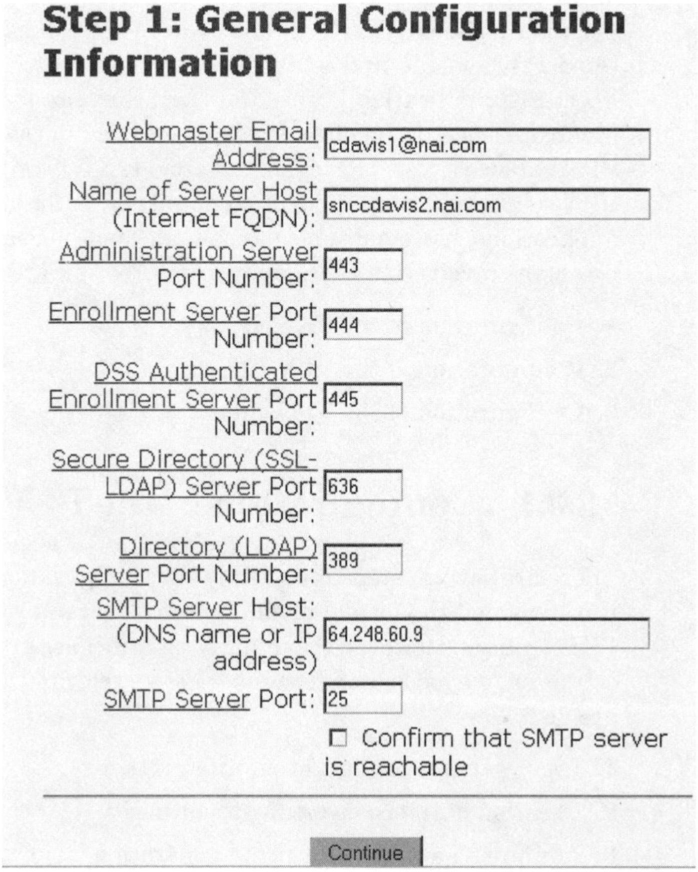

Figure 13-3
Information for General Configuration of PKI Server

Step 1: General Configuration Information

Webmaster Email Address:	cdavis1@nai.com
Name of Server Host (Internet FQDN):	snccdavis2.nai.com
Administration Server Port Number:	443
Enrollment Server Port Number:	444
DSS Authenticated Enrollment Server Port Number:	445
Secure Directory (SSL-LDAP) Server Port Number:	636
Directory (LDAP) Server Port Number:	389
SMTP Server Host: (DNS name or IP address)	64.248.60.9
SMTP Server Port:	25

☐ Confirm that SMTP server is reachable

Continue

- **Administration Server Port Number:** The NetTools PKI server has three portions and a separate interface for each portion: the administration, enrollment, and DSS authenticated enrollment servers, and their respective interfaces. The administration server is the portion that does the administrative tasks, such as generating, signing, issuing, and revoking of certificates. Only the PKI administrators (typically one or more CAs) should be allowed access to the interface for the administration server. The administration server listens on TCP port 443. The other portions of the NetTools PKI server are discussed below.

- **Enrollment Server Port Number:** The enrollment server is the second portion of the NetTools PKI server. It handles certificate requests from users and put them in the certificate request queue. The enrollment server listens on TCP port 444.

- **DSS Authenticated Enrollment Server Port Number:** This server is identical in function to the enrollment server. The only difference is that it serves certificates containing DSA (digital signature algorithm) keys, whereas the enrollment server serves certificates containing RSA keys. This server listens on TCP port 445.

- **Secure Directory (SSL-LDAP) Server Port Number:** The NetTools PKI directory server is a directory service which interfaces with the PKI database. It handles both LDAP and SSL-LDAP calls. The SSL-LDAP calls are used by the directory server to talk securely to the NetTools PKI database. The SSL-LDAP server listens on TCP port 636.

- **SMTP Server Host:** This field contains the DNS name or IP address of the mail server to which the PKI server should forward mail.

- **SMTP Server Port:** The port on the mail server to which mail should be directed. TCP port 25 is reserved for SMTP (Simple Mail Transfer Protocol).

Creation of a Root CA Certificate

The next step involves generating the root CA certificate. For details about the content of an X.509 certificate see Section 5.1.1. The root CA private key for the public key contained in the root CA certificate is used for the signing of CA certificates that the root CA issues. Figures 13-4 and 13-5 show screen shots of the web form eliciting the information for the creation of the root CA certificate.

Step 2: Root CA Creation

No problems were detected with the information provided in the previous step. Please proceed to provide information for the Root Certificate Authority.

- The Root CA will sign all SSL server certificates as well as the certificate of the Administrative CA.

Common Name (used as CA nickname) | `Root CA` **
 required **
E-mail Address | `cali@dsldesigns.com`
Organization Name | `Netfortify`
Organizational Unit | `Sales`
Locality | `Montreal`
State or Province | `Quebec`
2-letter Country Code | `CA`
Validity Period | `1100` days

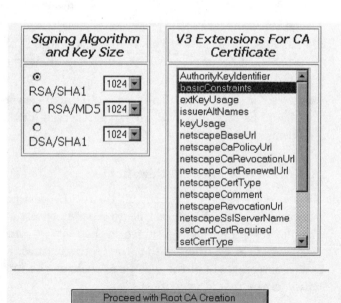

Signing Algorithm and Key Size

- ◉ RSA/SHA1 `1024`
- ○ RSA/MD5 `1024`
- ○ DSA/SHA1 `1024`

V3 Extensions For CA Certificate

- AuthorityKeyIdentifier
- basicConstraints
- extKeyUsage
- issuerAltNames
- keyUsage
- netscapeBaseUrl
- netscapeCaPolicyUrl
- netscapeCaRevocationUrl
- netscapeCertRenewalUrl
- netscapeCertType
- netscapeComment
- netscapeRevocationUrl
- netscapeSslServerName
- setCardCertRequired
- setCertType

Proceed with Root CA Creation

As shown in Figure 13-5, we selected a 1024-bit RSA key as our signing key; for the hash algorithm we selected SHA-1. The right-hand side of this figure indicates some of the X.509 version 3 extensions available for selection. We chose one extension: the basicConstraints extension. As explained in Chapter 5, the basicConstraints extension identifies whether the subject of the certificate is a CA, and if so, it specifies the depth of the certification path through this CA. The PKIX profile stipulates that this extension must appear as a critical extension in all CA certificates. However, it should not appear in non-CA certificates.

We are now ready to continue, so we press the Proceed with Root CA Creation button. The screen shot shown in Figure 13-6 is the result.

The web form shown in this screen shot allows us to select whether the extension should be critical or noncritical, indicates whether the certificate is a CA or end-entity certificate, and enters a value for the path length constraint. For the path length constraint, we enter a value of zero indicating that this is the root CA; therefore, no other CA certificates should follow this certificate in a certification path. See Section 5.1.2 for information about any of the other variables shown in this figure.

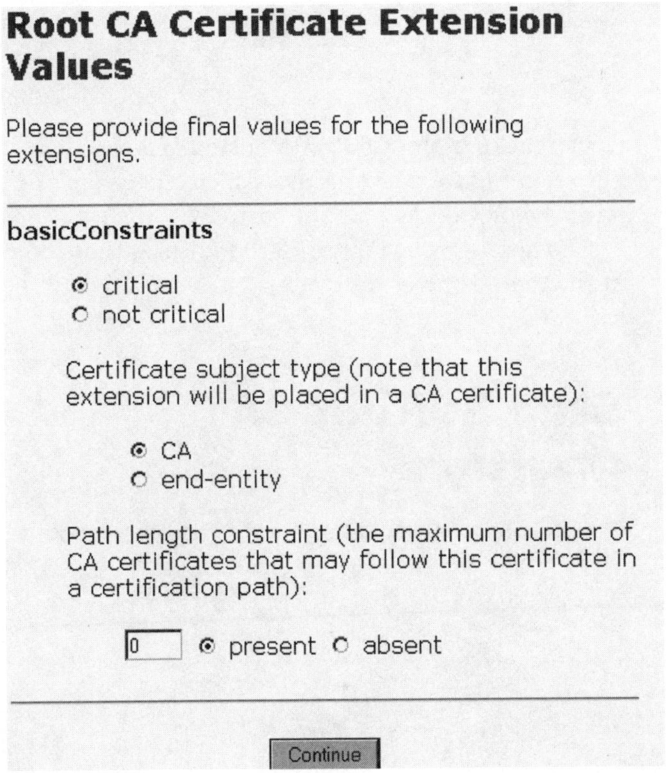

Figure 13-6
Information for Root
CA Extension

Root CA Certificate Extension Values

Please provide final values for the following extensions.

basicConstraints

  ⊙ critical
  ○ not critical

  Certificate subject type (note that this
  extension will be placed in a CA certificate):

    ⊙ CA
    ○ end-entity

  Path length constraint (the maximum number of
  CA certificates that may follow this certificate in
  a certification path):

    [0] ⊙ present ○ absent

[Continue]

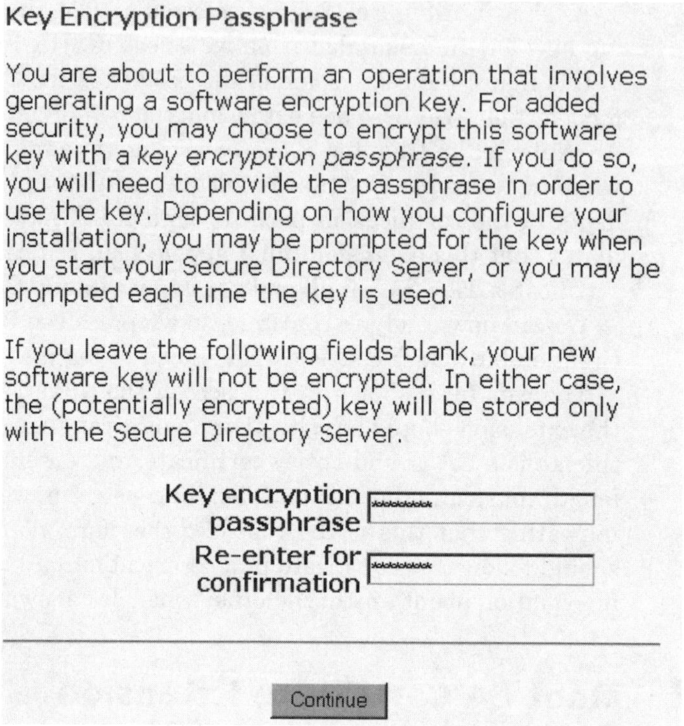

Figure 13-7

Information for
Encryption Pass-
Phrase for Root
CA Key

Key Encryption Passphrase

You are about to perform an operation that involves
generating a software encryption key. For added
security, you may choose to encrypt this software
key with a *key encryption passphrase*. If you do so,
you will need to provide the passphrase in order to
use the key. Depending on how you configure your
installation, you may be prompted for the key when
you start your Secure Directory Server, or you may be
prompted each time the key is used.

If you leave the following fields blank, your new
software key will not be encrypted. In either case,
the (potentially encrypted) key will be stored only
with the Secure Directory Server.

Key encryption passphrase [********]

Re-enter for confirmation [********]

[Continue]

On clicking the Continue button indicated in Figure 13-6, the form
shown in Figure 13-7 appears, which elicits a pass-phrase to be associated
with the private key for the root CA.

The next screen (Figure 13-8) indicates that the root CA certificate has
been created successfully.

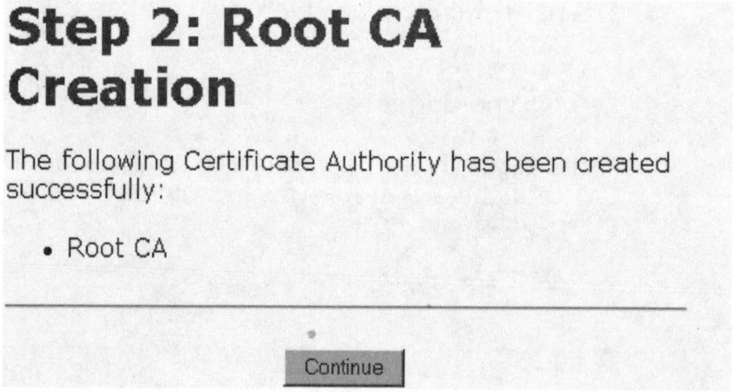

Figure 13-8

Information for the
Successful Creation
of the Root CA
Certificate

Step 2: Root CA Creation

The following Certificate Authority has been created
successfully:

- Root CA

[Continue]

Creation of an Administrative CA Certificate

Next we create the administrative CA certificate. The administrative CA private key will be used to sign clients' administrative certificates. Figures 13-9 to 13-13 show the screen shots relating the creation of the administrative CA certificate.

Figure 13-9
Information for the Ccreation of Administrative CA Certificate

Step 2b: Administrative CA Creation

Please proceed to provide information for the Administrative Certificate Authority.

- Client certificates issued by the Administrative CA will have access to the Net Tools PKI Server Administration server.

Common Name (used as CA nickname) required **	Administrative CA **
E-mail Address	PKIAdmin@netfortify.com
Organization Name	Netfortify
Organizational Unit	Sales
Locality	Montreal
State or Province	Quebec
2-letter Country Code	CA
Validity Period	1095 days

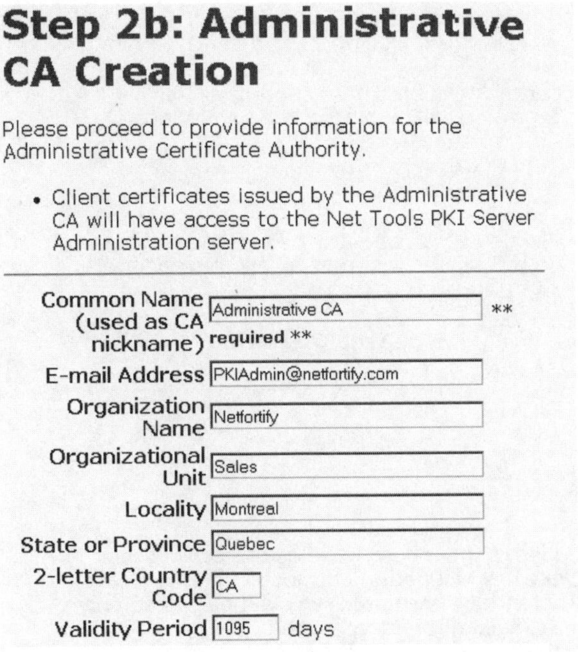

Figure 13-10
Information for the Creation of Administrative CA Certificate

Signing Algorithm and Key Size

- ◉ RSA/SHA1 [1024 ▼]
- ○ RSA/MD5 [1024 ▼]
- ○ DSA/SHA1 [1024 ▼]

V3 Extensions For CA Certificate

AuthorityKeyIdentifier
basicConstraints
extKeyUsage
issuerAltNames
keyUsage
netscapeBaseUrl
netscapeCaPolicyUrl
netscapeCaRevocationUrl
netscapeCertRenewalUrl
netscapeCertType
netscapeComment
netscapeRevocationUrl
netscapeSslServerName
setCardCertRequired
setCertType

[Continue]

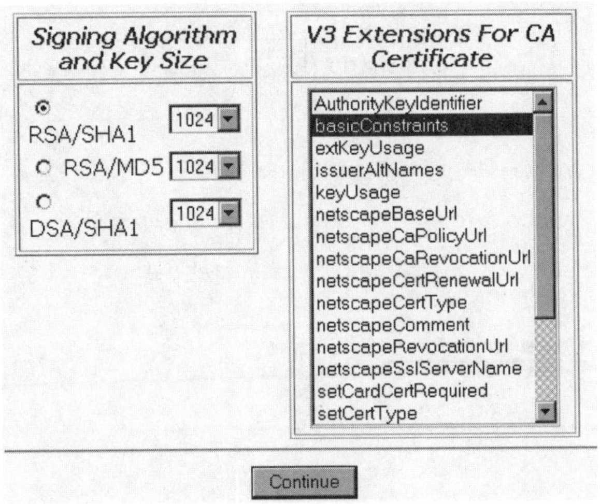

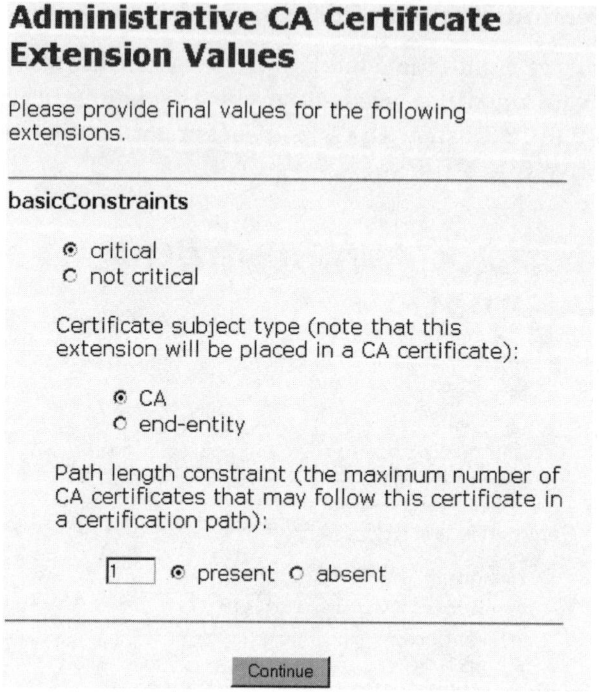

Figure 13-11
Information for
Administrative
CA Extension

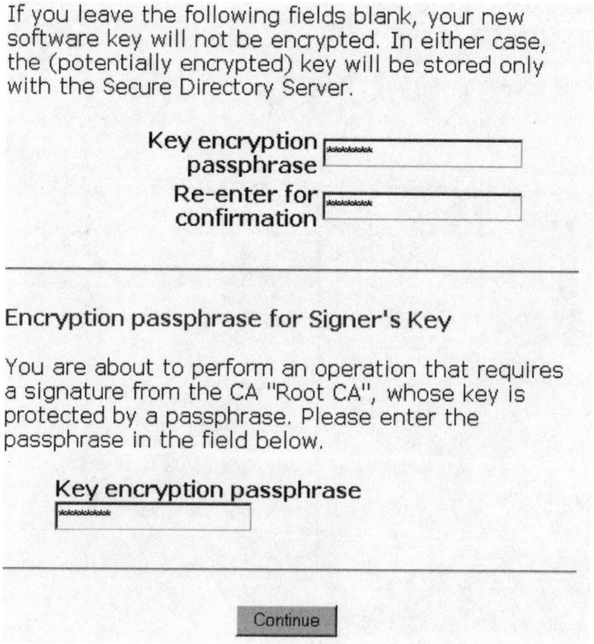

Administrative CA Certificate Extension Values

Please provide final values for the following extensions.

basicConstraints

◉ critical
○ not critical

Certificate subject type (note that this extension will be placed in a CA certificate):

◉ CA
○ end-entity

Path length constraint (the maximum number of CA certificates that may follow this certificate in a certification path):

[1] ◉ present ○ absent

[Continue]

Figure 13-12
Information for
Encryption
Pass-Phrase for
Administrative CA Key

If you leave the following fields blank, your new software key will not be encrypted. In either case, the (potentially encrypted) key will be stored only with the Secure Directory Server.

Key encryption passphrase [**********]
Re-enter for confirmation [**********]

Encryption passphrase for Signer's Key

You are about to perform an operation that requires a signature from the CA "Root CA", whose key is protected by a passphrase. Please enter the passphrase in the field below.

Key encryption passphrase
[**********]

[Continue]

Step 2b: Administrative CA Creation

The following Certificate Authority has been created successfully:

- Administrative CA

Continue

Note that for the path length constraint for the basic constraints extension for the administrative CA (Figure 13-11), we entered 1 indicating that one CA certificate (the root CA certificate) should follow this certificate in a certification path. All CA certificates typically require the signature of the root CA. The pass-phrase assigned to the root CA is required to access the private key associated with the public key contained in the root CA certificate. We inputted the root CA pass-phrase in the field shown in Figure 13-12.

Creation of Enrollment and Administrative Web Server Certificates

The next step in the PKI configuration process involves the creation of the enrollment and administrative web server certificates. These certificates will be used for access control to the enrollment and administrative servers. Figures 13-14 to 13-16 show the screen shots relating to the generation of these certificates.

The Enrollment Server

Common Name	Enrollment cert **
	**required **
Webmaster E-mail Address	cali@dsldesigns.com
Organization Name	Netfortify
Organizational Unit	Sales
Locality	Montreal
State or Province	Quebec
2-letter Country Code	CA
Key size (in bits)	1024

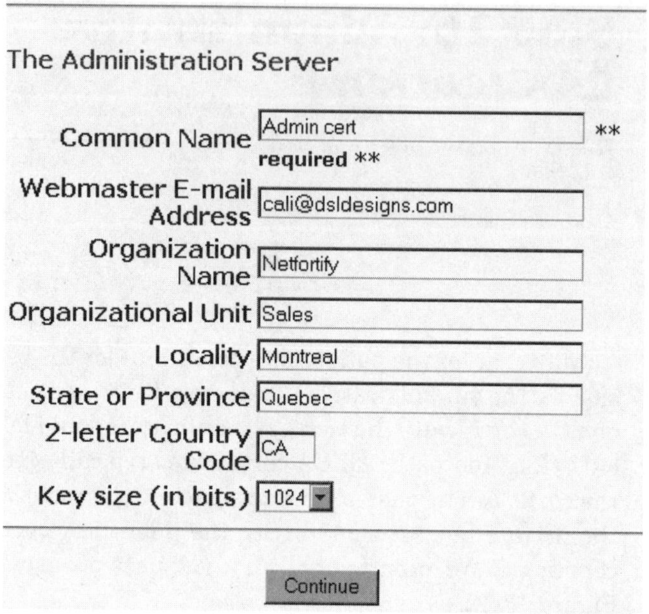

■ ■ ■ ■
Figure 13-15
Information for
Administrative Web
Server Certificate

The Administration Server

Common Name | Admin cert | **
required **

Webmaster E-mail Address | cali@dsldesigns.com

Organization Name | Netfortify

Organizational Unit | Sales

Locality | Montreal

State or Province | Quebec

2-letter Country Code | CA

Key size (in bits) | 1024 ▾

[Continue]

■ ■ ■ ■
Figure 13-16
Information Relating
to Pass-Phrase for
Enrollment and
Administrative Web
Server Certificates

Key Encryption Passphrase

You are about to perform an operation that involves
generating one or more software keys for certificates
to be used for SSL connections. These keys will be
written to files on your hard disk. For added security,
you may choose to encrypt the keys with a *key
encryption passphrase*.

If you leave the following fields blank, your new
software keys will not be encrypted.

Key encryption passphrase | ********

Re-enter for confirmation | ********

Encryption passphrase for Signer's Key

You are about to perform an operation that requires
a signature from the CA "Root CA", whose key is
protected by a passphrase. Please enter the
passphrase in the field below.

Key encryption passphrase

****

Generation of an Administrative Client Certificate}

As mentioned previously, only PKI server administrators should be able to connect to the administrative server. In order to force this access control, access to the administrative server is restricted to hosts that have an administrative client certificate signed by administrative CA. This step involves the creation of an administrative client certificate that is issued to the PKI server administrator. Figures 13-17 to 13-19 show the screen shots relating to the generation of this certificate.

Figure 13-17
Information Relating
to an Administrative
Client Certificate

Administrative Certificate Information

Since client authentication will be active for the administrative interface to Net Tools PKI Server, you will need an Administrative Client Certificate to manage your installation.

This form collects the information that will be used to generate this administrative certificate.

Name: `Administrator` **
Required **

Email: `PKIAdmin@netfortify.com`

Organization: `Netfortify`

Organization Unit: `Sales`

Locality: `Montreal`

State/Province (do not abbreviate): `Quebec`

Country Code (2 letter): `CA`

Continue

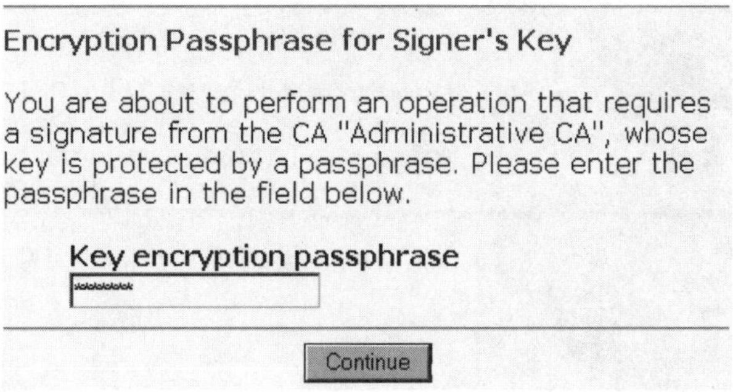

Figure 13-18
Pass-Phrase
Information

Encryption Passphrase for Signer's Key

You are about to perform an operation that requires a signature from the CA "Administrative CA", whose key is protected by a passphrase. Please enter the passphrase in the field below.

Key encryption passphrase

`********`

Continue

Figure 13-19
Enabling
Administrative
Certificate Access

Enable Administrative Certificate Access

1. Download your Administrative Client Certificate into your browser by clicking on the button below.

Please note:
> Your MSIE browser might require that you stop and restart it OR that you start a new copy of your browser, before a newly downloaded certificate can be used. If you decide to stop and restart your browser be sure to do this only AFTER downloading your Administrative Client Certificate.

Download Administrative Client Certificate...

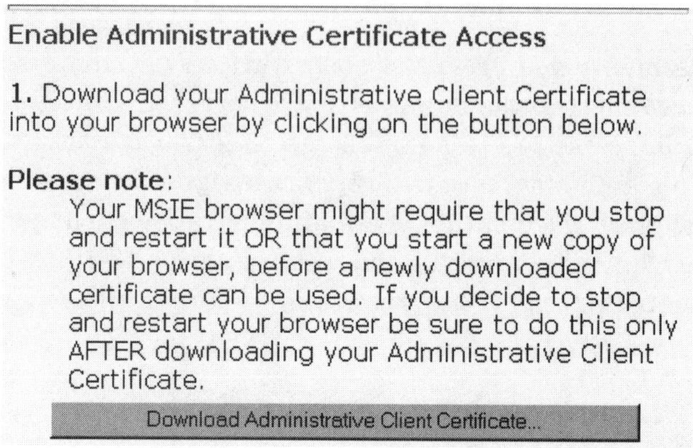

At the end of these steps, the PKI server is configured and ready to be used. Figures 13.20 and 13.21 show screen shots of the web interface to the administrative and enrollment servers, respectively.

Figure 13-20
Web Interface to
the NetTools PKI
Administrative Server

Figure 13-21
Web interface to
the NetTools PKI
Enrollment Server

Figure 13-21
Web interface to
the NetTools PKI
Enrollment Server

13.3.2 Configuration of the VPN Gateway

There are six principal steps involved in configuring the Gauntlet firewall
VPN gateway:

1. Create PKI components.
2. Download CA certificates.
3. Create a request for a firewall certificate.
4. Retrieve the firewall certificate from the PKI server when it is
   issued, and activate it.
5. Configure the VPN link.
6. Configure link settings.

Creating PKI Components

The Gauntlet firewall uses PKI components to interface with CAs and to
manage certificates issued by CAs. We need to create PKI components for
the root CA certificate. The steps involved are as follows:

1. Select Environment from the Gauntlet graphical user interface (GUI),
   and then click PKI. Figure 13-22 shows the resulting screen shot.

Figure 13-22
Gauntlet GUI

WebShield 300 E-ppliance joab
File Help
PKI
WebShield 300
Rules
Rule Elements
Services
Environment
Authentication
Content Scanning
Fwd Filter Rules
Local Filter Rules
NAT
Perimeter
PKI
SNMP Agent
Reports
Maintenance
VPNs
Name
CA Type
Add...
Modify...
Delete
Get CA Cert...
Create Cert Request...
Ready
Mod

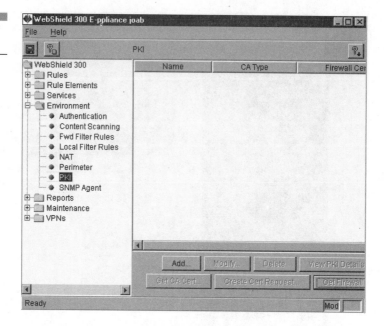

2. Next, click the Add button. Figure 13-23 shows the resulting screen with the inputted information.
3. Following this, we click the OK button. The resulting screen is shown in Figure 13-24.

Figure 13-23
Add PKI Component Screen

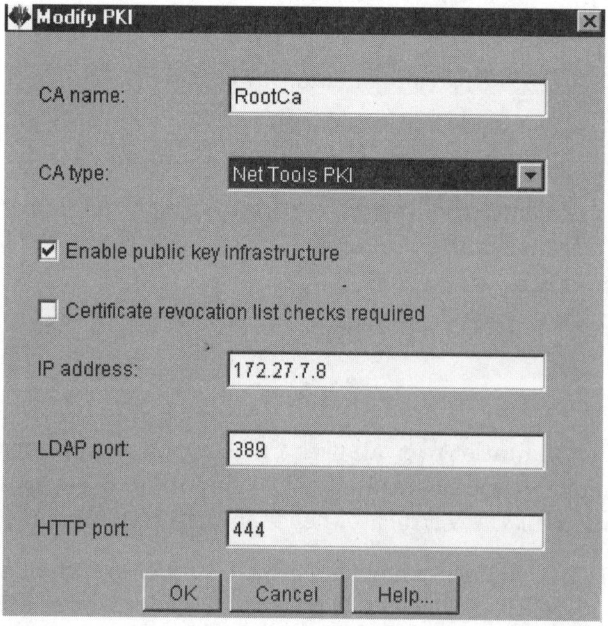

Modify PKI
CA name:
RootCa
CA type:
Net Tools PKI
Enable public key infrastructure
Certificate revocation list checks required
IP address:
172.27.7.8
LDAP port:
389
HTTP port:
444
OK
Cancel
Help...

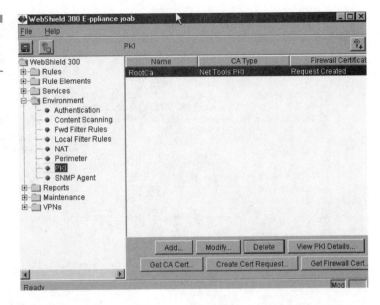

Figure 13-24
Add PKI Component
Screen

Downloading the CA Certificates

After creating the PKI components, we need to download the root CA certificate from the PKI server and load it on the firewall. The firewall needs this CA certificate to validate the VPN clients' certificates during the authentication process of the IKE SA negotiations. The steps involved in downloading the root CA certificate are as follows:

1. Click the Get CA Cert button. The resulting screen shot is shown in Figure 13-25. All the input fields, except the Common name

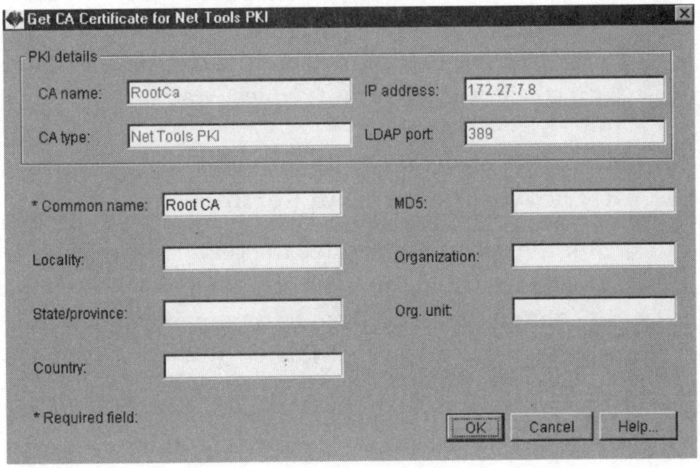

Figure 13-25
Get CA Certificate
Screen

Figure 13-26

NetTools PKI CA
Certificate

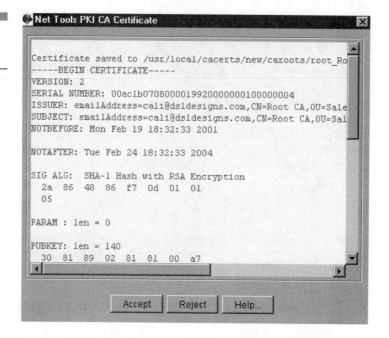

> **Net Tools PKI CA Certificate**
>
> ```
> Certificate saved to /usr/local/cacerts/new/caroots/root_Ro
> -----BEGIN CERTIFICATE-----
> VERSION: 2
> SERIAL NUMBER: 00ac1b07080000199200000000100000004
> ISSUER: emailAddress=cali@dsldesigns.com,CN=Root CA,OU=Sale
> SUBJECT: emailAddress=cali@dsldesigns.com,CN=Root CA,OU=Sal
> NOTBEFORE: Mon Feb 19 18:32:33 2001
>
> NOTAFTER: Tue Feb 24 18:32:33 2004
>
> SIG ALG:  SHA-1 Hash with RSA Encryption
>    2a  86  48  86  f7  0d  01  01
>    05
>
> PARAM : len = 0
>
> PUBKEY: len = 140
>    30  81  89  02  81  81  00  a7
> ```
>
> Accept   Reject   Help...

field, are optional. Input Root CA in this field and click the OK button. Figure 13-26 shows the resulting screen shot.

2. Next, click the Accept button to load the root CA certificate on the firewall.

Generating a Request for a Firewall Certificate

To generate a request for a firewall certificate, click the Create Cert Request button indicated in Figure 13-24. The resulting screen with the information inputted is shown in Figure 13-27.

On clicking the OK button, the display in Figure 13-28 appears, indicating that the certificate request was successfully generated and sent to the PKI server.

Retrieving the Firewall Certificate

After the firewall generates the certificate request and sends it to the PKI server, the root CA needs to create a certificate for the firewall, based on the information submitted in the certificate request. The CA can view the pending requests for certificates by clicking Manage pending requests on the web interface for the PKI administration server. The display shown in Figure 13-29 results.

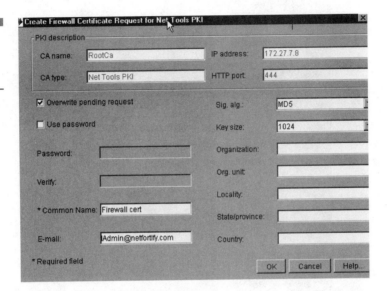

Figure 13-27
Create Firewall
Certificate Request
Screen

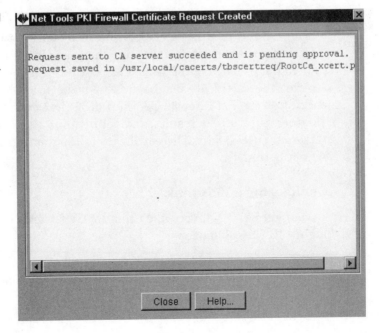

Figure 13-28
Firewall Certificate
Request Created

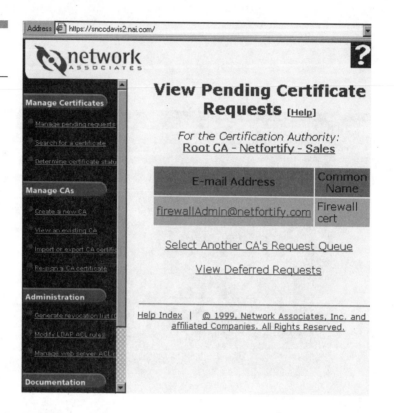

The CA can then issue the certificate by clicking the e-mail address address for the certificate, inputting the pass-phrase for the root CA, and confirming by clicking the Issue Cert button.

After the certificate has been issued, the firewall can retrieve it by clicking on the Get Firewall Cert button on the screen displayed in Figure 13-25. Figure 13-30 results, indicating that the certificate has been retrieved successfully. The certificate is then activated by pressing the Accept button.

Configuring a VPN Link

To configure a VPN link on the Gauntlet GUI, click VPNs and then Links; Figure 13-31 will appear.

1. On clicking the Add button, Figure 13-32 appears minus the information that was inputted. Let us take a look at some of the options in this figure:

   ■ Link type: There are three choices: Private, Trusted, and Pass Through. Private links provide privacy without trust;

Figure 13-30
Retrieving Firewall
Certificate

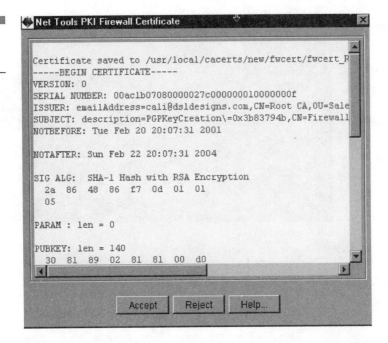

that is, the ESP confidentiality service is applied to the packets. However, when the packets get to the firewall, they are subjected to security screening rules as if the packets originated from an untrusted host. Trusted links provide both privacy and trust. They differ from private links in that the packets are not

Figure 13-31
Adding a VPN Link

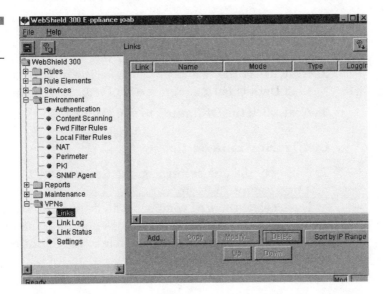

Figure 13-32
Add VPN Link
Configuration

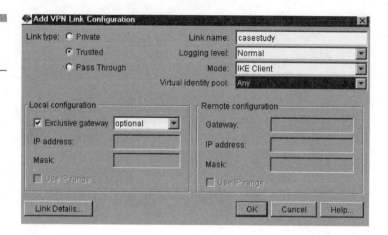

subjected to security screening rules when they arrive at the firewall. Pass through links allow packets that are part of a Gauntlet VPN to pass through the firewall without being altered or subjected to security screening rules.

- ▪ Exclusive gateway: This option can be used to force all VPN traffic to pass through the VPN gateway.

- ▪ Link name: A name to identify the VPN link.

- ▪ Mode: There are two choices: IKE Client mode and IKE Dynamic Key. IKE client mode is utilized for links with VPN clients that have dynamic IP addresses; IKE dynamic key mode is used for VPN peers with static IP addresses.

- ▪ Virtual identity pool: This is the pool of addresses for Mode config. The configuration information for the IP addresses is presented below.

2. Next, select the security options for the link by clicking on the Link Details button. Figure 13-33 indicates the selected choices.

3. Next, click the OK button to add the link.

Configuring Link Settings

To configure the link settings on the Gauntlet GUI, select VPNs and click Settings. Figure 13-34 appears.

Then, select the PKI component to be used to manage the certificates for this link by clicking PKI Settings and then the Add button to make the root CA PKI components available to the Gauntlet VPN. Figure 13-35 shows the resulting screen.

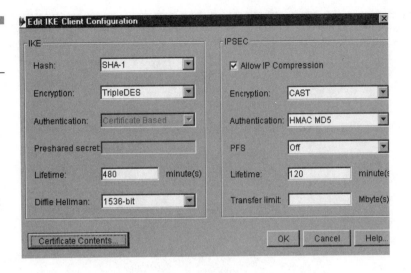

Figure 13-33
Selecting Security
Options

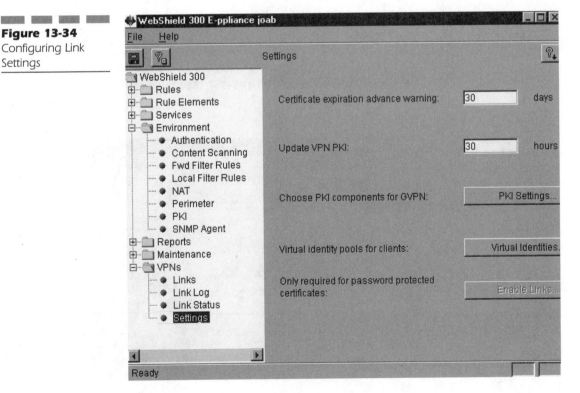

Figure 13-34
Configuring Link
Settings

Figure 13-35
Configuring PKI
Settings

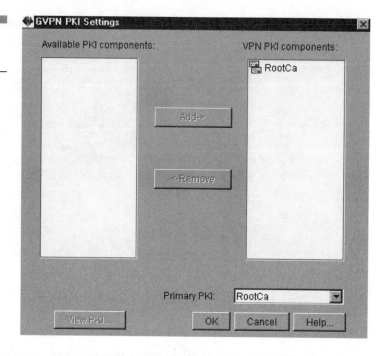

Next, configure the virtual identity (Mode config) address pool by clicking the Virtual Identities button indicated in Figure 13-34, click Add, and input the requested information. Figure 13-36 results.

Following this, click the Addresses button and add the IP address pool. Figure 13-37 results.

Figure 13-36
Adding Virtual Client
Identity Pool

Figure 13-37
Adding Virtual Client
Identity Pool

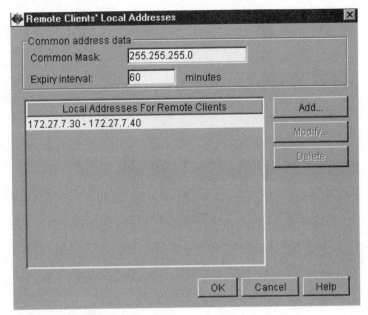

At the end of these steps, the VPN link on the Gauntlet is configured; any VPN client with a valid NetTools PKI certificate signed by the root CA we created should now be able to establish a VPN tunnel with the Gauntlet firewall VPN gateway.

We will now turn our attention to the configuration of the PGP VPN client.

13.3.3 Configuration of the VPN Client

The configuration of the PGP VPN client involves the following steps:

1. Obtain a digital certificate and add it to the key ring. This can be done as follows:

   ■ Retrieve the root CA certificate and add it to the key ring. Typically, this involves connecting via a web browser to the enrollment server, clicking on Download a CA certificate, clicking on Examine this CA cert, and copying the certificate and pasting it to the PGP key ring.

   ■ Configure the PGPnet CA panel. Figure 13-38 shows the CA panel with the configuration information.

Figure 13-38
Configuration of CA
Panel

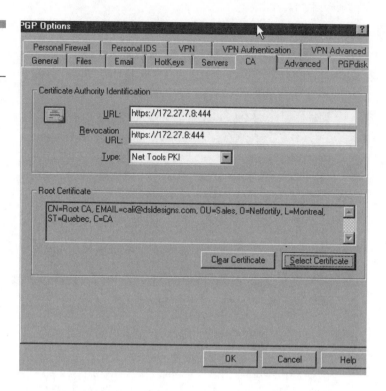

- Make a certificate request. Figure 13-39 shows the information submitted for the certificate request.

- When the certificate is issued, PGP receives the certificate automatically.

Figure 13-39
Certificate Request
Information

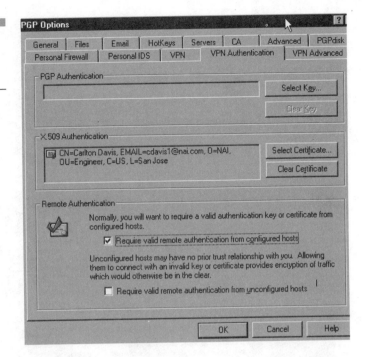

Figure 13-40
Selecting the
Authenticating
Certificate

2. Select the certificate that will be used for authentication to the VPN gateway. Figure 13-40 indicates this selection.

3. Add the VPN link. This can be done as follows: from the PGPnet GUI (Figure 13-41) click Add and select the required options. Figure 13-42 results.

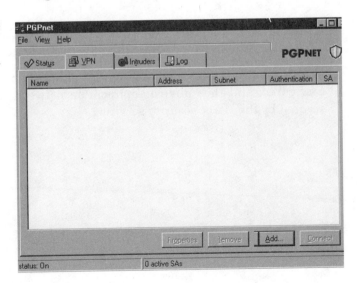

Figure 13-41
Adding a VPN Link

Figure 13-42
Configuring the VPN
Link

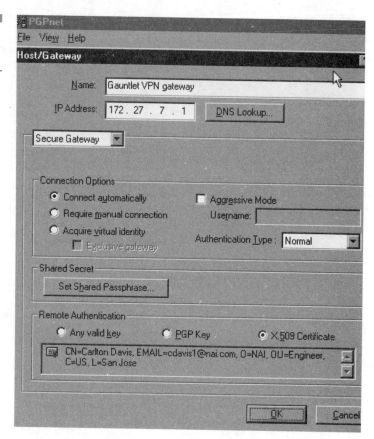

4. Configure the security policy database (SPD). Figure 13-43 shows the encryption and authentication algorithms selected.

At the end of these steps both the VPN gateway and the VPN client are configured, and thus any communication between these hosts will be secured by the IPSec security services.

Figure 13-43
Configuring the
Security Policy
Database

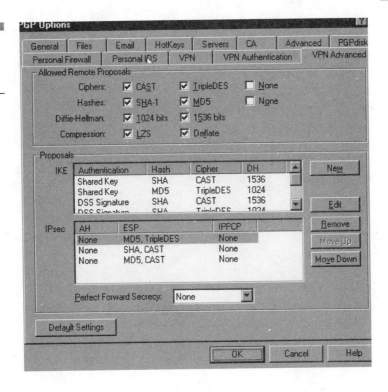

A Reference C Implementation for AES

Rijndael cryptographic algorithm was designated the Advance Encryption Standard (AES) by the National Institute of Standards and Technology (NIST) in September 2000. We would like to express our gratitude to the authors of Rijndael for giving us their permission to include this reference implementation of AES in our presentation.

The implementation consists of five files. We list the files below in the order we presented them.

1. rijndael-alg-ref.h: Contains the header file for the algorithm implementation.

2. rijndael-alg-ref.c: The algorithm implementation.

3. rijndael-api-ref.h: The header file for an interface to the C API.

4. rijndael-api-ref.c: Implementation for the interface to the C API.

5. boxes-ref.dat: Tables that are needed by the reference implementation. The tables implement the S-box and its inverse, and also some temporary tables needed for multiplying in the finite field $GF(2^8)$.

```
/* rijndael-alg-ref.h  v2.0  August '99
 * Reference ANSI C code
 * authors: Paulo Barreto
 *          Vincent Rijmen, K.U.Leuven
 */
#ifndef __RIJNDAEL_ALG_H
#define __RIJNDAEL_ALG_H

#define MAXBC                           (256/32)
#define MAXKC                           (256/32)
#define MAXROUNDS                       14


typedef unsigned char           word8;
typedef unsigned short          word16;
typedef unsigned long           word32;

int rijndaelKeySched (word8 k[4][MAXKC], int keyBits, int blockBits,
            word8 rk[MAXROUNDS+1][4][MAXBC]);
int rijndaelEncrypt (word8 a[4][MAXBC], int keyBits, int blockBits,
            word8 rk[MAXROUNDS+1][4][MAXBC]);
int rijndaelEncryptRound (word8 a[4][MAXBC], int keyBits, int blockBits,
            word8 rk[MAXROUNDS+1][4][MAXBC], int rounds);
int rijndaelDecrypt (word8 a[4][MAXBC], int keyBits, int blockBits,
            word8 rk[MAXROUNDS+1][4][MAXBC]);
int rijndaelDecryptRound (word8 a[4][MAXBC], int keyBits, int blockBits,
            word8 rk[MAXROUNDS+1][4][MAXBC], int rounds);


#endif /* __RIJNDAEL_ALG_H */




/* rijndael-alg-ref.c  v2.0  August '99
 * Reference ANSI C code
 * authors: Paulo Barreto
 *          Vincent Rijmen, K.U.Leuven
 *
 * This code is placed in the public domain.
 */

#include <stdio.h>
#include <stdlib.h>

#include "rijndael-alg-ref.h"

#define SC      ((BC - 4) >> 1)

#include "boxes-ref.dat"
```

```
static word8 shifts[3][4][2] = {
   0, 0,
   1, 3,
   2, 2,
   3, 1,

   0, 0,
   1, 5,
   2, 4,
   3, 3,

   0, 0,
   1, 7,
   3, 5,
   4, 4
};



word8 mul(word8 a, word8 b) {
   /* multiply two elements of GF(2^m)
    * needed for MixColumn and InvMixColumn
    */
       if (a && b) return Alogtable[(Logtable[a] + Logtable[b])%255];
       else return 0;
}


void KeyAddition(word8 a[4][MAXBC], word8 rk[4][MAXBC], word8 BC) {
       /* Exor corresponding text input and round key input bytes
        */
       int i, j;

       for(i = 0; i < 4; i++)
              for(j = 0; j < BC; j++) a[i][j] ^= rk[i][j];
}


void ShiftRow(word8 a[4][MAXBC], word8 d, word8 BC) {
       /* Row 0 remains unchanged
        * The other three rows are shifted a variable amount
        */
       word8 tmp[MAXBC];
       int i, j;

       for(i = 1; i < 4; i++) {
           for(j = 0; j < BC; j++) tmp[j] = a[i][(j + shifts[SC][i][d]) % BC];
              for(j = 0; j < BC; j++) a[i][j] = tmp[j];
       }
}
```

```c
void Substitution(word8 a[4][MAXBC], word8 box[256], word8 BC) {
        /* Replace every byte of the input by the byte at that place
         * in the nonlinear S-box
         */
        int i, j;

        for(i = 0; i < 4; i++)
                for(j = 0; j < BC; j++) a[i][j] = box[a[i][j]] ;
}

void MixColumn(word8 a[4][MAXBC], word8 BC) {
        /* Mix the four bytes of every column in a linear way
         */
        word8 b[4][MAXBC];
        int i, j;

        for(j = 0; j < BC; j++)
                for(i = 0; i < 4; i++)
                        b[i][j] = mul(2,a[i][j])
                                ^ mul(3,a[(i + 1) % 4][j])
                                ^ a[(i + 2) % 4][j]
                                ^ a[(i + 3) % 4][j];
        for(i = 0; i < 4; i++)
                for(j = 0; j < BC; j++) a[i][j] = b[i][j];
}

void InvMixColumn(word8 a[4][MAXBC], word8 BC) {
        /* Mix the four bytes of every column in a linear way
         * This is the opposite operation of Mixcolumn
         */
        word8 b[4][MAXBC];
        int i, j;

        for(j = 0; j < BC; j++)
        for(i = 0; i < 4; i++)
                b[i][j] = mul(0xe,a[i][j])
                        ^ mul(0xb,a[(i + 1) % 4][j])
                        ^ mul(0xd,a[(i + 2) % 4][j])
                        ^ mul(0x9,a[(i + 3) % 4][j]);
        for(i = 0; i < 4; i++)
                for(j = 0; j < BC; j++) a[i][j] = b[i][j];
}
```

```
int rijndaelKeySched (word8 k[4][MAXKC], int keyBits, int blockBits,
                      word8 W[MAXROUNDS+1][4][MAXBC]) {
        /* Calculate the necessary round keys
         * The number of calculations depends on keyBits and blockBits
         */
        int KC, BC, ROUNDS;
        int i, j, t, rconpointer = 0;
        word8 tk[4][MAXKC];

        switch (keyBits) {
        case 128: KC = 4; break;
        case 192: KC = 6; break;
        case 256: KC = 8; break;
        default : return (-1);
        }

        switch (blockBits) {
        case 128: BC = 4; break;
        case 192: BC = 6; break;
        case 256: BC = 8; break;
        default : return (-2);
        }

        switch (keyBits >= blockBits ? keyBits : blockBits) {
        case 128: ROUNDS = 10; break;
        case 192: ROUNDS = 12; break;
        case 256: ROUNDS = 14; break;
        default : return (-3); /* this cannot happen */
        }


        for(j = 0; j < KC; j++)
                for(i = 0; i < 4; i++)
                        tk[i][j] = k[i][j];
        t = 0;
        /* copy values into round key array */
        for(j = 0; (j < KC) && (t < (ROUNDS+1)*BC); j++, t++)
                for(i = 0; i < 4; i++) W[t / BC][i][t % BC] = tk[i][j];

        while (t < (ROUNDS+1)*BC) { /* while not enough round key
                                       material calculated */
            /* calculate new values */
            for(i = 0; i < 4; i++)
                tk[i][0] ^= S[tk[(i+1)%4][KC-1]];
            tk[0][0] ^= rcon[rconpointer++];

            if (KC != 8)
                for(j = 1; j < KC; j++)
                        for(i = 0; i < 4; i++) tk[i][j] ^= tk[i][j-1];
```

```
        else {
                for(j = 1; j < KC/2; j++)
                        for(i = 0; i < 4; i++) tk[i][j] ^= tk[i][j-1];
                for(i = 0; i < 4; i++) tk[i][KC/2] ^= S[tk[i][KC/2 - 1]];
                for(j = KC/2 + 1; j < KC; j++)
                        for(i = 0; i < 4; i++) tk[i][j] ^= tk[i][j-1];
        }
        /* copy values into round key array */
        for(j = 0; (j < KC) && (t < (ROUNDS+1)*BC); j++, t++)
                for(i = 0; i < 4; i++) W[t / BC][i][t % BC] = tk[i][j];
        }

        return 0;
}

int rijndaelEncrypt (word8 a[4][MAXBC], int keyBits, int blockBits,
                        word8 rk[MAXROUNDS+1][4][MAXBC])
{
        /* Encryption of one block.
         */
        int r, BC, ROUNDS;

        switch (blockBits) {
        case 128: BC = 4; break;
        case 192: BC = 6; break;
        case 256: BC = 8; break;
        default : return (-2);
        }

        switch (keyBits >= blockBits ? keyBits : blockBits) {
        case 128: ROUNDS = 10; break;
        case 192: ROUNDS = 12; break;
        case 256: ROUNDS = 14; break;
        default : return (-3); /* this cannot happen */
        }

        /* begin with a key addition
         */
        KeyAddition(a,rk[0],BC);

        /* ROUNDS-1 ordinary rounds
         */
        for(r = 1; r < ROUNDS; r++) {
                Substitution(a,S,BC);
                ShiftRow(a,0,BC);
                MixColumn(a,BC);
                KeyAddition(a,rk[r],BC);
        }
```

```
        /* Last round is special: there is no MixColumn
         */
        Substitution(a,S,BC);
        ShiftRow(a,0,BC);
        KeyAddition(a,rk[ROUNDS],BC);

        return 0;
}




int rijndaelEncryptRound (word8 a[4][MAXBC], int keyBits, int blockBits,
                word8 rk[MAXROUNDS+1][4][MAXBC], int rounds)
/* Encrypt only a certain number of rounds.
 * Only used in the Intermediate Value Known Answer Test.
 */
{
        int r, BC, ROUNDS;

        switch (blockBits) {
        case 128: BC = 4; break;
        case 192: BC = 6; break;
        case 256: BC = 8; break;
        default : return (-2);
        }

        switch (keyBits >= blockBits ? keyBits : blockBits) {
        case 128: ROUNDS = 10; break;
        case 192: ROUNDS = 12; break;
        case 256: ROUNDS = 14; break;
        default : return (-3); /* this cannot happen */
        }

        /* make number of rounds sane */
        if (rounds > ROUNDS) rounds = ROUNDS;

        /* begin with a key addition
         */
        KeyAddition(a,rk[0],BC);

        /* at most ROUNDS-1 ordinary rounds
         */
        for(r = 1; (r <= rounds) && (r < ROUNDS); r++) {
                Substitution(a,S,BC);
                ShiftRow(a,0,BC);
                MixColumn(a,BC);
                KeyAddition(a,rk[r],BC);
        }
```

```
        /* if necessary, do the last, special, round:
         */
        if (rounds == ROUNDS) {
                Substitution(a,S,BC);
                ShiftRow(a,0,BC);
                KeyAddition(a,rk[ROUNDS],BC);
        }

        return 0;
}


int rijndaelDecrypt (word8 a[4][MAXBC], int keyBits, int blockBits,
                        word8 rk[MAXROUNDS+1][4][MAXBC])
{
        int r, BC, ROUNDS;

        switch (blockBits) {
        case 128: BC = 4; break;
        case 192: BC = 6; break;
        case 256: BC = 8; break;
        default : return (-2);
        }

        switch (keyBits >= blockBits ? keyBits : blockBits) {
        case 128: ROUNDS = 10; break;
        case 192: ROUNDS = 12; break;
        case 256: ROUNDS = 14; break;
        default : return (-3); /* this cannot happen */
        }

        /* To decrypt: apply the inverse operations of the encrypt routine,
         *             in opposite order
         *
         * (KeyAddition is an involution: it 's equal to its inverse)
         * (the inverse of Substitution with table S is Substitution
         *   with the inverse table of S)
         * (the inverse of Shiftrow is Shiftrow over a suitable distance)
         */

        /* First the special round:
         *   without InvMixColumn
         *   with extra KeyAddition
         */
        KeyAddition(a,rk[ROUNDS],BC);
        Substitution(a,Si,BC);
        ShiftRow(a,1,BC);
```

```
        /* ROUNDS-1 ordinary rounds
         */
        for(r = ROUNDS-1; r > 0; r-) {
                KeyAddition(a,rk[r],BC);
                InvMixColumn(a,BC);
                Substitution(a,Si,BC);
                ShiftRow(a,1,BC);
        }

        /* End with the extra key addition
         */

        KeyAddition(a,rk[0],BC);

        return 0;
}


int rijndaelDecryptRound (word8 a[4][MAXBC], int keyBits, int blockBits,
        word8 rk[MAXROUNDS+1][4][MAXBC], int rounds)
/* Decrypt only a certain number of rounds.
 * Only used in the Intermediate Value Known Answer Test.
 * Operations rearranged such that the intermediate values of decryption
 * correspond with the intermediate values of encryption.
 */
{
        int r, BC, ROUNDS;

        switch (blockBits) {
        case 128: BC = 4; break;
        case 192: BC = 6; break;
        case 256: BC = 8; break;
        default : return (-2);
        }

        switch (keyBits >= blockBits ? keyBits : blockBits) {
        case 128: ROUNDS = 10; break;
        case 192: ROUNDS = 12; break;
        case 256: ROUNDS = 14; break;
        default : return (-3); /* this cannot happen */
        }


        /* make number of rounds sane */
        if (rounds > ROUNDS) rounds = ROUNDS;

        /* First the special round:
         *    without InvMixColumn
         *    with extra KeyAddition
         */
        KeyAddition(a,rk[ROUNDS],BC);
        Substitution(a,Si,BC);
        ShiftRow(a,1,BC);
```

```
        /* ROUNDS-1 ordinary rounds
         */
        for(r = ROUNDS-1; r > rounds; r—) {
                KeyAddition(a,rk[r],BC);
                InvMixColumn(a,BC);
                Substitution(a,Si,BC);
                ShiftRow(a,1,BC);
        }

        if (rounds == 0) {
                /* End with the extra key addition
                 */
                KeyAddition(a,rk[0],BC);
        }

        return 0;
}




/* rijndael-api-ref.h    v2.0    August '99
 * Reference ANSI C code
 */

/*  AES Cipher header file for ANSI C Submissions
        Lawrence E. Bassham III
        Computer Security Division
        National Institute of Standards and Technology

        April 15, 1998

    This sample is to assist implementers developing to the Cryptographic API
Profile for AES Candidate Algorithm Submissions. Please consult this document as
a cross-reference.

        ANY CHANGES, WHERE APPROPRIATE, TO INFORMATION PROVIDED IN THIS FILE MUST BE
DOCUMENTED. CHANGES ARE ONLY APPROPRIATE WHERE SPECIFIED WITH THE STRING "CHANGE
POSSIBLE". FUNCTION CALLS AND THEIR PARAMETERS CANNOT BE CHANGED. STRUCTURES CAN
BE ALTERED TO ALLOW IMPLEMENTERS TO INCLUDE IMPLEMENTATION SPECIFIC INFORMATION.
 */

/*  Includes:
        Standard include files
 */

#include <stdio.h>
#include "rijndael-alg-ref.h"
```

```
/*   Defines:
        Add any additional defines you need
*/


#define     DIR_ENCRYPT     0    /*  Are we encrpyting?  */
#define     DIR_DECRYPT     1    /*  Are we decrpyting?  */
#define     MODE_ECB        1    /*  Are we ciphering in ECB mode?   */
#define     MODE_CBC        2    /*  Are we ciphering in CBC mode?   */
#define     MODE_CFB1       3    /*  Are we ciphering in 1-bit CFB mode? */
#define     TRUE            1
#define     FALSE           0
#define BITSPERBLOCK        128  /* Default number of bits in a cipher block */


/*  Error Codes - CHANGE POSSIBLE: inclusion of additional error codes  */
#define     BAD_KEY_DIR         -1   /*  Key direction is invalid, e.g., unknown
                                            value */
#define     BAD_KEY_MAT         -2   /*  Key material not of correct length */
#define     BAD_KEY_INSTANCE    -3   /*  Key passed is not valid */
#define     BAD_CIPHER_MODE     -4   /*  Params struct passed to cipherInit
                                            invalid */
#define     BAD_CIPHER_STATE    -5   /*  Cipher in wrong state (e.g., not
                                            initialized) */
#define     BAD_CIPHER_INSTANCE  -7


/*  CHANGE POSSIBLE:  inclusion of algorithm specific defines  */
#define     MAX_KEY_SIZE        64   /* # of ASCII char's needed to represent a
                                            key */
#define     MAX_IV_SIZE         BITSPERBLOCK/8  /* # bytes needed to represent
                                            an IV  */


/*  Typedefs:

        Typedef'ed data storage elements. Add any algorithm specific parameters
at the bottom of the structs as appropriate.
*/


typedef     unsigned char    BYTE;


/*  The structure for key information */
typedef struct {
        BYTE   direction;  /*  Key used for encrypting or decrypting? */
        int    keyLen;      /*  Length of the key  */
        char   keyMaterial[MAX_KEY_SIZE+1];  /*  Raw key data in ASCII, e.g., user
                                        input or KAT values */
        /*  The following parameters are algorithm dependent, replace or add as
                necessary  */
        int    blockLen;   /* block length */
        word8 keySched[MAXROUNDS+1][4][MAXBC];    /* key schedule         */
        } keyInstance;
```

```
/*  The structure for cipher information */
typedef struct {
        BYTE    mode;                   /* MODE_ECB, MODE_CBC, or MODE_CFB1 */
        BYTE    IV[MAX_IV_SIZE]; /* A possible Initialization Vector for ciphering */
        /*  Add any algorithm specific parameters needed here   */
        int     blockLen;               /* Sample: Handles non-128 bit block sizes
                                                  (if available) */

        } cipherInstance;


/*  Function prototypes   */
/*  CHANGED: makeKey(): parameter blockLen added
                        this parameter is absolutely necessary if you want to
                        setup the round keys in a variable block length setting
            cipherInit(): parameter blockLen added (for obvious reasons) */
int makeKey(keyInstance *key, BYTE direction, int keyLen, char *keyMaterial);

int cipherInit(cipherInstance *cipher, BYTE mode, char *IV);

int blockEncrypt(cipherInstance *cipher, keyInstance *key, BYTE *input, int
                        inputLen, BYTE *outBuffer);

int blockDecrypt(cipherInstance *cipher, keyInstance *key, BYTE *input, int
                        inputLen, BYTE *outBuffer);
int cipherUpdateRounds(cipherInstance *cipher, keyInstance *key, BYTE *input,
                        int inputLen, BYTE *outBuffer, int Rounds);




/* rijndael-api-ref.c    v2.1    April 2000
 * Reference ANSI C code
 * authors: v2.0 Paulo Barreto
 *               Vincent Rijmen, K.U.Leuven
 *          v2.1 Vincent Rijmen, K.U.Leuven
 *
 * This code is placed in the public domain.
 */
#include <stdlib.h>
#include <string.h>

#include "rijndael-alg-ref.h"
#include "rijndael-api-ref.h"
```

```c
int makeKey(keyInstance *key, BYTE direction, int keyLen, char *keyMaterial)
{
        word8 k[4][MAXKC];
        int i, j, t;

        if (key == NULL) {
                return BAD_KEY_INSTANCE;
        }

        if ((direction == DIR_ENCRYPT) || (direction == DIR_DECRYPT)) {
                key->direction = direction;
        } else {
                return BAD_KEY_DIR;
        }

        if ((keyLen == 128) || (keyLen == 192) || (keyLen == 256)) {
                key->keyLen = keyLen;
        } else {
                return BAD_KEY_MAT;
        }

        if ( keyMaterial ) {
                strncpy(key->keyMaterial, keyMaterial, keyLen/4);
        }

        /* initialize key schedule: */
        for(i = 0; i < key->keyLen/8; i++) {
                t = key->keyMaterial[2*i];
                if ((t >= '0') && (t <= '9')) j = (t - '0') << 4;
                else if ((t >= 'a') && (t <= 'f')) j = (t - 'a' + 10) << 4;
                else if ((t >= 'A') && (t <= 'F')) j = (t - 'A' + 10) << 4;
                else return BAD_KEY_MAT;

                t = key->keyMaterial[2*i+1];
                if ((t >= '0') && (t <= '9')) j ^= (t - '0');
                else if ((t >= 'a') && (t <= 'f')) j ^= (t - 'a' + 10);
                else if ((t >= 'A') && (t <= 'F')) j ^= (t - 'A' + 10);
                else return BAD_KEY_MAT;

                k[i % 4][i / 4] = (word8) j;
        }

        rijndaelKeySched (k, key->keyLen, key->blockLen, key->keySched);

        return TRUE;
}
```

```c
int cipherInit(cipherInstance *cipher, BYTE mode, char *IV)
{
        int i, j, t;

        if ((mode == MODE_ECB) || (mode == MODE_CBC) || (mode == MODE_CFB1)) {
                cipher->mode = mode;
        } else {
                return BAD_CIPHER_MODE;
        }

        if (IV != NULL) {
                for(i = 0; i < cipher->blockLen/8; i++) {
                        t = IV[2*i];
                        if ((t >= '0') && (t <= '9'))
                                j = (t - '0') << 4;
                        else if ((t >= 'a') && (t <= 'f'))
                                j = (t - 'a' + 10) << 4;
                        else if ((t >= 'A') && (t <= 'F'))
                                j = (t - 'A' + 10) << 4;
                        else return BAD_CIPHER_INSTANCE;

                        t = IV[2*i+1];
                        if ((t >= '0') && (t <= '9'))
                                j ^= (t - '0');
                        else if ((t >= 'a') && (t <= 'f'))
                                j ^= (t - 'a' + 10);
                        else if ((t >= 'A') && (t <= 'F'))
                                j ^= (t - 'A' + 10);
                        else return BAD_CIPHER_INSTANCE;

                        cipher->IV[i] = (BYTE) j;
                }
        }

        return TRUE;
}


int blockEncrypt(cipherInstance *cipher,
        keyInstance *key, BYTE *input, int inputLen, BYTE *outBuffer)
{
        int i, j, t, numBlocks;
        word8 block[4][MAXBC];

        /* check parameter consistency: */
        if (key == NULL ||
                key->direction != DIR_ENCRYPT ||
                (key->keyLen != 128 && key->keyLen != 192
                  && key->keyLen != 256)) {
                return BAD_KEY_MAT;
        }
```

```
if (cipher == NULL ||
        (cipher->mode != MODE_ECB && cipher->mode != MODE_CBC
         && cipher->mode != MODE_CFB1) ||
        (cipher->blockLen != 128 && cipher->blockLen != 192
         && cipher->blockLen != 256)) {
        return BAD_CIPHER_STATE;
}


numBlocks = inputLen/cipher->blockLen;

switch (cipher->mode) {
case MODE_ECB:
        for (i = 0; i < numBlocks; i++) {
                for (j = 0; j < cipher->blockLen/32; j++) {
                        for(t = 0; t < 4; t++)
                        /* parse input stream into rectangular array */
                                block[t][j] = input[cipher->blockLen
                                                /8*i+4*j+t] & 0xFF;
                }
                rijndaelEncrypt (block, key->keyLen, cipher->blockLen,
                                key->keySched);
                for (j = 0; j < cipher->blockLen/32; j++) {
                        /* parse rectangular array into output
                           ciphertext bytes */
                        for(t = 0; t < 4; t++)
                                outBuffer[cipher->blockLen/8*i+4*j+t]
                                        = (BYTE) block[t][j];
                }
        }
        break;

case MODE_CBC:
        for (j = 0; j < cipher->blockLen/32; j++) {
                for(t = 0; t < 4; t++)
                /* parse initial value into rectangular array */
                        block[t][j] = cipher->IV[t+4*j] & 0xFF;
        }
        for (i = 0; i < numBlocks; i++) {
                for (j = 0; j < cipher->blockLen/32; j++) {
                        for(t = 0; t < 4; t++)
                        /* parse input stream into rectangular
                           array and exor with IV or the previous
                           ciphertext */
                                block[t][j] ^= input[cipher->blockLen
                                                /8*i+4*j+t] & 0xFF;
                }
                rijndaelEncrypt (block, key->keyLen, cipher->blockLen,
                                key->keySched);
                for (j = 0; j < cipher->blockLen/32; j++) {
                        /* parse rectangular array into output
                           ciphertext bytes */
```

```
                                    for(t = 0; t < 4; t++)
                                            outBuffer[cipher->blockLen/8*i+4*j+t]
                                                        = (BYTE) block[t][j];
                        }
                }
                break;

        default: return BAD_CIPHER_STATE;
        }

        return numBlocks*cipher->blockLen;
}


int blockDecrypt(cipherInstance *cipher,
        keyInstance *key, BYTE *input, int inputLen, BYTE *outBuffer)
{
        int i, j, t, numBlocks;
        word8 block[4][MAXBC];

        if (cipher == NULL ||
                key == NULL ||
                key->direction == DIR_ENCRYPT ||
                cipher->blockLen != key->blockLen) {
                return BAD_CIPHER_STATE;
        }

        /* check parameter consistency: */
        if (key == NULL ||
                key->direction != DIR_DECRYPT ||
                (key->keyLen != 128 && key->keyLen != 192
                                && key->keyLen != 256)) {
                return BAD_KEY_MAT;
        }
        if (cipher == NULL ||
                (cipher->mode != MODE_ECB && cipher->mode != MODE_CBC
                                        && cipher->mode != MODE_CFB1) ||
                (cipher->blockLen != 128 && cipher->blockLen != 192
                                        && cipher->blockLen != 256)) {
                return BAD_CIPHER_STATE;
        }


        numBlocks = inputLen/cipher->blockLen;

        switch (cipher->mode) {
        case MODE_ECB:
                for (i = 0; i < numBlocks; i++) {
                        for (j = 0; j < cipher->blockLen/32; j++) {
                                for(t = 0; t < 4; t++)
                                /* parse input stream into rectangular array */
                                        block[t][j] = input[cipher->blockLen
                                                        /8*i+4*j+t] & 0xFF;
                        }
```

```
            rijndaelDecrypt (block, key->keyLen, cipher->blockLen,
                            key->keySched);
            for (j = 0; j < cipher->blockLen/32; j++) {
                    /* parse rectangular array into output
                        ciphertext bytes */
                    for(t = 0; t < 4; t++)
                            outBuffer[cipher->blockLen/8*i+4*j+t]
                                    = (BYTE) block[t][j];
            }
        }
        break;

case MODE_CBC:
        /* first block */
        for (j = 0; j < cipher->blockLen/32; j++) {
                for(t = 0; t < 4; t++)
                /* parse input stream into rectangular array */
                        block[t][j] = input[4*j+t] & 0xFF;
        }
        rijndaelDecrypt (block, key->keyLen, cipher->blockLen,
                        key->keySched);

        for (j = 0; j < cipher->blockLen/32; j++) {
                /* exor the IV and parse rectangular array into output
                    ciphertext bytes */
                for(t = 0; t < 4; t++)
                        outBuffer[4*j+t] = (BYTE) (block[t][j]
                                                ^ cipher->IV[t+4*j]);
        }

        /* next blocks */
        for (i = 1; i < numBlocks; i++) {
                for (j = 0; j < cipher->blockLen/32; j++) {
                        for(t = 0; t < 4; t++)
                        /* parse input stream into rectangular array */
                                block[t][j] = input[cipher->blockLen
                                                /8*i+4*j+t] & 0xFF;
                }
                rijndaelDecrypt (block, key->keyLen, cipher->blockLen,
                                key->keySched);
```

```c
                    for (j = 0; j < cipher->blockLen/32; j++) {
                            /* exor previous ciphertext block and parse
                             rectangular array
                                into output ciphertext bytes */
                        for(t = 0; t < 4; t++)
                                outBuffer[cipher->blockLen/8*i+4*j+t]
                                    = (BYTE) (block[t][j] ^
                                        input[cipher->blockLen
                                        /8*i+4*j+t-4*cipher->blockLen
                                                                /32]);
                    }
                }
                break;

        default: return BAD_CIPHER_STATE;
        }

        return numBlocks*cipher->blockLen;
}


/**
 *      cipherUpdateRounds:
 *
 *      Encrypts/Decrypts exactly one full block a specified number of rounds.
 *      Only used in the Intermediate Value Known Answer Test.
 *
 *      Returns:
 *              TRUE - on success
 *              BAD_CIPHER_STATE - cipher in bad state (e.g., not initialized)
 */
int cipherUpdateRounds(cipherInstance *cipher,
        keyInstance *key, BYTE *input, int inputLen, BYTE *outBuffer, int rounds)
{
        int j, t;
        word8 block[4][MAXBC];

        if (cipher == NULL ||
                key == NULL ||
                cipher->blockLen != key->blockLen) {
                return BAD_CIPHER_STATE;
        }

        for (j = 0; j < cipher->blockLen/32; j++) {
                for(t = 0; t < 4; t++)
                        /* parse input stream into rectangular array */
                        block[t][j] = input[4*j+t] & 0xFF;
        }
```

```
        switch (key->direction) {
        case DIR_ENCRYPT:
                rijndaelEncryptRound (block, key->keyLen, cipher->blockLen,
                             key->keySched, rounds);
        break;

        case DIR_DECRYPT:
                rijndaelDecryptRound (block, key->keyLen, cipher->blockLen,
                             key->keySched, rounds);
        break;

        default: return BAD_KEY_DIR;
        }
        for (j = 0; j < cipher->blockLen/32; j++) {
                /* parse rectangular array into output ciphertext bytes */
                for(t = 0; t < 4; t++)
                        outBuffer[4*j+t] = (BYTE) block[t][j];
        }

        return TRUE;
}


/* boxes-ref.dat
 *
 *
 */


word8 Logtable[256] = {
  0,   0, 25,   1, 50,   2, 26, 198, 75, 199, 27, 104, 51, 238, 223,  3,
100,   4, 224, 14, 52,  141, 129, 239, 76, 113,   8, 200, 248, 105, 28, 193,
125, 194, 29, 181, 249, 185, 39, 106, 77, 228, 166, 114, 154, 201,  9, 120,
101, 47, 138,   5, 33, 15, 225, 36, 18, 240, 130, 69, 53, 147, 218, 142,
150, 143, 219, 189, 54, 208, 206, 148, 19, 92, 210, 241, 64, 70, 131, 56,
102, 221, 253, 48, 191,   6, 139, 98, 179, 37, 226, 152, 34, 136, 145, 16,
126, 110, 72, 195, 163, 182, 30, 66, 58, 107, 40, 84, 250, 133, 61, 186,
 43, 121, 10, 21, 155, 159, 94, 202, 78, 212, 172, 229, 243, 115, 167, 87,
175, 88, 168, 80, 244, 234, 214, 116, 79, 174, 233, 213, 231, 230, 173, 232,
 44, 215, 117, 122, 235, 22, 11, 245, 89, 203, 95, 176, 156, 169, 81, 160,
127, 12, 246, 111, 23, 196, 73, 236, 216, 67, 31, 45, 164, 118, 123, 183,
204, 187, 62, 90, 251, 96, 177, 134, 59, 82, 161, 108, 170, 85, 41, 157,
151, 178, 135, 144, 97, 190, 220, 252, 188, 149, 207, 205, 55, 63, 91, 209,
 83, 57, 132, 60, 65, 162, 109, 71, 20, 42, 158, 93, 86, 242, 211, 171,
 68, 17, 146, 217, 35, 32, 46, 137, 180, 124, 184, 38, 119, 153, 227, 165,
103, 74, 237, 222, 197, 49, 254, 24, 13, 99, 140, 128, 192, 247, 112,  7,
};
```

```
word8 Alogtable[256] = {
   1,   3,   5,  15,  17,  51,  85, 255,  26,  46, 114, 150, 161, 248,  19,  53,
  95, 225,  56,  72, 216, 115, 149, 164, 247,   2,   6,  10,  30,  34, 102, 170,
 229,  52,  92, 228,  55,  89, 235,  38, 106, 190, 217, 112, 144, 171, 230,  49,
  83, 245,   4,  12,  20,  60,  68, 204,  79, 209, 104, 184, 211, 110, 178, 205,
  76, 212, 103, 169, 224,  59,  77, 215,  98, 166, 241,   8,  24,  40, 120, 136,
 131, 158, 185, 208, 107, 189, 220, 127, 129, 152, 179, 206,  73, 219, 118, 154,
 181, 196,  87, 249,  16,  48,  80, 240,  11,  29,  39, 105, 187, 214,  97, 163,
 254,  25,  43, 125, 135, 146, 173, 236,  47, 113, 147, 174, 233,  32,  96, 160,
 251,  22,  58,  78, 210, 109, 183, 194,  93, 231,  50,  86, 250,  21,  63,  65,
 195,  94, 226,  61,  71, 201,  64, 192,  91, 237,  44, 116, 156, 191, 218, 117,
 159, 186, 213, 100, 172, 239,  42, 126, 130, 157, 188, 223, 122, 142, 137, 128,
 155, 182, 193,  88, 232,  35, 101, 175, 234,  37, 111, 177, 200,  67, 197,  84,
 252,  31,  33,  99, 165, 244,   7,   9,  27,  45, 119, 153, 176, 203,  70, 202,
  69, 207,  74, 222, 121, 139, 134, 145, 168, 227,  62,  66, 198,  81, 243,  14,
  18,  54,  90, 238,  41, 123, 141, 140, 143, 138, 133, 148, 167, 242,  13,  23,
  57,  75, 221, 124, 132, 151, 162, 253,  28,  36, 108, 180, 199,  82, 246,   1,
};

word8 S[256] = {
  99, 124, 119, 123, 242, 107, 111, 197,  48,   1, 103,  43, 254, 215, 171, 118,
 202, 130, 201, 125, 250,  89,  71, 240, 173, 212, 162, 175, 156, 164, 114, 192,
 183, 253, 147,  38,  54,  63, 247, 204,  52, 165, 229, 241, 113, 216,  49,  21,
   4, 199,  35, 195,  24, 150,   5, 154,   7,  18, 128, 226, 235,  39, 178, 117,
   9, 131,  44,  26,  27, 110,  90, 160,  82,  59, 214, 179,  41, 227,  47, 132,
  83, 209,   0, 237,  32, 252, 177,  91, 106, 203, 190,  57,  74,  76,  88, 207,
 208, 239, 170, 251,  67,  77,  51, 133,  69, 249,   2, 127,  80,  60, 159, 168,
  81, 163,  64, 143, 146, 157,  56, 245, 188, 182, 218,  33,  16, 255, 243, 210,
 205,  12,  19, 236,  95, 151,  68,  23, 196, 167, 126,  61, 100,  93,  25, 115,
  96, 129,  79, 220,  34,  42, 144, 136,  70, 238, 184,  20, 222,  94,  11, 219,
 224,  50,  58,  10,  73,   6,  36,  92, 194, 211, 172,  98, 145, 149, 228, 121,
 231, 200,  55, 109, 141, 213,  78, 169, 108,  86, 244, 234, 101, 122, 174,   8,
 186, 120,  37,  46,  28, 166, 180, 198, 232, 221, 116,  31,  75, 189, 139, 138,
 112,  62, 181, 102,  72,   3, 246,  14,  97,  53,  87, 185, 134, 193,  29, 158,
 225, 248, 152,  17, 105, 217, 142, 148, 155,  30, 135, 233, 206,  85,  40, 223,
 140, 161, 137,  13, 191, 230,  66, 104,  65, 153,  45,  15, 176,  84, 187,  22,
};
```

```
word8 Si[256] = {
 82,   9, 106, 213,  48,  54, 165,  56, 191,  64, 163, 158, 129, 243, 215, 251,
124, 227,  57, 130, 155,  47, 255, 135,  52, 142,  67,  68, 196, 222, 233, 203,
 84, 123, 148,  50, 166, 194,  35,  61, 238,  76, 149,  11,  66, 250, 195,  78,
  8,  46, 161, 102,  40, 217,  36, 178, 118,  91, 162,  73, 109, 139, 209,  37,
114, 248, 246, 100, 134, 104, 152,  22, 212, 164,  92, 204,  93, 101, 182, 146,
108, 112,  72,  80, 253, 237, 185, 218,  94,  21,  70,  87, 167, 141, 157, 132,
144, 216, 171,   0, 140, 188, 211,  10, 247, 228,  88,   5, 184, 179,  69,   6,
208,  44,  30, 143, 202,  63,  15,   2, 193, 175, 189,   3,   1,  19, 138, 107,
 58, 145,  17,  65,  79, 103, 220, 234, 151, 242, 207, 206, 240, 180, 230, 115,
150, 172, 116,  34, 231, 173,  53, 133, 226, 249,  55, 232,  28, 117, 223, 110,
 71, 241,  26, 113,  29,  41, 197, 137, 111, 183,  98,  14, 170,  24, 190,  27,
252,  86,  62,  75, 198, 210, 121,  32, 154, 219, 192, 254, 120, 205,  90, 244,
 31, 221, 168,  51, 136,   7, 199,  49, 177,  18,  16,  89,  39, 128, 236,  95,
 96,  81, 127, 169,  25, 181,  74,  13,  45, 229, 122, 159, 147, 201, 156, 239,
160, 224,  59,  77, 174,  42, 245, 176, 200, 235, 187,  60, 131,  83, 153,  97,
 23,  43,   4, 126, 186, 119, 214,  38, 225, 105,  20,  99,  85,  33,  12, 125,
};


word8 iG[4][4] = {
0x0e, 0x09, 0x0d, 0x0b,
0x0b, 0x0e, 0x09, 0x0d,
0x0d, 0x0b, 0x0e, 0x09,
0x09, 0x0d, 0x0b, 0x0e,
};


word32 rcon[30] = {
  0x01,0x02, 0x04, 0x08, 0x10, 0x20, 0x40, 0x80, 0x1b, 0x36, 0x6c,
  0xd8, 0xab, 0x4d, 0x9a, 0x2f, 0x5e, 0xbc, 0x63, 0xc6, 0x97, 0x35,
  0x6a, 0xd4, 0xb3, 0x7d, 0xfa, 0xef, 0xc5, 0x91, };
```

B

A Java Implementation of AES

With the authors permission, we present in this appendix, a java implementation of AES (Rijndael). The program consists of two files:

1. Rijndael_Algorithm.java: Rijndael Algorithm Java source.

2. Rijndael_Properties.java: Rijndael Properties support code.

We present the content of these files in the order shown above.

```
// $Id: $
//
// $Log: $
// Revision 1.1  1998/04/12  Paulo
// + optimized methods for the default 128-bit block size.
//
// Revision 1.0  1998/03/11  Raif
// + original version.
//
// $Endlog$
/*
 * Copyright (c) 1997, 1998 Systemics Ltd on behalf of the Cryptix Development
 * Team. All rights reserved.
 */
package Rijndael;

import java.io.PrintWriter;
import java.security.InvalidKeyException;


//.............................................................................
/**
 * Rijndael —pronounced Reindaal— is a variable block-size (128-, 192- and
 * 256-bit), variable key-size (128-, 192- and 256-bit) symmetric cipher.
 *
 * Rijndael was written by Vincent Rijmen (rijmen@esat.kuleuven.ac.be)
 * and Joan Daemen (Joan.Daemen@village.uunet.be)
 *
 * Portions of this code are Copyright; 1997, 1998
 * Systemics Ltd (http://www.systemics.com) on behalf of the
 * Cryptix Development Team (http://www.systemics.com/docs/cryptix/)
 * All rights reserved.
 *
 * $Revision: $
 * @author  Raif S. Naffah
 * @author  Paulo S. L. M. Barreto
 */
public final class Rijndael_Algorithm // implicit no-argument constructor
{
// Debugging methods and variables
//.............................................................................

    static final String NAME = "Rijndael_Algorithm";
    static final boolean IN = true, OUT = false;

    static final boolean DEBUG = Rijndael_Properties.GLOBAL_DEBUG;
    static final int debuglevel = DEBUG ? Rijndael_Properties.getLevel(NAME) : 0;
    static final PrintWriter err = DEBUG ? Rijndael_Properties.getOutput() : null;

    static final boolean TRACE = Rijndael_Properties.isTraceable(NAME);
```

```java
    static void debug (String s) { err.println(">> "+NAME+": "+s); }
    static void trace (boolean in, String s) {
        if (TRACE) err.println((in?"==> ":"<== ")+NAME+"."+s);
    }
    static void trace (String s) { if (TRACE) err.println("<=> "+NAME+"."+s); }
```

```java
// Constants and variables
//...................................................................................

    static final int BLOCK_SIZE = 16; // default block size in bytes

    static final int[] alog = new int[256];
    static final int[] log =  new int[256];

    static final byte[] S =  new byte[256];
    static final byte[] Si = new byte[256];
    static final int[] T1 = new int[256];
    static final int[] T2 = new int[256];
    static final int[] T3 = new int[256];
    static final int[] T4 = new int[256];
    static final int[] T5 = new int[256];
    static final int[] T6 = new int[256];
    static final int[] T7 = new int[256];
    static final int[] T8 = new int[256];
    static final int[] U1 = new int[256];
    static final int[] U2 = new int[256];
    static final int[] U3 = new int[256];
    static final int[] U4 = new int[256];
    static final byte[] rcon = new byte[30];

    static final int[][][] shifts = new int[][][] {
        { {0, 0}, {1, 3}, {2, 2}, {3, 1} },
        { {0, 0}, {1, 5}, {2, 4}, {3, 3} },
        { {0, 0}, {1, 7}, {3, 5}, {4, 4} }
    };

    private static final char[] HEX_DIGITS = {
        '0','1','2','3','4','5','6','7','8','9','A','B','C','D','E','F'
    };


// Static code - to intialise S-boxes and T-boxes
//...................................................................................

    static {
        long time = System.currentTimeMillis();

if (DEBUG && debuglevel > 6) {
System.out.println("Algorithm Name: "+Rijndael_Properties.FULL_NAME);
System.out.println("Electronic Codebook (ECB) Mode");
System.out.println();
}
```

```
int ROOT = 0x11B;
int i, j = 0;


//
// produce log and alog tables, needed for multiplying in the
// field GF(2^m) (generator = 3)
//
alog[0] = 1;
for (i = 1; i < 256; i++) {
    j = (alog[i-1] << 1) ^ alog[i-1];
    if ((j & 0x100) != 0) j ^= ROOT;
    alog[i] = j;
}
for (i = 1; i < 255; i++) log[alog[i]] = i;
byte[][] A = new byte[][] {
    {1, 1, 1, 1, 1, 0, 0, 0},
    {0, 1, 1, 1, 1, 1, 0, 0},
            {0, 0, 1, 1, 1, 1, 1, 0},
            {0, 0, 0, 1, 1, 1, 1, 1},
            {1, 0, 0, 0, 1, 1, 1, 1},
            {1, 1, 0, 0, 0, 1, 1, 1},
            {1, 1, 1, 0, 0, 0, 1, 1},
            {1, 1, 1, 1, 0, 0, 0, 1}
        };
byte[] B = new byte[] { 0, 1, 1, 0, 0, 0, 1, 1};


//
// substitution box based on F^{-1}(x)
//
int t;
byte[][] box = new byte[256][8];
box[1][7] = 1;
for (i = 2; i < 256; i++) {
    j = alog[255 - log[i]];
    for (t = 0; t < 8; t++)
        box[i][t] = (byte)((j >> (7 - t)) & 0x01);
}
//
// affine transform:  box[i] <- B + A*box[i]
//
byte[][] cox = new byte[256][8];
for (i = 0; i < 256; i++)
    for (t = 0; t < 8; t++) {
        cox[i][t] = B[t];
        for (j = 0; j < 8; j++)
            cox[i][t] ^= A[t][j] * box[i][j];
    }
//
```

```java
// S-boxes and inverse S-boxes
//
for (i = 0; i < 256; i++) {
    S[i] = (byte)(cox[i][0] << 7);
        for (t = 1; t < 8; t++)
            S[i] ^= cox[i][t] << (7-t);
    Si[S[i] & 0xFF] = (byte) i;
}
//
// T-boxes
//
byte[][] G = new byte[][] {
    {2, 1, 1, 3},
    {3, 2, 1, 1},
    {1, 3, 2, 1},
    {1, 1, 3, 2}
};
byte[][] AA = new byte[4][8];
for (i = 0; i < 4; i++) {
    for (j = 0; j < 4; j++) AA[i][j] = G[i][j];
    AA[i][i+4] = 1;
}
byte pivot, tmp;
byte[][] iG = new byte[4][4];
for (i = 0; i < 4; i++) {
    pivot = AA[i][i];
    if (pivot == 0) {
        t = i + 1;
        while ((AA[t][i] == 0) && (t < 4))
            t++;
        if (t == 4)
            throw new RuntimeException("G matrix is not invertible");
        else {
            for (j = 0; j < 8; j++) {
                tmp = AA[i][j];
                AA[i][j] = AA[t][j];
                AA[t][j] = (byte) tmp;
            }
            pivot = AA[i][i];
        }
    }
    for (j = 0; j < 8; j++)
        if (AA[i][j] != 0)
            AA[i][j] = (byte)
                alog[(255 + log[AA[i][j] & 0xFF] - log[pivot & 0xFF])
    for (t = 0; t < 4; t++)
        if (i != t) {
            for (j = i+1; j < 8; j++)
                AA[t][j] ^= mul(AA[i][j], AA[t][i]);
            AA[t][i] = 0;
        }
}
```

```
        for (i = 0; i < 4; i++)
            for (j = 0; j < 4; j++) iG[i][j] = AA[i][j + 4];

        int s;
        for (t = 0; t < 256; t++) {
            s = S[t];
            T1[t] = mul4(s, G[0]);
            T2[t] = mul4(s, G[1]);
            T3[t] = mul4(s, G[2]);
            T4[t] = mul4(s, G[3]);

            s = Si[t];
            T5[t] = mul4(s, iG[0]);
            T6[t] = mul4(s, iG[1]);
            T7[t] = mul4(s, iG[2]);
            T8[t] = mul4(s, iG[3]);

            U1[t] = mul4(t, iG[0]);
            U2[t] = mul4(t, iG[1]);
            U3[t] = mul4(t, iG[2]);
            U4[t] = mul4(t, iG[3]);
        }
        //
        // round constants
        //
        rcon[0] = 1;
        int r = 1;
        for (t = 1; t < 30; ) rcon[t++] = (byte)(r = mul(2, r));

        time = System.currentTimeMillis() - time;

if (DEBUG && debuglevel > 8) {
System.out.println("==========");
System.out.println();
System.out.println("Static Data");
System.out.println();
System.out.println("S[]:"); for(i=0;i<16;i++) { for(j=0;j<16;j++)
System.out.print("0x"+byteToString(S[i*16+j])+", ");
System.out.println();}
System.out.println();
System.out.println("Si[]:"); for(i=0;i<16;i++) { for(j=0;j<16;j++)
System.out.print("0x"+byteToString(Si[i*16+j])+", "); System.out.println();}

System.out.println();
System.out.println("iG[]:"); for(i=0;i<4;i++){for(j=0;j<4;j++)
System.out.print("0x"+byteToString(iG[i][j])+", "); System.out.println();}
```

```
System.out.println();
System.out.println("T1[]:"); for(i=0;i<64;i++){for(j=0;j<4;j++)
System.out.print("0x"+intToString(T1[i*4+j])+", "); System.out.println();}
System.out.println();
System.out.println("T2[]:"); for(i=0;i<64;i++){for(j=0;j<4;j++)
System.out.print("0x"+intToString(T2[i*4+j])+", "); System.out.println();}
System.out.println();
System.out.println("T3[]:"); for(i=0;i<64;i++){for(j=0;j<4;j++)
System.out.print("0x"+intToString(T3[i*4+j])+", "); System.out.println();}
System.out.println();
System.out.println("T4[]:"); for(i=0;i<64;i++){for(j=0;j<4;j++)
System.out.print("0x"+intToString(T4[i*4+j])+", "); System.out.println();}
System.out.println();
System.out.println("T5[]:"); for(i=0;i<64;i++){for(j=0;j<4;j++)
System.out.print("0x"+intToString(T5[i*4+j])+", "); System.out.println();}
System.out.println();
System.out.println("T6[]:"); for(i=0;i<64;i++){for(j=0;j<4;j++)
System.out.print("0x"+intToString(T6[i*4+j])+", "); System.out.println();}
System.out.println();
System.out.println("T7[]:"); for(i=0;i<64;i++){for(j=0;j<4;j++)
System.out.print("0x"+intToString(T7[i*4+j])+", "); System.out.println();}
System.out.println();
System.out.println("T8[]:"); for(i=0;i<64;i++){for(j=0;j<4;j++)
System.out.print("0x"+intToString(T8[i*4+j])+", "); System.out.println();}

System.out.println();
System.out.println("U1[]:"); for(i=0;i<64;i++){for(j=0;j<4;j++)
System.out.print("0x"+intToString(U1[i*4+j])+", "); System.out.println();}
System.out.println();
System.out.println("U2[]:"); for(i=0;i<64;i++){for(j=0;j<4;j++)
System.out.print("0x"+intToString(U2[i*4+j])+", "); System.out.println();}
System.out.println();
System.out.println("U3[]:"); for(i=0;i<64;i++){for(j=0;j<4;j++)
System.out.print("0x"+intToString(U3[i*4+j])+", "); System.out.println();}
System.out.println();
System.out.println("U4[]:"); for(i=0;i<64;i++){for(j=0;j<4;j++)
System.out.print("0x"+intToString(U4[i*4+j])+", "); System.out.println();}

System.out.println();
System.out.println("rcon[]:"); for(i=0;i<5;i++){for(j=0;j<6;j++)
System.out.print("0x"+byteToString(rcon[i*6+j])+", "); System.out.println();}

System.out.println();
System.out.println("Total initialization time: "+time+" ms.");
System.out.println();
}
    }
```

```
        // multiply two elements of GF(2^m)
        static final int mul (int a, int b) {
            return (a != 0 && b != 0) ?
                alog[(log[a & 0xFF] + log[b & 0xFF]) % 255] :
                0;
        }


        // convenience method used in generating Transposition boxes
        static final int mul4 (int a, byte[] b) {
            if (a == 0) return 0;
            a = log[a & 0xFF];
            int a0 = (b[0] != 0) ? alog[(a + log[b[0] & 0xFF]) % 255] & 0xFF : 0;
            int a1 = (b[1] != 0) ? alog[(a + log[b[1] & 0xFF]) % 255] & 0xFF : 0;
            int a2 = (b[2] != 0) ? alog[(a + log[b[2] & 0xFF]) % 255] & 0xFF : 0;
            int a3 = (b[3] != 0) ? alog[(a + log[b[3] & 0xFF]) % 255] & 0xFF : 0;
            return a0 << 24 | a1 << 16 | a2 << 8 | a3;
        }



// Basic API methods
//........................................................................

    /**
     * Convenience method to expand a user-supplied key material into a session
     * key, assuming Rijndael's default block size (128-bit).
     *
     * @param key The 128/192/256-bit user-key to use.
     * @exception  InvalidKeyException  If the key is invalid.
     */
    public static Object makeKey (byte[] k) throws InvalidKeyException {
        return makeKey(k, BLOCK_SIZE);
    }


    /**
     * Convenience method to encrypt exactly one block of plaintext, assuming
     * Rijndael's default block size (128-bit).
     *
     * @param  in          The plaintext.
     * @param  inOffset     Index of in from which to start considering data.
     * @param  sessionKey The session key to use for encryption.
     * @return The ciphertext generated from a plaintext using the session key.
     */
    public static byte[]
    blockEncrypt (byte[] in, int inOffset, Object sessionKey) {
if (DEBUG) trace(IN, "blockEncrypt("+in+", "+inOffset+", "+sessionKey+")");
        int[][] Ke = (int[][]) ((Object[]) sessionKey)[0];
        // extract encryption round keys
        int ROUNDS = Ke.length - 1;
        int[] Ker = Ke[0];
```

```java
            // plaintext to ints + key
            int t0   = ((in[inOffset++] & 0xFF) << 24 |
                        (in[inOffset++] & 0xFF) << 16 |
                        (in[inOffset++] & 0xFF) <<  8 |
                        (in[inOffset++] & 0xFF)          ) ^ Ker[0];
            int t1   = ((in[inOffset++] & 0xFF) << 24 |
                        (in[inOffset++] & 0xFF) << 16 |
                        (in[inOffset++] & 0xFF) <<  8 |
                        (in[inOffset++] & 0xFF)          ) ^ Ker[1];
            int t2   = ((in[inOffset++] & 0xFF) << 24 |
                        (in[inOffset++] & 0xFF) << 16 |
                        (in[inOffset++] & 0xFF) <<  8 |
                        (in[inOffset++] & 0xFF)          ) ^ Ker[2];
            int t3   = ((in[inOffset++] & 0xFF) << 24 |
                        (in[inOffset++] & 0xFF) << 16 |
                        (in[inOffset++] & 0xFF) <<  8 |
                        (in[inOffset++] & 0xFF)          ) ^ Ker[3];

            int a0, a1, a2, a3;
            for (int r = 1; r < ROUNDS; r++) {            // apply round transforms
                Ker = Ke[r];
                a0   = (T1[(t0 >> 24) & 0xFF] ^
                        T2[(t1 >> 16) & 0xFF] ^
                        T3[(t2 >>  8) & 0xFF] ^
                        T4[ t3        & 0xFF]   ) ^ Ker[0];
                a1   = (T1[(t1 >> 24) & 0xFF] ^
                        T2[(t2 >> 16) & 0xFF] ^
                        T3[(t3 >>  8) & 0xFF] ^
                        T4[ t0        & 0xFF]   ) ^ Ker[1];
                a2   = (T1[(t2 >> 24) & 0xFF] ^
                        T2[(t3 >> 16) & 0xFF] ^
                        T3[(t0 >>  8) & 0xFF] ^
                        T4[ t1        & 0xFF]   ) ^ Ker[2];
                a3   = (T1[(t3 >> 24) & 0xFF] ^
                        T2[(t0 >> 16) & 0xFF] ^
                        T3[(t1 >>  8) & 0xFF] ^
                        T4[ t2        & 0xFF]   ) ^ Ker[3];
                t0 = a0;
                t1 = a1;
                t2 = a2;
                t3 = a3;
if (DEBUG && debuglevel > 6)
                System.out.println("CT"+r+"="+intToString(t0)
                +intToString(t1)+intToString(t2)+intToString(t3));
            }
```

```
        // last round is special
        byte[] result = new byte[BLOCK_SIZE]; // the resulting ciphertext
        Ker = Ke[ROUNDS];
        int tt = Ker[0];
        result[ 0] = (byte)(S[(t0 >>> 24) & 0xFF] ^ (tt >>> 24));
        result[ 1] = (byte)(S[(t1 >>> 16) & 0xFF] ^ (tt >>> 16));
        result[ 2] = (byte)(S[(t2 >>>  8) & 0xFF] ^ (tt >>>  8));
        result[ 3] = (byte)(S[ t3         & 0xFF] ^  tt         );
        tt = Ker[1];
        result[ 4] = (byte)(S[(t1 >>> 24) & 0xFF] ^ (tt >>> 24));
        result[ 5] = (byte)(S[(t2 >>> 16) & 0xFF] ^ (tt >>> 16));
        result[ 6] = (byte)(S[(t3 >>>  8) & 0xFF] ^ (tt >>>  8));
        result[ 7] = (byte)(S[ t0         & 0xFF] ^  tt         );
        tt = Ker[2];
        result[ 8] = (byte)(S[(t2 >>> 24) & 0xFF] ^ (tt >>> 24));
        result[ 9] = (byte)(S[(t3 >>> 16) & 0xFF] ^ (tt >>> 16));
        result[10] = (byte)(S[(t0 >>>  8) & 0xFF] ^ (tt >>>  8));
        result[11] = (byte)(S[ t1         & 0xFF] ^  tt         );
        tt = Ker[3];
        result[12] = (byte)(S[(t3 >>> 24) & 0xFF] ^ (tt >>> 24));
        result[13] = (byte)(S[(t0 >>> 16) & 0xFF] ^ (tt >>> 16));
        result[14] = (byte)(S[(t1 >>>  8) & 0xFF] ^ (tt >>>  8));
        result[15] = (byte)(S[ t2         & 0xFF] ^  tt         );
if (DEBUG && debuglevel > 6) {
System.out.println("CT="+toString(result));
System.out.println();
}
if (DEBUG) trace(OUT, "blockEncrypt()");
        return result;
    }


    /**
     * Convenience method to decrypt exactly one block of plaintext, assuming
     * Rijndael's default block size (128-bit).
     *
     * @param  in        The ciphertext.
     * @param  inOffset  Index of in from which to start considering data.
     * @param  sessionKey The session key to use for decryption.
     * @return The plaintext generated from a ciphertext using the session key.
     */
    public static byte[]
    blockDecrypt (byte[] in, int inOffset, Object sessionKey) {
if (DEBUG) trace(IN, "blockDecrypt("+in+", "+inOffset+", "+sessionKey+")");
        int[][] Kd = (int[][]) ((Object[]) sessionKey)[1];
        // extract decryption round keys
        int ROUNDS = Kd.length - 1;
        int[] Kdr = Kd[0];
```

```
            // ciphertext to ints + key
    int t0   = ((in[inOffset++] & 0xFF) << 24 |
                (in[inOffset++] & 0xFF) << 16 |
                (in[inOffset++] & 0xFF) <<  8 |
                (in[inOffset++] & 0xFF)          ) ^ Kdr[0];
    int t1   = ((in[inOffset++] & 0xFF) << 24 |
                (in[inOffset++] & 0xFF) << 16 |
                (in[inOffset++] & 0xFF) <<  8 |
                (in[inOffset++] & 0xFF)          ) ^ Kdr[1];
    int t2   = ((in[inOffset++] & 0xFF) << 24 |
                (in[inOffset++] & 0xFF) << 16 |
                (in[inOffset++] & 0xFF) <<  8 |
                (in[inOffset++] & 0xFF)          ) ^ Kdr[2];
    int t3   = ((in[inOffset++] & 0xFF) << 24 |
                (in[inOffset++] & 0xFF) << 16 |
                (in[inOffset++] & 0xFF) <<  8 |
                (in[inOffset++] & 0xFF)          ) ^ Kdr[3];


    int a0, a1, a2, a3;
    for (int r = 1; r < ROUNDS; r++) {       // apply round transforms
        Kdr = Kd[r];
        a0   = (T5[(t0 >> 24) & 0xFF] ^
                T6[(t3 >> 16) & 0xFF] ^
                T7[(t2 >>  8) & 0xFF] ^
                T8[ t1        & 0xFF]  ) ^ Kdr[0];
        a1   = (T5[(t1 >> 24) & 0xFF] ^
                T6[(t0 >> 16) & 0xFF] ^
                T7[(t3 >>  8) & 0xFF] ^
                T8[ t2        & 0xFF]  ) ^ Kdr[1];
        a2   = (T5[(t2 >> 24) & 0xFF] ^
                T6[(t1 >> 16) & 0xFF] ^
                T7[(t0 >>  8) & 0xFF] ^
                T8[ t3        & 0xFF]  ) ^ Kdr[2];
        a3   = (T5[(t3 >> 24) & 0xFF] ^
                T6[(t2 >> 16) & 0xFF] ^
                T7[(t1 >>  8) & 0xFF] ^
                T8[ t0        & 0xFF]  ) ^ Kdr[3];
        t0 = a0;
        t1 = a1;
        t2 = a2;
        t3 = a3;
if (DEBUG && debuglevel > 6)
        System.out.println("PT"+r+"="+intToString(t0)
        +intToString(t1)+intToString(t2)+intToString(t3));
    }
```

```
                // last round is special
                byte[] result = new byte[16]; // the resulting plaintext
                Kdr = Kd[ROUNDS];
                int tt = Kdr[0];
                result[ 0] = (byte)(Si[(t0 >>> 24) & 0xFF] ^ (tt >>> 24));
                result[ 1] = (byte)(Si[(t3 >>> 16) & 0xFF] ^ (tt >>> 16));
                result[ 2] = (byte)(Si[(t2 >>>  8) & 0xFF] ^ (tt >>>  8));
                result[ 3] = (byte)(Si[ t1         & 0xFF] ^  tt         );
                tt = Kdr[1];
                result[ 4] = (byte)(Si[(t1 >>> 24) & 0xFF] ^ (tt >>> 24));
                result[ 5] = (byte)(Si[(t0 >>> 16) & 0xFF] ^ (tt >>> 16));
                result[ 6] = (byte)(Si[(t3 >>>  8) & 0xFF] ^ (tt >>>  8));
                result[ 7] = (byte)(Si[ t2         & 0xFF] ^  tt         );
                tt = Kdr[2];
                result[ 8] = (byte)(Si[(t2 >>> 24) & 0xFF] ^ (tt >>> 24));
                result[ 9] = (byte)(Si[(t1 >>> 16) & 0xFF] ^ (tt >>> 16));
                result[10] = (byte)(Si[(t0 >>>  8) & 0xFF] ^ (tt >>>  8));
                result[11] = (byte)(Si[ t3         & 0xFF] ^  tt         );
                tt = Kdr[3];
                result[12] = (byte)(Si[(t3 >>> 24) & 0xFF] ^ (tt >>> 24));
                result[13] = (byte)(Si[(t2 >>> 16) & 0xFF] ^ (tt >>> 16));
                result[14] = (byte)(Si[(t1 >>>  8) & 0xFF] ^ (tt >>>  8));
                result[15] = (byte)(Si[ t0         & 0xFF] ^  tt         );
if (DEBUG && debuglevel > 6) {
System.out.println("PT="+toString(result));
System.out.println();
}
if (DEBUG) trace(OUT, "blockDecrypt()");
                return result;
            }


    /** A basic symmetric encryption/decryption test. */
    public static boolean self_test() { return self_test(BLOCK_SIZE); }


// Rijndael own methods
//............................................................................


    /** @return The default length in bytes of the Algorithm input block. */
    public static int blockSize() { return BLOCK_SIZE; }

    /**
     * Expand a user-supplied key material into a session key.
     *
     * @param key       The 128/192/256-bit user-key to use.
     * @param blockSize  The block size in bytes of this Rijndael.
     * @exception  InvalidKeyException  If the key is invalid.
     */
    public static synchronized Object makeKey (byte[] k, int blockSize)
    throws InvalidKeyException {
```

```java
if (DEBUG) trace(IN, "makeKey("+k+", "+blockSize+")");
        if (k == null)
            throw new InvalidKeyException("Empty key");
        if (!(k.length == 16 || k.length == 24 || k.length == 32))
            throw new InvalidKeyException("Incorrect key length");
        int ROUNDS = getRounds(k.length, blockSize);
        int BC = blockSize / 4;
        int[][] Ke = new int[ROUNDS + 1][BC]; // encryption round keys
        int[][] Kd = new int[ROUNDS + 1][BC]; // decryption round keys
        int ROUND_KEY_COUNT = (ROUNDS + 1) * BC;
        int KC = k.length / 4;
        int[] tk = new int[KC];
        int i, j;

        // copy user material bytes into temporary ints
        for (i = 0, j = 0; i < KC; )
            tk[i++] = (k[j++] & 0xFF) << 24 |
                      (k[j++] & 0xFF) << 16 |
                      (k[j++] & 0xFF) <<  8 |
                      (k[j++] & 0xFF);
        // copy values into round key arrays
        int t = 0;
        for (j = 0; (j < KC) && (t < ROUND_KEY_COUNT); j++, t++) {
            Ke[t / BC][t % BC] = tk[j];
            Kd[ROUNDS - (t / BC)][t % BC] = tk[j];
        }
        int tt, rconpointer = 0;
        while (t < ROUND_KEY_COUNT) {
            // extrapolate using phi (the round key evolution function)
            tt = tk[KC - 1];
            tk[0] ^= (S[(tt >>> 16) & 0xFF] & 0xFF) << 24 ^
                     (S[(tt >>>  8) & 0xFF] & 0xFF) << 16 ^
                     (S[ tt         & 0xFF] & 0xFF) <<  8 ^
                     (S[(tt >>> 24) & 0xFF] & 0xFF)       ^
                     (rcon[rconpointer++]   & 0xFF) << 24;
            if (KC != 8)
                for (i = 1, j = 0; i < KC; ) tk[i++] ^= tk[j++];
            else {
                for (i = 1, j = 0; i < KC / 2; ) tk[i++] ^= tk[j++];
                tt = tk[KC / 2 - 1];
                tk[KC / 2] ^= (S[ tt         & 0xFF] & 0xFF)       ^
                              (S[(tt >>  8) & 0xFF] & 0xFF) <<  8 ^
                              (S[(tt >> 16) & 0xFF] & 0xFF) << 16 ^
                              (S[(tt >> 24) & 0xFF] & 0xFF) << 24;
                for (j = KC / 2, i = j + 1; i < KC; ) tk[i++] ^= tk[j++];
            }
            // copy values into round key arrays
            for (j = 0; (j < KC) && (t < ROUND_KEY_COUNT); j++, t++) {
                Ke[t / BC][t % BC] = tk[j];
                Kd[ROUNDS - (t / BC)][t % BC] = tk[j];
            }
        }
    }
```

```
        for (int r = 1; r < ROUNDS; r++)      // inverse MixColumn where needed
            for (j = 0; j < BC; j++) {
                tt = Kd[r][j];
                Kd[r][j] = U1[(tt >> 24) & 0xFF] ^
                           U2[(tt >> 16) & 0xFF] ^
                           U3[(tt >>  8) & 0xFF] ^
                           U4[ tt        & 0xFF];
            }
        // assemble the encryption (Ke) and decryption (Kd) round keys into
        // one sessionKey object
        Object[] sessionKey = new Object[] {Ke, Kd};
if (DEBUG) trace(OUT, "makeKey()");
        return sessionKey;
    }


    /**
     * Encrypt exactly one block of plaintext.
     *
     * @param  in         The plaintext.
     * @param  inOffset   Index of in from which to start considering data.
     * @param  sessionKey The session key to use for encryption.
     * @param  blockSize  The block size in bytes of this Rijndael.
     * @return The ciphertext generated from a plaintext using the session key.
     */
    public static byte[]
    blockEncrypt (byte[] in, int inOffset, Object sessionKey, int blockSize)
       {
        if (blockSize == BLOCK_SIZE)
            return blockEncrypt(in, inOffset, sessionKey);
if (DEBUG) trace(IN, "blockEncrypt("+in+", "+inOffset+", "+sessionKey+", "
                            +blockSize+")");
        Object[] sKey = (Object[]) sessionKey;
        // extract encryption round keys
        int[][] Ke = (int[][]) sKey[0];

        int BC = blockSize / 4;
        int ROUNDS = Ke.length - 1;
        int SC = BC == 4 ? 0 : (BC == 6 ? 1 : 2);
        int s1 = shifts[SC][1][0];
        int s2 = shifts[SC][2][0];
        int s3 = shifts[SC][3][0];
        int[] a = new int[BC];
        int[] t = new int[BC]; // temporary work array
        int i;
        byte[] result = new byte[blockSize]; // the resulting ciphertext
        int j = 0, tt;
```

```
            for (i = 0; i < BC; i++)         // plaintext to ints + key
                t[i] = ((in[inOffset++] & 0xFF) << 24 |
                        (in[inOffset++] & 0xFF) << 16 |
                        (in[inOffset++] & 0xFF) << 8 |
                        (in[inOffset++] & 0xFF)         ) ^ Ke[0][i];
            for (int r = 1; r < ROUNDS; r++) {    // apply round transforms
                for (i = 0; i < BC; i++)
                    a[i] = (T1[(t[ i            ] >> 24) & 0xFF] ^
                            T2[(t[(i + s1) % BC] >> 16) & 0xFF] ^
                            T3[(t[(i + s2) % BC] >>  8) & 0xFF] ^
                            T4[ t[(i + s3) % BC]        & 0xFF] ) ^ Ke[r][i];
                System.arraycopy(a, 0, t, 0, BC);
if (DEBUG && debuglevel > 6) System.out.println("CT"+r+"="+toString(t));
            }
            for (i = 0; i < BC; i++) {                    // last round is special
                tt = Ke[ROUNDS][i];
                result[j++] = (byte)(S[(t[ i            ] >>> 24) & 0xFF]
                                                             ^ (tt >>> 24));
                result[j++] = (byte)(S[(t[(i + s1) % BC] >>> 16) & 0xFF]
                                                             ^ (tt >>> 16));
                result[j++] = (byte)(S[(t[(i + s2) % BC] >>>  8) & 0xFF]
                                                             ^ (tt >>>  8));
                result[j++] = (byte)(S[ t[(i + s3) % BC]         & 0xFF] ^ tt);
            }
if (DEBUG && debuglevel > 6) {
System.out.println("CT="+toString(result));
System.out.println();
}
if (DEBUG) trace(OUT, "blockEncrypt()");
            return result;
        }


    /**
     * Decrypt exactly one block of ciphertext.
     *
     * @param  in         The ciphertext.
     * @param  inOffset   Index of in from which to start considering data.
     * @param  sessionKey The session key to use for decryption.
     * @param  blockSize  The block size in bytes of this Rijndael.
     * @return The plaintext generated from a ciphertext using the session key.
     */
    public static byte[]
    blockDecrypt (byte[] in, int inOffset, Object sessionKey, int blockSize)
        {
            if (blockSize == BLOCK_SIZE)
                return blockDecrypt(in, inOffset, sessionKey);
if (DEBUG) trace(IN, "blockDecrypt("+in+", "+inOffset+", "+sessionKey+", "
                 +blockSize+")");
            Object[] sKey = (Object[]) sessionKey;
            // extract decryption round keys
            int[][] Kd = (int[][]) sKey[1];
```

```
        int BC = blockSize / 4;
        int ROUNDS = Kd.length - 1;
        int SC = BC == 4 ? 0 : (BC == 6 ? 1 : 2);
        int s1 = shifts[SC][1][1];
        int s2 = shifts[SC][2][1];
        int s3 = shifts[SC][3][1];
        int[] a = new int[BC];
        int[] t = new int[BC]; // temporary work array
        int i;
        byte[] result = new byte[blockSize]; // the resulting plaintext
        int j = 0, tt;

        for (i = 0; i < BC; i++)                          // ciphertext to ints + key
            t[i] = ((in[inOffset++] & 0xFF) << 24 |
                    (in[inOffset++] & 0xFF) << 16 |
                    (in[inOffset++] & 0xFF) <<  8 |
                    (in[inOffset++] & 0xFF)        ) ^ Kd[0][i];
        for (int r = 1; r < ROUNDS; r++) {                // apply round transforms
            for (i = 0; i < BC; i++)
                a[i] = (T5[(t[ i           ] >>> 24) & 0xFF] ^
                        T6[(t[(i + s1) % BC] >>> 16) & 0xFF] ^
                        T7[(t[(i + s2) % BC] >>>  8) & 0xFF] ^
                        T8[ t[(i + s3) % BC]         & 0xFF]  ) ^ Kd[r][i];
            System.arraycopy(a, 0, t, 0, BC);                       .
if (DEBUG && debuglevel > 6) System.out.println("PT"+r+"="+toString(t));
        }
        for (i = 0; i < BC; i++) {                        // last round is special
            tt = Kd[ROUNDS][i];
            result[j++] = (byte)(Si[(t[ i           ] >>> 24) & 0xFF]
                                                      ^ (tt >>> 24));
            result[j++] = (byte)(Si[(t[(i + s1) % BC] >>> 16) & 0xFF]
                                                      ^ (tt >> 16));
            result[j++] = (byte)(Si[(t[(i + s2) % BC] >>>  8) & 0xFF]
                                                      ^ (tt >>>  8));
            result[j++] = (byte)(Si[ t[(i + s3) % BC]         & 0xFF] ^ tt);
        }
if (DEBUG && debuglevel > 6) {
System.out.println("PT="+toString(result));
System.out.println();
}
if (DEBUG) trace(OUT, "blockDecrypt()");
        return result;
    }


    /** A basic symmetric encryption/decryption test for a given key size. */
    private static boolean self_test (int keysize) {
if (DEBUG) trace(IN, "self_test("+keysize+")");
        boolean ok = false;
        try {
            byte[] kb = new byte[keysize];
            byte[] pt = new byte[BLOCK_SIZE];
            int i;
```

```
                  for (i = 0; i < keysize; i++)
                      kb[i] = (byte) i;
                  for (i = 0; i < BLOCK_SIZE; i++)
                      pt[i] = (byte) i;

if (DEBUG && debuglevel > 6) {
System.out.println("==========");
System.out.println();
System.out.println("KEYSIZE="+(8*keysize));
System.out.println("KEY="+toString(kb));
System.out.println();
}
              Object key = makeKey(kb, BLOCK_SIZE);

if (DEBUG && debuglevel > 6) {
System.out.println("Intermediate Ciphertext Values (Encryption)");
System.out.println();
System.out.println("PT="+toString(pt));
}
              byte[] ct = blockEncrypt(pt, 0, key, BLOCK_SIZE);

if (DEBUG && debuglevel > 6) {
System.out.println("Intermediate Plaintext Values (Decryption)");
System.out.println();
System.out.println("CT="+toString(ct));
}
              byte[] cpt = blockDecrypt(ct, 0, key, BLOCK_SIZE);

              ok = areEqual(pt, cpt);
              if (!ok)
                  throw new RuntimeException("Symmetric operation failed");
          }
          catch (Exception x) {
if (DEBUG && debuglevel > 0) {
    debug("Exception encountered during self-test: " + x.getMessage());
    x.printStackTrace();
}
          }
if (DEBUG && debuglevel > 0) debug("Self-test OK? " + ok);
if (DEBUG) trace(OUT, "self_test()");
          return ok;
      }

    /**
     * Return The number of rounds for a given Rijndael's key and block sizes.
     *
     * @param keySize    The size of the user key material in bytes.
     * @param blockSize  The desired block size in bytes.
     * @return The number of rounds for a given Rijndael's key and block sizes.
     */
```

```java
    public static int getRounds (int keySize, int blockSize) {
        switch (keySize) {
        case 16:
            return blockSize == 16 ? 10 : (blockSize == 24 ? 12 : 14);
        case 24:
            return blockSize != 32 ? 12 : 14;
        default: // 32 bytes = 256 bits
            return 14;
        }
    }


// utility static methods (from cryptix.util.core ArrayUtil and Hex classes)
//...............................................................................

    /**
     * Compares two byte arrays for equality.
     *
     * @return true if the arrays have identical contents
     */
    private static boolean areEqual (byte[] a, byte[] b) {
        int aLength = a.length;
        if (aLength != b.length)
            return false;
        for (int i = 0; i < aLength; i++)
            if (a[i] != b[i])
                return false;
        return true;
    }


    /**
     * Returns a string of 2 hexadecimal digits (most significant digit first)
     * corresponding to the lowest 8 bits of <i>n</i>.
     */
    private static String byteToString (int n) {
        char[] buf = {
            HEX_DIGITS[(n >>> 4) & 0x0F],
            HEX_DIGITS[ n        & 0x0F]
        };
        return new String(buf);
    }


    /**
     * Returns a string of 8 hexadecimal digits (most significant digit first)
     * corresponding to the integer <i>n</i>, which is treated as unsigned.
     */
    private static String intToString (int n) {
        char[] buf = new char[8];
        for (int i = 7; i >= 0; i--) {
            buf[i] = HEX_DIGITS[n & 0x0F];
            n >>>= 4;
        }
        return new String(buf);
    }
```

```java
/**
 * Returns a string of hexadecimal digits from a byte array. Each byte is
 * converted to 2 hex symbols.
 */
private static String toString (byte[] ba) {
    int length = ba.length;
    char[] buf = new char[length * 2];
    for (int i = 0, j = 0, k; i < length; ) {
        k = ba[i++];
        buf[j++] = HEX_DIGITS[(k >> 4) & 0x0F];
        buf[j++] = HEX_DIGITS[ k       & 0x0F];
    }
    return new String(buf);
}


/**
 * Returns a string of hexadecimal digits from an integer array. Each int
 * is converted to 4 hex symbols.
 */
private static String toString (int[] ia) {
    int length = ia.length;
    char[] buf = new char[length * 8];
    for (int i = 0, j = 0, k; i < length; i++) {
        k = ia[i];
        buf[j++] = HEX_DIGITS[(k >>> 28) & 0x0F];
        buf[j++] = HEX_DIGITS[(k >>> 24) & 0x0F];
        buf[j++] = HEX_DIGITS[(k >>> 20) & 0x0F];
        buf[j++] = HEX_DIGITS[(k >>> 16) & 0x0F];
        buf[j++] = HEX_DIGITS[(k >>> 12) & 0x0F];
        buf[j++] = HEX_DIGITS[(k >>>  8) & 0x0F];
        buf[j++] = HEX_DIGITS[(k >>>  4) & 0x0F];
        buf[j++] = HEX_DIGITS[ k         & 0x0F];
    }
    return new String(buf);
}


// main(): use to generate the Intermediate Values KAT
//................................................................

    public static void main (String[] args) {
        self_test(16);
        self_test(24);
        self_test(32);
    }
}
```

```
// $Id: $
//
// $Log: $
// Revision 1.0  1998/04/07  raif
// + original version.
//
// $Endlog$
/*
 * Copyright (c) 1997, 1998 Systemics Ltd on behalf of the Cryptix Development
 * Team. All rights reserved.
 */
package Rijndael;

import java.io.FileInputStream;
import java.io.FileNotFoundException;
import java.io.InputStream;
import java.io.IOException;
import java.io.PrintWriter;
import java.io.PrintStream;
import java.util.Enumeration;
import java.util.Properties;


/**
 * This class acts as a central repository for an algorithm specific properties.
 * It reads an (algorithm).properties file containing algorithm-specific
 * properties. When using the AES-Kit, this (algorithm).properties file is
 * located in the (algorithm).jar file produced by the "jarit" batch/script
 * command.
 *
 * Copyright; 1997, 1998
 * Systemics Ltd (http://www.systemics.com/) on behalf of the
 * Cryptix Development Team (http://www.systemics.com/docs/cryptix/)
 * All rights reserved.
 *
 * $Revision: $
 * @author  David Hopwood
 * @author  Jill Baker
 * @author  Raif S. Naffah
 */
public class Rijndael_Properties // implicit no-argument constructor
{
// Constants and variables with relevant static code
//................................................................................

    static final boolean GLOBAL_DEBUG = false;

    static final String ALGORITHM = "Rijndael";
    static final double VERSION = 0.1;
    static final String FULL_NAME = ALGORITHM + " ver. " + VERSION;
    static final String NAME = "Rijndael_Properties";
```

```
        static final Properties properties = new Properties();

        /** Default properties in case .properties file was not found. */
        private static final String[][] DEFAULT_PROPERTIES = {
            {"Trace.Rijndael_Algorithm",          "true"},
            {"Debug.Level.*",                      "1"},
            {"Debug.Level.Rijndael_Algorithm", "9"}},
        };


        static {
if (GLOBAL_DEBUG) System.err.println(">>> " + NAME + ": Looking for "
                        + ALGORITHM + " properties");
            String it = ALGORITHM + ".properties";
            InputStream is = Rijndael_Properties.class.getResourceAsStream(it);
            boolean ok = is != null;
            if (ok)
                try {
                    properties.load(is);
                    is.close();
if (GLOBAL_DEBUG) System.err.println(">>> " + NAME + ":
                                        Properties file loaded OK...");
                } catch (Exception x) {
                    ok = false;
                }
            if (!ok) {
if (GLOBAL_DEBUG) System.err.println(">>> " + NAME + ":
                WARNING: Unable to load \"" + it + "\" from CLASSPATH.");
if (GLOBAL_DEBUG) System.err.println(">>> " + NAME + ":
                                        Will use default values instead...");
                int n = DEFAULT_PROPERTIES.length;
                for (int i = 0; i < n; i++)
                    properties.put(
                        DEFAULT_PROPERTIES[i][0], DEFAULT_PROPERTIES[i][1]);
if (GLOBAL_DEBUG) System.err.println(">>> " + NAME + ":
                                        Default properties now set...");
            }
        }


// Properties methods (excluding load and save, which are deliberately not
// supported).
//....................................................................

        /** Get the value of a property for this algorithm. */
        public static String getProperty (String key) {
            return properties.getProperty(key);
        }
```

```java
/**
 * Get the value of a property for this algorithm, or return <i>value</i>
 * if the property was not set.
 */
public static String getProperty (String key, String value) {
    return properties.getProperty(key, value);
}


/** List algorithm properties to the PrintStream <i>out</i>. */
public static void list (PrintStream out) {
    list(new PrintWriter(out, true));
}


/** List algorithm properties to the PrintWriter <i>out</i>. */
public static void list (PrintWriter out) {
    out.println("#");
    out.println("# ----- Begin "+ALGORITHM+" properties -----");
    out.println("#");
    String key, value;
    Enumeration enum = properties.propertyNames();
    while (enum.hasMoreElements()) {
        key = (String) enum.nextElement();
        value = getProperty(key);
        out.println(key + " = " + value);
    }
    out.println("#");
    out.println("# ----- End "+ALGORITHM+" properties -----");
}

//    public synchronized void load(InputStream in) throws IOException {}

    public static Enumeration propertyNames() {
        return properties.propertyNames();
    }

//    public void save (OutputStream os, String comment) {}


// Developer support: Tracing and debugging enquiry methods (package-private)
//.............................................................................

    /**
     * Return true if tracing is requested for a given class.<p>
     *
     * User indicates this by setting the tracing <code>boolean</code> property
     * for <i>label</i> in the <code>(algorithm).properties</code> file. The
     * property's key is "<code>Trace.<i>label</i></code>".<p>
     *
     * @param label  The name of a class.
     * @return True iff a boolean true value is set for a property with
     *         the key <code>Trace.<i>label</i></code>.
     */
```

```java
static boolean isTraceable (String label) {
    String s = getProperty("Trace." + label);
    if (s == null)
        return false;
    return new Boolean(s).booleanValue();
}


/**
 * Return the debug level for a given class.<p>
 *
 * User indicates this by setting the numeric property with key
 * "<code>Debug.Level.<i>label</i></code>".<p>
 *
 * If this property is not set, "<code>Debug.Level.*</code>" is looked up
 * next. If neither property is set, or if the first property found is
 * not a valid decimal integer, then this method returns 0.
 *
 * @param label   The name of a class.
 * @return   The required debugging level for the designated class.
 */
static int getLevel(String label) {
    String s = getProperty("Debug.Level." + label);
    if (s == null) {
        s = getProperty("Debug.Level.*");
        if (s == null)
            return 0;
    }
    try {
        return Integer.parseInt(s);
    } catch (NumberFormatException e) {
        return 0;
    }
}


/**
 * Return the PrintWriter to which tracing and debugging output is to
 * be sent.<p>
 *
 * User indicates this by setting the property with key <code>Output</code>
 * to the literal <code>out</code> or <code>err</code>.<p>
 *
 * By default or if the set value is not allowed, <code>System.err</code>
 * will be used.
 */
static PrintWriter getOutput() {
    PrintWriter pw;
    String name = getProperty("Output");
    if (name != null && name.equals("out"))
        pw = new PrintWriter(System.out, true);
    else
        pw = new PrintWriter(System.err, true);
    return pw;
}
}
```

C

A Reference Implementation of MD5

We present in this appendix, a publicly available reference C source code for MD5: one of the most commonly used hash function. The program consists of three files:

1. global.h: The global header file

2. md5.h: Header file for MD5

3. md5c.: Source code for MD5

The content of these files are presented in the order shown above.

```
/* global.h
 *
 *   GLOBAL.H - RSAREF types and constants
 */


/* PROTOTYPES should be set to one if and only if the compiler supports
   function argument prototyping.
   The following makes PROTOTYPES default to 0 if it has not already been
   defined with C compiler flags.
*/

#ifndef PROTOTYPES
#define PROTOTYPES 0
#endif


/* POINTER defines a generic pointer type */
typedef unsigned char *POINTER;

/* UINT2 defines a two byte word */
typedef unsigned short int UINT2;

/* UINT4 defines a four byte word */
typedef unsigned long int UINT4;

/* PROTO_LIST is defined depending on how PROTOTYPES is defined above.
If using PROTOTYPES, then PROTO_LIST returns the list, otherwise it returns
   an empty list.
 */
#if PROTOTYPES
#define PROTO_LIST(list) list
#else
#define PROTO_LIST(list) ()
#endif




/* md5.h
 *
 * MD5.H - header file for MD5C.C
 */
```

```
/* MD5 context. */
typedef struct {
  UINT4 state[4];                                  /* state (ABCD) */
  UINT4 count[2];          /* number of bits, modulo 2^64 (lsb first) */
  unsigned char buffer[64];                        /* input buffer */
} MD5_CTX;

void MD5Init PROTO_LIST ((MD5_CTX *));
void MD5Update PROTO_LIST
  ((MD5_CTX *, unsigned char *, unsigned int));
void MD5Final PROTO_LIST ((unsigned char [16], MD5_CTX *));
```

```
/* md5c.c
 *
 * MD5C.C - RSA Data Security, Inc., MD5 message-digest algorithm
 */
```

These notices must be retained in any copies of any part of this documentation and/or software.
 */

```
#include "global.h"
#include "md5.h"

/* Constants for MD5Transform routine.
 */

#define S11 7
#define S12 12
#define S13 17
#define S14 22
#define S21 5
#define S22 9
#define S23 14
#define S24 20
#define S31 4
#define S32 11
#define S33 16
#define S34 23
#define S41 6
#define S42 10
#define S43 15
#define S44 21

static void MD5Transform PROTO_LIST ((UINT4 [4], unsigned char [64]));
static void Encode PROTO_LIST
  ((unsigned char *, UINT4 *, unsigned int));
static void Decode PROTO_LIST
  ((UINT4 *, unsigned char *, unsigned int));
static void MD5_memcpy PROTO_LIST ((POINTER, POINTER, unsigned int));
static void MD5_memset PROTO_LIST ((POINTER, int, unsigned int));

static unsigned char PADDING[64] = {
  0x80, 0, 0, 0, 0, 0, 0, 0, 0, 0, 0, 0, 0, 0, 0, 0, 0, 0, 0, 0, 0, 0,
  0, 0, 0, 0, 0, 0, 0, 0, 0, 0, 0, 0, 0, 0, 0, 0, 0, 0, 0, 0, 0, 0,
  0, 0, 0, 0, 0, 0, 0, 0, 0, 0, 0, 0, 0, 0, 0, 0, 0, 0, 0, 0
};

/* F, G, H and I are basic MD5 functions.
 */
#define F(x, y, z) (((x) & (y)) | ((~x) & (z)))
#define G(x, y, z) (((x) & (z)) | ((y) & (~z)))
#define H(x, y, z) ((x) ^ (y) ^ (z))
#define I(x, y, z) ((y) ^ ((x) | (~z)))

/* ROTATE_LEFT rotates x left n bits.
 */
#define ROTATE_LEFT(x, n) (((x) << (n)) | ((x) >> (32-(n))))
```

```
/* FF, GG, HH, and II transformations for rounds 1, 2, 3, and 4.
Rotation is separate from addition to prevent recomputation.
 */
#define FF(a, b, c, d, x, s, ac) { \
 (a) += F ((b), (c), (d)) + (x) + (UINT4)(ac); \
 (a) = ROTATE_LEFT ((a), (s)); \
(a) += (b); \
 }
#define GG(a, b, c, d, x, s, ac) { \
 (a) += G ((b), (c), (d)) + (x) + (UINT4)(ac); \
 (a) = ROTATE_LEFT ((a), (s)); \
 (a) += (b); \
 }
#define HH(a, b, c, d, x, s, ac) { \
 (a) += H ((b), (c), (d)) + (x) + (UINT4)(ac); \
 (a) = ROTATE_LEFT ((a), (s)); \
 (a) += (b); \
 }
#define II(a, b, c, d, x, s, ac) { \
 (a) += I ((b), (c), (d)) + (x) + (UINT4)(ac); \
 (a) = ROTATE_LEFT ((a), (s)); \
 (a) += (b); \
 }


/* MD5 initialization. Begins an MD5 operation, writing a new context.
 */
void MD5Init (context)
MD5_CTX *context;                                       /* context */
{
  context->count[0] = context->count[1] = 0;
  /* Load magic initialization constants.
*/
  context->state[0] = 0x67452301;
  context->state[1] = 0xefcdab89;
  context->state[2] = 0x98badcfe;
  context->state[3] = 0x10325476;
}


/* MD5 block update operation. Continues an MD5 message-digest operation,
  processing another message block, and updating the context.
 */
void MD5Update (context, input, inputLen)
MD5_CTX *context;                                       /* context */
unsigned char *input;                                   /* input block */
unsigned int inputLen;                          /* length of input block */
{
  unsigned int i, index, partLen;

  /* Compute number of bytes mod 64 */
  index = (unsigned int)((context->count[0] >> 3) & 0x3F);
```

```
  /* Update number of bits */
  if ((context->count[0] += ((UINT4)inputLen << 3))
                            < ((UINT4)inputLen << 3))
context->count[1]++;
  context->count[1] += ((UINT4)inputLen >> 29);

  partLen = 64 - index;

  /* Transform as many times as possible.
*/
  if (inputLen >= partLen) {
MD5_memcpy
    ((POINTER)&context->buffer[index], (POINTER)input, partLen);
MD5Transform (context->state, context->buffer);

  for (i = partLen; i + 63 < inputLen; i += 64)
    MD5Transform (context->state, &input[i]);

  index = 0;
   }
   else
i = 0;

  /* Buffer remaining input */
  MD5_memcpy
((POINTER)&context->buffer[index], (POINTER)&input[i], inputLen-i);
}

/* MD5 finalization. Ends an MD5 message-digest operation, writing the
  the message digest and zeroizing the context.
  */
void MD5Final (digest, context)
unsigned char digest[16];                            /* message digest */
MD5_CTX *context;                                    /* context */
{
  unsigned char bits[8];
  unsigned int index, padLen;

  /* Save number of bits */
  Encode (bits, context->count, 8);
```

```
  /* Pad out to 56 mod 64.
*/
  index = (unsigned int)((context->count[0] > 3) & 0x3f);
  padLen = (index < 56) ? (56 - index) : (120 - index);
  MD5Update (context, PADDING, padLen);

  /* Append length (before padding) */
  MD5Update (context, bits, 8);
  /* Store state in digest */
  Encode (digest, context->state, 16);

  /* Zeroize sensitive information.
*/
  MD5_memset ((POINTER)context, 0, sizeof (*context));
}

/* MD5 basic transformation. Transforms state based on block.
 */
static void MD5Transform (state, block)
UINT4 state[4];
unsigned char block[64];
{
  UINT4 a = state[0], b = state[1], c = state[2], d = state[3], x[16];

  Decode (x, block, 64);

  /* Round 1 */
  FF (a, b, c, d, x[ 0], S11, 0xd76aa478); /* 1 */
  FF (d, a, b, c, x[ 1], S12, 0xe8c7b756); /* 2 */
  FF (c, d, a, b, x[ 2], S13, 0x242070db); /* 3 */
  FF (b, c, d, a, x[ 3], S14, 0xc1bdceee); /* 4 */
  FF (a, b, c, d, x[ 4], S11, 0xf57c0faf); /* 5 */
  FF (d, a, b, c, x[ 5], S12, 0x4787c62a); /* 6 */
  FF (c, d, a, b, x[ 6], S13, 0xa8304613); /* 7 */
  FF (b, c, d, a, x[ 7], S14, 0xfd469501); /* 8 */
  FF (a, b, c, d, x[ 8], S11, 0x698098d8); /* 9 */
  FF (d, a, b, c, x[ 9], S12, 0x8b44f7af); /* 10 */
  FF (c, d, a, b, x[10], S13, 0xffff5bb1); /* 11 */
  FF (b, c, d, a, x[11], S14, 0x895cd7be); /* 12 */
  FF (a, b, c, d, x[12], S11, 0x6b901122); /* 13 */
  FF (d, a, b, c, x[13], S12, 0xfd987193); /* 14 */
  FF (c, d, a, b, x[14], S13, 0xa679438e); /* 15 */
  FF (b, c, d, a, x[15], S14, 0x49b40821); /* 16 */
```

```
/* Round 2 */
GG (a, b, c, d, x[ 1], S21, 0xf61e2562); /* 17 */
GG (d, a, b, c, x[ 6], S22, 0xc040b340); /* 18 */
GG (c, d, a, b, x[11], S23, 0x265e5a51); /* 19 */
GG (b, c, d, a, x[ 0], S24, 0xe9b6c7aa); /* 20 */
GG (a, b, c, d, x[ 5], S21, 0xd62f105d); /* 21 */
GG (d, a, b, c, x[10], S22,  0x2441453); /* 22 */
GG (c, d, a, b, x[15], S23, 0xd8a1e681); /* 23 */
GG (b, c, d, a, x[ 4], S24, 0xe7d3fbc8); /* 24 */
GG (a, b, c, d, x[ 9], S21, 0x21e1cde6); /* 25 */
GG (d, a, b, c, x[14], S22, 0xc33707d6); /* 26 */
GG (c, d, a, b, x[ 3], S23, 0xf4d50d87); /* 27 */
GG (b, c, d, a, x[ 8], S24, 0x455a14ed); /* 28 */
GG (a, b, c, d, x[13], S21, 0xa9e3e905); /* 29 */
GG (d, a, b, c, x[ 2], S22, 0xfcefa3f8); /* 30 */
GG (c, d, a, b, x[ 7], S23, 0x676f02d9); /* 31 */
GG (b, c, d, a, x[12], S24, 0x8d2a4c8a); /* 32 */


/* Round 3 */
HH (a, b, c, d, x[ 5], S31, 0xfffa3942); /* 33 */
HH (d, a, b, c, x[ 8], S32, 0x8771f681); /* 34 */
HH (c, d, a, b, x[11], S33, 0x6d9d6122); /* 35 */
HH (b, c, d, a, x[14], S34, 0xfde5380c); /* 36 */
HH (a, b, c, d, x[ 1], S31, 0xa4beea44); /* 37 */
HH (d, a, b, c, x[ 4], S32, 0x4bdecfa9); /* 38 */
HH (c, d, a, b, x[ 7], S33, 0xf6bb4b60); /* 39 */
HH (b, c, d, a, x[10], S34, 0xbebfbc70); /* 40 */
HH (a, b, c, d, x[13], S31, 0x289b7ec6); /* 41 */
HH (d, a, b, c, x[ 0], S32, 0xeaa127fa); /* 42 */
HH (c, d, a, b, x[ 3], S33, 0xd4ef3085); /* 43 */
HH (b, c, d, a, x[ 6], S34,  0x4881d05); /* 44 */
HH (a, b, c, d, x[ 9], S31, 0xd9d4d039); /* 45 */
HH (d, a, b, c, x[12], S32, 0xe6db99e5); /* 46 */
HH (c, d, a, b, x[15], S33, 0x1fa27cf8); /* 47 */
HH (b, c, d, a, x[ 2], S34, 0xc4ac5665); /* 48 */


/* Round 4 */
II (a, b, c, d, x[ 0], S41, 0xf4292244); /* 49 */
II (d, a, b, c, x[ 7], S42, 0x432aff97); /* 50 */
II (c, d, a, b, x[14], S43, 0xab9423a7); /* 51 */
II (b, c, d, a, x[ 5], S44, 0xfc93a039); /* 52 */
II (a, b, c, d, x[12], S41, 0x655b59c3); /* 53 */
II (d, a, b, c, x[ 3], S42, 0x8f0ccc92); /* 54 */
II (c, d, a, b, x[10], S43, 0xffeff47d); /* 55 */
II (b, c, d, a, x[ 1], S44, 0x85845dd1); /* 56 */
II (a, b, c, d, x[ 8], S41, 0x6fa87e4f); /* 57 */
II (d, a, b, c, x[15], S42, 0xfe2ce6e0); /* 58 */
II (c, d, a, b, x[ 6], S43, 0xa3014314); /* 59 */
II (b, c, d, a, x[13], S44, 0x4e0811a1); /* 60 */
II (a, b, c, d, x[ 4], S41, 0xf7537e82); /* 61 */
II (d, a, b, c, x[11], S42, 0xbd3af235); /* 62 */
II (c, d, a, b, x[ 2], S43, 0x2ad7d2bb); /* 63 */
II (b, c, d, a, x[ 9], S44, 0xeb86d391); /* 64 */
```

```
    state[0] += a;
    state[1] += b;
    state[2] += c;
    state[3] += d;

    /* Zeroize sensitive information. */
    MD5_memset ((POINTER)x, 0, sizeof (x));
}

/* Encodes input (UINT4) into output (unsigned char). Assumes len is
   a multiple of 4.
 */
static void Encode (output, input, len)
unsigned char *output;
UINT4 *input;
unsigned int len;
{
  unsigned int i, j;

  for (i = 0, j = 0; j < len; i++, j += 4) {
    output[j] = (unsigned char)(input[i] & 0xff);
    output[j+1] = (unsigned char)((input[i] >> 8) & 0xff);
    output[j+2] = (unsigned char)((input[i] >> 16) & 0xff);
    output[j+3] = (unsigned char)((input[i] >> 24) & 0xff);
  }
}

/* Decodes input (unsigned char) into output (UINT4). Assumes len is
   a multiple of 4.
 */
static void Decode (output, input, len)
UINT4 *output;
unsigned char *input;
unsigned int len;
{
  unsigned int i, j;

  for (i = 0, j = 0; j < len; i++, j += 4)
    output[i] = ((UINT4)input[j]) | (((UINT4)input[j+1]) << 8) |
      (((UINT4)input[j+2]) << 16) | (((UINT4)input[j+3]) << 24);
}

/* Note: Replace "for loop" with standard memcpy if possible.
 */
```

```
static void MD5_memcpy (output, input, len)
POINTER output;
POINTER input;
unsigned int len;
{
  unsigned int i;

  for (i = 0; i < len; i++)
      output[i] = input[i];
}

/* Note: Replace "for loop" with standard memset if possible.
 */
static void MD5_memset (output, value, len)
POINTER output;
int value;
unsigned int len;
{
  unsigned int i;

  for (i = 0; i < len; i++)
  ((char *)output)[i] = (char)value;
}
```

Bibliography

[ABK98]   Anderson, R., Biham, E., Knudsen, L., "Serpent:
              A Proposal for the Advanced Encryption
              Standard," *http://www.nist.gov/aes*, 1998.

[Ada97]   Adams, C., "The CAST-128 Encryption
              Algorithm," Request for Comments (RFC 2144),
              May 1997.

[AG99]   Adams, C., Gilchrist, J. "The CAST-256
              Encryption Algorithm," Request for Comments
              (RFC 2612), May 1999.

[Ano98]   Anonymous, "Maximum Security A Hacker's
              Guide to Protect Your Internet and Site
              Network," Sams Publishing, 2nd ed.,
              August 1998.

[BBP88]   Braden, R., Borman, D., and Partridge, C.,
              "Computing the Internet Checksum," Request
              for Comment (RFC 1071), September 1988.

[BLP93]   Buhler, J., Lenstra, H., Jr., and Pomerance, C.,
              "Factoring Integers with the Number Field
              Sieve", in The Development of the Number Field
              Sieve, Lecture Notes in Mathematics, Vol. 1554,
              Springer-Verlag, pp. 11–42, 1993.

[BP00]   Beaulieu, S., and Pereira, R., "Extended Authen-
              tication Within IKE (XAUTH)," Internet Draft
              Document: <draft-beaulieu-ike-xauth-00.txt>,
              October 2000.

[BR96]   Baldwin, R., Rivest, R., " The RC5, RC5-CBC,
              RC5-CBC-Pad, and RC5-CTS Algorithms,"
              Request for Comments (RFC 2040),
              October 1996.

[Bar64]   Baran, Paul, "On Distributed Communications:
              I. Introduction to Distributed Communications
              Network," MEMORANDUM RM-3420-PR,
              RAND Corporation, August 1964.

[BS93]   Biham, E. and Shamir, A., "Differential
             Cryptanalysis Data Encryption Standard,"
             New York: Springer-Verlag, 1993.

[CDFT98]   Callas, J., et al., "OpenPGP Message Format,"
             Request for Comments (RFC 2440), November
             1998.

[CK74]   Cerf, V. and Kahn R., "A Protocol for Packet
             Network Interconnection," IEEE Trans. on
             Communication, Vol. COM-22, pp. 637–648,
             May 1974.

[Cla88]   Clark, D.D., "The Design Philosophy of the
             DARPA Internet Protocols," Proc. SIGCOMM 88
             Conf., ACM, pp. 106–114, 1988.

[CQ93]   Carl-Mitchell, Smoot and Quarterman, John S.,
             "Practical Internetworking with TCP/IP and
             UNIX," Addison-Wesley Publishing Company,
             1993.

[DBP96]   Dobbertin, H., Bosselaer, A., and Preneel, B.,
             "RIPEMD-160: A Strengthened Version of
             RIPEMD" Fast Software Encryption, LNCS 1039,
             Springer-Verlag, pp. 71–82, 1996.

[Dee89]   Deering, S.E., "Host Extensions for IP Multi-
             casting," Request For Comments (RFC 1112),
             August 1989.

[DH95]   Deering, S.E. and Hinden, R., "Internet Protocol,
             Version 6 (IPv6) Specification ," Request for
             Comments (RFC 1883), December 1995.

[DH76]   Diffie, W. and Hellman, M., "Multiusers
             Cryptographic Techniques," Proceedings of
             the AFIPS National Computer Conference,
             June 1976.

[DP00]   Dukes, D., and Pereira, R., "The ISAKMP
             Configuration Method," INTERNET-DRAFT
             <draft-dukes-ike-mode-cfg-00.txt>, October 2000.

[DR99]   Daemen, J., Rijmen, V., "Rijndael Block Cipher," AES Proposal, *http://www.nist.gov/aes*, 1999.

[Dro97]   Droms, R., "Dynamic Host Configuration Protocol," Request for Comments (RFC 2131), March 1997.

[Eas99]   Eastlake, D., "Domain Name System Security Extensions," Request for Comments (RFC 2535), March 1999.

[EFRL99]   Ellison, C., et al., "SPKI Certificate Theory," Request for Comments (RFC 2693), September 1999.

[ElG85]   ElGamal, T., "A Public Key Cryptosystem and a Signature Scheme Based on Discrete Logarithms," IEE Transactions on Information Theory, Vol. 31, pp. 469–472, 1985.

[Fie73]   Feistel, Horst. "Cryptography and Computer Privacy," Scientific America, May 1973.

[FM98]   Friend, R., and Monsour, R., "IP Compression Using LZS," Request for Comments (RFC 2395), December 1998.

[FTMT84]   Finlayson, R., Timothy, M., Mogul, J., Theimer, M., "A Reverse Address Resolution Protocol," Network Working Group Request for Comments (RFC 903), June 1984.

[FWWD94]   Fischer, W., Wallmeier, E., Worster, T., Davis, S.P., Hayter, A., "Data Communication Using ATM: Architecture, Protocols and Resource Management," IEEE Communication Magazine, Vol. 32, pp. 24–33, August 1994.

[Gor95]   Goralski, W.J., "Introduction to ATM Networking," New York: McGraw-Hill, 1995.

[HC98]   Harkins, D., Carrel, D., "Internet Key Exchange
              (IKE)," Request for Comments (RFC 2409),
              November 1998.

[HFPS99]   Housley, R., Ford, W., Polk, W. and Solo, D.,
              "Internet X.509 Public Key Infracture Certificate
              and CRL Profile," Request for Comments (RFC
              2459), January 1999.

[HS97]   Howes, T., and Smith, M., "The LDAP URL
              Format," Request for Comments (RFC 2255),
              December 1997.

[How97]   Howes, T., "The String Representation of LDAP
              Search Filters," Request for Comments (RFC
              2254), December 1997.

[Hun98]   Hunt, Craig, "TCP/IP Network Administration,"
              O'Reilly and Associates Inc., 2nd ed., 1998.

[IANA00]   Internet Assigned Numbers Authority (IANA),
              "Protocol Numbers and Assigned Services",
              http://www.iana.org/numbers.html.

[IBM99]   Burwick, C., et al., "MARS—a candidate cipher
              for AES," IBM Corporation, September 1999,
              http://www.nist.gov/aes.

[JM99]   Jurisic, A., Memezes, A., "Elliptic Curves
              Cryptography," available at
              http://www.certicom.com.

[KA98]   Kent, S., Atkinson, R, "IP Authentication
              Header" Request for Comments (RFC 2402),
              November 1998.

[Kal98]   Kaliski, B., "PKCS #7: Cryptographic Message
              Syntax Version 1.5", Request for Comments
              (RFC 2315), March 1998.

[KBC97]   Krawczyk, H., Bellare, M., and Canetti, R.,
                   "HMAC: Keyed-Hashing for Message
                   Authentication," Request for Comments
                   (RFC 2104), February 1997.

[KK00]   Kivinen, T., and Kojo, M., "More MODP Diffie-
                   Hellman groups for IKE," INTERNET-DRAFT
                   <draft-ietf-ipsec-ike-modp-groups-01.txt>,
                   November 2000.

[KN93]   Kohl, J., and Neuman, C., "The Kerberos
                   Network Authentication Service (V5)," Request
                   for Comments (RFC 1510), September 1993.

[Kob87]   Koblitz, N., "Elliptic Curve Cryptosystems,"
                   Mathematics of Computation, Vol. 48,
                   pp. 203–209, 1987.

[Kra96]   Krawczyk, H., "SKEME: A versitile Secure Key
                   Exchange Mechanism for Internet", IEEE
                   Proceedings of Symposium on Network and
                   Distributed Systems Security, 1996.

[Kya95]   Kyas, O. "ATM Networks," London: International
                   Thompson Publishing, 1995.

[LM90]   Lia, X., and Massey, J., "A Proposal for a
                   New Block Encryption Standard," Proceedings,
                   EUROCRYPTO '90, Published by Springer-
                   Verlag, 1990.

[LM91]   Lia, X., and Massey, J., "Markov Cipher and
                   Cryptanalysis," Proceedings, EUROCRYPTO '91,
                   Published by Springer-Verlag, 1991.

[LRA92]   Latif, A., Rowlance, E.J., and Adams, R.H., "IBM
                   8209 LAN Bridge," IEEE Network Magazine,
                   Vol. 6, pp. 28–37, May/June 1992.

[LCPM85]   Leiner, B.M., Cole, R., Postel, J., and Mills, D.,
                   "The DARPA Internet Protocol Suite," IEEE
                   Communication Magazine, Vol. 23, pp. 29–34,
                   March 1985.

[Luc99]   Lucks, S., "Attacking Seven Rounds of
              Rijndael under 192-bit and 256-bit Keys"
              http://www.nist.gov/aes, 1999.

[Mat93]   Matsui, M., "Linear Cryptanalysis Method of
              DES Cipher," Proceedings, EUROCRYPT '93,
              1993.

[LSZ00]   Litvin, M., Shamir, R., and Zegman, T.,
              "A Hybrid Authentication Mode For IKE,"
              <draft-ietf-ipsec-isakmp-hybrid-auth.txt>,
              August 2000.

[MB76]   Metcalfe, R.M., and Boggs, D.R., "Ethernet:
              Distributed Packet Switching for local Computer
              Networks," Commun. of the ACM, Vol. 19,
              pp. 395–404, July 1976.

[Mil86]   Miller, V., "Uses of Elliptic Curves in Cryp-
              tography," Advance in Cryptology, CRYPTO 85
              Lecture Notes in Computer Science, Vol. 218,
              Springer-Verlag, pp. 417–426, 1986.

[MSST98]   Maughan, D., Schertler, M., Schneider, M.,
              Turner, J., "Internet Security Association
              and Key Management Protocol," Request for
              Comments (RFC 2408), November 1998.

[Mur90]   Murphy, S., "The Cryptanalysis of FEAL-4 with
              20 Choosen Plaintexts," Journal of Cryptology,
              No. 3, 1990.

[NIST93]   National Institute of Standard and Technology,
              "Secure Hash Standard," Federal Information
              Processing Standards Publication 180-1 (FIPS
              PUB 180-1), April 17, 1995.

[NIST98]   National Institute of Standard and Technology,
              "Digital Signature Standard (DSS)," Federal
              Information Processing Standards Publication
              186-1 (FIPS PUB 186-1), December 15, 1998.

[NIST99]   National Institute of Standard and Technology, "Data Encryption Standard (DES)," Federal Information Processing Standards Publication 46-3 (FIPS PUB 46-3), October 25, 1999.

[NKPC70]   Newkirk, J., Kraley, M., Postel, J., and Crocker, S.D, "Prototypical Implementation of the NCP," Network Working Group Request for Comments (RFC 55), June 1970.

[Orm98]   Orman, H., "Oakley Key Determination Protocol," Request for Comments (RFC 2412), November 1998.

[OCSP99]   Myers, M., et. al., "X.509 Internet Public Key Infrastructure Online Certificate Status Protocol–OCSP," Request for Comments (RFC 2560), June 1999.

[PAKG00]   Patel, B., Aboba, B., Kelly, S., and Gupta, V., "DHCP Configuration of IPSEC Tunnel Mode in IPv4," INTERNET-DRAFT <draft-ietf-ipsec-dhcp-07.txt>, October 2000.

[PC78]   Pollard, J., "Monte Carlo Methods for Index computation mod p", Mathematics of Computation, Vol. 32, pp. 918–924, 1978.

[Per]   Pereira, R., "IP Payload Compression Using DEFLATE," Request for Comments (RFC 2394), December 1998.

[PH78]   Pohlig, S., and Hellman, M., "An Improved Algorithm for Computing Logarithms Over GF(P) and its Cryptographic Significance," IEEE Transactions on Information Theory, Vol. 24, pp. 106–110, 1978.

[Plu82]   Plummer, David C., "Ethernet Address Resolution Protocol," Network Working Group Request for Comments (RFC826), November 1982.

[Pip98]   Piper, D., "The Internet IP Security Domain of Interpretation for ISAKMP," Request for Comments (RFC 2407), November 1998.

[Pos80]   Postel, J.B., "User Datagram Protocol," Request for Comments (RFC 768), August 1980.

[Pos81a]   Postel, J.B., "Internet Protocol," Request for Comments (RFC 791), September 1981.

[Pos81b]   Postel, J.B., "Internet Control Message Protocol," Request for Comments (RFC 792), September 1981.

[Pos81c]   Postel, J.B., "Transmission Control Protocol," Request for Comments (RFC 793), September 1981.

[RP88]   Reynolds, J. and Postel, J.B., "A Standard for the Transmission of IP Datagram Over IEEE 802 Networks," Request for Comments (RFC 1042), February 88.

[RP94]   Reynolds, J. and Postel, J.B., "Assigned Numbers," Request for Comments (RFC 1700), October 1994.

[Riv92a]   Rivest, R., "The MD5 Message—Digest Algorithm," Request for Comments (RFC 1321), April 1992.

[Riv92b]   Rivest, R., "The MD4 Message—Digest Algorithm," Request for Comments (RFC 1320), April 1992.

[Riv94]   Rivest, R., "RC5 Encryption Algorithm," Proceedings, Second International Workshop on Fast Software Encryption, Published by Springer-Verlag, December 1994.

[Riv97]   Rivest, R., et al. "RC6 Block Cipher," AES Submission, *http://www.nist.gov/aes*, 1997.

[RSA78]   Rivest, R., Shamir, A., and Adleman, L., "A
                    Method for Obtaining Digital Signatures and
                    Public Key Cryptosystems," Communications
                    of the ACM, February 1978.

[Riv98]   Rivest, R., "A Description of the RC2(r)
                    Encryption Algorithm," Request for Comments
                    (RFC 2268), March 1998.

[RSA97]   RSA Data Security Inc., "Government Encryption
                    Standard Takes a Fall." RSA Data Press Release,
                    June 17, 1997.

[SA98]   Kent, S., Atkinson, R., "IP Encapsulatin Security
                    Payload (ESP)," Request for Comments (RFC
                    2406), September 1998.

[Sch93]   Schneier, B., "Description of a New Variable-
                    Length Key, 64-bit Block Cipher (Blowfish),"
                    Proceedings, Workshop on Fast Software
                    Encryption, Published by Springer-Verlag,
                    December 1993.

[SEC99]   Standards for Efficient Cryptography, "SEC 1:
                    Elliptic Curve Cryptography" Working Draft,
                    September 1999, Version 0.5.

[SKW98]   Schneier, B., et al., "Twofish: A 128-Bit
                    Block Cipher," AES submission,
                    http://www.nist.gov/aes, 1998.

[SMPT98]   Shacham, A., Monsour, R., Pereira, R., and
                    Thomas, M. "IP Payload Compression Protocol
                    (IPComp)," Request for Comments (RFC 2393),
                    December 1998.

[SPBN00]   Santesson, S., Polk, W., Barzin, P., and Nystrom,
                    M., "Internet X.509 Public Key Infrastructure
                    Qualified Certificates Profile," PKIX Working
                    Group INTERNET-DRAFT, August 2000.

[Sta99]   Stallings, William, "Cryptography and Network Security: Principle and Practice," Prentice Hall Inc., 2nd ed., 1999.

[Ste94]   Stevens, W. Richards, "TCP/IP Illustrated, Vol. 1, The Protocols," Addison-Wesley Publishing Company, 1994.

[Sti95]   Stinson, D., R., "Cryptography Theory and Practice," CRC Press LLC, 1995.

[SW00]   Schneier, B., Whiting, D., "A Performance Comparison of the Five AES Finalists," *http://www.nist.gov/aes*, 2000.

[Tan96]   Tanenbaum, Andrew S., "Computer Networks," Prentice-Hall Inc., 3rd ed., 1996.

[Wah97]   Wahl, M., "A Summary of the X.500(96) User Schema for use with LDAPv3," Request for Comment (RFC 2256), December 1997.

[WZ99]   Wiener, M., Zuccherato R., "Fast Attacks on Elliptic Curve Cryptosystems," Fifth Annual Work-shop on Selected Areas in Cryptography: SAC '98, pp. 190–200, 1999.

[X.208]   International Telecommunication Union, Recommendation X.208 ISO/IEC 8824: ASN.1 Basic Notation, 1988, available at *http://www.itu.org*.

[X.500]   International Telecommunication Union, Recommendation X.500: Information technology–Open systems Interconnection–The Directory, November 1993, available at *http://www.itu.org*.

INDEX

Q

R

INTERNATIONAL CONTACT INFORMATION

AUSTRALIA
McGraw-Hill Book Company Australia Pty. Ltd.
TEL +61-2-9417-9899
FAX +61-2-9417-5687
http://www.mcgraw-hill.com.au
books-it_sydney@mcgraw-hill.com

CANADA
McGraw-Hill Ryerson Ltd.
TEL +905-430-5000
FAX +905-430-5020
http://www.mcgrawhill.ca

**GREECE, MIDDLE EAST,
NORTHERN AFRICA**
McGraw-Hill Hellas
TEL +30-1-656-0990-3-4
FAX +30-1-654-5525

MEXICO (Also serving Latin America)
McGraw-Hill Interamericana Editores S.A. de C.V.
TEL +525-117-1583
FAX +525-117-1589
http://www.mcgraw-hill.com.mx
fernando_castellanos@mcgraw-hill.com

SINGAPORE (Serving Asia)
McGraw-Hill Book Company
TEL +65-863-1580
FAX +65-862-3354
http://www.mcgraw-hill.com.sg
mghasia@mcgraw-hill.com

SOUTH AFRICA
McGraw-Hill South Africa
TEL +27-11-622-7512
FAX +27-11-622-9045
robyn_swanepoel@mcgraw-hill.com

**UNITED KINGDOM & EUROPE
(Excluding Southern Europe)**
McGraw-Hill Publishing Company
TEL +44-1-628-502500
FAX +44-1-628-770224
http://www.mcgraw-hill.co.uk
computing_neurope@mcgraw-hill.com

ALL OTHER INQUIRIES Contact:
Osborne/McGraw-Hill
TEL +1-510-549-6600
FAX +1-510-883-7600
http://www.osborne.com
omg_international@mcgraw-hill.com

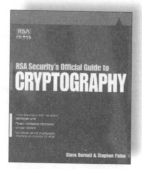

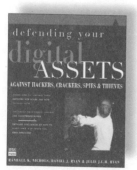

The Company

RSA Security Inc. is the most trusted name in e-security, helping organizations build secure, trusted foundations for e-business through its two-factor authentication, encryption and public key management systems. RSA Security has the market reach, proven leadership and unrivaled technical and systems experience to address the changing security needs of e-business and bring trust to the new online economy.

A truly global company with more than 8,000 customers, RSA Security is renowned for providing technologies that help organizations conduct e-business with confidence. Headquartered in Bedford, Mass., and with offices around the world, RSA Security is a public company (NASDAQ: RSAS) with 2000 revenues of $280 million.

Our Markets and Products

With the proliferation of the Internet and revolutionary new e-business practices, there has never been a more critical need for sophisticated security technologies and solutions. Today, as public and private networks merge and organizations increasingly expand their businesses to the Internet, RSA Security's core offerings are continually evolving to address the critical need for e-security. As the inventor of leading security technologies, RSA Security is focused on three core disciplines of e-security, including:

Public Key Infrastructure RSA Keon® public key infrastructure (PKI) solutions are a family of interoperable, standards-based PKI software modules for managing digital certificates and creating an environment for authenticated, private and legally binding electronic communications and transactions. RSA Keon software is designed to be easy to use and interoperable with other standards-based PKI solutions, and to feature enhanced security through its synergy with the RSA SecurID authentication and RSA BSAFE encryption product families.

Authentication RSA SecurID® systems are a leading solution for two-factor user authentication. RSA SecurID software is designed to protect valuable network resources by helping to ensure that only authorized users are granted access to e-mail, Web servers, intranets, extranets, network operating systems and other resources. The RSA SecurID family offers a wide range of easy-to-use authenticators, from time-synchronous tokens to smart cards, that help to create a strong barrier against unauthorized access, helping to safeguard network resources from potentially devastating accidental or malicious intrusion.

Encryption   RSA BSAFE® software is embedded in today's most successful Internet applications, including Web browsers, wireless devices, commerce servers, e-mail systems and virtual private network products. Built to provide implementations of standards such as SSL, S/MIME, WTLS, IPSec and PKCS, RSA BSAFE products can save developers time and risk in their development schedules, and have the security that only comes from a decade of proven, robust performance.

Commitment to Interoperability

RSA Security's offerings represent a set of open, standards-based products and technologies that integrate easily into organizations' IT environments, with minimal modification to existing applications and network systems. These solutions and technologies are designed to help organizations deploy new applications securely, while maintaining corporate investments in existing infrastructure. In addition, the Company maintains active, strategic partnerships with other leading IT vendors to promote interoperability and enhanced functionality.

Strategic Partnerships

RSA Security has built its business through its commitment to interoperability. Today, through its various partnering programs, the Company has strategic relationships with hundreds of industry-leading companies—including 3COM, AOL/Netscape, Ascend, AT&T, Nortel Networks, Cisco Systems, Compaq, IBM, Oracle, Microsoft and Intel—who are delivering integrated, RSA Security technology in more than 1,000 products.

Customers

RSA Security customers span a wide range of industries, including an extensive presence in the e-commerce, banking, government, telecommunications, aerospace, university and healthcare arenas. Today, more that 8 million users across 7,000 organizations—including more than half of the Fortune 100—use RSA SecurID authentication products to protect corporate data. Additionally, more than 500 companies embed RSA BSAFE software in some 1,000 applications, with a combined distribution of approximately one billion units worldwide.

Worldwide Service and Support

RSA Security offers a full complement of world-class service and support offerings to ensure the success of each customer's project or deployment through a range of ongoing customer support and professional services including assessments, project consulting, implementation, education and training, and developer support. RSA Security's Technical Support organization is known for resolving requests in the shortest possible time, gaining customers' confidence and exceeding expectations

Distribution

RSA Security has established a multi-channel distribution and sales network to serve the enterprise and data security markets. The Company sells and licenses its products directly to end users through its direct sales force and indirectly through an extensive network of OEMs, VARs and distributors. RSA Security supports its direct and indirect sales effort through strategic marketing relationships and programs.

Global Presence

RSA Security is a truly global e-security provider with major offices in the US, United Kingdom, Singapore and Tokyo, and representation in nearly 50 countries with additional international expansion underway. The RSA SecurWorld channel program brings RSA Security's products to value-added resellers and distributors worldwide, including locations in Europe, the Middle East, Africa, the Americas and Asia-Pacific.

For more information about RSA Security, please visit us at http://www.rsasecurity.com.

RSA BSAFE®

ENCRYPTION FROM THE MOST TRUSTED NAME IN e-SECURITY

Whether you need core cryptography routines, digital certificate management components, or fully implemented protocol for your application, the RSA BSAFE SDKs provide you with all of the components you need to make your applications absolutely safe and secure. By using RSA BSAFE products, your staff can save months of development time, enabling you to roll out mission-critical systems earlier and with more confidence. Contact RSA Security, your choice for authentication, encryption and PKI.

SECURITY™

The Most Trusted Name in e-Security®

How Do I Choose
The Right
PKI Solution?

Public Key Infrastructure (PKI) and digital certificates provide the best security foundation for e-business. But how do you choose the right PKI? The wrong decision could result in lost time and money. And put your reputation at risk in the process.

There's a lot at stake. That's why your best choice is PKI from the most trusted name in e-security, RSA Security. We've been the e-security industry leader for over 20 years. We pioneered public key cryptography and we know what you need in a PKI solution. That's why RSA Keon is the first truly interoperable PKI based entirely on open standards. And its modular approach allows for flexible implementation.

More than 7,000 organizations worldwide already trust us with their e-security. So for PKI you can trust, the right decision is RSA Keon. Contact RSA Security, your source for authentication, encryption and PKI.

www.rsasecurity.com/go/rsapress/IPSEC

SECURITY™

The Most Trusted Name in e-Security®

Who's
on the other end of your VPN?

There's only one way to know: replace passwords with RSA SecurID.

You've set up a rock-solid VPN that guarantees private, encrypted communication. But if your VPN relies on passwords for security, how can you be sure who's on the line? After all, passwords can be found, guessed, stolen and hacked.

RSA SecurID's two-factor authentication combines a one-time code, refreshed every 60 seconds, with a private PIN to ensure that you know who's on your network at all times.

The security of your mission critical applications is at stake. That's why products from leading VPN vendors are compatible with RSA SecurID. Contact RSA Security, your source for authentication, encryption and PKI.

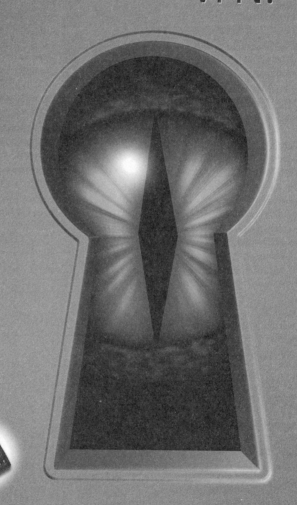

RSA
SECURITY™
The Most Trusted Name in e-Security®

www.rsasecurity.com/go/rsapress/IPSEC